Inequality and Growth

The CESifo Seminar Series
Hans-Werner Sinn, editor

Inequality and Growth: Theory and Policy Implications, ed. Theo S. Eicher and Stephen J. Turnovsky (2003)

Public Finance and Public Policy in the New Century, ed. Sijbren Cnossen and Hans-Werner Sinn (2003)

Inequality and Growth

Theory and Policy Implications

Theo S. Eicher and
Stephen J. Turnovsky,
editors

CESifo Seminar Series

The MIT Press
Cambridge, Massachusetts
London, England

This book was set in Palatino on 3B2 by Asco Typesetters, Hong Kong, and was printed and bound in the United States of America.

Library of Congress Cataloging-in-Publication Data

Inequality and growth : theory and policy implications / Theo S. Eicher and
  Stephen J. Turnovsky, editors.
    p.   cm. — (The CESifo seminar series ; 1)
  Conference papers.
  Includes bibliographical references and index.
  ISBN 0-262-05069-2 (hc. : alk. paper)
    1. Income distribution—Congresses. 2. Economic development—Congresses.
  I. Eicher, Theo S. II. Turnovsky, Stephen J. III. CESifo (Organization). IV. Series.
  HC79.I5I493   2003
  339.2′2—dc21   2002043162

Contents

Series Foreword

This book is part of the CESifo Seminar Series in Economic Policy, which aims to cover topical policy issues in economics from a largely European perspective. The books in this series are the products of the papers presented and discussed at seminars hosted by CESifo, an international research network of renowned economists supported jointly by the Center for Economic Studies at Ludwig-Maximilians-Universität, Munich, and the Ifo Institute for Economic Research. All publications in this series have been carefully selected and refereed by members of the CESifo research network.

Hans-Werner Sinn

Preface

Economists and policymakers alike are inherently interested in the process of economic growth. As Nobel Laureate Robert E. Lucas (1988) pointed out in "On the Mechanics of Economic Development," the nature of growth is such that the welfare implications of small (and possibly simple) policy changes can be staggering. Even minute increases in the growth rate can compound into dramatic changes in living standards over just one generation. However, the precise nature of such growth enhancing policies is often elusive, which highlights that the execution of such policies presupposes a clear understanding of the mechanics of economic growth.

Even if growth is achieved, its benefits may not be shared equally. Some may gain more or less than others, and a fraction of the population may actually be disadvantaged by the enhanced growth performance of the aggregate economy. The relationship between inequality and growth is especially topical since the most recent economic literature reports both positive and negative relationships between growth and inequality across nations (for a review, see Aghion, Caroli, and García-Peñalosa 1999). If policies are designed to foster growth, what is their impact on inequality? Aside from possible normative desires to reduce inequality, does (in)equality by itself facilitate or detract from economic growth, and does it amplify or diminish policy effectiveness? Once the relationship between growth and inequality is clarified, one can attempt to answer these questions and inquire about the role for public policy in enhancing growth and equality.

The questions we raise here have generated great interest in both academic journals and in the popular press. In this volume we seek to provide a forum for economists to examine the theoretical, empirical, and policy issues involved. The ultimate goal is to provide a framework for an informed policy debate based on sound analytical frameworks and solid empirical evidence.

The chapters that comprise this volume illuminate the range of economic fundamentals and policies that influence growth and equality positively. However, two features stand out as almost common among all chapters. The first is the unusual diversity of contexts within which the issue of inequality and growth is discussed. The chapters in this volume encompass topics from natural resources, taxation, fertility, redistribution, technological change, transition, labor markets, to education in both developed and developing countries. We believe that this indicates the breadth of the theory and policy implications that are the subject of inequality and growth. On the other hand, despite the diversity of topics, one policy prescription is virtually common among just about all papers: It is the importance of education in reducing inequality and increasing economic growth.

François Bourguignon (chapter 1) demonstrates that both the level of development and the degree of inequality influence the speed by which economic growth reduces poverty. Growth is shown to generate more rapid poverty reduction in low-inequality, high-income countries. These results show a strong bias against the poorest, most unequal economies, as growth is shown to be least effective in alleviating poverty in countries that need it most. On the other hand, Bourguignon highlights the double dividend of redistribution, which increases growth as well as the speed with which growth decreases poverty. Danny Quah (chapter 2) takes Bourguignon's argument one step further to address directly the concerns of those who worry exclusively about the impact of growth on poverty. He documents that neither the belief that "inequality drives growth," nor the assertion that "growth generates inequality," has support in economic data. Quah reminds us that much of the variation in inequality is across countries, but that over time, this variation does not change much. Conversely, growth rates hardly vary across countries, but vary dramatically over time. Using India and China between 1980 and 1992 as examples, Quah uses simple arithmetic to show that, even if growth increased inequality, more than 300 million were helped out of poverty.

Avner Ahituv and Omer Moav (chapter 3) highlight the importance of education in increasing growth and decreasing fertility. The authors provide both theory and empirical evidence to support the hypothesis that reductions in fertility improve growth and increase education. The effect is amplified by a positive feedback: More educated parents become progressively better at providing excellent education. Policy implications are clear: Subsidies to parents should focus on educational incentives rather than simple child support. Jean-Marie Viaene and Itzhak Zilcha (chapter 4) show how different types of education affect human capital accumulation and respond to technical change. They warn of the dangers of a digital divide, where technical change in the computer industry could lead to greater heterogeneity that would hamper growth.

Instead of relying on aggregate data, Michael P. Keane and Eswar S. Prasad (chapter 5) examine actual records of Polish budget survey microdata to construct estimates of inequality that are significantly smaller than those previously reported. Large transfer payments have long been considered detrimental to the transition process, but the authors show, using the microdata, that Polish shock therapy worked because of smart redistribution not only to the very poor but also to the structurally unemployed. Large and specifically targeted transfers to pensioners increased the political support for reforms of those who were potentially most hurt. At the same time, these specifically targeted transfers increased productivity, since they served as incentives for retirement of the least productive. Taking the analysis from Poland to the entire group of transition countries, Oleksiy Ivanschenko (chapter 6) highlights the differences in European and the former Soviet Union (FSU) inequality and growth contributors. Inflation is a major issue in the FSU. However, in the more stable macroeconomic environments, reform indicators are much more significant in determining growth and inequality. The precise relationship is shown to be a function of income thresholds.

Günther Rehme (chapter 7) examines alternative education mechanics from Viaene and Zilcha, to focus on the dual function of education as a public institution and as a means of redistribution. Essentially he shows that the benefits from redistribution via education significantly outweigh those associated with simple income distribution. Theo Eicher, Stephen J. Turnovsky, and Maria Carme Riera Prunera (chapter 8) employ a formal growth model that includes the incentives to invest in education to simulate both short- and long-term policy experiments, such as the Reagan tax cuts. They conclude that the recent, second generation of endogenous growth models is well suited to predict growth and inequality in the short and long term.

Thorvaldur Gylfason and Gylfi Zoega (chapter 9) sharpen the growing literature popularized by Sachs and Warner (1995) on natural resources and growth. The contribution of the chapter is to demonstrate how increased dependence on natural resources tends to go along with less economic growth and greater inequality in the distribution of income within countries. The apparently inverse empirical relationship between growth and inequality may hence not imply any causal relationship between the two. Instead, natural resource dependence may be affecting both equality and growth. Subsidies to education can mitigate the negative effect of natural resources and their unequal distribution. Finally, Campbell Leith, Chol-Won Li, and Cecilia García-Peñalosa (chapter 10) investigate how the impact of technical change on inequality and growth is amplified by labor market frictions. They show that when technology generates job destruction, relative wages rise or fall depending on the magnitude of the labor market frictions. Such dynamics are shown to be capable of explaining U.S./European unemployment and relative wage differentials. Most interesting is that the authors highlight the dilemma of policymakers. While job protection may lower inequality and increase growth, it would hurt those workers who are now stuck longer in structural unemployment.

The two conferences on Inequality and Growth that preceded this volume were made possible in large part by the support of Hans-Werner Sinn and the CESifo network. We thank him for his unwavering support. The quality of the conferences and papers was assured by extensive comments from discussants including Daniele Checchi, Rafael Domenech, Walter Fisher, Carola Grün, Raji Jayaraman, Louise Keely, Henryk Kierzkowski, Stephan Klasen, Antonio Garcia Pascual, Cecilia García-Peñalosa, Maria Carme Riera Prunera, Ray Riezman, Mathias Thoenig, Gylfi Zoega, and a number of anonymous referees. CESifo, and specifically Roisin Hearn and Frank Westermann, provided excellent and efficient administrative support throughout, and they were ably assisted by Silke Übelmesser and Marko Köthenbürger. The Castor Endowment at the University of Washington also supported this project, a subject in which Cecil and Jane Castor held a lifelong interest. Financial support was also provided by the European Union Center at the University of Washington. We are grateful to all contributors for making this venture possible and worthwhile. Finally we would like to extend our deep appreciation to our wives, Regina Lyons and Michelle Turnovsky, for their loving support during the completion of this volume.

References

Aghion, Philippe, Eve Caroli, and Cecilia García-Peñalosa. 1999. "Inequality and Economic Growth: The Perspective of the New Growth Theories." *Journal of Economic Literature* 37(4): 1615–1660.

Lucas, Robert E. 1988. "On the Mechanics of Economic Development." *Journal of Monetary Economics* 22(1): 3–42.

Sachs, Jeffrey D., and Andrew M. Warner. 1995. "Natural Resource Abundance and Economic Growth." National Bureau of Economic Research Working Paper no. 5398.

I

Measuring the Impact of Growth on Inequality

1

The Growth Elasticity of Poverty Reduction: Explaining Heterogeneity across Countries and Time Periods

François Bourguignon

1.1 Introduction

Part of the ongoing debate on poverty reduction strategies bears on the issue of the actual contribution of economic growth to poverty reduction. There is no doubt that faster economic growth is associated with faster poverty reduction. But what is the corresponding elasticity? If it is reasonably high, then poverty reductions strategies almost exclusively relying on economic growth are probably justified. If it is low, however, ambitious poverty reduction strategies might have to combine both economic growth and some kind of redistribution. Ravallion and Chen (1997) estimated that, on average on a sample of developing countries, the growth elasticity of poverty, as measured by the number of individuals below the conventional $1-a-day threshold, was around 3—namely, a 1 percent increase in mean income or consumption expenditures in the population reduces the proportion of people living below the poverty line by 3 percent. As emphasized in *Attacking Poverty, World Development Report 2000/2001*, however, there is very much cross-country heterogeneity behind this average figure—which, as a matter of fact, was found there closer to 2 than 3.[1] Several countries knew only limited changes in poverty despite satisfactory growth performances whereas poverty fell in some countries where growth had yet been disappointing. Understanding the causes of that heterogeneity is clearly crucial for the design of poverty reduction strategies.

To get some idea of the actual heterogeneity in the relationship between changes in poverty and changes in income, and of the ambiguity of average cross-sectional data, figure 1.1 plots observations that come from a sample of growth spells taken over various periods in selected countries. These spells are essentially defined by

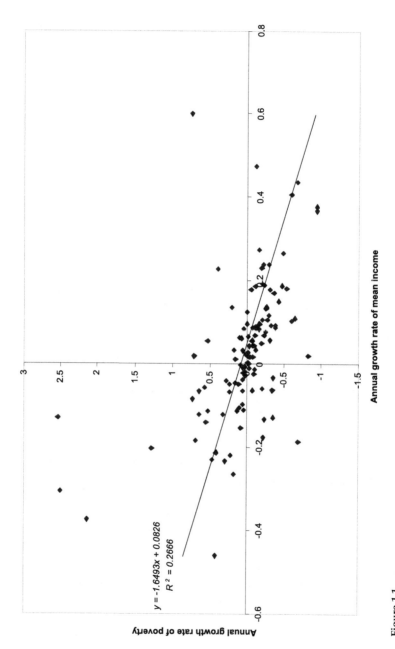

Figure 1.1
The relationship between poverty reduction and growth in a sample of growth spells

the availability of fully comparable household surveys at the two ends of the spell, only the most distant ends being considered in the case of adjacent annual observations. The sample comprises 114 spells covering approximately 50 countries—see the list in the appendix. The common poverty line that is used is the $1-a-day line after local currency expenditures data have been translated into dollars and PPP correction.[2] The poverty measure being used is the headcount ratio, that is the proportion of the population below the poverty line. As expected, the scatter of observations shows a declining relationship between the change in poverty and the change in the mean income. The fitted OLS straight line has a slope equal to −1.6, suggesting an average elasticity somewhat below the value of 2 reported in World Bank (2000). Differences in the mean elasticity in different samples of countries or growth spells is not the issue, however. The issue is the difference across countries or growth spells. From that point of view figure 1.1 is disappointing. Changes in the mean income of the population explain only 26 percent of the variance of observed changes in poverty headcounts. If this figure is taken seriously, would it make sense to base poverty reduction so much on growth strategies, as is often suggested? Wouldn't it be better to identify first the nature of the remaining 74 percent and then the reason why poverty in various countries tend to react very differently to the same increase in the mean income of the population?

Analytically, an *identity* links the growth of the mean income in a given population, the change in the distribution of relative incomes, and the reduction of poverty. Formally, the relationship between poverty and growth may be obtained from that identity in the case where there would be no change in the distribution of relative individual incomes, or, in other words, if income growth were the same in all segments of society. Even in that case, however, the growth-poverty relationship is not simple and the corresponding elasticity is certainly not constant across countries and across the various ways of measuring poverty. In effect, the growth elasticity of poverty is a decreasing function of the development level of a country and of the degree of inequality of the income distribution, this function depending itself on the poverty index that is being used. A rather precise characterization of that relationship is offered in this chapter under some simplifying assumption about the underlying distribution of income.

The second source of heterogeneity is of course the change in the distribution of relative incomes over time. Measuring the actual contribution of that source to the observed evolution of poverty is of utmost importance since this should give an indication of the practical relevance of distributional concerns in comparison with pure growth concerns in poverty reduction policies. Because the actual contribution of growth to poverty reduction is not precisely identified by the practice that consists of assuming a constant elasticity, it follows that the contribution of the distributional component is also imprecisely estimated. The methodology proposed in this chapter permits correcting that imprecision too and has implications for the interpretation of available evidence on the growth-poverty relationship.

Many recent papers focused on the statistical relationship between economic growth and poverty reduction across countries and time periods. Many of them—see, for instance, de Janvry and Sadoulet (1995, 2000), Ravallion and Chen (1997), Dollar and Kraay (2000)— are based on linear regressions where the evolution of some poverty measure between two points of time is explained by the growth of income or GDP per capita and a host of other variables, the main issue being the importance of GDP and these other variables in determining poverty reduction. By adopting a linear regression framework, or by investing too little in functional specification testing, however, these papers miss the earlier point, that is that of a complex but yet identity-related relationship between mean income growth and poverty change. On the contrary, other authors —for instance, Ravallion and Huppi (1991), Datt and Ravallion (1992), Kakwani (1993)[3]—fully take into account the poverty/mean-income/distribution identity in studying the evolution of poverty and its causes. In particular, they are all quite careful in distinguishing precisely the effects on poverty reduction of growth on the one hand and distributional changes on the other. At the same time, their analysis is generally restricted to a specific country or a limited number of countries or regions: Indonesia, regions of Brazil and India, the Cote d'Ivoire, respectively.

This chapter stands midway between these two approaches. Ideally, international comparisons in the evolution of poverty should all rely on the methodology based on the poverty/mean-income/ distribution identity. But, because it requires using the full microeconomic information on the distribution of income or expenditures in each country or region, it may seem cumbersome. Instead, this chapter proposes a methodology that is less demanding. It relies on functional approximations of the identity, and in particular on an approximation based on the assumption that the distribution of income or consumption expenditure is lognormal.

A simple application to the sample of growth spells shown in figure 1.1 shows that these approximations fit the data extremely well and do incomparably better than the linear model that is generally used. It also suggests that only half of the observed changes in poverty in the sample may be explained by economic growth, the remaining half being the result of changes in the distribution of relative incomes.

The chapter is organized as follows. Section 1.2 introduces and discusses the analytical identity that links poverty, growth, and distribution. Closed-form formulae for the growth elasticity of poverty when the distribution is lognormal are derived. They are used to analyze in some detail the theoretical relationship that exists among poverty reduction, the level of development, and the inequality of the distribution when the distribution of income is remaining constant over time. Section 1.3 tests the empirical validity of various approximations to the preceding identity, including the lognormal approximation, and compares the results with the standard linear specification. A concluding section 1.4 draws several implications of the main argument in the chapter for the empirical analysis of the relationship between growth and poverty and for the design of poverty reduction strategies.

1.2 The Arithmetic of Distributional and Poverty Changes

Any poverty index may be seen as a statistics defined on all individuals in a population whose standard of living lies below some predetermined limit. In what follows, it is assumed that there is no ambiguity on the definition of that "poverty line"; that is, whether it is defined in terms of income or consumption, the kind of equivalence scale being used to account for heterogeneity in household composition, and indeed the level of that poverty line. This poverty line will also be assumed to be constant over time—at least during the period being analyzed. Since the argument will implicitly refer to international comparisons, it makes also sense to assume that this poverty line is defined in "absolute" terms and the same across countries, for instance, the familiar $1 or $2 a day after correction for purchasing power parity.

Given this definition of poverty, let y be a measure of individual living standard—say, income per adult equivalent—and let z be the poverty line. In a given country, the distribution of income at some point of time, t, is represented by the cumulative distribution function $F_t(Y)$, which stands for the proportion of individuals in the population with living standard, or income, y, less than Y. The most widely used poverty index is simply the proportion of individuals in the population below the poverty line, z. This index is generally referred to as the "headcount." With the preceding notations, it may be formally defined as

$$H_t = F_t(z). \tag{1}$$

For the sake of simplicity, the analysis will be momentarily restricted to that single poverty index.

The definition of the headcount poverty index implies the following definition of change in poverty between two points of time, t and t':

$$\Delta H = H_{t'} - H_t = F_{t'}(z) - F_t(z).$$

To show the contribution of growth to the change in poverty, it is convenient to define the distribution of *relative income* at time t as the distribution of incomes after normalizing by the population mean. This is equivalent with defining the distribution of income in a way that is independent of the scale of incomes. Let $\tilde{F}_t(X)$ be that distribution. With this definition, any change in the distribution of income may then be decomposed into (a) a proportional change in all incomes that leaves the distribution of relative income, $\tilde{F}_t(X)$, unchanged; and (b) a change in the distribution of relative incomes, which, by definition, is independent of the mean. For obvious reasons, the first change will be referred to as the "growth" effect whereas the second one will be termed the "distributional" effect.

This decomposition was discussed in some detail by Datt and Ravallion (1992) and Kakwani (1993). It is illustrated in figure 1.2. This figure shows the density of the distribution of income—that is, the number of individuals at each level of income represented on a logarithmic scale on the horizontal axis. In that figure, the function $F(\ )$ appears only indirectly as the area under the density curves. The move from the initial to the new distribution goes through an

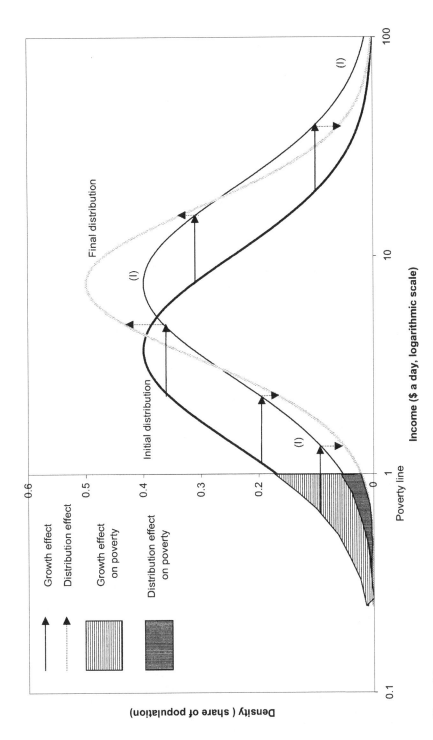

Figure 1.2
Decomposition of change in distribution and poverty into growth and distributional effects

intermediate step, which is the horizontal translation of the initial density curve to curve (I). Because of the logarithmic scale on the horizontal axis, this change corresponds to the same proportional increase of all incomes in the population and thus stands for the "growth effect." Then, moving from curve (I) to the new distribution curve occurs at constant mean income. This movement thus corresponds to the change in the distribution of "relative" income, or the "distribution" effect. Of course, there is some path dependence in that decomposition. Instead of moving first rightward and then up and down as in figure 1.2, it would have been possible to move first up and down and to have the distribution effect based on the mean income observed in the initial period, and then to move rightward. Presumably, these two paths are not necessarily equivalent except for infinitesimal changes. This issue is ignored in what follows, assuming in effect that all changes are sufficiently small for path dependence not to be a problem.[4]

Figure 1.2 illustrates the natural decomposition of the change in the whole distribution of income between two points of time. Things are somewhat simpler if the focus is exclusively on poverty, as measured by the headcount. In figure 1.2, the poverty headcount is simply the area under the density curve at the left of the poverty line, arbitrarily set at \$1 a day. The move from the initial curve to the intermediate curve (I) and then from that curve to the new distribution curve have natural counterparts in terms of changes in this area. More formally, this decomposition may be written as

$$\Delta H = H_{t'} - H_t = \left[\tilde{F}_t \left(\frac{z}{\bar{y}_{t'}} \right) - \tilde{F}_t \left(\frac{z}{\bar{y}_t} \right) \right] + \left[\tilde{F}_{t'} \left(\frac{z}{\bar{y}_{t'}} \right) - \tilde{F}_t \left(\frac{z}{\bar{y}_{t'}} \right) \right]. \tag{2}$$

This expression is the direct application in the case of the headcount poverty index of the general formula proposed by Datt and Ravallion (1992), which they applied to Brazilian and Indian distribution data. It is indeed a simple *identity* since it consists of adding and subtracting the same term $\tilde{F}_t(z/\bar{y}_{t'})$ in the original definition of the change in poverty. The first expression in square bracket in (2) corresponds to the growth effect at "constant" relative income distribution, $\tilde{F}_t(\ )$, that is the translation of the density curve along the horizontal axis in figure 1.2, whereas the second square bracket formalizes the distribution effect—that is, the change in the relative income distribution, $\tilde{F}_{t'}(X) - \tilde{F}_t(X)$, at the new level of the "relative" poverty line, that is the ratio of the absolute poverty line and the mean income, $X = z/\bar{y}_{t'}$.

Shifting to elasticity concepts, the growth elasticity of poverty may thus be defined as

$$\varepsilon = \lim_{t' \to t} \frac{\left[\tilde{F}_t\left(\frac{z}{\bar{y}_{t'}}\right) - \tilde{F}_t\left(\frac{z}{\bar{y}_t}\right)\right] / \tilde{F}_t\left(\frac{z}{\bar{y}_t}\right)}{(\bar{y}_{t'} - \bar{y}_t)/\bar{y}_t}. \tag{3}$$

The distribution effect is more difficult to translate in terms of elasticity because it generally cannot be represented by a scalar.

The terms entering the decomposition identity (2) may be evaluated as long as one observes some continuous approximation of the distribution functions $F(\ )$ at the two points of time t and t'. Continuous kernel approximations of the density and cumulative relative distribution functions may be computed from available microeconomic data. With this kind of tool, evaluating the decomposition identity for any growth spell for which distribution data are available at the two ends of the spell should not be difficult. In a cross-country framework, however, this might require manipulating a large number of microeconomic data sets and may be found cumbersome.

Interestingly enough, a very simple approximation of (2) may be obtained in the case where the distributions may be assumed to be lognormal, probably the most standard approximation of empirical distributions in the applied literature. The relative income distribution writes in that case:

$$\tilde{F}_t(X) = \Pi\left[\frac{\log(X)}{\sigma} + \frac{1}{2}\sigma\right],$$

where $\Pi(\ )$ is the cumulative distribution function of the standard normal and σ is the standard deviation of the logarithm of income. Substituting this expression in (2) shows that the change in poverty headcount between time t and t' depends on the level of mean income at these two dates, $\bar{y}/z$, expressed as a proportion of the poverty line, and on the standard deviation, σ, of the logarithm of income at the two dates. Allowing t' to be close to t and taking limits as in (3) then leads to

$$\frac{\Delta H}{H_t} = \lambda\left[\frac{\log(z/\bar{y}_t)}{\sigma} + \frac{1}{2}\sigma\right] \cdot \left[-\frac{\Delta \log(\bar{y})}{\sigma} + \left(\frac{1}{2} - \frac{\log(z/\bar{y}_t)}{\sigma^2}\right)\Delta\sigma\right], \tag{2'}$$

where $\lambda(\ )$ stands for the ratio of the density to the cumulative function—or hazard rate—of the standard normal, $\Delta \log(\bar{y})$ is the growth rate of the economy and $\Delta\sigma$ is the variation in the standard deviation of the logarithm of income. Based on that expression and following (3), the growth elasticity of poverty, ε, may be defined as the relative change in the poverty headcount for 1 percent growth in mean income, for constant relative inequality, σ:

$$\varepsilon = \frac{\Delta H}{\Delta \log(\bar{y})H_t} = \frac{1}{\sigma}\lambda\left[\frac{\log(z/\bar{y}_t)}{\sigma} + \frac{1}{2}\sigma\right]. \tag{3'}$$

In that expression, the growth elasticity of poverty appears explicitly as an increasing function of the level of development, as measured by the inverse of the ratio $z/\bar{y}_t$, and a decreasing function of the degree of relative income inequality as measured by the standard deviation of the logarithm of income, σ.[5]

The preceding relationship is represented in figure 1.3 by curves in the development inequality space along which the growth elasticity of poverty is constant. The inverse of the development level is measured along the horizontal axis by the ratio of the poverty line to the mean income of the population. Inequality is measured along the vertical axis by the Gini coefficient of the distribution of relative income rather than the standard deviation of logarithm. This measure of inequality is more familiar than σ but is known to be an increasing function of it.[6]

Figure 1.3 is useful to get some direct and quick estimate of the growth elasticity of poverty. Consider, for instance, the case of a poor country where the mean income is only twice the poverty line at the right end of the figure. Reading the figure, it may be seen that the growth elasticity is around 3 if inequality is low—namely, a Gini coefficient around 0.3—but it is only 2 if the Gini coefficient is around the more common value of 0.4. If the economy gets richer, then the elasticity increases. But at the same time it becomes more sensitive to the level of inequality. For instance, when the mean income of the population is four times the poverty line, the growth elasticity of poverty is 5 for low-income inequality—namely, a Gini equal to 0.3—but 2 again if inequality is high—namely, a Gini coefficient equal to 0.5. These various combinations are illustrated by the example of a few countries in the mid-1980s. The ratio of the poverty line to the mean income is taken to be the $1-a-day line related to

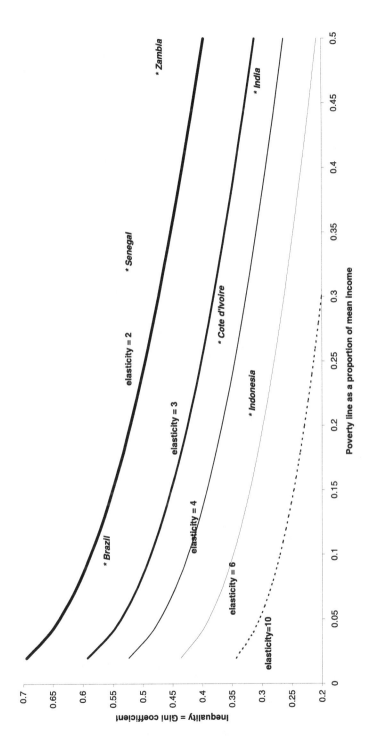

Figure 1.3
Poverty (headcount)/growth elasticity as a function of mean income and income inequality, under the assumption of constant (lognormal) distribution

GDP per capita, whereas Gini coefficients are taken from the Deininger and Squire (1996) database. Growth elasticities of poverty reduction consistent with the lognormal assumption vary between 5 for a country like Indonesia to 3 for India and the Cote d'Ivoire, which were poorer and/or had a higher level of inequality. The elasticity is around 2 for Brazil, despite the fact that it is considerably richer than the other countries. Income inequality makes the difference. Finally, the elasticity is much below 2 in the case of Senegal and Zambia, both of which are poor and unequal.

Figure 1.3 and the underlying lognormal approximation to the growth elasticity of poverty in (5) refers to the headcount as the poverty index. Similar expressions and curves may be obtained using alternative indices. For instance, the poverty gap is a measure of poverty obtained by multiplying the headcount by the average relative distance at which the poor are from the poverty line. The advantage of that measure over the headcount is obviously that it takes into account not only the proportion of people being poor but also the intensity of poverty. Under the lognormal assumption, it may be shown that the growth elasticity of the poverty gap is given by the following formula:[7]

$$\varepsilon_y^{PG} = -\frac{\Pi[\log(z/\bar{y}_t)/\sigma - \sigma/2]}{(z/\bar{y}_t) * \Pi[\log(z/\bar{y}_t)/\sigma + \sigma/2] - \Pi[\log(z/\bar{y}_t)/\sigma - \sigma/2]}, \qquad (4)$$

whereas the elasticity with respect to the standard deviation of the logarithm of income is given by

$$\varepsilon_\sigma^{PG} = -\frac{\sigma \cdot \pi[\log(z/\bar{y}_t)/\sigma - \sigma/2]}{(z/\bar{y}_t) * \Pi[\log(z/\bar{y}_t)/\sigma + \sigma/2] - \Pi[\log(z/\bar{y}_t)/\sigma - \sigma/2]},$$

where $\Pi(\ )$ and $\pi(\ )$ are respectively the cumulative distribution and the density functions of the standard normal variable. As before, the growth elasticity depends on the level of development as measured by the ratio $z/\bar{y}_t$ and the inequality of the distribution of income as given by the standard deviation of the logarithm of income. Although not shown here, the iso elasticity contours in the development/inequality space corresponding to function (4) are very similar to what was shown in figure 1.3 for the headcount index. Equivalent formulas and similar figures could be derived for other poverty measures, in particular those belonging to the well-known P_α family—see Foster, Greer, and Thorbecke (1984).[8]

1.3 Revisiting the Empirical Evidence on the Growth-Poverty Relationship

The identity linking growth, poverty reduction, and distributional changes should be readily apparent from data on growth-poverty spells. This section shows that this is indeed the case, provided the adequate specification is used. In particular the lognormal approximation proves to be extremely precise.

The data being used are the same as those used for figure 1.1. The sample includes mostly developing countries but a few transition economies are also present. The only modification made to the original data was to eliminate all spells where the percentage change in the poverty headcount was abnormally large in relative value. Cases left aside essentially correspond to situations where the poverty headcount went from zero or an almost negligible figure to some positive value, or the opposite, in a few years. This was made in order to comply with the definition of the elasticity concepts given earlier and the corresponding requirement of "small" changes.[9] The mean annual growth in mean income over all these spells is 2.7 percent, the mean relative change in the poverty headcount—with a $1-a-day poverty line—is close to zero and the mean change in the Gini coefficient is −.0022.

Based on this data set, four different models are compared against each other. The first corresponds to the naive view alluded to above that there is a constant elasticity between poverty reduction and growth. It consists of regressing observed changes in the poverty headcount on observed changes in mean income. The second model, which is termed the "standard" model in table 1.1 includes the observed change in income inequality, as measured by the Gini coefficient as an additional explanatory variable. It is thus consistent with a decomposition of type (2) above, except for the fact that both the growth elasticity and the Gini elasticity of poverty reduction are taken to be constant. The third model improves on the previous one by allowing the growth elasticity to depend on the inverse level of development, as measured by the poverty-line/mean-income ratio, and on the initial degree of inequality as measured by the Gini coefficient. Nothing is imposed a priori on that relationship, though. Finding the optimal functional specification is left to econometrics. To do so, two additional variables are introduced in the regression: the interaction between growth and the preceding two variables. The final model relies on the lognormal approximation discussed earlier. The explanatory variables are the theoretical elasticity defined in (3′) times the observed growth rate of mean income[10] and the change in the Gini coefficient. If the lognormal approximation discussed earlier is not too unsatisfactory, then one should find that the coefficient of the theoretical elasticity in that regression is not significantly different from unity.

The estimation of these four models is reported in the first four columns of table 1.1. Results fully confirm the identity relationship discussed in this chapter. First, one can see that the naive model suggests a significant negative elasticity of poverty with respect to growth but its explanatory power is low. This strictly corresponds to the fitted line in figure 1.1 with a R^2 equal to 26 percent. Things improve quite substantially when one shifts to the standard model by adding distributional changes in the regression equation. Adding the change in the Gini coefficient in the linear specification practically doubles the R^2 coefficient, suggesting that the heterogeneity in distributional changes is as much responsible for variation in poverty reduction across growth spells as the heterogeneity in growth rates itself.

Interacting growth with the initial poverty-line/mean-income ratio and the initial Gini coefficient in the "improved standard model 1" yields still another significant improvement in explanatory power. The two interaction terms are very significant and go in the right direction. As expected, both a lesser level of development and a higher level of inequality reduce the growth elasticity of poverty. Both effects are significant and sizable. At the mean point of the sample—namely, for a growth spell leading to an annual 2.7 percent rise in mean income—an increase of the initial level of development by one standard deviation of the poverty-line/mean-income variable increases poverty reduction by some 3 percentage points annually. In the same conditions, an increase in the initial Gini coefficient by one standard deviation diminishes poverty reduction by a little less than 1 percentage point.

No assumption is made in the preceding regression on the way income growth, the development level and the initial degree of inequality interact to determine poverty reduction. In the fourth column of table 1.1, on the contrary, it is assumed that the joint effect of these three variables is in accordance with the theoretical elasticity

Table 1.1
Explaining the evolution of poverty across growth spells[a]
(dependent variable = percentage change in poverty headcount during growth spell)

Explanatory variables	Naive model (1)	Standard model (2)	Improved standard model 1 (3)	Identity check: Lognormal model 1 (4)	Improved standard model 2 (5)	Identity check: Lognormal model 2 (6)
Intercept	0.0826 *0.0434*	0.0972 *0.0364*	0.0837 *0.0349*	0.0752 *0.0325*	0.0977 *0.0321*	0.0692 *0.0281*
Y = percentage change in mean income	-1.6493 *0.2585*	-2.0124 *0.2223*	-6.3518 *1.2451*		-7.8706 *1.1310*	
DGini = Variation in Gini coefficient		4.7178 *0.6731*	5.2863 *0.6529*	5.0769 *0.6118*	21.5606 *4.1205*	
Y * poverty-line / mean-income			3.9678 *1.1662*		3.9481 *1.0286*	
Y * initial Gini coefficient			7.0039 *2.4586*		9.6869 *2.2104*	
DGini * poverty-line / mean-income					-16.3898 *2.8255*	
DGini * initial Gini coefficient					-20.3600 *7.4388*	
Y * theoretical value of growth elasticity under lognormal assumption[b]				-0.8727 *0.0778*		-0.9261 *0.0679*
DSigma * theoretical value of poverty inequality elasticity under lognormal assumption[b]						0.6824 *0.0601*
R²	0.2666	0.4916	0.555	0.5857	0.6651	0.6892

[a]Ordinary least squares estimates, standard errors in italics. The sample includes the 114 growth spells listed in the appendix. All coefficients are significantly different from zero at the 1 percent probability level except the intercept.
[b]Switching from the coefficient of Gini to the standard deviation of the logarithm of income is done through the formula in note 6.

derived in the preceding section under the assumption that the underlying distribution of relative income is lognormal. The resulting explanatory variable in the poverty reduction regression thus is this theoretical elasticity times the observed growth of the mean income. This test of the identity that links poverty reduction and growth is very successful. On the one hand, the R^2 coefficient proves to be substantially higher than when the various explanatory variables are entered without functional restriction as in the preceding regression, despite less degrees of freedom being used. On the other hand, the coefficient of the theoretical value of the elasticity proves to be only slightly below unity. Overall, it must then be concluded that the best "single" explanation of observed poverty reduction in a sample of growth spells is indeed provided by the identity that logically links poverty and growth under the lognormal assumption.

In all the preceding regressions, no care is taken of the fact that, according to the identity discussed above, the role of the change in inequality on poverty reduction is unlikely to be linear. The last two columns of table 1.1 correct the preceding results for this. In column (5) the effect of the distributional change on poverty reduction is assumed to depend both on the initial level of development and the initial level of inequality. In column (6), the two explanatory variables are the growth and inequality elasticities, as defined in (2′) under the lognormal assumption, multiplied respectively by the relative change in mean income and the change in the Gini coefficient. The "improved standard model 2" in column (5) proves to do much better than the improved standard model 1 in column (3) where distributional changes were only captured by the change in the Gini coefficient. The R^2 coefficient gains more than 10 percentage points, solely because of the interaction terms between the change in the Gini coefficient and the two key level variables, the initial inequality level and the initial development level. Surprisingly enough, still a better score is achieved in column (6) with the lognormal approximation with only two explanatory variables that stand for the growth and inequality elasticity of poverty. It may be seen, moreover, that the coefficient of the growth-elasticity term is not significantly different from unity, something that would seem to be in favor of the lognormal approximation. Unfortunately, this is not true of the inequality-elasticity variable, which in effect would lead to reject that approximation. Note, however, that an additional hypothesis that cannot be tested independently of the lognormality is the infinitesimal approximation behind all types of elasticity calculation. As may be seen in figure 1.1, some observations are such that the annual absolute relative change in the mean income of the population is greater then 25 percent. It is not clear that the standard elasticity calculation would apply in this case. Yet, no attempt has been made in this chapter to use nondifferential expressions.

That the lognormal approximation plays an effective role in the R^2 of the last column of table 1.1 being still far from unity is confirmed when the preceding exercise is repeated with the poverty gap, rather than the poverty headcount. Table 1.2 is the equivalent of table 1.1 with the poverty index being the poverty gap rather than the poverty headcount. The striking feature there is of course that all R^2 are much lower than what was found with the poverty headcount, and also that the improvement in the fit of poverty reduction observations due to the approximations discussed in this chapter is less dramatic.

This last set of results may be somewhat disappointing but they are easily understandable. Using the headcount leads somehow to make predictions or simulations that concerns the value of the cumulative distribution function of income, $\tilde{F}_t(X)$, at a single point, namely, $X = z/\bar{y}_t$. Using the poverty gap, on the contrary, requires using predictions on the mean value of income for all people below $z/\bar{y}_t$, that is about the full range of values of $F_t(X)$ below the value X. This is much more demanding. The lognormal approximation may not perform too badly at a specific point close to the poverty line. It may do much worse if all incomes below that value are to be taken into account too.

This experiment is interesting because it suggests that, if one wants to go beyond the poverty headcount in poverty measurement, then functional approximations to growth and distribution elasticities of poverty reduction may simply be unsatisfactory. Dealing with the issue of the determinants of poverty reduction will then require working with the full distribution of income or living standards rather than a few summary measures. This will probably prove to be the only satisfactory solution in the long run and the sooner poverty specialists will get used to dealing systematically with distribution data, rather than inequality or poverty summary measures, at the national level, the better it will be.

Table 1.2
Explaining the evolution of poverty across growth spells (poverty gap)[a]
(dependent variable = percentage change in poverty gap during growth spell)

Explanatory variables	Naive model (1)	Standard model (2)	Improved standard model 1 (3)	Identity check: Lognormal model 1 (4)	Improved standard model 2 (5)	Identity check: Lognormal model 2 (6)
Intercept	0.1434 *0.0857*	0.1660 *0.0777*	0.1683 *0.0796*	0.1412 *0.0787*	0.1823 *0.0812*	0.1272 *0.0759*
Y = percentage change in mean income	-1.2388 *0.5101*	-1.8003 *0.4747*	-0.4101 *2.8388*		-2.3059 *2.8658*	
Variation in Gini coefficient		7.2962 *1.4375*	7.1231 *1.4885*	7.1781 *1.4806*	27.8647 *10.4411*	
Y * poverty-line/mean-income			-0.9647 *2.6588*		-0.9486 *2.6065*	
Y * initial Gini coefficient			-2.4774 *5.6055*		0.8514 *5.6010*	
DGini * poverty-line/mean-income					-20.0988 *7.1598*	
DGini * initial Gini coefficient					-26.8577 *18.8496*	
Y * theoretical value of growth elasticity under lognormal assumption				-0.4961 *0.1661*		-0.5750 *0.1627*
DSigma * theoretical value of poverty inequality elasticity under lognormal assumption[b]						0.7035 *0.1218*
R²	0.05	0.229	0.2308	0.1938	0.2849	0.249

[a]Ordinary least squares estimates, standard errors in italics. The sample includes the 114 growth spells listed in the appendix. All coefficients are significantly different from zero at the 1 percent probability level except the intercept.
[b]Switching from the coefficient of Gini to the standard deviation of the logarithm of income is done through the formula in note 6.

1.4   Some Implications

This being said, the identity that links poverty reduction, mean income growth, and distributional change has several implications for policymaking and economic analysis in the field of poverty that are worth stressing.

On the policy side, it was shown in this chapter that this identity permits identifying precisely the potential contribution of growth and distributional change to poverty reduction. However, it also introduces a point that is often overlooked in the debate of growth vs. redistribution as poverty reduction strategies—an exception being Ravallion (1997). To the extent that growth is sustainable in the long run whereas there is a natural limit to redistribution, it may reasonably be argued that an effective long-run policy of poverty reduction should rely primarily on sustained growth. According to the basic identity analyzed in this chapter, however, income redistribution plays essentially two roles in poverty reduction. A permanent redistribution of income reduces poverty instantaneously through what was identified as the "distribution effect." But, in addition it also contributes to a permanent increase in the elasticity of poverty reduction with respect to growth and therefore to *an acceleration of poverty reduction* for a given rate of economic growth. This is quite independent of the phenomenon emphasized in the recent growth-inequality literature according to which growth would tend to be faster in a less inegalitarian environment.[11] If this were true, there would then be a kind of "double dividend" associated with redistribution policy since it would at the same time accelerate growth and accelerate the speed at which growth spills over onto poverty reduction.

From the point of view of economic analysis, the basic argument in this chapter has clear implications for the understanding of poverty reduction. The common practice of trying to explain the evolution of some poverty measure over time, or across various countries, as a function of a host of variables including economic growth has something tautological. The preceding section has shown that the actual growth elasticity of poverty reduction in a given country could be estimated with considerable precision, even under the lognormal approximation. Running a regression like the "standard model" above where growth appears among the regressors would thus make sense only in the case where one does not observe the actual determinants of the theoretical value of the growth-poverty elasticity, that is the level of development and inequality. This would seem very unlikely, though, and it must be admitted that the way poverty reduction depends on growth is in effect perfectly known. Under these conditions, the only thing that remains to be explained in the basic poverty reduction decomposition formula is the pure "distributional change" effect. Somehow, all the variables that may be added in the regression after the growth effect has been rigorously taken into account should track the change in the distribution and its effects on poverty. In other words, the only thing that poverty change regressions should try to do is really to identify the causes of distributional changes and their effects on poverty indices.

This last remark relates to an earlier point about the nature of poverty being analyzed. In an international context, it seems natural that cross-country comparisons of poverty reduction bears on an "absolute" concept of poverty—namely, $1 or $2 a day. However, most of the argument in this chapter can be reinterpreted as saying that changes in absolute poverty may be decomposed into changes in the mean income of the population and changes in "relative poverty," as measured for instance by the number of people below some fixed proportion of the mean or median income, or simply the poorest x percent of the population. Viewed in this way, the argument in the preceding paragraph basically says that, in understanding the evolution of absolute poverty, the main object of analysis should really be the evolution of relative poverty, as the effect of a change in the mean income on absolute poverty is practically tautological. Although they do not formulate it in this way, this is what Dollar and Kraay (2000) attempt to do by focusing on the mean income or the income share of the bottom 20 percent of the population. When they show that this income share does not seem to move in any systematic direction with growth across countries, they in effect validate the use of the identity relationship to compute the effect of growth on absolute poverty reduction.

1.5 Appendix

The countries and growth spells used in the empirical part of this chapter appear in the following table. Spells are defined by the initial and terminal years.

Table 1.A.1
Countries and spells in database

Country	Spell	Country	Spell
Algeria	88–95	Honduras	94–96
Bangladesh	84–85	India	83–86
Bangladesh	85–88	India	86–87
Bangladesh	88–92	India	87–88
Bangladesh	92–96	India	88–89
Brazil	85–88	India	89–90
Brazil	88–89	India	90–92
Brazil	89–93	India	92–94
Brazil	93–95	India	94–95
Brazil	95–96	India	95–96
Chile	87–90	India	96–97
Chile	90–92	Indonesia	84–87
Chile	92–94	Indonesia	87–90
China	92–93	Indonesia	90–93
China	93–94	Indonesia	93–96
China	94–95	Indonesia	96–99
China	95–96	Jamaica	89–90
China	96–97	Jamaica	93–96
China	97–98	Jordan	92–97
Colombia	88–91	Kazakhstan	93–96
Colombia	95–96	Kenya	92–94
Costa Rica	86–90	Kyrgyz Republic	93–97
Costa Rica	90–93	Lesotho	86–93
Costa Rica	93–96	Madagascar	80–93
Cote D'Ivoire	87–88	Malaysia	84–87
Cote D'Ivoire	88–93	Malaysia	87–89
Cote D'Ivoire	93–95	Malaysia	89–92
Dominican Rep	89–96	Malaysia	92–95
Ecuador	88–94	Mauritania	88–93
Ecuador	94–95	Mauritania	93–95
Egypt	91–95	Mexico	84–92
El Salvador	89–95	Mexico	89–95
El Salvador	95–96	Morocco	85–90
Estonia	93–95	Nepal	85–95
Ethiopia	81–95	Niger	92–95
Ghana	87–89	Nigeria	85–92
Ghana	89–92	Nigeria	92–97
Guatemala	87–89	Pakistan	87–90
Honduras	89–90	Pakistan	90–93
Honduras	92–94	Pakistan	93–96

Table 1.A.1
(continued)

Country	Spell	Country	Spell
Panama	89–91	Thailand	88 (2)–92
Panama	91–95	Thailand	92–96
Panama	95–96	Thailand	96–98
Panama	96–97	Trinidad and Tobago	88–92
Paraguay	90–95	Tunisia	85–90
Peru	94–96	Turkey	87–94
Philippines	85–88	Uganda	89–92
Philippines	88–91	Ukraine	95–96
Philippines	91–94	Venezuela	81–87
Philippines	94–97	Venezuela	87–89
Romania	92–94	Venezuela	89–93
Russia	93–96	Venezuela	93–95
Russia	96–98	Venezuela	95–96
Senegal	91–94	Yemen?	92–98
Sri Lanka	85–90	Zambia	91–93
Sri Lanka	90–95	Zambia	93–96
Thailand	81–88 (1)		

Notes

A preliminary version of this chapter was presented at the conference World Poverty: A Challenge for the Private Sector, organized by the Amsterdam Institute for International Development, Amsterdam, October 3–4, 2000. The present version benefited from comments made by participants to a seminar at CESIfo (Munich, May 2001) and by participants to LACEA 2001 in Montevideo. I am particularly indebted to Daniele Checchi, Gylfi Zoega, and an anonymous referee. I am also indebted to Martin Ravallion for making the data set used in this chapter available to me. Of course, I remain solely responsible for any remaining error. Views expressed in this chapter are those of the author and should not be attributed to the World Bank or any affiliated organization.

1. See World Bank (2000, 47).

2. For a full description of these data, see Chen and Ravallion (2000).

3. See also the presentation of that methodology in the short literature survey provided by Fields (2001).

4. Figure 1.2 provides a very handy general representation of distributional changes and has been used in a number of circumstances. See, for instance, Quah (chapter 2).

5. These properties derive from the fact that $\lambda(\ )$ is known to be an increasing function in the case of the standard normal distribution. Indeed it may be shown that $\lambda(x)$ is the incomplete mean of the standard normal variable over the range (α, x).

6. In the case of a lognormal distribution, both magnitudes are related by the following relationship (see Aitchinson and Brown 1966): $G = 2\Pi(\sigma/2^{1/2}) - 1$.

7. It is also known that $\varepsilon_y^{PG} = (PG - H)/PG$, where PG is the poverty gap.

8. Instead of considering poverty measures, it would also be interesting to consider aggregate measures of social welfare. From that point of view, the measure $W = \bar{y} \cdot (1 - G)$, where $\bar{y}$ is the mean income and G is the Gini coefficient that was originally proposed by Sen, lends itself to the same simple decomposition into growth and distribution effects as the poverty indices considered here.

9. Of course, it would have been possible to keep these observations if the original decomposition formula (2) with the lognormal approximation, rather than (2′), had been used in the econometric analysis that follows.

10. Expression (3′) relies on the standard deviation of the logarithm of income whereas inequality is measured by the Gini coefficient in the data set. However, a one-to-one relationship exists between these two magnitudes when the underlying distribution is lognormal (see note 5). That relationship was used to derive σ from the observed value of the Gini.

11. On this see the survey by Aghion, Caroli, and García-Peñalosa. (1999).

References

Aghion, P., E. Caroli, and C. García-Peñalosa. 1999. Inequality and economic growth: The perspective of new growth theories. *Journal of Economic Literature* 37(4): 1615–1660.

Aitchison, J., and J. Brown. 1966. *The Log-Normal Distribution*. Cambridge: Cambridge University Press.

Chen, S., and M. Ravallion. 2000. How did the world's poorest fare in the 1990s? Mimeo., The World Bank.

Datt, G., and M. Ravallion. 1992. Growth and redistribution components of changes in poverty measures: A decomposition with application to Brazil and India in the 1980s. *Journal of Development Economics* 38(2): 275–295.

de Janvry, A., and E. Sadoulet. 1995. Poverty alleviation, income redistribution and growth during adjustment. In *Coping with Austerity: Poverty and Inequality in Latin America*, ed. N. Lustig. Washington, DC: Brookings Institution.

de Janvry, A., and E. Sadoulet. 2000. Growth, poverty, and inequality in Latin America: A causal analysis, 1970–94. *Review of Income and Wealth* 46(3): 267–287.

Deininger, K., and L. Squire. 1996. A new data set measuring income inequality. *The World Bank Economic Review* 10: 565–591.

Dollar, D., and A. Kraay. 2000. Growth is good for the poor. Mimeo., The World Bank.

Fields, G. 2001. *Distribution and Development: A New Look at the Developing World*. Cambridge: The MIT Press.

Foster, J., J. Greer, and E. Thorbecke. 1984. A class of decomposable poverty measures, *Econometrica* 52: 761–766.

Kakwani, N. 1993. Poverty and economic growth with application to Cote d'Ivoire. *Review of Income and Wealth* 39: 121–139.

Ravallion, M. 1997. Can high-inequality developing countries escape absolute poverty? *Economic Letters* 56: 51–57.

Ravallion, M., and S. Chen. 1997. What can new survey data tell us about recent changes in distribution and poverty? *The World Bank Economic Review* 11: 357–382.

Ravallion M., and M. Huppi. 1991. Measuring changes in poverty: A methodological case study of Indonesia during an adjustment period. *The World Bank Economic Review* 5: 57–82.

World Bank. 2000. *Attacking Poverty, World Development Report 2000/2001*. Oxford: Oxford University Press.

2   One Third of the World's Growth and Inequality

Danny Quah

2.1   Introduction

Three concerns underlie all research on income inequality and economic growth. First, inequality might be causal for growth, raising or lowering an economy's growth rate. Understanding the mechanism then becomes paramount. How do alternative structures of political economy and taxation matter for this relation between inequality and growth? Does income inequality increase the rate of capital investment and therefore growth? Do credit and capital market imperfections magnify potentially adverse impacts of inequality, thereby worsening economic performance and growth? For concreteness, I refer to this circle of related questions as the *mechanism* concern.

Second, even as economic growth occurs, the simultaneous rise in inequality—sometimes hypothesized, other times asserted— might be so steep that the very poor suffer a decline in their incomes. This is one of a set of beliefs underlying the anti-capitalism, anti-globalization, anti-growth movement. Although, not exhaustively descriptive, *anti-globalization* is the term I use to refer to this second concern.

Third is an all-else category of analyses that fall outside the first two. This incorporates concerns such as envy, equity, risk, peer group effects, or the economics of superstars (where the distribution of outcomes turns out more skewed than that of the important underlying characteristics). Thus, this category includes the more traditional motivations in research on income distribution and inequality, but that have become less emphasized in recent research that focus more on the mechanism and anti-globalization concerns.

This chapter is part of a body of research that argues that the mechanism and anti-globalization concerns are empirically untenable. It seeks to sharpen the general points made in Quah (2001b) by concentrating on the world's two most populous nation states, China and India—only two points in a cross-country analysis, but fully one-third of the world's population.

The remainder of this chapter is organized as follows. Section 2.2 describes related literature, and section 2.3 develops the class of probability models underlying the approach in this chapter. Sections 2.4 and 2.5 present the empirical results. Section 2.6 concludes. The technical appendix, section 2.7, contains details on the estimation and data.

2.2 Related Literature

A conventional wisdom recently emerged from empirical research on inequality and growth is how fragile empirical findings are, varying with auxiliary conditioning information, functional form specification, assumed patterns of causality, and so on (e.g., Banerjee and Duflo 2000).

This state of affairs is unlike that at the origins of inequality and growth as a distinct field of study. Then, Kuznets (1955) had asked if personal income inequality increased or declined in the course of economic growth. He documented both: Looking across countries, from poorest to richest, he noted that within-country income inequality first rose and then fell.

Since most of the work there entailed defining and collecting data, it was painstaking and laborious. By contrast, modern researchers now using readily available observations on growth and inequality can easily and routinely reexamine Kuznets's inverted U-shaped curve (e.g., Deininger and Squire 1998). Interest therefore has shifted to more subtle issues: causality and mechanisms relating inequality and growth—see, for example, Aghion, Caroli, and García-Peñalosa (1999), Bénabou (1996), Galor and Zeira (1993), and the literature surveyed in Bertola (1999).

On these more complex questions, however, the data have given a less clearcut message. Results have varied, depending on auxiliary conditioning information and econometric technique. For instance, Alesina and Rodrik (1994), Perotti (1996), and Persson and Tabellini (1994) concluded that inequality and growth are negatively related, while Barro (2000), Forbes (2000), and Li and Zou (1998) reported a positive or varying relation. To some researchers, the situation has seemed so bad that they have simply concluded the data are not informative for interesting issues in inequality and growth, and have attempted to explain why this is so, within a particular model of inequality and growth (e.g., Banerjee and Duflo 2000). In this view, the data are noisy.

This chapter takes no explicit stance on causality between inequality and growth, nor on the functional form relating them. Instead, it models inequality and growth jointly as part of a vector stochastic process, and calibrates the impact each has on a range of welfare indicators and on the individual income distributions—first within China and India, and then taking the two countries together. The chapter addresses simpler questions than those treated in the ambitious work attempting to trace out causality across growth and inequality.

This chapter asks, When growth occurs, how do the poor fare? What difference have the historical dynamics of inequality and growth made for the incomes of one third of the world's population? If inequality were, indeed, to fall when growth is lower, does it fall enough to overcome the negative impact on the poor of slower economic growth overall? Alternatively, if within-country inequality were to rise, does that occur simultaneously with Chinese and India per capita incomes converging, so that overall individual income inequality across these two economies is falling?

Given the data extant, arithmetic alone suffices to retrieve useful answers to these questions. Here, the data are loud, not noisy: For a universe comprising China and India—one-third of the world—for understanding the secular dynamics of personal incomes against a setting of cross-country inequalities, those forces of first-order importance are macroeconomic ones determining national patterns of growth and convergence. Rising average incomes dominate everything else. Within-country inequality dynamics are insignificant for determining inequality across people internationally.

Several earlier papers motivate my approach here. Deininger and Squire (1998) addressed questions closely related to those I've just posed. They used regression analysis and more elaborate data, in contrast to the minimalist, arithmetic approach of this chapter. They concluded, though, much the same as I do below: The poor benefit more from increasing aggregate growth by a range of factors than from reducing inequality through redistribution. Deininger and Squire's view of growth and inequality as the joint outcome of some underlying, unobserved development process matches that in section 2.3.

Dollar and Kraay (2001) studied directly average incomes of the poorest fifth of the population across many different economies. They noted those incomes rise proportionally with overall average incomes, for a wide range of factors generating economic growth. Put differently, it is difficult to find anything raising average incomes that doesn't also increase incomes for the very poor. They concluded, as I will in what follows, that the poor benefit from aggregate economic growth, whatever is driving the latter. Similarly, Ravallion and Chen (1997) found in survey data that changes in inequality are orthogonal to changes in average living standards.

All these papers, in my interpretation, point to a consistent, quantitatively important characterization of the relation between growth and inequality. The characterization is one naturally viewed in terms of figure 2.2 below and rounded out by the arithmetic calculations in this chapter and in Quah (2001b).

More recent papers are related as well. Bourguignon (chapter 1) performed calculations like those in section 2.7.4.1. Sala-i-Martin (2002) used within-country income shares as vector $\mathscr{I}$ (section 2.3 below) and therefore was able to specialize the calculations from what I give in sections 2.3 and 2.7. Although his techniques and emphases differ from those in this chapter and in Quah (2001b), our motivations and conclusions are close and complement each other's. Finally, Heston and Summers (1999), Milanovic (2002), and Sala-i-Martin (2002) constructed world income distributions—namely, across over a hundred countries, not just those for the two I use here—but that similarly put together individual country statistics. Their methods, approaches, and data sources differ from mine, but the underlying ideas are the same.

Critics of this work have pointed out that income inequality statistics such as Gini coefficients, 90-10 ratios, mean-median income ratio, log standard deviations, and so on were never intended for examining the kinds of issues that I treat in what follows nor for merging with the per capita income and population measures that I analyze. Thus, for instance, more detailed investigations into the very poor in any single country, made possible from surveys, field research, or other individual-level microeconomic data, could well display tendencies different from those I derive—see, for example,

Atkinson and Brandolini (2001) or Dreze and Sen (1995). My calculations then, it is asserted, do no more than reveal the misleading nature of many income inequality statistics.

Perhaps so. However, it is also exactly these same statistics with which Bénabou (1996) begins his powerful and influential statement on how inequality matters importantly in economic growth—merging inequality and aggregate statistics, comparing Korea and the Philippines, in a similar spirit to what I do in what follows. If measures like those I use mislead, then all such research is flawed (which I don't believe)—not just those studies, like the current one, that argue inequality is unimportant. The single set of data that researchers all use has different dimensions to it, and we cannot selectively ignore some and heed only others—thereby imposing biases based on whether certain conclusions seem a priori sensible.

2.3   Probability Models for Income Distribution Dynamics

Fix a country at a point in time, and let Y denote income, $\mathscr{I}$ a vector of income inequality measures, and F the distribution of Y across individuals. One entry in $\mathscr{I}$ might be the Gini coefficient; another might be the mean-median income ratio; yet a third might be the standard deviation of log incomes; further entries might be (within-country) income shares; and so on. Each element of $\mathscr{I}$ is a functional or a statistic of the distribution F. To emphasize that per capita income is the *arithmetic mean* or *expectation* of F, write it as $\mathscr{E}$. Economic growth is $\dot{\mathscr{E}}/\mathscr{E}$.

Asking about causality between growth and inequality is asking about the functions

$$\dot{\mathscr{E}}/\mathscr{E} = \phi(\mathscr{I}) \quad \text{or} \quad (\mathscr{I}) = \psi(\dot{\mathscr{E}}/\mathscr{E})$$

(as in, e.g., figure 2.1). If that is the interest, econometric analysis can trace out ϕ and ψ.

By contrast, this chapter models $\dot{\mathscr{E}}/\mathscr{E}$ and $\mathscr{I}$ jointly, taking them to be elements of equal standing in a vector stochastic process Z. Let Z_0 denote the vector of other variables in the system, including population P, so that

$$\{Z(t) : t \geq 0\}, \quad \text{with } Z \overset{\text{def}}{=} \begin{pmatrix} \dot{\mathscr{E}}/\mathscr{E} \\ \mathscr{I} \\ Z_0 \end{pmatrix}$$

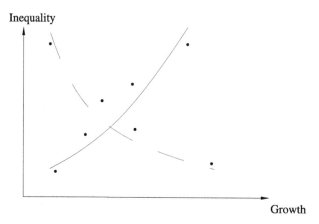

Figure 2.1
Inequality and growth

constitutes the object to investigate. The current study can be viewed as describing an unrestricted vector autoregression in Z; it makes no assumptions on causality relations across the different entries of Z. The law of motion describing the dynamics of the income distribution F implies a law of motion for the vector Z. Conversely, when Z_0 is sufficiently extensive, Z's dynamics imply F's; when Z_0 is not complete, Z's dynamics restrict but do not fully specify F's.

Figure 2.2 illustrates this. The right side shows the density f corresponding to the distribution F, at two time points t_0 and t_1, with the dashed line indicating f at t_0, the earlier time, and the solid line indicating that at time point t_1. Associated with f_0 is its mean $\mathscr{E}_0$; similarly, associated with f_1 is its mean $\mathscr{E}_1$. Figure 2.2 has, as an illustration, $\mathscr{E}_1 > \mathscr{E}_0$ so that economic growth, as measured by national income statistics, has occurred. If $\underline{Y}$ is some arbitrary but fixed income level, one can estimate the fraction of the population that remains with income below $\underline{Y}$ by calculating $\int_{Y \le \underline{Y}} f(Y) \, dY$ from knowledge of f, from time t_0 to time t_1. If one knows the population P as well, then one can use this calculation to estimate the number of people living at incomes less than $\underline{Y}$. In the inequality literature, the statistic $\int_{Y \le \underline{Y}} f(Y) \, dY$ is sometimes called the *poverty headcount index*, and written $HC_{\underline{Y}}$; while the size of the population with incomes at most $\underline{Y}$ is written $P_{\underline{Y}}$ (e.g., equations (14) and (15) in section 2.7).

The problem is one typically has only incomplete information on Z and f. But the researcher can use knowledge on Z to infer restrictions on f, and then estimate statistics of interest like $HC_{\underline{Y}}$ and $P_{\underline{Y}}$.

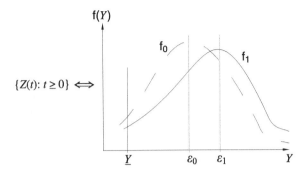

Figure 2.2
Income distribution dynamics

To illustrate the idea, suppose F were assumed (or otherwise inferred) to be Pareto, and known up to the two parameters θ_1 and θ_2:

$$F(y) = 1 - (\theta_1 y^{-1})^{\theta_2}, \qquad \theta_1 > 0, y \geq \theta_1, \theta_2 > 1. \tag{1}$$

What restrictions does knowledge of Z imply for F? Equation (1) gives per capita income $\mathscr{E}$ and Gini coefficient $\mathscr{I}_G$ as

$$\mathscr{E} \stackrel{\text{def}}{=} \int_{-\infty}^{\infty} y \, dF(y) = (\theta_2 - 1)^{-1} \theta_2 \theta_1,$$

$$\mathscr{I}_G \stackrel{\text{def}}{=} [2^{-1}\mathscr{E}(F)]^{-1} \int_{-\infty}^{\infty} \left(F(y) - \frac{1}{2}\right) y \, dF(y) = (2\theta_2 - 1)^{-1},$$

so that knowledge of the first two entries of Z alone gives

$$\hat{\theta}_2 = (1 + \mathscr{I}_G^{-1})/2,$$

$$\hat{\theta}_1 = (1 - \hat{\theta}_2^{-1})\mathscr{E}.$$

With more information in Z, the researcher can either estimate θ more precisely, using a method of moments technique as described in section 2.7.1 below, or alternatively, relax the Pareto assumption for F. In either case, HC_Y and P_Y can then be estimated straighforwardly.

Putting together the implied F's for different countries in the world would allow mapping the worldwide income distribution (Quah 2001b). To appreciate the value of doing this, consider figure 2.3, which shows what has sometimes been referred to as an *emerging twin peaks* in cross-country income distribution dynamics (e.g.,

Income distributions

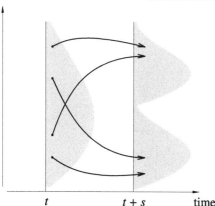

Figure 2.3
Emerging twin peaks

Quah 2001a). This twin-peaks characterization, as many others in the macroeconomic growth literature, takes a country as a unit of observation. Thus, countries as large as China are treated the same way as those as small as Singapore, and income distributions *within* countries are ignored—the analysis takes everyone in the economy to have the same (per capita, average) income.

Information on income distributions within a country allow enriching the picture in figure 2.3 to something like figure 2.4. The black dots at time *t* indicate the per capita incomes of two hypothetical countries, with the darker shaded area around each depicting within-country individual income distributions. Thus, even as national per capita incomes evolve according to an emergent twin-peaks dynamic law, the distribution of incomes across people, within and across countries, can evolve and overlap in intricate ways.

2.4 China and India

China and India—although only two countries out of over one hundred in figure 2.3—carry within them a third of the world's population. They thus provide substantial insight into the dynamics in figure 2.4.

Table 2.1 records that between 1980 and 1992 China's per capita income grew from US$972 to US$1,493, an annual growth rate of

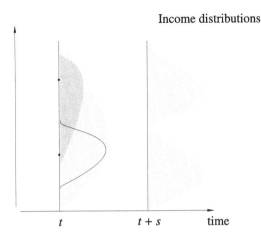

Income distributions

t $t + s$ time

Figure 2.4
Individual income distributions

Table 2.1
Aggregate income and population dynamics: China, India, and the United States

	Per capita incomes (US$)			Population ($\times 10^6$)	
	1980	1992	$\dot{\mathscr{E}}/\mathscr{E}$	1980	1992
China	972	1493	3.58%	981	1162
India	882	1282	3.12%	687	884
United States	15295	17945	1.33%	228	255

3.58 percent. Over this period, India grew at a lower annual rate of 3.12 percent, increasing its per capita income from US$882 to US$1,282. (Per capita incomes are purchasing power parity adjusted real GDP per capita in constant dollars at 1985 prices, series `rgdpch` from Summers and Heston 1991.) For comparison, table 2.1 also contains a row for the United States, showing its 1.33 percent annual growth over 1980–1992, taking per U.S. capita income from US$15,295 to US$17,945. The last two columns of table 2.1 contain population figures, again from Summers and Heston (1991). By 1992, China had grown to over 1.1 billion people, with India approaching 0.9 billion.

It has been remarked many times elsewhere that China's fast-increasing per capita income came together with rises in inequality. Table 2.2 shows Gini coefficients for the same three countries, China, India, and the United States, over 1980–1992. Inequality in China, as

Table 2.2
Inequality in China, India, and the United States, by Gini coefficient (from Deininger and Squire 1996)

	Gini coefficient $\mathscr{I}_G$		
	1980	1992	Min. (year)
China	0.32	0.38	0.26 (1984)
India	0.32	0.32	0.30 (1990)
US	0.35	0.38	0.35 (1982)

Table 2.3
Fraction of population and number of people with incomes less than US$2 per day. The range of estimates spans the different distributional assumptions described in section 2.7.4.

	$\underline{Y} = 2;\ HC_{\underline{Y}}(P_{\underline{Y}}, 10^6)$	
	1980	1992
China	0.37–0.54 (360–530)	0.14–0.17 (158–192)
India	0.48–0.62 (326–426)	0.12–0.19 (110–166)

measured by the Gini coefficient, increased from 0.32 to 0.38, while that in India remained constant at 0.32. While the last column of table 2.2 shows the increase in China's inequality is not monotone and India's inequality was not constant throughout—China had its low Gini coefficient of 0.26 over this period in 1984, while India's low was 0.30 in 1990—it is tempting to conclude from looking cross-sectionally at China and India that a fast-growing economy also has its inequality rise rapidly, while a slower-growing economy can keep inequality in check.

But what do tables 2.1 and 2.2 imply for, say, the number of people in China and India living below a specific fixed income level? How rapidly were people exiting low-income states, given aggregate growth and actual changes in measured inequality? If, counterfactually, inequality had remained unchanged, how would aggregate growth alone have changed conditions for the poor? Or, again counterfactually, how much would inequality have had to increase, for the poor not to have benefited at all from aggregate growth?

Tables 2.3 and 2.4 provide answers to these questions, obtained using the calculations detailed below in section 2.7. First, from the actual historical record in per capita income growth $(\dot{\mathscr{E}}/\mathscr{E})$, population, and Gini coefficients, one can, with weak additional assumptions on the parametric form of density f, work out how the entire distribution of individual income shifted between 1980 and 1992. Table 2.3 shows how the situation for the very poor changed over this time period. The fraction of the population living on less than US$2 per day (US$730 annually) varied from 0.37 to 0.54 in China in 1980; this corresponded to between 360 million to 530 million people.[1] By 1992, the fraction of population in that income range had fallen to 0.14 to 0.17, implying only between 158 million to 192 million people, given the population size then. In other words, over 1980–1992 China reduced the population in this very poor income range by between 210 million to 338 million people, even as inequality and total population rose.

The situation for India is less surprising, as measured inequality there remained constant, and only aggregate economic growth occurred.[2] But since the total Indian population also rose, it might well have been that the poor did increase in number. Table 2.3 shows that did not happen. Between 1980 and 1992, the number of Indians living on less than US$2 a day fell from 326–426 million to less than half that, 110–166 million. The fraction of the Indian population in this income range fell from approximately half to perhaps one-fifth, likely less. India reduced the population living in the very poor income range by about a quarter of a billion, a number comparable to the change in China.

If the world comprised only China and India put together, it would show a number of interesting features. First, the country that grew faster on aggregate also had inequality rise more—the upward-sloping schedule in figure 2.1 is that that is relevant. Second, however, even despite this positive relation between growth and inequality, overall the world's poor benefited dramatically from economic growth. Over the course of little more than a decade, about half a billion people—out of a total population across the two countries of about 1.6 to 1.9 billion—exited the state of extreme poverty. This decline in sheer numbers of the very poor divided about equally between China and India.

Table 2.4 takes the argument further. Suppose population were held constant at 1980 levels in China and India. The left panel in the table shows that if inequality too were held constant at its 1980 levels, then aggregate growth alone would have removed from being

Table 2.4
From 1980 perspective: Given aggregate growth, reduction in numbers of poor if inequality unchanged, and proportional inequality increase per year to maintain poverty numbers

	$\mathscr{I}_G$, P constant: $-\dot{P}_{\underline{Y}}$	$HC_{\underline{Y}}$ constant: $\dot{\mathscr{I}}_G/\mathscr{I}_G$
China	33 million/year	8.3%/year
India	17 million/year	8.8%/year

very poor 33 million people a year in China, and 17 million people a year in India. The right panel shows that to keep constant the number of people living on incomes less than US$2 a day as aggregate growth proceeded, the Gini coefficient would have had to rise at a proportional growth rate of 8.3 percent per year in China, and 8.8 percent per year in India. Such rapid and large increases in inequality are unprecedented in world history.[3] China's increase in inequality would have had to more than double, and be kept at that rate for a dozen years, to nullify the beneficial effects of its high aggregate growth rate.

I conclude from the discussion here that, given the historical experience in China and India, aggregate economic growth might well come about only with increases in inequality. However, given magnitudes that are historically reasonable, growth is unambiguously beneficial—especially for the poor in general, and even for the poor in particular when inequality rises.

2.5   Extensions

This section expands on the discussion in section 2.4 above. It provides further quantification and illustration to the conclusions there.

Deininger and Squire (1996), Li, Squire, and Zou (1998), and Quah (2001b) have presented calculations formalizing how most of the variation in measured inequality is *across* countries. Inequality changes hardly at all in time. It is not that inequality—for physical reasons or otherwise—cannot vary much; it is that the workings of economies lead to inequality hardly changing through time. Honduras's 1968 income inequality of 62 percent (Gini coefficient) is 2.4 times that of Belgium's 26 percent in 1985. But at the same time, over the entire postwar era, income inequality in Belgium never rose above 28 percent while Honduras's never fell below 50 percent.

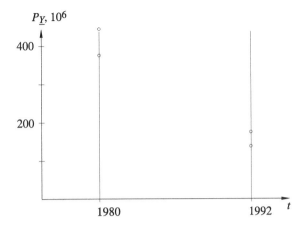

Figure 2.5
Estimated absolute poverty reduction

This fact has implications for panel data analyses of inequality and growth (Quah 2001b). Panel data econometric methods that condition out individual effects—almost all do—end up removing all the important variation in inequality data. Moreover, since economic growth has its principal variation in the orthogonal direction—in time rather than across countries (e.g., Easterly et al. 1993)—panel data methods shoehorn inequality and growth data into spuriously better fit with each other. In other words, econometric methods that condition out individual effects represent here a methodologically suspect attempt to remove statistical biases. That justification has often been simply imported from other fields of economics, without due attention to why applying such techniques to study inequality and growth might be inappropriate.

From table 2.3 one concludes that China and India together reduced the number of people living on less than US$2 a day by between 36 million and 50 million each year. Figure 2.5 graphs this same reduction from 1980 to 1992 in the number of people with incomes less than US$2 per day, given the actual historical outcomes in income inequality and economic growth. China and India alone shifted 508 million people, more than 12 percent of the world's population, about one-third of the world's then-poor, out of poverty.

Figure 2.6 shows, for each economy, the amount of poverty reduction per year that would have occurred from aggregate growth alone, had inequality and population size remained constant at their

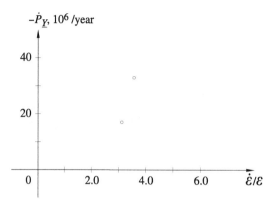

Figure 2.6
Growth alone

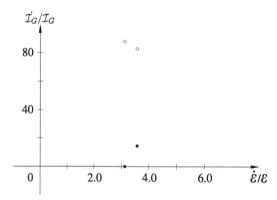

Figure 2.7
Inequality to nullify growth

1980 values. Obviously, the faster is economic growth, the faster would P_Y fall. The figure emphasizes that to reduce poverty worldwide it is in the very large economies like China and India where high growth is needed.

Figure 2.7 shows, again for each economy, the proportional growth rate of inequality that would be required to nullify the benefits of growth, had population remained constant at its 1980 value. The dark dots toward the bottom of the figure shows the actual growth rate in inequality that occurred over the sample. (These numbers would be lower than those in note 3, for the multiple/

single time-period reason described there.) Counterfactual increases in inequality of the magnitude that would be needed to overcome the poverty-reducing impact of economic growth—the upper part of the picture, in light dots—are far outside the range of historical realization.

Quah (2001b) presents counterparts of figures 2.5–2.7 for the 100 or so countries for which data are available. The previous conclusions are reinforced; unsurprisingly, China and India dominate the picture.

2.6 Conclusions

Much recent research on inequality and growth has taken one of two possible approaches: The first is explicit, and that is to see if inequality causes growth. The second, typically left implicit, is to see if, even as growth occurs, the poor might be disadvantaged anyway, because inequality has risen so dramatically. This chapter has shown that for China and India—only two points in a cross-section but one third of the world's population—neither of these possibilities is empirically tenable.

More traditional motivations—risk, poverty, equity—for studying inequality, however, remain. Indeed, they are reinforced as worldwide inequality continues to evolve, driven by powerful economic forces. But these motivations have little to do with the more recent analyses of the relation between inequality and growth.

This chapter has applied a simple arithmetic approach to obtain its findings. It has asked, given historical patterns of growth and inequality, how have income distributions evolved in China and in India and across both countries? How have the poor fared in the two countries as per capita incomes and rich-poor differences have changed? Whether the growth and inequality data are unable to speak clearly on questions of causality or whether they only imply weak empirical relations, the data are unequivocal on the questions I posed. The data are loud, not noisy.

The principal finding of the chapter is twofold: First, only under inconceivably high increases in inequality would economic growth not benefit the poor. The magnitudes of improvement in living standards due to aggregate economic growth simply overwhelm any putative deterioration due to increases in inequality. Second, any mechanism where inequality causes economic growth, positively or negatively, is empirically irrelevant for determining outcomes for individual income distributions. I have obtained these results for China and India in this chapter. A complete study—rounding out the remaining two-thirds left over from the title of this chapter—is in Quah (2001b).

This chapter has taken care to assume no single view on the causal mechanisms relating inequality and growth. It has pointed out that whatever it is that drives economic growth in the large, those forces—be they macroeconomic, technological, political, or institutional—are dramatically important for improving the lot of the poor when they lead to economic growth. And similarly so in the opposite direction when they lead to economic stagnation.

What might seem an appealing possibility to raise here is that income inequality could, positively or negatively, truly cause aggregate economic growth, so that this chapter's principal finding would then only reinforce the importance of distributional and inequality concerns over macroeconomic growth. However, even in reduced-form regressions of growth on inequality, the R^2 fit can never be very high: The directions of principal variation in the two variables are just too different (Quah 2001b). Therefore, even in the best of circumstances, even with no ambiguity on the direction of causality, many other factors beyond inequality influence economic growth. And *all* of them, through their impact on the aggregate income level, affect the poor—independent of inequality's effect on economic growth.

Finally, it is not a telling criticism of the work in this chapter to say that because it uses Gini coefficients or other standard inequality measures, it does not get at the true nature of inequality, whatever that might mean. Because the chapter's methods characterize the entire income distribution, the focus on specific inequality measures is only for practical convenience, not conceptual necessity. However, precisely the same measures are used in all other studies of growth and inequality I know—in particular, in the many regression studies that claim to show one causal relation or another between these two quantities. If the data used are inappropriate here, then they are similarly so there too. Indeed, one might view the calculations here as simply taking a logical step prior to other work in its drawing out an interpretation to the indexes used in studies of inequality and growth.

2.7   Technical Appendix

If data existed on individual incomes accruing to different economic agents, at each point in time, then the empirical analysis would be straightforward. One can directly estimate the entire income distribution across agents on the planet, and characterize its dynamics through time. The problem, however, is that such data are unavailable and are unlikely to be produced anytime soon.

I develop here an alternative empirical framework that is general, flexible, and convenient. The approach is designed to be capable of incorporating a wide range of alternative distributional hypotheses and a variety of measurements on different characteristics of income inequality. Thus, the empirical analysis is intended to apply readily as more and better data on income inequality characteristics become available.

I seek to uncover characteristics of the global distribution of income across individuals. One knows characteristics of income distributions *within* countries, over time for a number of countries. A traditional approach then to analyzing inequalities across progressively larger subsets of individual incomes—proceeding from yet finer subgroups—is to ask if the inequality index *aggregates* (e.g., Milanovic 2002). The approach I take here differs. It begins with noting that if one had the actual distribution $F_{j,t}$ for economy j at time t, where the population size is $P_{j,t}$, then the worldwide income distribution $F_{W,t}$, in a world of economies $j = 1, 2, \ldots, N$, is

$$F_{W,t}(y) = P_{W,t}^{-1} \sum_{j=1}^{N} F_{j,t}(y) \times P_{j,t}, \qquad y \in (0, \infty) \tag{2}$$

with the world population

$$P_{W,t} = \sum_{j=1}^{N} P_{j,t}.$$

Differentiating (2) with respect to y gives the implied density for the worldwide distribution of income as the weighted average of individual country income distribution densities:

$$f_{W,t}(y) = \sum_{j=1}^{N} f_{j,t}(y) \times (P_{j,t}/P_{W,t}), \qquad y \in (0, \infty). \tag{3}$$

Knowing the distribution F_W means one can calculate directly all the inequality indexes one wishes—whether or not particular indexes aggregate becomes irrelevant.

2.7.1 Estimating Individual Income Distributions

Given the quantities on the right of equation (3) the worldwide income distribution is straightforward to calculate. However, the individual distributions $F_{j,t}$ are, generally, unknown. Instead, typically, the researcher has data on a number of diverse functionals of them—for example, Gini coefficients, quintile shares, averages, and so on. This section describes obtaining an estimate for F_j from data on such functionals.

Since the remainder of this section concentrates on what happens with a single economy, the j subscript is taken as understood and deleted to ease notation.

Fix an economy j. Suppose in each period t, one observes realizations on (P_t, X_t), where P is the population size and $X_t \in \mathbb{R}^d$ is a d-dimensional vector of functionals of the underlying unobservable income distribution F_t and population P_t. For example, when the first entry of X_t is the average or per capita income, then

$$X_{1,t} = \int_{-\infty}^{+\infty} y \, dF_t(y) = \int_{0}^{+\infty} y \, dF_t(y).$$

Let $(\mathbb{R}, \mathscr{R})$ denote the pair comprised of the real line $\mathbb{R}$ together with the collection $\mathscr{R}$ of its Borel sets. Let $\mathbf{B}(\mathbb{R}, \mathscr{R})$ denote the Banach space of bounded finitely additive set functions on the measurable space $(\mathbb{R}, \mathscr{R})$ endowed with total variation norm

$$\forall \varphi \text{ in } \mathbf{B}(\mathbb{R}, \mathscr{R}): \qquad |\varphi| = \sup \sum_k |\varphi(A_k)|,$$

where the supremum in this definition is taken over all

$$\{A_k : j = 1, 2, \ldots, n\}$$

finite measurable partitions of $\mathbb{R}$.

Distributions on $\mathbb{R}$ can be identified with probability measures on $(\mathbb{R}, \mathscr{R})$. Those are, in turn, just countably additive elements in $\mathbf{B}(\mathbb{R}, \mathscr{R})$ assigning value 1 to the entire space $\mathbb{R}$. Let $\mathfrak{B}$ denote the Borel sigma-algebra generated by the open subsets (relative to total variation norm topology) of $\mathbf{B}(\mathbb{R}, \mathscr{R})$. Then $(\mathbf{B}, \mathfrak{B})$ is another measurable space.

Write the vector of potentially observable functionals as a collection

$$\mathbf{T}_l : (\mathbf{B} \times \mathbb{R}, \mathfrak{B} \times \mathscr{R}) \to (\mathbb{R}, \mathscr{R}), \qquad l = 1, 2, \ldots, d$$

(where $\mathfrak{B} \times \mathscr{R}$ denotes the sigma-algebra generated by the Cartesian product of $\mathfrak{B}$ and $\mathscr{R}$). Thus, for distribution F_t associated with probability measure $\varphi_t \in (\mathbf{B}, \mathfrak{B})$,

$$X_{l,t} = \mathbf{T}_l(\varphi_t, P_t), \qquad l = 1, 2, \ldots, d. \tag{4}$$

Without loss or ambiguity, I also write $\mathbf{T}_l(F_t, P_t)$ to denote the right hand side of (4). Write $\mathbf{T}$ to denote the vector of observed functionals, that is,

$$\mathbf{T}(F_t, P_t) = (\mathbf{T}_1(F_t, P_t), \mathbf{T}_2(F_t, P_t), \ldots, \mathbf{T}_d(F_t, P_t))'.$$

Assume, finally, that the distribution F_t is known up to a p-dimensional vector $\theta_t \in \mathbb{R}^p$,

$$F_t = F(\cdot \mid \theta_t) \stackrel{\text{def}}{=} \mathsf{F}_{\theta_t}. \tag{5}$$

(In equation (5) the symbol F is used to mean a number of different mathematical objects, but this will be without ambiguity, as the context will always be revealing.)

Equation (5) restricts in two distinct ways. First, the functional form F_t is assumed known. Second, time variation in the sequence of distributions F_t is assumed mediated entirely through the finite-dimensional parameter vector θ_t.

If for *some* θ_t^*, distribution F_{θ_t} is the true model, then

$$\mathbf{T}_l(\mathsf{F}_{\theta_t^*}, P_t) = X_{l,t}, \qquad l = 1, 2, \ldots, d.$$

At fixed t, define the estimator $\hat{\theta}_t$ for θ_t^* as

$$\hat{\theta}_t \stackrel{\text{def}}{=} \arg\min_{\theta \in \mathbb{R}^p} (\mathbf{T}(\mathsf{F}_\theta, P_t) - X_t)' \Omega (\mathbf{T}(\mathsf{F}_\theta, P_t) - X_t),$$

$$\Omega \ d \times d \ \text{positive definite}. \tag{6}$$

Each different weighting matrix Ω—including, notably, the identity matrix—produces a different estimator. Under standard regularity conditions (as in GMM or related analogue estimation; e.g., Hansen 1982; Manski 1988), each Ω-associated estimator is consistent when

X_t is itself replaced with a consistent estimator for the underlying population quantity. Moreover, defining the minimand

$$Q_{X_t}(\theta) = (\mathbf{T}(\mathsf{F}_\theta, P_t) - X_t)'\Omega(\mathbf{T}(\mathsf{F}_\theta, P_t) - X_t), \tag{7}$$

and denoting $\theta_{t,0}$ as the probability limit of (6), standard reasoning using

$$\hat{\theta}_t - \theta_{t,0} = -\left(\left.\frac{d^2Q}{d\theta\,d\theta'}\right|_{\theta_{t,0}}\right)^{-1}\left.\frac{dQ}{d\theta}\right|_{\theta_{t,0}},$$

allows a limit distribution theory for these estimators, provided the quantities X_t have a characterizable distribution around their underlying population counterparts.

Using θ_t from the estimating equation (6) in (5) gives an estimator for F_t in each economy j. Plugging the result for each j in turn into (2)–(3) gives an estimator for the worldwide distribution of income. Tracking $\theta_{j,t}$ as they evolve through time then gives worldwide individual income distribution dynamics.

Section 2.7.4 provides some explicit analytically worked out examples of this procedure.

2.7.2 Alternative Functionals T_l

This section provides examples of some candidate functionals T_l. When observations on them are available—as assumed in the notation for section 2.7.1—they are readily used in estimating and characterizing the distributions $F_{j,t}$. Conversely, if they are not observable but an estimate of $F_{j,t}$ is available, then estimates for T_l can, instead, be induced.

For *mean* or *per capita income*, take

$$\mathscr{E}(\mathsf{F}, P) \stackrel{\mathrm{def}}{=} \int_{-\infty}^{\infty} y\,d\mathsf{F}(y). \tag{8}$$

The *Gini coefficient* is standard in analysis of income inequality. Associate with it the functional

$$\mathscr{I}_G(\mathsf{F}, P) \stackrel{\mathrm{def}}{=} [2^{-1}\mathscr{E}(\mathsf{F})]^{-1} \int_{-\infty}^{\infty} \left(\mathsf{F}(y) - \frac{1}{2}\right) y\,d\mathsf{F}(y) \tag{9}$$

(see, e.g., Cowell 2000).

A different set of functionals standard in inequality analyses is the set of *cumulative quintile shares*. To define these, set for integer i from

1 to 4,

$$Y_{0.2i}(\mathsf{F}, P) \overset{\text{def}}{=} \sup_{y \in \mathbb{R}} \{y \mid \mathsf{F}(y) \le 0.2i\}, \tag{10}$$

$$S_{0.2i}(\mathsf{F}) \overset{\text{def}}{=} \left(\int_{-\infty}^{Y_{0.2i}(\mathsf{F}, P)} y \, d\mathsf{F}(y) \right) \times \mathscr{E}(\mathsf{F}, P)^{-1}. \tag{11}$$

The first of these, equation (10), defines the $(20 \times i)$-th percentile income level; the left-hand side is also known as the i-th quintile. The pair (10)–(11) generalizes to arbitrary percentile shares, but in practice the more general versions are rarely used (see, however, equations (12), (13), and (17)).

Concepts (9)–(11) are those traditionally used in studies on inequality. Reliable observations on them are now widely available across time and economies (Deininger and Squire 1996).

Recently, Milanovic (2002) has used household data to construct *within-decile average incomes* across many different countries. These fit within the framework as follows. Define

$$Y_{0.1i}(\mathsf{F}, P) \overset{\text{def}}{=} \sup_{y \in \mathbb{R}} \{y \mid \mathsf{F}(y) \le 0.1i\}, \qquad i = 0, 1, \ldots, 9, \tag{12}$$

and let

$$\mathscr{E}_{0.1i}(\mathsf{F}, P) \overset{\text{def}}{=} \int_{Y_{0.1 \times (i-1)}}^{Y_{0.1i}} y \, d\mathsf{F}(y), \qquad i = 1, \ldots, 9,$$

$$\mathscr{E}_1(\mathsf{F}, P) \overset{\text{def}}{=} \int_{Y_{0.9}}^{\infty} y \, d\mathsf{F}(y). \tag{13}$$

Similar to (10) above, equation (12) defines the $(10 \times i)$-th percentile income level, with the left-hand side also known as the i-th decile. The analysis in Milanovic (2002) can thus be merged with that which follows if one uses the decile averages $\mathscr{E}_{0.1i}$ from (13) (or even the deciles themselves $Y_{0.1i}$ in (12)) as candidate T_l's.

Yet other ways to extract or summarize information from (F, P) are relevant when interest lies in poverty specifically (e.g., Ravallion 1997; Ravallion and Chen 1997; World Bank 1990). Fix a low but otherwise arbitrary level of income $\underline{Y}$, and let

$$HC_{\underline{Y}}(\mathsf{F}, P) \overset{\text{def}}{=} \mathsf{F}(\underline{Y}) = \int_{-\infty}^{\underline{Y}} d\mathsf{F}(y). \tag{14}$$

Equation (14) gives a *poverty headcount index*, namely, the fraction of population below a given income level $\underline{Y}$. Record also the absolute size of the population with those incomes:

$$P_{\underline{Y}}(\mathsf{F}, P) \stackrel{\text{def}}{=} P \times \mathsf{F}(\underline{Y}).\tag{15}$$

Finally, define

$$PGI_{\underline{Y}}(\mathsf{F}, P) \stackrel{\text{def}}{=} \frac{\int_{-\infty}^{\underline{Y}} y \, d\mathsf{F}(y)}{\underline{Y}}.\tag{16}$$

This is a *poverty gap index*, namely, a (normalized) average income distance from a given income level $\underline{Y}$.

When researchers are interested in whether a gap is emerging between groups of high-income and low-income individuals, a concept more useful than just inequality is polarization (e.g., Esteban and Ray 1994; Quah 1993, 1997; Wolfson 1994). To obtain a functional that captures such an effect, follow the notation of (10) and let $Y_{0.5}$ denote the *median*

$$Y_{0.5}(\mathsf{F}, P) \stackrel{\text{def}}{=} \sup_{y \in \mathbb{R}} \left\{ y \mid \mathsf{F}(y) \leq \frac{1}{2} \right\},\tag{17}$$

and then, using (8), (9), and (17), define a *polarization index*

$$P_Z(\mathsf{F}, P) \stackrel{\text{def}}{=} \left[(1 - \mathscr{I}_G)\mathscr{E} - \frac{\int_{-\infty}^{Y_{0.5}} y \, d\mathsf{F}(y)}{\int_{-\infty}^{Y_{0.5}} d\mathsf{F}(y)} \right] \times \frac{2}{Y_{0.5}}.\tag{18}$$

The first term in square brackets is the Gini-adjusted per capita income; the second is the average level of incomes below the median (this is a special case of a conditional expectation that appears again in what follows). The greater this separation, the higher will be the value taken by the polarization index in (18).

All the functionals so far considered—apart from $P_{\underline{Y}}$ in (15)—vary only with the distribution F, and not the size of the population P. The next functional takes both into account; it describes a dynamic property of the evolving distributions. From the headcount index (14), one might be interested in the rate of flow of people past the fixed income level $\underline{Y}$. This is

$$Fl_{\underline{Y}}(\mathsf{F}_{\theta_t}, P_t) \stackrel{\text{def}}{=} -\frac{d}{dt}(\mathsf{F}_{\theta_t}(\underline{Y}) \cdot P_t)$$

$$= -\left[P_t \frac{d}{dt} \mathsf{F}_{\theta_t}(\underline{Y}) + \mathsf{F}_{\theta_t}(\underline{Y}) \frac{dP_t}{dt} \right].\tag{19}$$

Equation (19) shows interaction among a range of factors, including in particular per capita income growth $\dot{\mathcal{E}}/\mathcal{E}$ and static, point-in-time inequality $\mathcal{I}_G$. I use this simultaneous relationship in sections 2.7.4.1 and 2.7.4.2. Using different techniques, it is exactly this interaction that Ravallion (1997) studies for developing countries, using household survey data with direct observations on Fl_Y.

The previous examples should certainly not be viewed to be exhaustive. I have given explicit $\mathbf{T}_l$ calculations only for those functionals readily found in the empirical literature and for which observations are available. As progressively more refined income distribution data are constructed, the reasoning here is easily extended to take those into account.

2.7.3 Distribution F as Organizing Principle

As the discussion makes clear, my approach in this chapter is to use the distribution dynamics in $F_{W,t}$ as the core concept around which I organize all subsequent discussion. Equation (2) is the key compositional relation from individual economies to the world. All induced statistics—Gini coefficients, poverty headcounts, poverty gap indexes, polarization indexes, and so on—derive from it. In this exercise, it is not key whether those statistics retain compositional integrity, or have an axiomatic justification, or satisfy other reasonable criteria. They are not special in this analysis. I use them in what follows because they are easily interpretable and are standard in discussions on income distributions, thus allowing to reduce the dimensionality of (the information in) estimated distribution dynamics. As formulated here, when independently available, these statistics can be used to augment the estimation (6); when not, they can be straightforwardly derived from an estimate of $F_{j,t}$. Everything centers on the distributions.

Admittedly, backing out estimates of individual-economy distributions $F_{j,t}$—as in equation (6)—might be viewed as a contrived problem. If a researcher had the original individual-level incomes data, then $F_{j,t}$ (and thus $F_{W,t}$) could be estimated directly by standard methods (e.g., Milanovic 2002; Silverman 1981). One should never need to construct any of (9)–(19), and go through (6), to characterize the distribution $F_{j,t}$. It is because such individual-level data are not readily available—instead statistical agencies have calculated and made available only different, aggregative statistics of the underlying data—that one is led to estimation by (6).

By the same token, one might wish to take care not to view θ as "deep structural parameters" in any sense of the term. Instead, a useful perspective is to treat the θ's as simply convenient ways—hyperparameters—to keep control on the high-dimensional calculations that would be otherwise involved in tracing through distribution dynamics. The analysis in this chapter is obviously not one that sets out to test a multivariate regression or simultaneous equations model. It studies historical tendencies, not—to a large degree—the effects of artificial growth paths and inequality dynamics.

Standard econometric analysis of (6)–(7) allows consistency and limit distribution results for the hyperparameters θ. Measurement errors in the data X_t, in sample, do not logically pose any difficulties. However, whether X_t can be guaranteed to converge to underlying population quantities, and in a manner where the limiting distribution can be characterized falls outside the domain of analysis in this chapter.

Finally, to state the obvious, this approach is one that makes sense when the individual distributions $F_{j,t}$ are comparable. If they are not, then the whole enterprise of trying to study worldwide inequality is flawed from the beginning, regardless of the approach taken.

2.7.4 Induced Statistics and Parametric Examples

I now turn to some explicit parametric examples to provide intuition for the remainder of the analysis. In describing the distribution dynamics, it is useful to establish some additional notation.

Suppose that in a given economy per capita income $\mathscr{E}$ increases at a positive constant proportional growth rate:

$$\dot{\mathscr{E}}/\mathscr{E} = \xi > 0. \tag{20}$$

I wish to compare dynamically evolving income distributions against a fixed (feasible and low, but otherwise arbitrary) threshold income level $\underline{Y}$. One statistic I am concerned with in particular is the rate of flow of people past $\underline{Y}$, namely, equation (19). I am interested in the value of (19) when inequality, as measured by the Gini coefficient $\mathscr{I}_G$ say, is held constant. Alternatively, I am interested in finding how fast $\mathscr{I}_G$ has to change to set (19) to zero.

Write F_θ to denote a parametrized income distribution function, and let f_θ be its associated density function

$$F_\theta(y) = \int_{-\infty}^{y} f_\theta(\tilde{y})\, d\tilde{y}, \qquad y \in \mathbb{R}.$$

Any given distribution also implies the conditional expectation function

$$E_\theta(Y \mid Y \text{ in set } \mathscr{A}) = \frac{\int_{\mathscr{A}} y\, dF_\theta(y)}{\int_{\mathscr{A}} dF_\theta(y)}.$$

This is the expectation of a random variable Y, distributed F_θ, conditional on Y falling in set $\mathscr{A}$ of possible values.

I abuse notation by using subscripts such as $N(\theta)$, $L(\theta)$, or $P(\theta)$ to the functions F, f, and E, to denote specific functional forms—in this case the normal, the lognormal, and the Pareto type 1 distributions, respectively. In the general case (with no explicit functional form restriction), the subscript will be simply θ.

To begin discussing explicitly parametrized distributions, record that the normal distribution characterized by mean θ_1 and variance θ_2 has density

$$f_{N(\theta)}(y) = (2\pi\theta_2)^{-1/2} \times \exp\left\{-\frac{1}{2\theta_2}(y - \theta_1)^2\right\}, \qquad \theta_2 > 0.$$

The *standard normal* sets $\theta_1 = 0$ and $\theta_2 = 1$ so that then

$$F_{N(0,1)}(y) = \int_{-\infty}^{y} (2\pi)^{-1/2} \exp\left\{-\frac{1}{2}\tilde{y}^2\right\} d\tilde{y}.$$

2.7.4.1 Lognormal
The lognormal distribution is widely used in traditional studies of personal income distributions. Its density is

$$f_{L(\theta)}(y) = (2\pi\theta_2)^{-1/2} \cdot y^{-1} \times \exp\left\{-\frac{1}{2\theta_2}(\log y - \theta_1)^2\right\}, \qquad \theta_2 > 0, y > 0.$$

For this distribution the **T** functionals in (8)–(11) of section 2.7.2 are

$$\mathscr{E}(F_{L(\theta)}) = \exp\left(\theta_1 + \tfrac{1}{2}\theta_2\right),$$

$$\mathscr{I}_G(F_{L(\theta)}) = 2 \times F_{N(0,1)}(\theta_2^{1/2}/\sqrt{2}) - 1,$$

$$S_{0.2i}(F_{L(\theta)}) = F_{L(\theta_1+\theta_2, \theta_2)}(Y_{0.2i}(F_{L(\theta)})),$$

with

$$Y_{0.2i}(F_{L(\theta)}) = \exp\{F^{-1}_{N(0,1)}(0.2i) \cdot \theta_2^{1/2} + \theta_1\}.$$

An alternative expression for the cumulative quintile share is

$$S_{0.2i}(F_{L(\theta)}) = F_{N(0,1)}\left(\frac{\log Y_{0.2i} - (\theta_1 + \theta_2)}{\theta_2^{1/2}}\right)$$

$$= F_{N(0,1)}(F^{-1}_{N(0,1)}(0.2i) - \theta_2^{1/2}).$$

If estimation (6) used only $\mathscr{E}$ and $\mathscr{I}_G$, and ignored information on other elements of T (or if those observations were unavailable), then an exact analytical formula for the estimator can be given as follows:

$$\hat{\theta}_2 = [F^{-1}_{N(0,1)}((\mathscr{I}_G + 1)/2)]^2 \times 2,$$

$$\hat{\theta}_1 = \log \mathscr{E} - \hat{\theta}_2/2.$$

These can be used, in any case, as starting values in an iterative solution to (6). Heston and Summers (1999) used these as the estimates for their study.

Explicit formulas for some of the dynamics are then available:

$$\dot{\mathscr{E}}/\mathscr{E} = \dot{\theta}_1 + \tfrac{1}{2}\dot{\theta}_2,$$

$$\dot{\mathscr{I}}_G/\mathscr{I}_G = \frac{f_{N(0,1)}([\theta_2/2]^{1/2})}{2F_{N(0,1)}([\theta_2/2]^{1/2}) - 1} \cdot (\theta_2/2)^{1/2} \times \dot{\theta}_2/\theta_2,$$

and

$$\frac{d}{dt}F_{L(\theta)}(\underline{Y}) = \int_0^{\underline{Y}} \frac{d}{dt}f_{L(\theta)}\,dy.$$

(The Pareto case that follows permits explicit calculation for all the dynamics of interest, in particular, for all the numerical results in section 2.4. Other distributional hypotheses will, as with the lognormal, require at least some of the results calculated numerically as closed-form expressions are intractable.)

When $\mathscr{I}_G$ is held fixed, $\dot{\theta}_2$ is zero. Then

$$\dot{\theta}_1 = \dot{\mathscr{E}}/\mathscr{E} = \xi,$$

so that for any fixed y,

$$\frac{d}{dt} f_{L(\theta)}(y) = -(2\pi\theta_2)^{-1/2} \cdot y^{-1} \exp\left\{ -\frac{1}{2\theta_2}(\log y - \theta_1)^2 \right\}$$

$$\times (-\theta_2^{-1}) \cdot (\log y - \theta_1)(-\dot{\theta}_1)$$

$$= \theta_2^{-1/2} f_{L(\theta)}(y) \times \left(\frac{\log y - \theta_1}{\sqrt{\theta_2}} \right) \dot{\theta}_1.$$

But then,

$$-\frac{d}{dt} F_{L(\theta)}(\underline{Y}) = -\theta_2^{-1/2} \left(\int_0^{\underline{Y}} \left(\frac{\log y - \theta_1}{\sqrt{\theta_2}} \right) f_{L(\theta)}(y) \right) \times \xi$$

$$= -\theta_2^{-1/2} E_{N(0,1)} \left(Z \,|\, Z \leq \frac{\log \underline{Y} - \theta_1}{\sqrt{\theta_2}} \right)$$

$$\times F_{N(0,1)} \left(\frac{\log \underline{Y} - \theta_1}{\sqrt{\theta_2}} \right) \cdot \xi.$$

With fixed inequality at a constant $\mathscr{I}_G$, this expression says that the flow of population past a given threshold level $\underline{Y}$ is proportional to the aggregate growth rate ξ. The constant of proportionality, moreover, is easily calculated from knowledge of θ.

The value of $\dot{\mathscr{I}}_G/\mathscr{I}_G$ that sets the flow $dF_{L(\theta)}(\underline{Y})/dt$ to zero can be obtained only by numerical simulation.

2.7.4.2 Pareto (Type 1)

A different widely used parametrization for personal income distributions is the Pareto (type 1) distribution:

$$F_{P(\theta)}(y) = 1 - (\theta_1 y^{-1})^{\theta_2}, \qquad \theta_1 > 0, y \geq \theta_1, \theta_2 > 1,$$

with density

$$f_{P(\theta)}(y) = \begin{cases} 0 & \text{if } y \leq 0, \\ \theta_2(\theta_1 y^{-1})^{\theta_2} y^{-1} & \text{otherwise.} \end{cases}$$

The implied **T** functionals in (8)–(11) of section 2.7.2 then are

$$\mathscr{E}(F_{P(\theta)}) = (\theta_2 - 1)^{-1} \theta_2 \theta_1,$$

$$\mathscr{I}_G(F_{P(\theta)}) = (2\theta_2 - 1)^{-1},$$

$$Y_{0.2i}(F_{P(\theta)}) = F_{P(\theta_1, \theta_2 - 1)}(S_{0.2i}),$$

with

$$S_{0.2i}(\mathsf{F}_{\mathsf{P}(\theta)}) = (1 - 0.2i)^{-1/\theta_2} \cdot \theta_1.$$

As with the previous lognormal (similarly having two parameters), an exact formula for the estimator (6) is available when only $\mathscr{E}$ and $\mathscr{I}_G$ are observed:

$$\hat{\theta}_2 = (1 + \mathscr{I}_G^{-1})/2,$$

$$\hat{\theta}_1 = (1 - \hat{\theta}_2^{-1})\mathscr{E}.$$

In this case the dynamics in θ and $(\mathscr{E}, \mathscr{I}_G)$ can be easily seen to be related by

$$\dot{\mathscr{E}}/\mathscr{E} = \frac{\dot{\theta}_1}{\theta_1} - (\theta_2 - 1)^{-1}\frac{\dot{\theta}_2}{\theta_2},$$

$$\dot{\mathscr{I}}_G/\mathscr{I}_G = \left(\frac{-2\theta_2}{2\theta_2 - 1}\right)\frac{\dot{\theta}_2}{\theta_2}.$$

Moreover, direct calculation shows

$$-\frac{d}{dt}\mathsf{F}_{\mathsf{P}(\theta)}(\underline{Y}) = \frac{d}{dt}\left[\left(\frac{\theta_1}{\underline{Y}}\right)^{\theta_2}\right]$$

$$= (1 - \mathsf{F}_{\mathsf{P}(\theta)}(\underline{Y}))\theta_2 \times \left[\frac{\dot{\theta}_1}{\theta_1} + \log\left(\frac{\theta_1}{\underline{Y}}\right)\frac{\dot{\theta}_2}{\theta_2}\right].$$

When inequality in the form of $\mathscr{I}_G$ is held fixed, one has

$$\frac{\dot{\theta}_1}{\theta_1} = \frac{\dot{\mathscr{E}}}{\mathscr{E}} = \xi$$

and

$$-\frac{d}{dt}\mathsf{F}_{\mathsf{P}(\theta)}(\underline{Y}) = (1 - \mathsf{F}_{\mathsf{P}(\theta)}(\underline{Y}))\theta_2 \cdot \xi.$$

Alternatively, to fix $\mathsf{F}_{\mathsf{P}(\theta)}(\underline{Y})$ instead, require

$$\dot{\theta}_1/\theta_1 = -\log(\theta_1/\underline{Y})\dot{\theta}_2/\theta_2$$

or

$$\dot{\theta}_2/\theta_2 = -\left[\log(\theta_1/\underline{Y}) + (\theta_2 - 1)^{-1}\right]^{-1}\xi.$$

To achieve this, one needs

$$\dot{\mathscr{I}}_G/\mathscr{I}_G = \left(\frac{2\theta_2}{2\theta_2 - 1}\right)\left[\log(\theta_1/\underline{Y}) + (\theta_2 - 1)^{-1}\right]^{-1}\xi. \tag{21}$$

Equation (21) shows, at a given aggregate growth rate ξ, the rate of change in inequality required to hold fixed the proportion of the population below income $\underline{Y}$. The increase in $\mathscr{I}_G$ is proportional to ξ. When $\underline{Y}$ is sufficiently low, namely, when

$$F_{P(\theta)}(\underline{Y}) < 1 - \exp\left\{\frac{-\theta_2}{\theta_2 - 1}\right\}$$

(which happens to be the case of interest), the constant of proportionality is necessarily positive.

For the purposes of this chapter, the lognormal and Pareto cases are interesting only because they permit explicit (closed-form) analyses of the distribution dynamics of interest. They provide intuition for how the general case will work. In the latter, typically only numerical solutions are available.

2.7.5 Data

This chapter merges data from Deininger and Squire (1996), Summers and Heston (1991), and UNU (2000). The updated and expanded inequality data in Deininger and Squire (2002) are not, as of this writing, yet distributed for general use.

Notes

I thank the MacArthur Foundation for financial support. I have received many helpful suggestions from colleagues, including Abhijit Banerjee, Tim Besley, Richard Blundell, Andrew Chesher, Frank Cowell, Bill Easterly, Theo Eicher, Raquel Fernandez, Chico Ferreira, James Feyrer, Oded Galor, Cecilia García-Peñalosa, Louise Keely, and Branko Milanovic. Also useful were Clarissa Yeap's research assistance in the early stages of this work and Claudia Biancotti's Ec473 LSE seminar presentation, in the spring of 2001. All calculations and graphs were produced using L^ATEX and the author's econometrics shell tsrf.

1. Each entry in table 2.3 is a range rather than just a single number since alternative distributional assumptions can be used in the calculation; see section 2.7.4.

2. See again, however, the discussion at the end of section 2.2 and the more detailed picture available from studies such as Dreze and Sen (1995).

3. The only possible exceptions are the transition economies and Russia after the collapse of the Soviet Union: see, for example, Ivaschenko (chapter 6) and Shorrocks and Kolenikov (2001). The seven instances that Li, Squire, and Zou (1998) identified with statistically and quantitatively significant time trends in Gini coefficients only saw proportional growth rates of 1.02 percent (Australia), 1.04 percent (Chile), 3.18 percent (China), −1.71 percent (France), −1.18 percent (Italy), 1.61 percent (New Zealand), and

1.46 percent (Poland) (this author's calculations, from Table 4 in Li, Squire, and Zou (1998)) taken linearly over a single time period—multiple time periods would imply yet smaller growth rates.

References

Aghion, Philippe, Eve Caroli, and Cecilia García-Peñalosa. 1999. "Inequality and economic growth: The perspective of the new growth theories." *Journal of Economic Literature* 37(4): 1615–1660, December.

Alesina, Alberto, and Dani Rodrik. 1994. "Distributive politics and economic growth." *Quarterly Journal of Economics* 109(2): 465–490, May.

Atkinson, Anthony B., and Andrea Brandolini. 2001. "Promise and pitfalls in the use of secondary datasets: Income inequality in OECD countries as a case study." *Journal of Economic Literature* 39(3): 771–799, September.

Banerjee, Abhijit V., and Esther Duflo. 2000. "Inequality and growth: What can the data say?" Working Paper, Economics Department, MIT, May.

Barro, Robert J. 2000. "Inequality and growth in a panel of countries." *Journal of Economic Growth* 5(1): 5–32, March.

Bénabou, Roland. 1996. "Inequality and growth." In *Macroeconomics Annual*, vol. 11, ed. Ben Bernanke and Julio Rotemberg, 11–74. Cambridge: The MIT Press.

Bertola, Giuseppe. 1999. "Macroeconomics of distribution and growth." In *Handbook of Income Distribution*, vol. 1, ed. Anthony B. Atkinson and François Bourguignon, 477–540. Amsterdam: North-Holland/Elsevier Science.

Cowell, Frank. 2000. "Measurement of inequality." In *Handbook of Income Distribution*, vol. 1, ed. Anthony B. Atkinson and Francois Bourguignon, 87–166. Amsterdam: North-Holland/Elsevier Science.

Deininger, Klaus, and Lyn Squire. 1996. "A new data set measuring income inequality." *World Bank Economic Review* 10(3): 565–591, September.

Deininger, Klaus, and Lyn Squire. 1998. "New ways of looking at old issues: Inequality and growth." *Journal of Development Economics* 57: 259–287.

Deininger, Klaus, and Lyn Squire. 2002. "Revisiting inequality: New data, new results." Working Paper, The World Bank, Washington, DC, March.

Dollar, David, and Art Kraay. 2001. "Growth is good for the poor." Working paper, DRG, The World Bank, Washington, DC, March.

Dreze, Jean, and Amartya Sen. 1995. *India: Economic Development and Social Opportunity*. Oxford: Oxford University Press.

Easterly, William, Michael Kremer, Lant Pritchett, and Lawrence H. Summers. 1993. "Good policy or good luck? Country growth performance and temporary shocks." *Journal of Monetary Economics* 32(3): 459–483.

Esteban, Joan-María, and Debraj Ray. 1994. "On the measurement of polarization." *Econometrica* 62(4): 819–851, July.

Forbes, Kristin J. 2000. "A reassessment of the relationship between inequality and growth." *American Economic Review* 90(5): 869–887, December.

Galor, Oded, and Joseph Zeira. 1993. "Income distribution and macroeconomics." *Review of Economic Studies* 60(1): 35–52, January.

Hansen, Lars Peter. 1982. "Large sample properties of generalized method of moments estimators." *Econometrica* 50(4): 1029–1054, July.

Heston, Alan, and Robert Summers. 1999. "The world distribution of income: A synthesis of intercountry and intracountry data to measure worldwide material well-being." Working paper, University of Pennsylvania, Philadelphia, August.

Kuznets, Simon. 1955. "Economic growth and income inequality." *American Economic Review* 45(1): 1–28, March.

Li, Hongyi, and Hengfu Zou. 1998. "Income inequality is not harmful for growth: Theory and evidence." *Review of Development Economics* 2(3): 318–334, October.

Li, Hongyi, Lyn Squire, and Hengfu Zou. 1998. "Explaining international and inter-temporal variations in income inequality." *Economic Journal* 108, 1–18, January.

Manski, Charles F. 1988. *Analog Estimation Methods in Econometrics*. London: Chapman and Hall.

Milanovic, Branko. 2002. "True world income distribution, 1988 and 1993: First calculation based on household surveys alone." *Economic Journal* 112(476): 51–92, January.

Perotti, Roberto. 1996. "Growth, income distribution, and democracy: What the data say." *Journal of Economic Growth* 1(2): 149–187, June.

Persson, Torsten, and Guido Tabellini. 1994. "Is inequality harmful for growth?" *American Economic Review* 84(3): 600–621, June.

Quah, Danny. 1993. "Empirical cross-section dynamics in economic growth." *European Economic Review* 37(2/3): 426–434, April.

Quah, Danny. 1997. "Empirics for growth and distribution: Polarization, stratification, and convergence clubs." *Journal of Economic Growth* 2(1): 27–59, March.

Quah, Danny. 2001a. "Cross-country growth comparison: Theory to empirics." In *Advances in Macroeconomic Theory*, vol. 133 of *Proceedings of the Twelfth World Congress of the International Economic Association, Buenos Aires*, ed. Jacques Dreze, 332–351. London: Palgrave.

Quah, Danny. 2001b. "Some simple arithmetic on how income inequality and economic growth matter." Working paper, Economics Department, LSE, London, June. Given as the first *Journal of Applied Econometrics Lecture* at the Econometric Society Meetings, Auckland, New Zealand, July.

Ravallion, Martin. 1997. "Can high-inequality developing countries escape absolute poverty?" *Economics Letters* 56(1): 51–57.

Ravallion, Martin, and Shaohua Chen. 1997. "What can new survey data tell us about recent changes in distribution and poverty?" *World Bank Economic Review* 11(2): 357–382, June.

Sala-i-Martin, Xavier. 2002. "The disturbing 'rise' of world inequality." Working paper, Columbia University, New York, March.

Shorrocks, Anthony F., and Stanislav Kolenikov. 2001. "Poverty trends in Russia during the transition." Working paper, United Nations University/WIDER, Helsinki, May.

Silverman, Bernard W. 1981. "Using kernel density estimates to investigate multimodality." *Journal of the Royal Statistical Society, Series B* 43(1): 97–99.

Summers, Robert, and Alan Heston. 1991. "The Penn World Table (Mark 5): An expanded set of international comparisons, 1950–1988." *Quarterly Journal of Economics* 106(2): 327–368, May.

UNU. 2000. UNU/WIDER-UNDP World Income Inequality Database. Version 1.0. United Nations University/WIDER, Helsinki.

Wolfson, Michael (1994) "Diverging inequalities." *American Economic Review* 84(2): 353–358, May.

World Bank. 1990. *World Development Report: Poverty*. New York: Oxford University Press.

II

Population, Education, and Inequality

3

Fertility Clubs and Economic Growth

Avner Ahituv and
Omer Moav

3.1 Introduction

This chapter offers an empirical and theoretical investigation of the relationships among fertility, education, and economic growth. The theoretical model offers an explanation to the positive cross-country relationship between education and growth and the negative cross-country relationship between fertility and growth. The model also offers some insights explaining dramatic demographic transitions observed in some countries in the last few decades and bears policy implications for the promotion of economic growth. We examine the model's predictions empirically using a rich panel data set. We find significant negative relationships between fertility and economic growth and between fertility and education. In addition, consistent with the model, we find that improvements in education have increased the probability that a country would experience a demographic transition of fertility reduction that may pave the way to improved economic performance.

A comparison of living standards among countries shows wide diversity in both income and fertility levels. For example, the mean value of GDP per capita, for our sample of 114 countries, in 1985 was $4,204, with a larger standard deviation of $4,381. The richest country was the United States with $16,559 and the poorest was Ethiopia with only $283. The average number of children per woman was 4.43, with standard deviation of 2.03. Rwanda was highest, with 7.74 children; West Germany and Italy were lowest, with 1.41 children each. Thus, one woman in Rwanda produces the same number of children as five women in Italy.

More important, fertility and education have a strong negative correlation across countries, and education has a positive strong correlation with income per capita. As shown by Ahituv (2001) in low-income countries—with GDP of less than $1,000 per capita— the average fertility rate was 6.5 children per woman in 1965, as opposed to only 3.7 in the high-income group with income above $2,500. During the same period only 6.0 percent of the relevant school age children were enrolled in secondary school in low-income countries, compared to 49.2 percent in the high-income group of countries. Twenty years later, the picture was very similar. In 1985 the average fertility rate in the low-income countries was still above six, and in the high-income group the average had declined to 2.4. These facts, along with the aforementioned dramatic demographic transitions experienced by some countries, motivate the model, which is based on Moav (2001), and generates a high-income equilibrium, characterized by high investment in education and low fertility, along with a poverty trap equilibrium characterized by low investment in education and high fertility. At the same time, the theoretical model offers insights into the understanding of the economic forces leading to the demographic transitions that are observed in the data and suggests policy measures that will trigger and enhance these processes. In particular, the theory highlights the policy measures that would encourage a shift in household resource allocation from child quantity (fertility) to child quality (education), starting a process that may eventually lead to a catch-up of the poor countries with the rich.

Households, in the model, optimally allocate resources between the quality and quantity of children, capital transfers, and consumption. These decisions made by households in the economy determine subsequent aggregate supply of production factors. Due to the trade-off between child quality and quantity, economies characterized by high fertility rates sustain low levels of human capital and therefore low income per capita. The high fertility rates in the poor countries further dilute the accumulation of physical capital per capita, amplifying the impact of child quality choice on economic development. As a result of the assumption that human capital has a positive effect on the productivity in teaching, it is shown in the model that high-wage (educated) individuals have a comparative advantage in raising quality children, whereas the poor have a comparative advantage in child quantity. Thus, households in poor economies choose high fertility rates with low investment in their offspring's education and low levels of capital transfers; and therefore, poverty persists. In contrast, families in the rich countries choose low fertility rates with high investment in education and high levels of capital transfers, and therefore, high income also persists.

The microfoundations of the model follow the principle observation of Becker and Lewis (1973) that the cost of an additional child increases with the desired level of child quality. In contrast to Becker and Lewis who assume high-income elasticity for child quality, here the key assumption is that individuals' productivity in educating children increases with their own human capital. For instance, individuals' effectiveness in helping their children with homework, in contrast to feeding a child, increases with their own level of education. This assumption is consistent with empirical evidence. Lam and Duryea (1999) argue that mothers with more schooling, despite the increase in their market wages, do not increase their labor supply because of their higher productivity in producing well-educated children. In addition, Psacharopoulos, Valenzuela, and Arends (1996) find that teachers in Latin American countries are rewarded for their education similarly to the average reward in the economy. Card and Krueger (1992) argue that schooling rates of return are higher for individuals from states with better-educated teachers and Angrist and Lavy (2001) find that teachers' training led to an improvement in students' test scores.

Economic growth models of fertility designed to explain the possibility of multiple equilibria with persistence of poverty go back to Nelson (1956). He shows that in an environment in which fertility and saving rates increase with income, an underdevelopment trap with low savings is plausible. In this trap, even if capital is accumulated, population rises at an equal rate. More recently, Becker, Murphy, and Tamura (1990) have developed a model in which individuals face the trade-off between the quality and quantity of their offspring.[1] Their model generates multiple steady states consistent with the cross-country relationship between fertility, education, and growth. The source of multiplicity of equilibria in their model is the assumption that the return to education is lower in poor economies. In particular, they assume that the return to human capital increases with its aggregate level in society. Their approach suffers from both theoretical and empirical limitations. The poverty trap equilibrium is a result of a market failure in a framework in which education has a positive externality, where existing evidence contradicts the underlying assumption of increasing returns on education with income.[2] Furthermore, while fertility decisions in the analysis of Becker, Murphy, and Tamura (1990) may amplify the negative impact of low education investment on per capita income, they are not the source of multiple equilibria. In this chapter, in contrast, a simple dynamical system generates multiple steady states that emerge from the comparative advantage of educated individuals in the production of educated children. The model is based neither on restrictive assumptions concerning preferences, or the return on human capital, nor on any nonconvexity in the production process.[3]

The model offers explanations for cross-country output differences and for the phenomenon of club convergence.[4] Consistent with the evidence, as shown for instance by Quah (1997), countries in the club of the rich converge to a high-income per capita steady state, whereas countries in the club of the poor converge to a low income level. The poor countries, as consistent with the observation of Cohen (1996), fail to catch up with the rich because of insufficient progress in education, which, according to the model, is due to high fertility rates. Cross-section observations from 1965 suggest that countries in the club of the poor are also the countries in the high-fertility club, and the club of the rich consists of the countries that have low fertility rates. Our empirical investigation of the fertility trends, however, shows a different pattern than Quah's (1997) findings of increased polarization over time. On the one hand, fertility rates have further declined in the rich countries, but on the other, many of the high-fertility countries have dramatically reduced fertility rates, joining the club of the low-fertility countries. Based on our theory, we predict that some of these countries will eventually also converge to the club of the rich, which is now only a subset of the club of the low-fertility countries.

The empirical section of this chapter examines the model's predictions and implications. Our data contains rich social, demographic, political, and income indicators from 1965 to 1989, and fertility rates up to 2000, across 114 countries. Using this data, we first show an inverse relationship between fertility and GDP. Then we present evidence supporting the existence of a poverty trap and the phenomenon of club convergence. Finally, the analysis turns to the documentation of the various demographic transitions that have recently occurred in many of the poor countries of the world. We find that education, and in particular women's education, initiates fertility reduction and consequently brings about faster economic growth. These findings offer an explanation for the significant negative effect that fertility has on long-term economic growth, and the nonsignificant effect on short-term growth, as shown by Barro (1991).

The chapter proceeds as follows: Section 3.2 develops the basic model of fertility, capital accumulation, and child educational choices and discusses the results. Section 3.3 presents the empirical results. It first shows that fertility differs by economic cluster. Then it describes results of simple regression analysis that examine the interplay among the previous three variables. Section 3.4 concludes.

3.2   The Model

We develop a closed economy model of homogenous individuals following Moav (2001). The homogeneity assumption fits well the focus of this chapter: differences across countries and trends of countries over time, where it should be noted that empirical evidence show that fertility rates are indeed more heterogeneous across countries than within a country. Consider an overlapping generation economy in which activity extends over infinite discrete time. In every period the economy produces a single homogenous good, using two factors of production: physical and human capital. The supply of human capital is determined by households' decisions in the preceding period regarding the number of their children and the level of education investment in each child; the supply of physical capital is determined by individuals' choice of bequest.

3.2.1   Production

Production occurs within a period according to a neoclassical, constant-returns-to-scale, production technology. The output produced at time t, Y_t, is given by

$$Y_t = F(K_t, H_t) \equiv H_t f(k_t) = H_t A k_t^{\alpha}, \qquad k_t \equiv K_t / H_t, \tag{1}$$

where H_t and K_t are human (measured in efficiency units of labor) and physical capital employed in production in period t.

Producers operate in a perfectly competitive environment and therefore production factors are paid according to their marginal products,

$$w_t = (1 - \alpha)Ak^\alpha \equiv w(k_t),$$

$$r_t = \alpha Ak^{\alpha-1} \equiv r(k_t),$$

(2)

where w_t is the wage rate per efficiency unit of labor in time t, and r_t is the capital rate of return. For sake of simplicity, physical capital is assumed to fully depreciate at the end of each period.

3.2.2 Individuals

In each period a generation of individuals, who each has a single parent, is born. Individuals live two periods: In childhood they acquire human capital; in adulthood they are endowed with one unit of time, which they allocate between child rearing and participation in the labor force.

The preferences of members of generation t (born in $t - 1$) are defined over consumption as well as over the quality and quantity of their children, where quality is measured by their offspring's full income (potential income). Preferences are represented by the utility function

$$u_t = (1 - \beta) \log c_t + \beta[\log n_t + \log(w_{t+1}h_{t+1} + r_{t+1}s_{t+1})],$$

(3)

where $\beta \in (0, 1)$, c_t is the consumption in the household of members of generation t, n_t is the number of children in this household, h_{t+1} is the level of human capital of each child measured in efficiency units, and s_{t+1} is physical capital transferred to each child.

3.2.3 The Formation of Human Capital

In the first period of their lives individuals devote their entire time for the acquisition of human capital (measured in efficiency units of labor). The acquired level of human capital increases if their time investment is supplemented by investment in education. However, even in the absence of investment in education, individuals acquire one efficiency unit of labor—basic skills. The level of investment in education of each individual in period t, e_{t+1}, is measured in efficiency units of labor. The resulting number of efficiency units of labor in period $t + 1$, h_{t+1}, is a strictly increasing, strictly concave function of investment in education in period t, e_{t+1},

$$h_{t+1} = h(e_{t+1}),$$

(4)

where $h(0) = 1$, $\lim_{e \to 0^+} h'(e_t) = \gamma$, $\lim_{e \to \infty} h(e_t) > 1/\tau\gamma$,[5] and $\lim_{e \to \infty} h'(e_t) = 0$. The assumption that the slope of the production function of human capital is finite at the origin, along with the ability of individuals to supply some minimal level of labor regardless of the investment in human capital (beyond time), assure that under some conditions raising quality children is not optimal.[6] Since e_{t+1} is measured in efficiency units of labor, the real cost of the investment in education is $w_t e_{t+1}$.[7]

3.2.4 Budget Constraint

Let τ be the minimum time cost required for raising a child; additional time allocated to children positively affects their quality. That is, τ is the fraction of the individual's unit of time endowment that is required in order to raise a child, regardless of quality. Following Becker and Lewis (1973), Rosenzweig and Wolpin (1980), and Galor and Weil (2000), it is assumed for the sake of simplicity that the "quantity cost" per child does not vary with family size. The economic force behind the fertility gap between rich and poor is the lower quantity cost faced by the poor. Therefore, incorporating a range of decreasing quantity cost would increase the marginal cost difference faced by poor and rich, amplifying the fertility gap, and thus strengthening the results. Increasing returns to investment in quality would work in the opposite direction, but, up to a limit, should not have a qualitative effect on the model's results.[8] As will become apparent, fertility rates are bounded from above by β/τ, therefore it is assumed that $\tau < \beta$. It is further assumed that τ is sufficiently small, so that individuals with a low level of human capital choose the corner solution of zero investment in child education,

$$\tau < 1/\gamma. \tag{A1}$$

Consider an adult agent of generation t who is endowed with h_t efficiency units of labor and s_t units of capital. Full income, $w_t h_t + r_t s_t$, is divided between expenditure on child rearing (including bequests) and consumption, c_t. The (opportunity) cost of raising each child, regardless of quality, is equal to $w_t h_t \tau$, and the cost of quality of each child is equal to $w_t e_{t+1}$. The cost of raising n_t children, with an education level of e_{t+1} and a bequest s_{t+1} is given therefore, by $n_t[w_t h_t \tau + w_t e_{t+1} + s_{t+1}]$, and the individual faces the budget constraint

$$n_t[w_t h_t \tau + w_t e_{t+1} + s_{t+1}] + c_t \leq w_t h_t + r_t s_t, \tag{5}$$

where $w_t h_t + r_t s_t$ is full income of each individual in period t, and $h_t = h(e_t)$. As captured by the budget constraint, given in equation (5), the cost of child quantity, $w_t h_t \tau$, in contrast to the cost of child quality, $w_t e_{t+1}$, increases with the level of human capital of the t genereation agent, h_t. This is a result of the assumption that individuals' productivity as educators, in contrast to their productivity in child quantity, increases with their own human capital.

3.2.5 Optimization

Members of generation t choose the number, n_t, and quality, e_{t+1}, of their children, the quantity of physical capital they transfer to each child, s_{t+1}, and the household consumption, c_t, so as to maximize their utility. It follows from the optimization that consumption is

$$c_t = (1 - \beta)[w_t h_t + r_t s_t], \tag{6}$$

that is, a fraction $1 - \beta$ of full income is devoted to consumption and hence a fraction β of full income is devoted to child rearing in terms of quality and quantity.

The optimization with respect to capital transfers, s_{t+1}, is given by

$$\frac{h(e_{t+1})w_{t+1}}{(\tau h_t + e_{t+1})w_t} - r_{t+1} \begin{cases} > 0 & s_{t+1} = 0, \\ = 0 & s_{t+1} \in [0, \infty), \\ < 0 & s_{t+1} \to \infty. \end{cases} \tag{7}$$

where $s_{t+1} \to \infty$ implies that $n_t \to 0$. In equilibrium, however, since all individuals are identical, it follows from (7) that

$$\frac{h(e_{t+1})w_{t+1}}{(\tau h_t + e_{t+1})w_t} = r_{t+1}. \tag{8}$$

Otherwise, if the left-hand side is larger (smaller), there is no physical (human) capital in period $t + 1$, and the left-hand side is smaller (larger) in contradiction. Given (8), it follows from the optimization with respect to e_{t+1} that[9]

$$\frac{h(e_{t+1})}{\tau h(e_t) + e_{t+1}} - h'(e_{t+1}) \begin{cases} \geq 0 & \text{if } e_{t+1} = 0, \\ = 0 & \text{if } e_{t+1} > 0. \end{cases} \tag{9}$$

It follows, therefore, that the equilibrium level of investment in education in period t, e_{t+1}, is uniquely determined by the investment in education in the previous period, e_t.

Lemma 1 Under (A1) there exists a single valued function $\phi(e_t)$ such that

$$e_{t+1} = \phi(e_t) \begin{cases} = 0 & \text{if } e_t \leq \hat{e}, \\ > 0 & \text{if } e_t > \hat{e}, \end{cases}$$

where $\phi'(e_t) > 0$ for $e_t > \hat{e}$ and $\hat{e} > 0$ is unique and given by $1/\gamma = \tau h(\hat{e})$.

Proof   Define $G(e_{t+1}) \equiv h(e_{t+1})/\theta h'(e_{t+1})$. It follows from (9) that

$$G(e_{t+1}) \geq \tau h(e_t) + e_{t+1}. \tag{10}$$

As follows from (A1), $\partial G(e_{t+1})/\partial e_t = 0$, $\partial[\tau h(e_t) + e_{t+1}]/\partial e_t > 0$, and $G(0) = 1/\gamma > \tau h(0) = \tau$, and as follows from the properties of (4) $G(0) = 1/\gamma < \lim_{e \to \infty} \tau h(e_t)$, and $h'(e_t) > 0$. Therefore, as follows from the intermediate value theorem, there exists a unique $e_t = \hat{e} > 0$, given by $1/\gamma = \tau h(\hat{e})$, such that $G(0) = \tau h(\hat{e})$ and $G(0) >(<) \tau h(e_t)$ for all $e_t <(>) \hat{e}$ implying that $\phi(e_t) = 0$ for all $e_t \leq \hat{e}$ and $\phi(e_t) > 0$ otherwise.

As follows from implicit differentiation of the first-order condition of the maximization problem as given by (9), noting that second-order condition hold for a maximum, $\phi(e_t)$ is single valued and $\phi'(e_t) > 0$ for $e_t > \hat{e}$. □

It follows from lemma 1, and equations (5) and (6) that the number of children of each member of generation t, n_t is given by

$$n_t = n(e_t) = \begin{cases} \beta/\tau & \text{if } e_t \leq \hat{e}, \\ \beta h(e_t)/[\tau h(e_t) + \phi(e_t)] & \text{if } e_t > \hat{e}, \end{cases} \tag{11}$$

where $\beta/\tau \geq \beta h(e_t)/[\tau h(e_t) + \phi(e_t)]$. That is, fertility rates in low education economies ($e_t \leq \hat{e}$), where there is no investment in the quality of children, are higher than in those countries with higher education levels who invest in children's education.

3.2.6   The Evolution of the Economy

Figure 3.1 depicts the evolution of education in the economy, $\phi(e_t)$; (A1) assures the existence of a low education steady state, $\phi(0) = 0$.

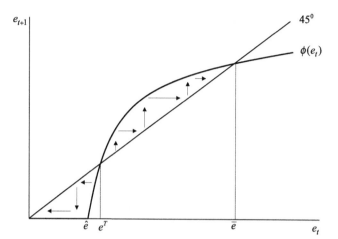

Figure 3.1
The evolution of education

However, in order for $\phi(e_t)$ to generate a high education steady state, there must exist a range of e_t in which $\phi(e_t)$ is sufficiently sensitive to changes in e_t. That is, a range must exist in which small changes in the parent's education bring about large changes in the offspring education and as a result $\phi(e_t) > e_t$ for some e_t.

Proposition 1 There exists a human capital production function, that satisfies (A1) and the properties of $h(e_t)$, in equation (4), such that, $\phi(e_t)$, is characterized by multiple steady states.

Proof The proof follows from an example. Consider the following human capital production function:

$$h_{t+1} = h(e_{t+1}) = \begin{cases} 1 + \gamma e_{t+1} & \text{if } e_{t+1} < \bar{e}, \\ 1 + \gamma \bar{e} & \text{if } e_{t+1} \geq \bar{e}, \end{cases} \tag{12}$$

where $\bar{e} > (1 - \tau\gamma)/\tau\gamma^2$. Hence, it follows from the optimization problem of a member i of generation t, that is endowed with $h(e_t)$ efficiency units of human capital that

$$e_{t+1} = \bar{\phi}(e_t) \begin{cases} = 0 & \text{if } e_t < \hat{e}, \\ \in [0, \bar{e}] & \text{if } e_t = \hat{e}, \\ = \bar{e} & \text{if } e_t > \hat{e}, \end{cases} \tag{13}$$

where as follows from (12) and (A1) $\hat{e} = (1 - \tau\gamma)/\tau\gamma^2 > 0$ and $\bar{e} > \hat{e}$. The dynamic system $\bar{\phi}(e_t)$ is characterized by two stable steady states, $\bar{e}$ and 0, and an unstable steady state $\hat{e}$, which is the threshold level of education. The lemma thus follows from continuity considerations.[10] $\square$

It follows from (2), (8), (9), and lemma 1 that the dynamical system governing the evolution of the economy is uniquely determined by the sequence $\{k_t, e_t\}_{t=0}^{\infty}$, such that

$$\begin{cases} e_{t+1} = \phi(e_t), \\ k_{t+1} = \psi(e_t, k_t) = \alpha A k_t^{\alpha} [\tau h(e_t) + \phi(e_t)]/h(\phi(e_t)), \end{cases} \tag{14}$$

where k_0 and e_0 are given. Note that k_t is the physical human capital ratio, and that physical capital per worker is equal to $h(e_t)k_t = s_t > k_t$. Output per worker, y_t, as follows from (1), is therefore uniquely determined by the dynamical system

$$y_t = h(e_t)Ak_t^{\alpha} = Ah_t^{1-\alpha}s_t^{\alpha}.$$

3.2.6.1 The kk Locus
Let kk be the locus of all pairs (k_t, e_t) such that physical capital per efficiency unit of labor, k_t, is in a steady state: $kk \equiv \{(k_t, e_t) : k_{t+1} = k_t\}$. As follows from (14) there exists a function

$$k^{kk}(e_t) = \left(\frac{\alpha A[\tau h(e_t) + \phi(e_t)]}{h(\phi(e_t))} \right)^{1/(1-\alpha)}, \tag{15}$$

such that if $k_t = k^{kk}(e_t)$, then $k_{t+1} = \psi(e_t, k_t) = k_t$—that is, the kk locus consists of all the pairs $(k^{kk}(e_t), e_t)$.

Lemma 2 $dk^{kk}(e_t)/de_t > 0$. That is, as depicted in figure 3.2, the kk locus is strictly increasing in the plan (e_t, k_t).

Proof   For $e_t \leq \hat{e}$, as follows from lemma 1, $\phi(e_t) = 0$, and therefore, $h(\phi(e_t)) = 1$, and since $h'(e_t) > 0$, it follows that $dk^{kk}(e_t)/de_t > 0$ for $e_t \leq \hat{e}$.
For $e_t > \hat{e}$, it follows from (9) and lemma 1 that $h(\phi(e_t))/[\tau h(e_t) + \phi(e_t)] = h'(\phi(e_t))$. Furthermore, as established in lemma 1 $\phi'(e_t) > 0$ for $e_t > \hat{e}$, and since $h''(e_t) < 0$ it follows that $h(\phi(e_t))/[\tau h(e_t) + \phi(e_t)]$ is strictly decreasing with e_t, and therefore $dk^{kk}(e_t)/de_t > 0$ for $e_t > \hat{e}$. $\square$

3.2.6.2 The ee Locus
Let ee be the locus of all pairs (k_t, e_t) such that the level of investment in human capital per capita, e_t, is in a steady state: $ee \equiv \{(k_t, e_t) :$

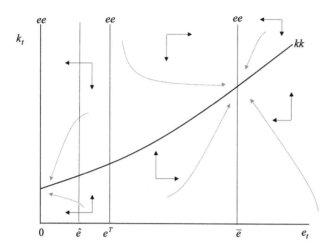

Figure 3.2
The dynamical system

$e_{t+1} = e_t\}$. However, as follows from (14), the evolution of e_t is independent of the evolution of the physical human capital ratio, and hence $ee \equiv \{e_t : \phi(e_t) = e_t\}$. As follows from the properties of $\phi(e_t)$ and as depicted in figure 3.1, $e_t = \phi(e_t)$ for $e_t = 0$, $e_t = e^T$, and $e_t = \bar{e}$, therefore the ee locus consists of three vertical lines in figure 3.2: $e = 0$, $e = e^T$, and $e = \bar{e}$.

The evolution of e_t as follows from (14) and depicted in figure 3.1 is given by $e_t = \phi(e_t)$. Therefore, as depicted in figure 3.2, $e_{t+1} > e_t$ for all $e_t \in (e^T, \bar{e})$, whereas $e_{t+1} < e_t$ for all $e_t < e^T$ and all $e_t > \bar{e}$. The dynamics of k_t follow from (14). As depicted in figure 3.2, $k_{t+1} > k_t$ for all $k_t < k^{kk}(e_t)$, and vice versa. Hence, k_t is increasing below the kk locus and decreasing above it.

3.2.7 Steady States and Implications of the Model

The model generates two locally stable steady states. If the initial level of education is above the threshold level, $e_0 > e^T$, the economy converges monotonically to the high capital labor ratio, high education steady state, characterized by a low fertility rate. If however $e_0 < e^T$, the economy converges to the low capital labor ratio, low education steady state—the poverty trap—that is characterized by a high fertility rate.

The mechanism generating multiple steady states is based on the effect of parental education on child quantity cost. The lower the parents' education, that is, the cheaper the parents' time, the cheaper the children and the parents' choice shifts to higher fertility rates and lower investment in offspring's human capital. Note that a decline in parental education, and hence in their income, leaves less resources for children's education even if their number is unchanged. The increased fertility further reduces investment in education that is, in addition, divided between more children. Therefore, consistent with proposition 1, differences in parental education can be amplified when it comes to differences in offspring education. The effect of quality choice on output per capita is amplified by its consequence on fertility and the diluting effect fertility has on capital accumulation. In the poverty trap, therefore, the high fertility rate yields a low capital labor ratio.

It is interesting to note that in the context of a closed economy, the low output steady state is not a result of capital market imperfections nor any other market failure, and resource allocation is dynamically efficient—the marginal return to education is not higher than the marginal return to physical capital. Hence, even if individuals could borrow to finance their own education they choose not to do so. A shift of the economy from the low- to the high-output steady state can be achieved only if one generation gives up child quantity in favor of child quality and suffers from a utility cost. Of course, if countries differ from each other, in particular, if some economies are in the high output steady state, than the low output steady state is an outcome of imperfection in international capital markets (taken to the extreme of closed economies in the model).

The effect of changes in the quantity cost parameter, τ, on the dynamical system and its steady states follows from equation (9) and lemma 1. An increase in τ increases the relative cost of quantity, inducing a shift to child quality. Hence, it reduces the level of the threshold below which individuals choose not to purchase any education for their offspring, $\hat{e}$, and increases the level of human capital, $\phi(e_t)$, above $\hat{e}$. This implies that the dynamical system depicted in figure 3.1 shifts upward, the threshold level, e^T, declines, and the high-income steady state, $\bar{e}$, increases. Therefore, the ee locus, depicted in figure 3.2, shifts accordingly, that is, the vertical line at $\bar{e}$ shifts to the right, while the vertical threshold line at e^T shifts to the left. Furthermore, since $\phi(e_t)$ increases with τ for $e > \hat{e}$, and since it is constant with respect to e_t for $e \leq \hat{e}$, it follows from lemma 1, the concavity of $h(e_t)$, (9) and (15) that the kk locus, depicted in figure 3.2, shifts upward as a result of an increase in τ. Hence, in the extended model, the impact of changes in the cost of child quantity is amplified by the diluting effect on physical capital (the change in the kk locus). Furthermore, since the threshold level of education, e^T, declines with τ, a sufficient increase in the quantity cost can facilitate a demographic transition and release the economy from the poverty trap.

The effect of changes in the cost of education is not so straightforward. The analysis of public schooling on fertility and education follows.[11] Suppose the government supplies schooling free of charge at a level e_t^g, which is financed by foreign aid or taxation.[12] It follows from (9) that if $\phi(e_t) < e_t^g$ parental investment in education would be zero, or otherwise it would equal $\phi(e_t) - e_t^g$. Public schooling has, therefore, a positive effect on the offspring level of education (for $\phi(e_t) < e_t^g$), but it also reduces parental expenditure on education if $\phi(e_t) > 0$ and therefore gives rise to a reallocation of resources for increased fertility. In the long run, however, if $e_t^g > e^T$, public schooling will shift the economy to a path of increased education and income and reduced fertility.

3.3   Evidence on Fertility and Economics Growth

The empirical part of the chapter uses aggregate international data from the United Nations Statistical Yearbook. We start with descriptive statistics that portray the joint time trends of fertility, education, and income of the last three decades—a period associated with rapid demographic transition in many countries around the world. Then, we use regression analysis to test whether the cross-country relationships between these variables are consistent with the predictions of the model.

We use a panel of data containing rich social, demographic, political, and income indicators from 1965 to 1989, in addition to fertility rates up to 2000, across 114 countries. The database for this study covers approximately fifty indicators. For each country, the data set contains annual time-series data from 1960 to 1989. Most of the analyses presented in this chapter use only six data points (1965, 1970, 1975, 1980, 1985, and 1989), because the early years are used as lag variables, and five-year spans are less likely to be serially corre-lated. The variables in this database are divided into four categories: (1) national account variables related to expenditure and income; (2) social and demographic indicators, including school and fertility; (3) political indicators, indexing political instability, regime and market distortions; and (4) geographic regions in which the country is located. Most of the variables are in time-variant format, but some of them, mainly the political and geographic regions, are time-invariant.

In 1965, the average number of children per woman—the fertility rate—was above 6 in more than half of the countries sampled, while in only six countries they were below 2.5. Even in 2000, in some East African countries fertility rates are still above seven. On the other hand in many countries (such as Spain, Italy, and Korea) they are well below 1.5. Figure 3.3 displays the distributions of fertility rates across countries and over time, showing a sharp decrease in fertility rates, and interesting changes in the shape of the distribution. In 1965, there were, roughly speaking, two separate groups of countries with respect to fertility levels. The distribution peaks around seven, capturing the mass of high-fertility countries, and it also peaks below three children per woman capturing the mass of the low fer-tility countries. Surprisingly, only a few countries had fertility rates between four and six children per woman. This twin-peak structure did not change during the next twenty-five years, in spite of the fact that many countries experienced a rapid demographic transition, and thus the mass of countries in the high fertility range has declined. These facts support the basic result of the model that there are strong economic forces driving toward polarization in fertility rates.

Since 1965, fertility declined in all but twelve African counties in our 114-country sample. Interestingly, fertility in the group of the rich countries, which was low in 1965, further declined. At the same time, many poor countries went through a major demographic tran-sition, significantly reducing their fertility rates and improving their education. In 2000, fertility rates are below 3 in more than sixty countries, and below 1.5 in twelve, which is significantly below the replacement rate. On the other spectrum, only twenty-five countries have fertility rates above 5, and only four of them still have fertility rates of above 7 children per woman. These observations raise inter-

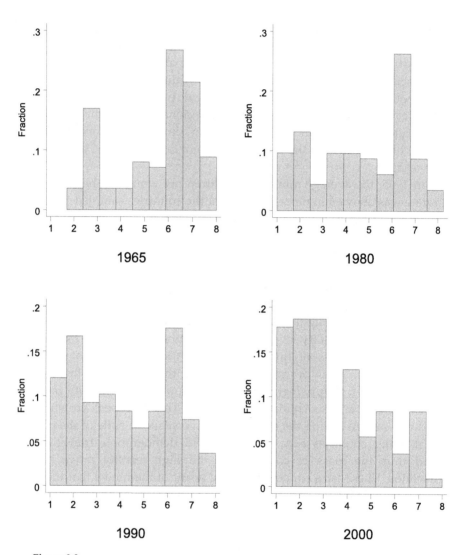

Figure 3.3
Fertility rates across countries

Table 3.1
Means of fertility by country group

	Low-income economies	Middle-income economies	High-income economies
1965	6.51	6.26	3.69
1980	6.41	5.07	2.64
1989	5.89	4.42	2.32
2001	4.90	3.42	1.89
Number of countries in each group	34	39	38

Note: The three groups are based on GDP per capita in 1965. Group 1: 0–1000; Group 2: 1001–2500; Group 3: 2501+.

esting questions. What are the economic forces or policy measures initiating the demographic transition? What will be the long-run consequences of these policies? Could this transition take place without outside intervention, from the United Nations and the developed countries?

We add income as our next stage of the analysis, to study the evolution of fertility rates by income group. Table 3.1 shows that fertility and GDP are closely related by displaying figures for four representative years. Low-income countries had 6.5 children per woman in 1965, as opposed to only 3.7 in the high-income group. Until 1980, fertility rates in the low-income countries did not change, while those in the two other groups declined significantly. During the last decade, however, fertility rates have been dropping in the low-income countries also, converging at 4.9 children per woman in 2000—approximately the rate in the middle-income group twenty years earlier. Fertility rates in the middle-income group declined during that period to 3.4, similar to those of the high-income countries in the early 1970s. The evidence reveals that the transition from high to lower fertility occurred in different periods across these three groups. In the high-income group the transition occurred before World War II; in the middle-income group the sharper decline started in the late 1960s, while in the low-income groups the transition started during the last ten years.

Table 3.2 shows results complementary to those in table 3.1, by presenting indicators for economic activities by groups of countries based on their fertility rates in 1965. The first line shows that economic growth declines with fertility rates. The trend, however, is not

Table 3.2
Summery of selected indicators by fertility rates

	Fertility rates					
	1–3	3–4	4–5	5–6	6–7	7–9
1. Annual GDP growth (65–85 avg.)	2.70%	2.60%	3.20%	2.09%	0.90%	1.25%
2. Changes in fertility rates (65–85)	−0.83	−1.07	−1.49	−0.86	−0.92	−0.81
3. Secondary school enrollment (65)	60%	53%	30%	14%	12%	12%
4. Secondary school enrollment (85)	89%	86%	62%	32%	28%	34%
5. Log of physical capital (65)	9.27	8.82	7.65	6.43	6.48	6.61
6. Log of physical capital (85)	10.33	9.91	9.03	7.74	7.49	7.75
Number of countries in each group	19	9	10	14	43	17

linear. While the rates of economic growth in the low-fertility countries are very similar to those in the middle-fertility group, the countries with high-fertility experienced significantly lower rates of economic growth. The second line shows that middle-fertility countries experienced a sharper reduction in fertility. This is consistent with the model's prediction of two steady states. Lines 3 and 4 show that enrollment in secondary school improved dramatically across all countries, leading, according to our theory, to the observed fertility declines of the 1990s. Finally when we compare physical capital across groups, we see a strong negative correlation with fertility rates, suggesting that capital accumulation, as consistent with our model, is diluted by fertility.

Table 3.3 adds a conditional correlation analysis to our descriptive examination. The table presents results from regressions in which the dependent variables are log-fertility, log-GDP, and school enrollment (a proxy for education) as well as 1965 to 1985 growth rates of these indicators (columns 4–6). The first three regressions, in which the explained variables are the levels of log-fertility, log-GDP, and school enrollment, are panel regressions with six observations per country. The main focus here is to display the interrelation between these three variables, controlling for other characteristics of each country. The growth regressions—the growth rates of these three variables—are cross-section regressions, where the values of the independent variables are from the initial year (1965). The main focus here is to examine the effects of the initial condition on the country's growth rates.

The results presented in columns 1–3 support one of our main hypotheses by showing clearly that fertility is inversely correlated with physical capital, GDP and education. In addition, countries with a wide gender education gap have higher fertility, and countries with long life expectancy have lower fertility rates. Controlling for a country's characteristics, fertility rates in Europe are still lower, while in Latin America and the Muslim countries they are significantly higher. The political conditions of the countries (civil liberties, number of revolutions, and social regime) do not have a significant effect on fertility rates. In addition to the negative effect of fertility on income, we also find a positive effect of education, and a negative effect of Africa and civil liberties. The regression in school enrollment reveals positive correlation with physical capital, again similar to the prediction of the model.

Shifting our analysis to the determinants of the growth rates of these three indicators, we find that initial GDP does not have a significant effect on fertility changes.[13] On the other hand, education has a strong negative effect on fertility changes, suggesting that the timing and speed of the demographic transition is affected by the initial level of education more than the initial level of GDP. This suggests that investment in education is an important element in initiating the fertility transition. Focusing on the other coefficients, fertility rates in African, Muslim, and socialist countries decline more slowly than in the rest of the world.

According to our theory, countries that are in a poverty trap characterized by high fertility will not exhibit high growth rates. Countries that manage, however, to escape the poverty trap will benefit from high growth rates. Accordingly, the effect of initial fertility rates on growth depends on the subsequent behavior of the economy in terms of changes in fertility rates. Our data shows that initial fertility has a negative effect, but not a very significant one, on economic growth. The coefficient of the changes in fertility, when we add this variable to the right hand side of the regression (not shown in table 3.3) is indeed significant and negative. In addition, countries that have not reduced their fertility rates are concentrated in Africa, and, indeed, the coefficient in African countries in explaining growth

Table 3.3
Coefficient estimates from cross-country regressions

Dependent variable	(1) Log fertility	(2) Log GDP	(3) Secondary school enrollment	(4) Fertility growth (1965–1985)	(5) GDP growth (1965–1985)	(6) Growth of secondary school enrollment (1965–1985)
Log fertility		−0.198 (3.34)**	−0.208 (10.21)**	−0.355 (3.35)**	−0.232 (1.27)	−0.644 (0.66)
Log GDP				−0.033 (0.83)	−0.226 (3.25)**	0.044 (0.12)
Log capital	−0.023 (2.27)*	0.453 (28.25)**	0.053 (9.23)**			
Secondary school enrollment	−0.550 (7.87)**	0.291 (2.60)**		−0.414 (2.16)*	0.271 (0.82)	−3.838 (2.12)*
Years of school attainment	−0.021 (3.30)**	0.009 (1.00)				
Gender gap in secondary school	0.438 (5.26)**					−5.465 (2.24)*
Life expectancy	−0.011 (6.29)**	0.003 (1.24)	0.008 (8.89)**			−0.037 (1.09)
EUROPE	−0.231 (7.98)**	0.019 (0.4)	−0.031 (1.77)	−0.052 (0.67)	−0.045 (0.34)	0.357 (0.51)
AFRICA	0.019 (0.73)	−0.092 (2.26)*	−0.047 (3.08)**	0.218 (3.49)**	−0.459 (4.26)**	0.553 (0.92)
Latin-America	0.103 (2.69)**	0.063 (1.06)	−0.073 (3.27)**	0.084 (0.89)	−0.248 (0.53)	−0.436 (0.51)

CATHOLIC	0.013 (0.39)	-0.036 (0.72)	0.013 (0.69)	-0.04 (0.51)	0.008 (0.06)	-0.031 (0.04)
MUSLIM	0.115 (5.00)**	0.065 (1.78)	0.032 (2.22)*	0.104 (1.83)	-0.023 (0.23)	0.718 (1.38)
Civil liberties (index)	0.012 (1.52)	-0.05 (4.17)**	-0.009 (2.08)*	0.029 (1.49)	-0.007 (0.20)	-0.017 (0.11)
Number of revolution and coups	0.017 (0.49)	0.041 (0.02)	0.043 (2.07)*	0.078 (0.90)	-0.401 (2.70)**	-0.377 (0.51)
Socialist economy	0.046 (1.94)	0.041 (1.09)	0.029 (2.06)*	0.117 (2.03)*	-0.079 (0.79)	-0.562 (1.11)
Constant	2.423 (23.59)**	4.226 (19.48)**	-0.138 (1.71)	0.403 (1.05)	2.693 (4.07)**	5.82 (1.59)
R^2	0.86	0.92	0.86	0.58	0.38	0.39
Number of observations	675	675	675	112	112	112

Note: Absolute value of t-statistics in parentheses.

*significant at 5 percent level; ** significant at 1 percent level

is negative and significant. Surprisingly, most of the coefficients in school enrollment growth are insignificant. The only two significant coefficients are the negative sign on initial values of school enrollment and wide gender education gap. We do not have good explanations for these last results.[14]

The analysis in this section provides evidence supporting the building blocks of the model, and its main results. It shows an inverse relationship between fertility and education and a positive relationship between education and economic performance, supporting our presumption that there exists a trade-off between child quality and quantity, and that education has a positive effect on economic growth.[15] In addition, the fact that twenty-five countries in our sample are still characterized by fertility rates of above 5 children per women and by very low levels of education and income suggests that poverty is indeed persistent and highly related to fertility rates. Moreover, the rapid demographic transition experienced by many countries, combined with the fact that only a few countries are characterized by intermediate levels of fertility, supports the theoretical result of two locally stable equilibria.[16] These observations suggest that the next decade can bring significant economic growth in many countries that have recently experienced a rapid demographic transition.

3.4 Concluding Remarks

This chapter offers an empirical and theoretical investigation of the relationships among fertility, education, and economic growth. It argues that the trade-off between child quality and quantity, along with the comparative advantage of the poor in child quantity, in contrast to the comparative advantage of the rich in child quality, clusters countries into two fertility clubs. The club of high fertility, in contrast to the club of low fertility, is characterized by low investment in education, low capital ratios, and low income. Moreover, we show that improvements in education have increased the probability that a country will experience a sharp reduction in the fertility rates, joining the club of low-fertility countries. We suggest that these demographic transitions, experienced in the last few decades in many of the world's poor countries, will eventually pave the way to significant improvements in economic performance.

The theory presented in this chapter has interesting policy implications. An increase in the cost of quantity—the cost of a child regardless of the child's quality—induces a reallocation of resources to child quality. It therefore reduces the threshold above which economies reach the high-income steady state, allowing an easier escape from poverty. It would, in addition, further increase the investment in education, and hence increase income in the high-income steady state. Hence, an increase in the quantity cost positively affects economic growth and could, furthermore, release an economy from the trap of poverty, setting the stage for a demographic transition and economic growth. Thus, policies that reduce the quantity cost, such as tax discounts on large families, child allowances, and subsidized daycare and meals, have, according to the theory, a negative effect on income in the long run. Therefore, though not in harmony (at least in the short run) with a humanitarian approach, policy implications are straightforward—canceling or even reversing the aforementioned policies. Furthermore, since public schooling can release the economy from the poverty trap, growth-encouraging policies include the reallocation of government or foreign aid resources from quantity-cost reduction measures to the finance of schooling. The finding that a temporary improvement in education opportunities could have a permanent effect on the economy was established in previous literature (e.g., Galor and Zeira 1993). The contribution of this chapter, in this respect, is the linking of education to fertility, amplifying the economic consequences of the education policy.

Notes

We wish to thank Eric Gould, Joram Mayshar, M. Carme Riera Prunera, Mathias Thoenig, an anonymous referee and participants in CESifo conference on Growth and Inequality: Issues and Policy Implications, Munich 2001 and Elmau 2002, for helpful discussions.

1. See also Hazan and Berdugo (2002), who study the relationship between child labor, fertility, and growth, and Kremer and Chen (2002), who study the effect of income inequality on economic growth in an endogenous fertility framework. In addition, Veloso (1999) analyzes the effect of different compositions of wealth and human capital on education. Finally, some recent literature focuses on the long-run phenomena of fertility and the take-off from economic stagnation to sustained economic growth, including the work of Kremer (1993), Tamura (1996), Galor and Weil (1996, 2000), Dahan and Tsiddon (1998), Morand (1999), Hansen and Prescott (2002), Lagerloff (2000), Jones (2001), and Galor and Moav (2002).

2. See, for instance, Psacharopoulos (1994), Angrist (1995), and Acemoglu and Angrist (2000).

3. In contrast to this chapter's thesis, existing literature explaining poverty traps is based on nonconvexities in the technology. In particular, Banerjee and Newman (1993), Galor and Zeira (1993), Bénabou (1996), Durlauf (1996a), Piketty (1997), Maoz and Moav (1999), Ghatak and Jiang (2002), and Mookherjee and Ray (2000) show that credit constraints combined with investment thresholds generate persistence of poverty. In the model developed by Piketty (1997), the effort level, rather than capital investment, is indivisible. Mookherjee and Ray (2000) show that while inequality persists irrespective of the divisibility of investment, the multiplicity of steady states requires indivisibilities in the return to education. An exception is presented by Moav (2002), where increasing saving rates with income, replace the role of nonconvexities in the technology in generating multiple steady states.

4. See Azariadis (1996) and Galor (1996) for surveys of the theoretical and empirical literature and the summery by Durlauf (1996b).

5. Where τ, formally defined in what follows, is the time cost for raising a child.

6. The Inada conditions are typically designed to simplify the exposition by avoiding a corner solution, but they are surely not realistic assumptions.

7. Note that the cost of education is $w_t e_{t+1}^i$, whether this is viewed as a direct cost of hiring a teacher or an opportunity cost of teaching one's own children.

8. It is implicitly assumed that the time cost of raising a child can not be reduced by child care employment.

9. Note that individuals' optimization assures efficient investment. The marginal return to physical capital and human capital are equal in an interior solution and the return to physical is larger in a case of a corner solution with no investment in human capital.

10. While the model is not designed to perform calibrations, a numerical illustration reveals that reasonable parameters, in particular, the lifetime dollar return to each dollar invested in education, as given by γ (see Psacharopoulos 1994) can generate multiple equilibria. For $\gamma = 2$, $\theta = 1$, $\tau = 0.15$, $\beta = 1/2$ and $\bar{e} = 1.5$. earnings at the high-income equilibrium are four times higher than earnings at the low-income equilibrium, and fertility rates are 1.9 children per household (of two parents) in the high-income equilibrium and 6.6 at the low. Note that multiplicity will hold for any set of parameters restricted by (A1) and $\bar{e} > \hat{e}$.

11. The analysis abstracts from the potential effect of public schooling on the quantity cost.

12. An indirect consumption tax, for instance, will not have an impact on the quality and quantity choice of individuals.

13. Most countries have negative fertility growth, and the minus sign means faster decline in fertility.

14. As previously reported in the literature, for example, Barro (1991), initial GDP has a negative effect on GDP growth, supporting the conditional convergence hypothesis.

15. This is consistent with the findings of Rosenzweig and Wolpin (1980) and Hanushek (1992), who provide evidence that there exists a trade-off between quantity and quality of children.

16. Consistent with our theoretical argument and with our empirical findings, Altonji and Dunn (1996) find that parents' education positively affects children's education, supporting the existence of persistence of low education. In addition, Behrman et al. (1999) find that increases in the schooling of women enhance the human capital of the next generation, and, consistent with the underlying mechanism developed here, they argue that a component of the significant and positive relationship between maternal literacy and child schooling reflects the productivity effect of home teaching.

References

Acemoglu, D., and J. D. Angrist. 2000. "How Large Are the External Returns to Education? Evidence from Compulsory Schooling Laws." *NBER Macroannual* 15: 9–59.

Ahituv, A. 2001. "Be Fruitful or Multiply: On the Interplay between Fertility and Economic Development." *Journal of Population Economics* 14: 51–71.

Altonji, J. G., and T. A. Dunn. 1996. "The Effect of Family Characteristics on the Return to Education." *Review of Economics and Statistics* 78: 692–704.

Angrist, J. D. 1995. "The Economic Returns to Schooling in the West Bank and Gaza Strip." *American Economic Review* 85: 1065–1087.

Angrist, J. D., and V. Lavy. 2001. "Does Teacher Training Affect Pupil Learning? Evidence from Matched Comparisons in Jerusalem Public Schools." *Journal of Labor Economics* 19: 343–369.

Azariadis, C. 1996. "The Economics of Poverty Traps, Part One: Complete Markets." *Journal of Economic Growth* 1: 449–486.

Banerjee, A., and A. Newman. 1993. "Occupational Choice and the Process of Development." *Journal of Political Economy* 101: 274–298.

Barro, R. J. 1991. "Economic Growth in a Cross Section of Countries." *Quarterly Journal of Economics* 106: 407–443.

Becker, G. S., and H. G. Lewis. 1973. "On the Interaction between Quantity and Quality of Children." *Journal of Political Economy* 82: S279–S288.

Becker, G. S., K. M. Murphy, and R. F. Tamura. 1990. "Human Capital, Fertility, and Economic Growth." *Journal of Political Economy* 98: S12–S37.

Behrman, J. R., A. D. Foster, M. R. Rosenzweig, and P. Vashishtha. 1999. "Women's Schooling, Home Teaching, and Economic Growth." *Journal of Political Economy* 107: 682–714.

Bénabou, R. 1996. "Equity and Efficiency in Human Capital Investment: The Local Connection." *Review of Economic Studies* 63: 267–264.

Card, D., and A. B. Krueger. 1992. "Does School Quality Matter—Returns to Education and the Characteristics of Public-Schools in the United States." *Journal of Political Economy* 100: 1–40.

Cohen, D. 1996. "Tests of the "Convergence Hypothesis": Some Further Results." *Journal of Economic Growth* 1: 351–361.

Dahan, M., and D. Tsiddon. 1998. "Demographic Transition, Income Distribution, and Economic Growth." *Journal of Economic Growth* 3: 29–52.

Durlauf, S. N. 1996a. "A Theory of Persistent Income Inequality." *Journal of Economic Growth* 1: 75–93.

Durlauf, S. N. 1996b. "Controversy—On the Convergence and Divergence of Growth Rates—An Introduction." *Economic Journal* 106: 1016–1018.

Galor, O. 1996. "Convergence? Inferences from Theoretical Models." *Economic Journal* 106: 1056–1069.

Galor, O., and O. Moav. 2002. "Natural Selection and the Origin of Economic Growth." *Quarterly Journal of Economics* 117: 1133–1191.

Galor, O., and D. Weil. 1996. "The Gender Gap, Fertility and Growth." *American Economic Review* 86: 931–953.

Galor, O., and D. Weil. 2000. "Population, Technology, and Growth: From Malthusian Stagnation to Demographic Transition and Beyond." *American Economic Review* 90: 806–828.

Galor, O., and J. Zeira. 1993. "Income Distribution and Macroeconomics." *Review of Economic Studies* 60: 35–52.

Ghatak, M., and N. H. Jiang. 2002. "A Simple Model of Inequality, Occupational Choice and Development." *Journal of Development Economics* 69: 205–226.

Hansen, G., and E. Prescott. 2002. "Malthus to Solow." *American Economic Review* 92: 1205–1217.

Hanushek, E. A. 1992. "The Trade-Off between Child Quantity and Quality." *Journal of Political Economy* 100: 84–117.

Hazan, M., and B. Berdugo. 2002. "Child Labor, Fertility, and Economic Growth." *Economic Journal* 112: 810–828.

Jones, C. I. 2001. "Was the Industrial Revolution Inevitable? Economic Growth over the Very Long Run." *Advances in Macroeconomics* 1, Article 1. Available online.

Kremer, M. 1993. "Population Growth and Technological Change: One Million B.C. to 1990." *Quarterly Journal of Economics* 108: 681–716.

Kremer, M., and D. Chen. 2002. "Income Distribution Dynamics with Endogenous Fertility." *Journal of Economic Growth* 7: 227–258.

Lagerloff, N. P. 2000. "From Malthus to Modern Growth: The Three Regimes Revisited." Mimeo., Sydney.

Lam, D., and S. Duryea. 1999. "Effects of Schooling on Fertility, Labor Supply and Investments in Children, with Evidence from Brazil." *Journal of Human Resources* 34: 160–192.

Maoz, Y. D., and O. Moav. 1999. "Intergenerational Mobility and the Process of Development." *Economic Journal* 109: 677–697.

Moav, O. 2001. "Cheap Children and the Persistence of Poverty." CEPR Discussion Paper No. 3059.

Moav, O. 2002. "Income Distribution and Macroeconomics: The Persistence of Inequality in a Convex Technology Framework." *Economics Letters* 75: 187–192.

Morand, O. F. 1999. "Endogenous Fertility, Income Distribution, and Growth." *Journal of Economic Growth* 4: 331–349.

Mookherjee, D., and D. Ray. 2000. "Persistent Inequality." Mimeo., Boston University.

Nelson, R. R. 1956. "A Theory of Low-Level Equilibrium Trap in Underdeveloped Economies." *American Economic Review* 46: 894–908.

Piketty, T. 1997. "The Dynamics of the Wealth Distribution and Interest Rate with Credit-Rationing." *Review of Economic Studies* 64: 173–189.

Psacharopoulos, G. 1994. "Returns to Investment in Education—A Global Update." *World Development* 22: 1325–1343.

Psacharopoulos, G., J. Valenzuela, and M. Arends. 1996. "Teacher Salaries in Latin America: A Review." *Economics of Education Review* 15: 401–406.

Quah, D. T. 1997. "Empirics for Growth and Distribution: Stratification, Polarization, and Convergence Clubs." *Journal of Economic Growth* 2: 27–59.

Rosenzweig, M. R., and K. I. Wolpin. 1980. "Testing the Quantity-Quality Fertility Model: The Use of Twins as a Natural Experiment." *Econometrica* 48: 227–240.

Tamura, R. 1996. "From Decay to Growth: A Demographic Transition to Economic Growth." *Journal of Economic Dynamics and Control* 20: 1237–1261.

Veloso, F. A. 1999. "Wealth Composition, Endogenous Fertility and the Dynamics of Income Inequality." Mimeo., University of Chicago.

4

Human Capital Formation, Income Inequality, and Growth

Jean-Marie Viaene and
Itzhak Zilcha

4.1 Introduction

It has been established in many studies by economists (and sociologists) that education plays a significant role in shaping the income distribution and the growth process. We observe in recent decades increasing awareness of governments in the education process and, consequently, in enhancing investments to promote human capital skills. In recent years, as information technology advances and computors are being integrated into the learning technology, we are witnessing some important technological progress in the process of human capital formation. In this chapter we investigate the effects of various kinds of technological improvements on growth and the intragenerational distribution of income.

Education/training lies in the heart of our model, and it is composed of two parts: the parental role that takes place at "home," mainly during the period of "youth," and the "out of home" schooling, or the "public part" that, in most cases, is provided by the government and influenced by the "environment." Home education is provided by the close family, and it is carried out through parental tutoring, social interaction, learning devices available at home (such as computors), and so forth. In this case the human capital of parents and the time they dedicate to teaching/tutoring play an important role. The government in our economy has two main tasks: first, in organizing the public provision of education and determining the "level" of public schooling and, second, in financing the public provision of education via taxes on wage income. We do not attempt in this chapter, except in our numerical simulations, to study the process that determines the "level of public schooling," but rather take it as given in each period. Clearly, given the initial distribution of human capital (and of income), some democratic process will lead to certain decisions, based on the principle that education is provided equally to the younger generation, while the taxes paid by each individual to finance public education depend on his level of income.

We consider an overlapping generations economy that produces a single good using two types of production factors: physical capital and human capital. It starts at date 0 with some given initial distribution of human capital and physical capital stock. Due to investments in human capital of the younger generation, the economy exhibits endogenous growth. Each individual lives for three periods: the "youth" period in which no economic decisions are made but education is acquired, the "working period" where this individual earns wage income, and the "retirement period" in which only consumption takes place. Intergenerational transfers in our economy take place only in the form of investment, made by parents, in educating their offspring and in the provision of public education.

When looking at the effects of technological changes in human capital formation, we find that in some cases a more equal intragenerational income distribution coincides with higher output, while in other cases certain technological improvements enhance growth but make income distribution less equal. Basically, an important result of this work is to point out that the way in which technological progress affects the process of human capital accumulation matters. If improvements occur mainly in "home education," we find that growth increases while inequality in income distributions increases. On the other hand, when the technological improvement affects mostly "public education," then we witness higher growth but less inequality in income distribution.

The remainder of the chapter is organized as follows. The next section reviews some related literature. Section 4.3 presents a process of human capital formation that is part of an OLG model with altruistic heterogenous agents and characterizes the equilibrium of a closed economy. Numerical simulations illustrate the properties of the model. Section 4.4 studies and simulates the effects of changes in educational technology and externalities on growth and intragenerational income distributions. Section 4.5 presents numerical simulations of our dynamic general equilibrium model when majority voting determines the level of public schooling. Section 4.6 spells out the policy implications of the chapter, and the appendix contains proofs to facilitate the reading.

4.2 Related Literature

Endogenous growth models have attracted tremendous attention in economics in the last two decades. As was demonstrated in various ways in the literature, they provide an extremely efficient analytical tool in studying issues related to growth, convergence, and distribution of income in equilibrium (see, e.g., Loury 1981; Becker and Tomes 1986; Lucas 1988; Azariadis and Drazen 1990; Tamura 1991; Glomm and Ravikumar 1992; Eckstein and Zilcha 1994; Fischer and Serra 1996; Eicher 1996; Fernandez and Rogerson 1998; van Marrewijk 1999; Galor and Moav 2000; Viaene and Zilcha 2002a). A central feature in all these studies is the way in which the evolution process of human capital is modeled. This process is complex since the accumulation of human capital or skills depends not only on parents, the "environment," teachers, schools, and investment in education, but also on technology and culture. However, the production function for human capital used in economic models concentrate, for tractability reasons, on very few parameters (see, e.g., Jovanovic and Nyarko 1995). Like that part of the literature, production in our framework is constrained by education and work experience. Our model in the stationary state is an AK-type endogenous growth model where all variables grow at the same rate as effective labor. The advantage of our OLG framework is that, in contrast to the existing literature, it allows for a comparison, period by period, of nonstationary competitive equilibria.

Statistical offices of international organizations compile extensive lists of indicators that describe and compare educational achievements across countries (see, e.g., OECD 1997). While these features vary from country to country and thus there may not be a single theory that characterizes all the observed developments, two main common elements have inspired our framework of analysis. First, the production function for human capital exhibits the property that individuals from below-average families have a greater return to human capital investment derived from public schooling than those from above-average human capital families. Also, the effort, and therefore cost, of acquiring human capital for the younger generation is smaller for societies endowed with relatively higher levels of human capital (see, e.g., Tamura 1991; Fischer and Serra 1996). Second, parental tutoring plays an important role. For example, Glaeser (1994) divides the education's positive effects on economic growth into parts and concludes that children in families with educated parents seem to obtain a better education than do those children without that supportive context. Also, Burnhill, Garner, and Mc-Pherson (1990) find that parental education influences entry to higher education in Scotland over and above the influence of parental social class. A reason that is put forward is that parental education elicits more parental involvement at home. An important difference between our process of human capital accumulation and most cases discussed in the literature is the representation of private and public inputs via time in the production of human capital. Our approach suggests that the *time spent learning*, coupled with the human capital of the instructors, and not the expenditures on education, should be the relevant variables in this process. This distinction is important since in a dynamic framework the cost of financing a particular level of human capital fluctuates with relative factor rewards.

There is some analogy between the objectives of our chapter and those analyzed in Eicher (1996). The latter looks at the endogenous absorption of new technologies into production on endogenous growth and the wage of skilled relative to nonskilled labor. While technological change is exogenous in our model, we have a continuum of skills that provides insight into how technological change influences the equilibrium income distribution, partly through incentives to acquire human capital. Unlike Eicher (1996), individuals do not invest in their own human capital. With compulsory schooling in mind, it seems that the acts of training are not fully decided by the young generations.

Income distribution is another key economic issue, and its importance is forcing economists and policymakers to improve their understanding of its underlying determinants. Evidence of a rise in income inequality has been observed in a large number of OECD countries. Some believe that social norms are crucial determinants of earnings inequality (e.g., Atkinson 1999; Corneo and Jeanne 2001). In contrast, there is a widely held belief that this rise is driven by events like progress in information technology and integration of world trade and financial markets. The role of human capital accumulation on income distribution was thoroughly studied by many researchers in various contexts (see, e.g., Loury 1981; Becker and Tomes 1986; Galor and Zeira 1993; Fernandez and Rogerson 1998; Viaene and Zilcha 2002a). Others have shown great interest in the impact of income inequality on economic systems. For example, it was shown by Glomm and Ravikumar (1992) that majority voting results in a public educational system as long as the income distribution is negatively skewed. Cardak (1999) strenghens this result by considering a voting mechanism where the median preference for education expenditure, rather than median income household, is the decisive voter. There is also the popular claim that income inequality is harmful to economic growth. Some empirical findings indicate indeed that the conjecture of a negative effect holds (see, e.g., Persson and Tabellini 1994). More recent evidence differs, however, depending on the sample period, on the sample of countries and on whether time-series or cross-section estimation techniques are used (see, e.g., Forbes 2000), a fact that is also obtained in our theoretical work.

4.3 The Model

4.3.1 Human Capital Formation

Consider an overlapping generations economy with a continuum of consumers in each generation, each living for three periods. During the first period, each child gets education but takes no economic decision. Individuals are economically active during a single working period, which is followed by the retirement period. At the beginning of the "working period," each parent gives birth to one offspring. An agent is characterized by his or her family name $\omega \in [0, 1]$, population is normalized to unity. Denote by Ω the set of families in each generation: Ω is time independent since we assume no population growth. Denote by μ the Lebesgue measure on Ω.

Agents are endowed with two units of time in their second period: one is inelastically supplied to the labor market, while the other is allocated between leisure and time invested in generating human capital of the offspring. The motivation for parental tutoring is the utility parents derive from the future lifetime income of their child. Besides self-educating their own child, parents also pay (by taxes) for formal education, to enhance the human capital of their child.

Consider generation t—namely, all individuals ω born at the outset of date t, denoted G_t—and denote by $h_{t+1}(\omega)$ the level of human capital of family ω's child. We assume that the production function for human capital is composed of two components: informal education provided by the parents, and public education provided by "teachers" and the social environment. Informal education depends on the time allocated by the parents to this purpose, denoted by $e_t(\omega)$, and on the "quality of tutoring" represented by the parents' human capital level $h_t(\omega)$. The time allocated to schooling by the public education system is denoted by e_{gt}, and we assume that the human capital of the teachers determines the "quality" of this contribution to the formation of human capital. We assume that, for some constants $\beta_1 > 1$, $\beta_2 > 1$, $v > 0$ and $\eta > 0$, a family's human capital evolves as follows:

$$h_{t+1}(\omega) = \beta_1 e_t(\omega) h_t^v(\omega) + \beta_2 e_{gt} \bar{h}_t^\eta, \tag{1}$$

where the average human capital of "teachers" is the *average* human capital of generation t, denoted $\bar{h}_t$. This can be justified if we assume that the individuals engaged in education in each generation, called "teachers," are chosen randomly from the population of that generation. The parameters v and η measure the intensity of the externalities derived from parents' and society's human capital, respectively. The constants β_1 and β_2 represent how efficiently parental and public education produce human capital: β_1 is affected by facilities and the environment at home, while β_2 is affected by facilities, the schooling system, the neighborhood, social interactions, organization, and so forth. A similar human capital formation process to this one has been used in Eckstein and Zilcha (1994).

The assumption that teachers have the average level of human capital has a number of implications for our analysis. On the one hand, it allows a feedback to occur between the rest of the model and teacher quality, an element of complication. On the other hand, it leads to a simplification in that the tax rate on labor is equal to time allocated to schooling by the public education. To see that, consider the lifetime income of individual ω, denoted by $y_t(\omega)$. Since the human capital of a worker is observable and constitutes the only source of income, it depends on the effective labor supply

$$y_t(\omega) = w_t(1 - \tau_t) h_t(\omega), \tag{2}$$

where w_t is the wage rate in period t and τ_t is the tax rate on labor income.[1] Under the public education regime taxes on incomes finance the costs of educating the young generation. Making use of (1) and (2), balanced government budget means

$$\int_\Omega w_t e_{gt} \overline{h}_t \, d\mu(\omega) = \int_\Omega \tau_t w_t h_t(\omega) \, d\mu(\omega),$$

or equivalently,

$$e_{gt} = \tau_t, \tag{3}$$

that is, the tax rate on labor is equal to the proportion of the economy's effective labor used for public education.[2]

4.3.2 Equilibrium

Production in this economy is carried out by competitive firms that produce a single commodity, using effective labor and physical capital. This commodity serves for consumption and also as an input in production. There is a full depreciation of the physical capital. The per capita human capital in date t, h_t (not including the human capital devoted to formal education), is an input in the production process. In particular, we take the aggregate production function to be

$$q_t = F(k_t, (1 - e_{gt})h_t), \tag{4}$$

where k_t is the capital stock and $(1 - e_{gt})h_t = (1 - \tau_t)h_t$ is the effective human capital used in the production process. $F(\cdot, \cdot)$ is assumed to exhibit constant returns to scale, it is strictly increasing, concave, and continuously differentiable and satisfies $F_k(0, (1 - \tau_t)h_t) = \infty$, $F_h(k_t, 0) = \infty$, $F(0, (1 - \tau_t)h_t) = F(k_t, 0) = 0$.

Each agent ω at time t maximizes the following lifetime utility:

$$\max_{e_t, s_t} u_t(\omega) = c_{1t}(\omega)^{\alpha_1} c_{2t}(\omega)^{\alpha_2} y_{t+1}(\omega)^{\alpha_3} [1 - e_t(\omega)]^{\alpha_4}, \tag{5}$$

subject to

$$c_{1t}(\omega) = y_t(\omega) - s_t(\omega) \geq 0, \tag{6}$$

$$c_{2t}(\omega) = (1 + r_{t+1})s_t(\omega). \tag{7}$$

Given the optimum for (e_t, s_t) in (5)–(7), the following equilibrium conditions hold:

$$w_t = F_h(k_t, (1 - e_{gt})h_t), \tag{8}$$

$$(1 + r_t) = F_k(k_t, (1 - e_{gt})h_t), \tag{9}$$

$$k_{t+1} = \int_\Omega s_t(\omega) \, d\mu(\omega), \tag{10}$$

where income $y_t(\omega)$ is defined by (2) and human capital $h_{t+1}(\omega)$ is given by (1). The α_is are known parameters and $\alpha_i > 0$ for $i = 1, 2, 3, 4$; $c_{1t}(\omega)$ and $c_{2t}(\omega)$ denote, respectively, consumption in first and second period of the individual's life; $s_t(\omega)$ represents savings; leisure is given by $(1 - e_t(\omega))$; $(1 + r_t)$ is the interest factor at date t. The offspring's income, given by $y_{t+1}(\omega)$, enters parents' preferences directly and represents the motivation for parents' tutoring and formal education expenditure. Equation (6) is individual ω's budget constraint. Equations (8) and (9) are the clearing conditions on factor markets. Condition (10) is a market-clearing condition for physical capital, equating the aggregate capital stock at date $t + 1$ to the aggregate savings at date t.

After substituting the constraints, the first-order conditions that lead to the necessary and sufficient conditions for optimum are

$$\frac{c_{1t}}{c_{2t}} = \frac{\alpha_1}{\alpha_2(1 + r_{t+1})}, \tag{11}$$

$$\frac{\alpha_4}{(1 - e_t(\omega))} = \frac{\beta_1 \alpha_3(1 - \tau_{t+1})w_{t+1}h_t^v(\omega)}{y_{t+1}(\omega)}, \qquad \text{if } e_t(\omega) > 0, \tag{12}$$

$$\geq \qquad \text{if } e_t(\omega) = 0. \tag{13}$$

The last equation allocates the unit of nonworking time between leisure and the time spent on education by the parents. The latter, $e_t(\omega)$, increases with the parents' human capital h_t^v and the wage, net of taxes, at the future date. Equation (12) establishes a negative relationship between types of education, that is, public education substitutes for parental tutoring as τ_{t+1} increases. Hence, for each individual there exists a particular value of the tax rate such that $e_t(\omega) = 0$. This is obtained when the marginal utility of leisure is larger than the net future wage received from a marginal increase in the human capital of the younger generation as a result of parental tutoring. From (6), (7), and (11), we also obtain

$$c_{1t}(\omega) = \left(\frac{\alpha_1}{\alpha_1 + \alpha_2}\right) y_t(\omega), \tag{14}$$

$$s_t(\omega) = \left(\frac{\alpha_2}{\alpha_1 + \alpha_2}\right) y_t(\omega). \tag{15}$$

It is useful to derive the evolution of human capital from the first order conditions. Making use of (12), the human capital of a dynasty given by (1) can be rewritten as follows:

$$h_{t+1}(\omega) = \left(\frac{\alpha_3}{\alpha_3 + \alpha_4}\right) [\beta_1 h_t^v(\omega) + \beta_2 \tau_t \bar{h}_t^\eta]. \tag{16}$$

Define the growth factor of aggregate labor as

$$\gamma_t \equiv \frac{h_{t+1}}{h_t} \equiv \frac{\int_\Omega h_{t+1}(\omega)\, d\mu(\omega)}{\int_\Omega h_t(\omega)\, d\mu(\omega)}. \tag{17}$$

Substitution of (16) in (17) gives us an alternative expression for γ_t:

$$\gamma_t = \left(\frac{\alpha_3}{\alpha_3 + \alpha_4}\right) \left[\beta_1 \frac{\int_\Omega h_t^v(\omega)\, d\mu(\omega)}{\int_\Omega h_t(\omega)\, d\mu(\omega)} + \beta_2 \tau_t \bar{h}_t^{\eta-1}\right]. \tag{18}$$

It is clear from (18) that the growth factor of effective labor is the sum of two terms, one representing the contribution of parental tutoring, the other the contribution of public education. While the latter is influenced by the tax rate the former depends upon the distribution of human capital at each date.

4.3.3 Numerical Simulations

The aim of this section is to introduce a dynamic computable general equilibrium model with heterogenous agents and to characterize the properties of the equilibria of the model discussed so far. In particular, we are interested in establishing the relationship between changes in some parameters, and the growth and distribution of income that can be sustained in equilibrium. To facilitate the interpretation of our theoretical results, the first set of numerical simulations assumes that the sequence of τ_t is exogenously given. Later in section 4.5, we allow for the tax rate to be endogenously determined through majority voting.

In our numerical examples, we replace (4) by the Cobb-Douglas production function $q_t = A k_t^\theta (1 - \tau_t)^{1-\theta} h_t^{1-\theta}$, that is, $w_t = A(1 - \theta)$ $(k_t/(1 - \tau_t)h_t)^\theta$ and $(1 + r_t) = A\theta((1 - \tau_t)h_t/k_t)^{1-\theta}$. In the baseline case, we assume that the economy is in a steady state. To characterize the latter, consider equations (2), (10), (15), and the Cobb-Douglas production function to obtain

$$\frac{k_{t+1}}{k_t} = \frac{(1 - \theta)\alpha_2}{\theta(\alpha_1 + \alpha_2)}(1 + r_t). \tag{19}$$

Making use of (17) and of the expression for the rental rate:

$$\frac{k_{t+1}}{h_{t+1}} = \frac{A\alpha_2(1 - \theta)}{(\alpha_1 + \alpha_2)}(1 - \tau_t)^{1-\theta}(\gamma_t)^{-1}\left(\frac{k_t}{h_t}\right)^\theta, \tag{20}$$

which describes the dynamic path of the capital-labor ratio of the economy. In the long run, $k_{t+1}/h_{t+1} = k_t/h_t$ is a constant k/h if $\tau_t = \tau$ and $\gamma_t = \gamma$. The time independence of γ can be obtained by incorporating externalities that yield constant returns to scale to parents' and society's human capital in (1), namely, assuming $v = \eta = 1$. In that case, we obtain the long-run capital-labor ratio from (20):

$$\frac{k}{h} = (1 - \tau)\left[\frac{\alpha_2(1 - \theta)A}{\gamma(\alpha_1 + \alpha_2)}\right]^{1/(1-\theta)}. \tag{21}$$

From the previous equations, we obtain the expression for long-run output and income growth:

$$\frac{q_{t+1}}{q_t} = \frac{\int_\Omega y_{t+1}(\omega)\,d\mu(\omega)}{\int_\Omega y_t(\omega)\,d\mu(\omega)} = \frac{\alpha_2(1 - \theta)A}{(\alpha_1 + \alpha_2)}\left(\frac{h(1 - \tau)}{k}\right)^{1-\theta}.$$

Substituting (21) in this last expression gives

$$\frac{q_{t+1}}{q_t} = \gamma.$$

Long-run economic growth coincides with the growth factor of effective labor (γ), regardless of initial conditions. Our model in the stationary state is therefore an AK-type endogenous growth model where all variables grow at the rate ($\gamma - 1$).

Besides $v = \eta = 1$, we assume that the other baseline parameters are $k_{-1} = 70.019$, $\tau = 0.2$, $\alpha_1 = \alpha_2 = \alpha_4 = 1$, $\alpha_3 = 2$, $A = 4$, $\theta = 0.3$, and $\beta_1 = \beta_2 = 1.6$. We consider a discrete number of heterogenous families, namely, 11, with a human capital at $t = -1$ taking the values

$1, 2, \ldots, 8, 11, 14, 16$. The initial endowments in physical and human capital were chosen with three criteria in mind. First, the values of the endogenous variables that follow from these initial conditions and parameter values are long-run values at all dates. Second, the initial heterogeneity in human capital calibrates an exact Gini coefficient close to the European average, namely 0.309 in period 0. Third, the distribution of human capital is negatively skewed, a fact that is observed in many countries. The median lies therefore to the left of the mean. The following formula for the Gini coefficient is used:

$$g_t = \frac{1}{2n^2 \bar{y}_t} \sum_{i=1}^{n} \sum_{j=1}^{n} |y_i - y_j|, \tag{22}$$

where n represents the number of families, $\bar{y}_t$ is average income, y_i and y_j are individual incomes.

Given the set of baseline parameters of the model, the equilibrium path of all variables belonging to a particular family is obtained in two steps. First, the human capital of any individual at date t is given by (16). Aggregating the levels of human capital across individuals and equating the aggregate capital stock at date t to the aggregate savings at date $t - 1$ (see (10)), we obtain aggregate production q_t, the equilibrium w_t and $(1 + r_t)$. Upon this information, each individual derives his or her income $y_t(\omega)$ from (2) and summary statistics like the Gini coefficient can be computed. Second, given the time path of wages, marginal returns to physical capital, and income of each dynasty, each individual can compute $e_t(\omega)$, $c_{1t}(\omega)$, $c_{2t}(\omega)$, and $u_t(\omega)$.

Table 4.1 presents the solution for our baseline case and the equilibrium corresponding to a 10 percent increase in each parameter of the utility function. Changes in other parameters are emphasized in the next section. In the numerical simulations, given the chosen parameters, we solve the model for two hundred periods. As patterns emerge within twenty periods we discard the last 180 periods and compute the relevant statistics averaging over the first ten periods and over the second ten periods.

A feature of the baseline in column 1 is the decreasing inequality among dynasties. Though families start in period 0 with very different endowments, they tend to be similar after twenty periods. This shows the strength of public education relative to parental tutoring in the accumulation of human capital. This result is obtained even

Table 4.1
Baseline and parameters of the utility function

	(1) $\alpha_1 = \alpha_2 = 1$ $\alpha_3 = 2$ $\alpha_4 = 1$	(2) $\alpha_1 = 1.1$	(3) $\alpha_2 = 1.1$	(4) $\alpha_3 = 2.2$	(5) $\alpha_4 = 1.1$
Relative factor	0.471	0.504	0.442	0.492	0.451
returns $(1 + r_t)/w_t$	0.471	0.505	0.441	0.493	0.450
Gini coefficient (g_t)	0.155	0.155	0.155	0.155	0.155
	0.025	0.025	0.025	0.025	0.025
Growth rate (%)	28	27.7	28.3	31.8	24
(aggr. output)	28	28	28	32	23.9
Parental education (e_t)					
Poorest agent	0.550	0.550	0.550	0.578	0.521
	0.596	0.596	0.596	0.621	0.570
Richest agent	0.622	0.622	0.622	0.646	0.598
	0.605	0.605	0.605	0.630	0.580

Note: Column 1 is the baseline scenario assuming $\tau = 0.2$, $\alpha_1 = \alpha_2 = \alpha_4 = 1$, $\alpha_3 = 2$, $A = 4$, $\theta = 0.3$, $\beta_1 = \beta_2 = 1.6$, $v = \eta = 1$. Each row reports the average over the first ten periods and the average of the second ten periods.

though families have different degrees of parental tutoring as indicated by the last two rows. Changes in the parameters of the utility function do not affect the income distribution results. Though they modify individual income levels, these are modified in the same proportion as all families share the same utility function. Results in columns 2 and 3 can be best explained by referring to (14) and (15). While an increase in α_1 is conducive to less savings and more current consumption, an increase in α_2 leads to the reverse. While an increase in α_1 leads to somewhat lesser growth in the short run and higher rental rates when compared to the baseline solution, the opposite occurs in column 3. Columns 4 and 5 contrast stronger altruistic preferences with stronger preferences for leisure, respectively. It is important to note the marked differences in growth rates and parental education. More altruism leads to higher levels of human capital via more parental efforts in education and ultimately to higher long-run growth rates. The opposite occurs with a higher α_4.

4.4   Income Distribution and Growth

The focus of this section is to consider the inequality in the intra-generational income distribution, in equilibrium, and relate it to the various parameters of our dynamic model. At the same time, we wish to explore the relationship between inequality and growth. Our explanation is based on the extent of efficiencies and externalities in the process of human capital accumulation.

We use the relations that we derived in the previous section to obtain an expression for income at date $t+1$, $y_{t+1}(\omega)$. To that end, isolate $y_{t+1}(\omega)$ in (13) and make use of (1), (2), and (3) to obtain

$$y_{t+1}(\omega) = \left(\frac{\alpha_3}{\alpha_3 + \alpha_4}\right)(1 - \tau_{t+1})w_{t+1}\left[\beta_1 h_t^v(\omega) + \beta_2 e_{gt}\bar{h}_t^\eta\right]. \tag{23}$$

Equation (23) determines income at the future date in terms of the net wage at date $t+1$, the parents' and society's level of human capital at date t, the current education input ($\tau_t = e_{gt}$), and the externalities in education. Note that in this framework there is no direct dependence of incomes across generations.

We use a definition to compare distribution functions. Let X and W be two random variables with values in a bounded interval in $(-\infty, \infty)$ and let m_x and m_w denote their respective means. Define $\hat{X} = X/m_x$ and $\hat{W} = W/m_w$. Denote by F_x and F_w the cumulative distribution functions of $\hat{X}$ and $\hat{W}$, respectively. Let $[a, b]$ be the smallest interval containing the supports of $\hat{X}$ and $\hat{W}$.

Definition F_x is more equal than F_w if, for all $t \in [a, b]$, $\int_a^t [F_x(s) - F_w(s)]\, ds \leq 0$.

Thus, F_x is more equal than F_w if F_x *dominates* in the second-degree stochastic dominance F_w. This definition, due to Atkinson (1970), is equivalent to the requirement that the Lorenz curve corresponding to X is everywhere above that of W. We say that X is *more equal* than W if the cumulative distribution function (c.d.f.) of $\hat{X}$ and $\hat{W}$ satisfy: F_x is more equal than F_w. Henceforth the relation X is more equal than W is denoted $X \gg W$. We say that X is equivalent to W, and denote this relation by $X \approx W$, if $X \gg W$ and $W \gg X$.

4.4.1 Initial Conditions

Consider two similar economies that differ only in the initial distributions of human capital: One economy has higher levels of human capital but the same inequality of human capital distribution. Can we compare the equilibrium intragenerational income distributions of these two economies over time? The next proposition provides an answer.

Proposition 1 Consider two economies that differ only in their initial human capital distributions, $h_0(\omega)$ and $h_0^*(\omega)$. Assume that $h_0^*(\omega) > h_0(\omega)$ for all ω, but $h_0^*(\omega) \approx h_0(\omega)$, namely, these two distributions have the same level of inequality. Then, the equilibrium from $h_0^*(\omega)$ will have less unequal intragenerational income distributions at all dates t, $t = 1, 2, 3, \ldots$

Proof See the appendix.

This result indicates that a country that starts with higher levels of human capital, not necessarily more equal, has a better chance to maintain more equality in its future income distributions. A larger endowment of human capital increases the contribution of public education to human capital relative to that of parental tutoring. This evens the family attributes and reduces income inequality because, as public education is common to all, below-average families have a greater return to public schooling than above-average families. In general, policy and parameter changes of this model will reduce (increase) income inequality when the weight of public education in human capital formation increases (decreases).

4.4.2 Public Education

Throughout this section, we assume that public provision of education is determined by the government, say, by elections or other social decision mechanism, and it is equal to e_{gt} in date t and financed by taxing labor income at a fixed rate $\tau_t > 0$. From now on we assume that $v \leq 1$ and that $\eta \leq 1$. Let us consider the variation over time of the inequality in the distribution of income.

Proposition 2 If the same tax rate applies to all periods, the inequality in intragenerational income distribution at date $t + 1$ is smaller than the inequality at date t.

Proof See the appendix.

Column 1 of table 4.1 indicated already that under the assumption that the tax rate is the same for all levels of income, inequality declines over time. The inequality in income distribution at date $t + 1$

is indeed smaller than the inequality in income distribution at date t and in the limit families tend to the same level of human capital and income. Let us show now that a higher provision of public education reduces inequality in the distribution of income in each generation.

Proposition 3 In the previous economy, let $h_0(\omega)$ be the initial human capital distribution. Increasing the public provision of education results in less inequality in the intragenerational income distribution in each date.

Proof See the appendix.

This result may not be surprising since public education is provided equally to all young individuals (of the same generation), while it is financed by a flat tax rate on wage income. However, its importance lies in the fact that it is proved in equilibrium and that it holds in all future periods. It is also clear from (18) that, when $v = \eta = 1$, more public education contributes to a higher long-run growth rate of effective labor.

These results are quantified in the two columns of table 4.2 where τ_t takes two values, 0.20 and 0.22, respectively. Besides increasing the long-run growth rate of output and decreasing the inequality in the income distribution, table 4.2 confirms the substitution among education types. Public education crowds out parental tutoring though the elasticity computed at steady-state values is about -0.1 and thus quite small.

Table 4.2
Baseline and public education

	(1) $\tau = 0.2$	(2) $\tau = 0.22$
Relative factor returns	0.471	0.493
$(1 + r_t)/w_t$	0.471	0.495
Gini coefficient (g_t)	0.155	0.145
	0.025	0.020
Growth rate (%)	28	29.7
(aggr. output)	28	30.1
Parental education (e_t)		
Poorest agent	0.550	0.543
	0.596	0.590
Richest agent	0.622	0.616
	0.605	0.598

4.4.3 Efficiencies and Externalities

Consider some technological change that affects the production of human capital. We say that the provision of *public* education becomes *more efficient* if, in the human capital process (1), β_2/β_1 becomes *larger* without lowering neither β_1 nor β_2.[3] We say that the *private* provision of education becomes *more efficient* if, in the process (1), β_1/β_2 becomes *larger* while neither β_1 nor β_2 declines. Likewise, a technological improvement in the production of human capital is said to be *neutral* if the ratio β_2/β_1 remains unchanged while both parameters increase. Let us consider now the effects of each type of technological improvement in the education process on intragenerational income inequality.

Proposition 4 Consider the previous economy. A technological improvement in the production of human capital, given by equation (1), results in

a. If public provision of education becomes more efficient, the intragenerational distribution of income becomes less unequal in all periods.

b. If private provision of education becomes more efficient, income inequality becomes larger in all periods.

c. If the technological improvement is neutral, the inequality in income distribution remains unchanged at period 1 but declines for all periods afterward.

Proof See the appendix.

Let us consider now another type of a change in the "home-component" of the production of human capital and its economic implications in equilibrium. Observe the process represented by (1). Let us vary the parameters v and η, which relate to the role played by human capital of the parents or the "environment." Since we assume that $v \leq 1$ and $\eta \leq 1$, let us consider the effect that lower values will have on the inequality in income distributions in equilibrium.

Proposition 5 Consider the process of production of human capital given by (1). Then

a. Comparing two economies which differ only in this parameter v, we find that the economy with the lower v will have less inequality in the intragenerational income distribution in all periods.

b. Comparing two economies which differ only in the parameter η, we find that the economy with the lower value of η will have more inequality in the income distribution in all periods.

Proof See the appendix.

Let us consider now the effect that technological improvement in the production of human capital will have on output in equilibrium. Consider (1) and remember that we call the first term on the RHS, $\beta_1 e_t(\omega) h_t^v(\omega)$, the *home component*, and the second term, $\beta_2 e_{gt} \bar{h}_t^\eta$, the *public component*. Now we prove:

Proposition 6 Consider the human capital production process given by (1) and the following types of technological improvements:

a. Increasing β_1, or increasing v or both, will increase output in all dates.

b. Increasing β_2, or increasing η or both, will result in higher output in all periods.

If we consider the computor information revolution as a technological improvement in enhancing knowledge, then we ask whether the home component benefits more than the public component in the formation process of human capital. We believe that computors and the Internet have enhanced home education considerably, while schools benefit only in a limited manner. The following corollary may provide some explanation to the recent widespread phenomena (mostly during the 1990s) that in the OECD countries, economic growth is accompanied by increasing inequality in the distribution of income.

Corollary 7 (a) In the following two cases of technological improvement in the home component, we obtain higher economic growth coupled with *more* inequality in the distribution of income: (i) an increase in β_1, (ii) an increase in v.

(b) In the following two cases of technological improvement in the public component, we obtain higher economic growth coupled with

Table 4.3
Baseline and other specification externalities

Externalities	(1)	(2)	(3)	(4)	(5)
v	1	0.9	1	1.1	1
η	1	1	0.9	1	1.1
Relative factor returns	0.471	0.366	0.445	0.816	0.513
$(1 + r_t)/w_t$	0.471	0.345	0.430	3.29	0.581
Gini coefficient (g_t)	0.155	0.095	0.182	0.288	0.129
	0.025	0.003	0.050	0.327	0.008
Growth rate (%)	28	7.1	23.0	86.9	35.9
(aggr. output)	28	2.9	20.0	large	48.1
Parental education (e_t)					
Poorest agent	0.550	0.550	0.570	0.548	0.518
	0.596	0.578	0.621	0.633	0.527
Richest agent	0.622	0.598	0.636	0.649	0.597
	0.605	0.580	0.632	0.661	0.533

less inequality in the distribution of income: (i) an increase in β_2, (ii) an increase in η.

In terms of results, it is remarkable that both cases of technological improvement yield similar predictions on growth but opposite on income distribution. In this regard, table 4.3 adds that inequality as measured by Gini coefficients is more sensitive to externalities arising from the home component than from those arising from the public part of human capital formation. Decreasing returns in parents' human capital (column 2) reduce inequality substantially, all individuals becoming equal in the long run. In contrast, substantial income inequality is observed with increasing returns (column 4).[4] Columns 2 and 4 establish a positive correlation between growth and income inequality. In column 2, decreased inequality is obtained at the expense of growth, whether measured in terms of income or human capital (not shown), and vice versa in column 4. In contrast, when looking at changes in η, the correlation between growth and income inequality is negative as indicated in columns 3 and 5.

Table 4.4 looks at a technological improvement in human capital formation represented here by rises in the β's. Columns 2 to 4 show that a greater efficiency in education is always conducive to growth while hardly affecting income distributions. A comparison of columns 2 and 3 shows the stronger impact that parental education has on output growth.

Table 4.4
Baseline and other specification efficiency

Efficiency	(1)	(2)	(3)	(4)
β_1	1.6	1.76	1.6	1.76
β_2	1.6	1.6	1.76	1.76
Relative factor returns	0.471	0.526	0.482	0.537
$(1 + r_t)/w_t$	0.471	0.528	0.483	0.540
Gini coefficient (g_t)	0.155	0.166	0.145	0.155
	0.025	0.031	0.020	0.025
Growth rate (%)	28	38.2	30.0	40.2
(aggr. output)	28	38.7	30.1	40.8
Parental education (e_t)				
Poorest agent	0.550	0.556	0.543	0.550
	0.596	0.601	0.590	0.596
Richest agent	0.622	0.627	0.616	0.622
	0.605	0.612	0.598	0.605

4.5 Majority Voting

Though there is a growing awareness of governments in education, enhancing human capital skills require financial resources to cover the investment. Though the majority of constituents recognize the importance of learning, they are not prepared to contribute financially via income taxes in the same way. To establish the preferences of each individual with respect to $\tau_t(\omega)$ let us compute the reduced-form utility of each agent. Substituting the first-order conditions in (5), lifetime utility of agent ω can be rewritten as

$$u_t(\omega) = \Omega_t(1 - \tau_t(\omega))^{\alpha_1 + \alpha_2}(1 - \tau_{t+1}(\omega))^{\alpha_3}(\beta_1 h_t(\omega)^v + \beta_2 \tau_t(\omega)\bar{h}_t^\eta)^{\alpha_3 + \alpha_4}$$

$$(24)$$

where Ω_t groups all parameters and variables like factor rewards that are given to atomistic individuals. Knowing that each agent cannot enforce any tax rate at the future date, namely, $\tau_{t+1}(\omega)$ is given to him, the maximization of (24) with respect to $\tau_t(\omega)$ gives

$$\tau_t(\omega) = \frac{(\alpha_3 + \alpha_4)}{(\alpha_1 + \alpha_2 + \alpha_3 + \alpha_4)} - \frac{(\alpha_1 + \alpha_2)}{(\alpha_1 + \alpha_2 + \alpha_3 + \alpha_4)} \frac{\beta_1 h_t(\omega)^v}{\beta_2 \bar{h}_t^\eta}. \qquad (25)$$

Each agent chooses the optimal $\tau_t(\omega)$ such that the cost of current spending on education (in terms of foregone current and future consumption) is equal to the reward of a marginal increase in the human capital of their children. It is clear that the heterogeneity in

Table 4.5
Externalities and median voter

Externalities	(1)	(2)	(3)	(4)	(5)
v	1	0.9	1	1.1	1
η	1	1	0.9	1	1.1
Tax rate (τ_t)	0.222	0.299	0.109	0.101	0.347
	0.203	0.323	0.031	0.019	0.460
Relative factor returns	0.496	0.447	0.384	0.684	0.751
$(1 + r_t)/w_t$	0.476	0.440	0.315	2.31	1.67
Gini coefficient (g_t)	0.143	0.079	0.213	0.338	0.096
	0.021	0.001	0.127	0.586	0.001
Growth rate (%)	30.1	12.4	9.3	80.6	52.8
(aggr. output)	28.6	8.5	10.3	large	large
Parental education (e_t)					
Poorest agent	0.539	0.496	0.602	0.585	0.422
	0.595	0.511	0.657	0.641	0.189
Richest agent	0.616	0.556	0.651	0.657	0.519
	0.603	0.511	0.662	0.666	0.191

$\tau_t(\omega)$ derives from the heterogeneity in human capital. When $\eta \leq 1$ and $v \leq 1$ above-average agents are willing to pay a lower tax rate than below-average agents. In terms of numerical results, the first step in our simulations computes a vector of $\tau_t(\omega)$ based on (25). Given this vector of individual preferences for education expenditure, we assume that the level of public schooling is obtained at each date through majority voting. Numerically, majority voting boils down to identifying the median voter's preference for public schooling.

Tables 4.5 and 4.6 repeat the exercises performed in tables 4.3 and 4.4, now with endogenous public education. What difference does it make? Baseline is different because the distribution of human capital being negatively skewed, the median voter's human capital lies to the left of the mean and therefore he or she wishes a higher tax rate. Tables 4.5 and 4.6 reproduce the substitution in equilibrium between public education and parental education observed before: Any increase in τ_t decreases the time spent on parental education e_t and hence, raises leisure. This substitution among types of provision of education has a number of implications, one of them being that Gini coefficients vary more. It is important to note that simulation results confirm the robustness of corollary 7 whose results apply also to the case of endogenous public education. A positive correlation

Table 4.6
Efficiency and median voter

Efficiency	(1)	(2)	(3)	(4)
β_1	1.6	1.76	1.6	1.76
β_2	1.6	1.6	1.76	1.76
Tax rate (τ_t)	0.222	0.188	0.254	0.222
	0.203	0.166	0.238	0.203
Relative factor returns	0.496	0.516	0.545	0.565
$(1 + r_t)/w_t$	0.476	0.490	0.532	0.546
Gini coefficient (g_t)	0.143	0.166	0.124	0.143
	0.021	0.037	0.011	0.021
Growth rate (%)	30.1	37.8	35.0	42.6
(aggr. output)	28.6	35.4	34.7	41.4
Parental education (e_t)				
Poorest agent	0.539	0.560	0.517	0.539
	0.595	0.611	0.577	0.595
Richest agent	0.616	0.630	0.600	0.616
	0.603	0.622	0.583	0.603

between income inequality and income growth is obtained when externalities or efficiencies arising from parents' human capital vary. In contrast, this correlation is negative when externalities or efficiencies in the public contribution to human capital are considered.

4.6   Policy Implications

The chapter has studied the determinants of income distribution and growth in an overlapping generations economy with heterogenous households. Heterogenity results simply from the initial nondegenerate distribution of human capital across individuals. Both parental tutoring and public education contribute to human capital accumulation. Theoretical and numerical results from this model are consistent with some key features of the data.

A first effect analyzed in this chapter is the role of initial conditions. We find that a country that starts with a higher level of human capital, not necessarily less equal, has a better chance to maintain less inequality in the future. Hence, communities that create a culture of literacy and knowledge are more likely to experience lower income inequality. In this regard, International Adult Literacy Surveys show that between one-quarter and three-quarters of adults in a comparison of OECD countries fail to attain a literacy level considered by experts as a suitable minimum to cope with the demands of contemporanous societies. Our first proposition suggests that these cross-country differences in literacy skills may be important determinants of the observed cross-country differences in income inequality.

There is an important role for public education. Under the assumption that the tax rate that finances education is positive and fixed over time, inequality declines over time. Increasing this tax rate in an attempt to enhance the provision of public education results in less income inequality. These theoretical results do not depend on the levels of public educations, $\{e_{gt}\}$. However, most governments are concerned with the optimality of the resources invested in education (see, e.g., Viaene and Zilcha 2002b). In economic theory, the choice of some "optimal" level of public education requires some social welfare function that, due to the heterogeneity of households, may not represent a political equilibrium. Instead, the majority voting criterion is widely used and one can determine this level by using the median voter's optimal choice. Our numerical simulations make use of this concept to endogenize public education. It follows that the median voter's preferred tax rate to finance public schooling is *increasing* in (1) the negative skewness of the distribution of human capital, (2) the externality derived from society's human capital, (3) the efficiency of public schooling, and (4) the parameters of altruism and leisure in the utility function. The prefered tax rate is *decreasing* in (1) the externality derived from family's human capital, (2) the efficiency of parental tutoring, and (3) the parameters for current and future consumption in the utility function.

The claim that income inequality is harmful to economic growth has been tested in a number of empirical studies. While the first evidence indicated that the conjecture of a negative sign indeed holds, more recent empirical studies find the effect to be ambiguous, a fact that is also obtained in our work. If technological improvements in the human capital accumulation process occur mainly in home education, both growth and income inequality increase. In contrast, if the technological improvement affects mostly public education then higher growth and less income inequality are obtained. In terms of results, it is remarkable that both types of technological changes yield dissimilar predictions on income inequality. This creates challenges for policymakers because independent policies affecting parental education only cannot serve two masters at the same time while those affecting public education can. For example, policies aimed at the use of computers and telecommunication in homes (via tax deductions) magnify differences in family attributes while the same policies in schools diminish them.

The information revolution of the last decade is said to lead to a digital divide. This phenomenon means a split of a country's population between those without and those with Internet access, which are mainly the better-educated groups. A divide may also arise globally as the Internet density is higher in industrial countries than elsewhere. In both cases, this may enhance the existing intragenerational socioeconomic disparities within the world's population. In our framework, a divide is obtained when human capital formation is characterized by increasing returns to scale in family's human capital. In this case, income inequality increases (see column 4 of tables 4.3 and 4.5): Some families experience an ever increasing human capital and some face a development trap. That is, the latter have too low an endowment of human capital and, as a result, experience a continuous decrease in their human capital over time. The existence of a development trap gives a role for public education to offset this gap. Numerically, we can show that, even in the presence of externalities in family's human capital, there exists a level of public education sufficient to lead to a drop in income inequality.

Many industrialized countries are experiencing an increase in income inequality. Using Gini coefficients, there is evidence of a sharp rise for the United States, the United Kingdom, and New Zealand. Increased inequality is not uniform across the OECD as some countries like France and Canada experience decreasing inequality. Our framework offers a simple explanation that focuses mainly on education technology and education policy: It depends on the size of the public component of education relative to the home contribution. For example, increased inequality is explained by the decline through time of the relative contribution of public education whereby family attributes gain a larger role. As indicated in tables 4.2–4.4, this could be the result of numerous factors or any combination of them. Likely explanations are the lower quality of public education due to lower scholastic standards, lower quality of teachers, lower efficiency or disorganization of the schooling system, and technological improvement in parental education. As for the digital divide, another possible explanation is the presence of increasing returns to scale in family's human capital that, if combined with increases in public education, can duplicate the erratic pattern of inequality shown in the data of some countries.

Our model makes some specific and simplifying assumptions, and it is therefore subject to the robustness issue. First, the production function for human capital is additive in the contributions of parental tutoring and public education. Though this specification is quite standard, there is hardly no empirical test of the assumed functional form. It follows that both types of education are substitutes and that our theoretical results on inequality depend on the weight of public education (common to all), relative to parental tutoring (which is family-specific). Second, it is important to note that introducing intergenerational monetary transfers in our model will modify the results. In such a case, we lose the one to one relationship between the distribution of income and the distribution of human capital. Technological progress in the aggregate production function may have different effects on the intragenerational income distributions (see Karni and Zilcha 1994). Likewise, the framework can be generalized by introducing an additional redistributive measure by the government, such as social security. This may also vary some of our conclusions.

4.7 Appendix

Proof of Proposition 1   Consider two equilibria in which human capital accumulation is described by (1). Variables under the second equilibrium are marked by "*". Let us rewrite equation (23) for both equilibria:

$$y_{t+1}(\omega) = C_t\left[h_t^v(\omega) + \frac{\beta_2}{\beta_1}e_{gt}\bar{h}_t^\eta\right],$$

$$y_{t+1}^*(\omega) = C_t^*\left[h_t^{*v}(\omega) + \frac{\beta_2}{\beta_1}e_{gt}\bar{h}_t^{*\eta}\right]$$

where C_t and C_t^* are positive constants. Since h_0 and h_0^* are equally distributed, the same holds for $h_0^v(\omega)$ and $[h_0^*(\omega)]^v$, since $v \leq 1$. Moreover, since $\bar{h}_0 < \bar{h}_0^*$ we obtain that $h_1^*(\omega)$ is more equal than $h_1(\omega)$ (see Lemma 2 in Karni and Zilcha 1994). It is easy to verify from (18) that $h_1(\omega)$ are lower than $h_1^*(\omega)$ for all ω. In particular, we obtain that $[h_1^*(\omega)]^v$ is more equal than $[h_1(\omega)]^v$ (see Shaked and

Shanthikumar 1994, Theorem 3.A.5). Also we have $[\bar{h}_1]^\eta < [\bar{h}_1^*]^\eta$. This implies, using (16), that $h_2^*(\omega)$ is more equal than $h_2(\omega)$. It is easy to see that this process can be continued to generalize this to all periods. □

Proof of Proposition 2 Let us show first that in each generation individuals with higher level of human capital choose at the optimum higher level of time to be allocated for private education of their offspring. To see this, let us derive from the first-order conditions, using some manipulation, the following equation:

$$1 - \left[1 + \frac{\beta_1 \alpha_4}{\alpha_3}\right] e_t(\omega) = \frac{\alpha_4 \beta_2}{\alpha_3} e_{gt} \bar{h}_t^\eta [h_t^{-v}(\omega)], \tag{26}$$

which demonstrates that higher $h_t(\omega)$ implies higher level of $e_t(\omega)$. Let us show that such a property generates less equality in the distribution of $y_{t+1}(\omega)$ compared to that of $y_t(\omega)$. It is useful however, to apply (16) for this issue. In fact it represents the period $t+1$ income $y_{t+1}(\omega)$ as a function of the date t income $y_t(\omega)$ via the human capital evolution. Define the function $Q : R \to R$ such that $Q[h_t(\omega)] = h_{t+1}(\omega)$ using (16). This monotone-increasing function satisfies: $Q(x) > 0$ for any $x > 0$ and $Q(x)/x$ is decreasing in x. Therefore (see Shaked and Shanthikumar 1994), the human capital distribution $h_{t+1}(\omega)$ is more equal than the distribution in date t, $h_t(\omega)$. This implies that $y_{t+1}(\omega)$ is more equal than $y_t(\omega)$. □

Proof of Proposition 3 Let us consider equation (16) for $t = 0$. Since $h_0(\omega)$ is given, $h_0^v(\omega)$ and $\bar{h}_0$ are fixed. By raising e_{g0} the distribution of the human capital for generation 1, $h_1(\omega)$ becomes more equal. This follows from Lemma 2 in Karni and Zilcha (1994). Moreover, we claim from (16) that the average human capital in generation 1 increases as well. Increasing e_{g0} will result in higher $h_1(\omega)$ for all ω and higher level of $\bar{h}_1$. Moreover, it also implies that $h_1^v(\omega)$ will have a *more equal* distribution (see Shaked and Shanthikumar 1994, Theorem 3.A.5).

Now, let us consider $t = 1$. Increasing e_{g1} will imply the following facts: $h_1^v(\omega)$ becomes more equal and $\beta_2 e_{g1} \bar{h}_1^\eta$ is larger than its value before we increase the levels of public education. Using (16) and the same lemma as before, we obtain that $h_2(\omega)$ becomes more equal. This process can be continued for $t = 3, 4, \ldots$, which establishes our claim. □

Proof of Proposition 4 Let the initial distribution of human capital
$h_0(\omega)$ be given. Compare the following two equilibria from the same
initial conditions: one with the human capital formation process
given by (1), and another with the same process but β_2 is replaced by
a larger coefficient $\beta_2^* > \beta_2$. Clearly, we keep β_1 unchanged. Let us
rewrite equation (23) as follows:

$$y_{t+1}(\omega) = C_t\left[h_t^v(\omega) + \frac{\beta_2}{\beta_1}e_{gt}\bar{h}_t^\eta\right],$$

$$y_{t+1}^*(\omega) = C_t^*\left[h_t^{*v}(\omega) + \frac{\beta_2^*}{\beta_1}e_{gt}\bar{h}_t^{*\eta}\right],$$

where C_t and C_t^* are some positive constants. Since $h_0(\omega)$ is fixed at
date $t = 0$ we find (using once again Lemma 2 from Karni and Zilcha
1994) that $\beta_2^*/\beta_1 > \beta_2/\beta_1$ imply that $y_1^*(\omega)$ is more equal than $y_1(\omega)$.
We also derive that $h_1(\omega)$ are lower than $h_1^*(\omega)$ for all ω and, hence,
$\bar{h}_1 < \bar{h}_1^*$. By (16), using the same argument as in the last proof, $h_1^{*v}(\omega)$
is more equal than $h_1^v(\omega)$ and $(\beta_2^*/\beta_1)e_{g1}\bar{h}_1^{*\eta} > (\beta_2/\beta_1)e_{g1}\bar{h}_1^\eta$, hence
$h_2^*(\omega)$ is more equal than $h_2(\omega)$. This same argument can be con-
tinued for all dates $t = 3, 4, 5, \ldots$, which completes the proof of part
(a) of this proposition. The proof of part (b) follows from the same
types of arguments using the fact that if $\beta_1 < \beta_1^*$ then $\beta_2/\beta_1 > \beta_2^*/\beta_1$
and, hence, $h_1(\omega)$ is more equal than $h_1^*(\omega)$ and $\bar{h}_1 > \bar{h}_1^*$. This process
leads, using similar arguments as before, to $y_t(\omega)$ more equal than
$y_t^*(\omega)$ for all periods t. Consider now the claim in part (c). From
(16) we see that inequality in the distribution of $h_1(\omega)$ remains
unchanged even though all levels of $h_1(\omega)$ increase due to this technological improvement. In particular, $\bar{h}_1$ increases. Now, since inequality of $h_1^v(\omega)$ did not vary but the second term in the RHS of (16)
has increased due to the higher value of $\bar{h}_1$, we obtain more equal
distribution of $h_2(\omega)$. Now, this argument can be used again at dates
$3, 4, \ldots$, which completes the proof. $\square$

Proof of Proposition 5 Assume, without loss of generality, that
$h_0(\omega) \geq 1$ for all ω. Since the two economies have the same initial
distribution of human capital $h_0(\omega)$ the process that determines $h_1(\omega)$
differs only in the parameter v. Denote by $v^* < v \leq 1$ the parameters,
then it is clear that $[h_0(\omega)]^{v^*}$ is more equal than $[h_0(\omega)]^v$ since it is
attained by a strictly concave transformation (see Shaked and Shanthikumar 1994, Theorem 3.A.5). Likewise, the human capital distri-

bution $h_1^*(\omega)$ is more equal than the distribution $h_1(\omega)$. This implies that $y_1^*(\omega)$ is more equal than $y_1(\omega)$. Now we can apply the same argument to date 1: The distribution of $[h_1^*(\omega)]^{v^*}$ is more equal than that of $[h_1(\omega)]^v$; hence, using (16) and Shaked and Shanthikumar (1994), we derive that the distribution of $[h_2^*(\omega)]^{v^*}$ is more equal than that of $[h_2(\omega)]^v$. This process can be continued for all t.

When we lower the value of η, keeping all other parameters constant, we basically lower the second term in (16), $[\bar{h}_0]^\eta$, while $[h_0(\omega)]^v$ remains unchanged. By Lemma 2 in Karni and Zilcha (1994), we obtain that the distribution of $h_1(\omega)$ becomes less equal. This can be continued for $t = 2$ as well since it is easy to verify that $[\bar{h}_1]^\eta$ decreases while $[h_1(\omega)]^v$ becomes less equal. This process can be extended to $t = 2, 3, \ldots$, which complete the proof. $\square$

Proof of Proposition 6   Let us just sketch the proof of this claim. Any technological improvement, either in the public component or the home component, will imply higher human capital stock as of period 1 and on. Since, the initial capital stock is given this will increase the output in date 1 and, hence, the aggregate savings in this period. Thus the output in date 2 will be higher and hence the capital stock to be used as well. This process continues in all coming periods. $\square$

Notes

We are grateful to the participants of the CESifo conferences on Growth and Inequality: Issues and Policy Implications for contributing remarks. We also wish to express our thanks to an anonymous referee and to T. Eicher, H. Kierzkowski, H. de Kruijk, R. Riezman, H.-W. Sinn, O. Swank, and S. Turnovsky for numerous suggestions. Research assistance by D. Ottens is gratefully acknowledged.

1. The heterogeneity of consumers stems from the heterogeneity of income. As w_t and τ_t are common to all agents, (2) clearly indicates that heterogeneity of incomes derives from the distribution of human capital across individuals.

2. In contrast, under a decentralized system, both $\tau_t(\omega)$ and $e_{gt}(\omega)$ are decision variables of agents and the individual's budget constraint on private education is

$$\tau_t(\omega)w_t h_t(\omega) = w_t e_{gt}(\omega)\bar{h}_t,$$

where the level of teachers' instruction is chosen freely from the market but their average human capital is the same as the economy's. Aggregate resources invested in education then become

$$\int_\Omega e_{gt}(\omega)\,d\mu(\omega) = \frac{1}{\bar{h}_t}\int_\Omega \tau_t(\omega)h_t(\omega)\,d\mu(\omega),$$

which depend upon the distribution of human capital in each date. This is not the case under public education.

3. A growing empirical literature has given much attention to efficiency of public education on pupils' current and later achievements. One issue that has been highlighted is the causal effect of class size on human capital. For example, Lindahl (2001) finds that smaller classes in Sweden generate higher educational attainments.

4. Externalities that yield increasing returns to scale to parents' human capital, that is $v > 1$, have been observed in China (Knight and Shi 1996) and are therefore not a mere theoretical curiosum.

References

Atkinson, A. B. 1970. On the measurement of inequality. *Journal of Economic Theory* 2: 244–263.

Atkinson, A. B. 1999. Is rising income inequality inevitable? A critique of the Transatlantic Consensus. *UNU/WIDER Publication WAL3*.

Azariadis, C., and A. Drazen. 1990. Threshold externalities in economic development. *Quarterly Journal of Economics* 105: 501–526.

Becker, G. S., and N. Tomes. 1986. Human capital and the rise and fall of families. *Journal of Labor Economics* 4(3): S1–S39.

Burnhill, P., C. Garner, and A. McPherson. 1990. Parental education, social class and entry to higher education 1976–86. *Journal of the Royal Statistical Association, Series A* 153(2): 233–248.

Cardak, B. A. 1999. Heteregeneous preferences, education expenditures and income distribution. *The Economic Record* 75(228): 63–76.

Corneo, G., and O. Jeanne. 2001. Status, the distribution of wealth, and growth. *The Scandinavian Journal of Economics* 103(2): 283–293.

Eckstein, Z., and I. Zilcha. 1994. The effects of compulsory schooling on growth, income distribution and welfare. *Journal of Public Economics* 54: 339–359.

Eicher, T. S. 1996. Interaction between endogenous human capital and technological change. *Review of Economic Studies* 63: 127–144.

Fernandez, R., and R. Rogerson. 1998. Public education and income distribution: A quantitative dynamic evaluation of education-finance reform. *American Economic Review* 88(4): 813–833.

Fischer, R. D., and P. J. Serra. 1996. Income convergence within and between countries. *International Economic Review* 37(3): 531–551.

Forbes, K. J. 2000. A reassessment of the relationship between inequality and growth. *American Economic Review* 90(4): 865–887.

Galor, O., and O. Moav. 2000. Ability biased technological transition, wage inequality and growth. *Quarterly Journal of Economics* 115: 469–497.

Galor, O., and J. Zeira. 1993. Income distribution and macroeconomics. *Review of Economic Studies* 60: 35–52.

Glaeser, E. L. 1994. Why does schooling generate economic growth? *Economics Letters* 44(3): 333–337.

Glomm, G., and B. Ravikumar. 1992. Public versus private investment in human capital: Endogenous growth and income inequality. *Journal of Political Economy* 100: 818–834.

Jovanovic, B., and Y. Nyarko. 1995. The transfer of human capital. *Journal of Economic Dynamics and Control* 19: 1033–1064.

Karni, E., and I. Zilcha. 1994. Technological progress and income inequality: A model with human capital and bequests. In *The Changing Distribution of Income in an Open U.S. Economy*, ed. J. H. Bergstrand et al., 279–297. Amsterdam: North-Holland.

Knight, J., and L. Shi. 1996. Educational attainment and the rural-urban divide in China. *Oxford Bulletin of Economics and Statistics* 58(1): 83–117.

Lindahl, M. 2001. Home versus school learning: A new approach to estimating the effects of class size on achievement. *Discussion Paper No. 261.* IZA (Bonn).

Loury, G. 1981. Intergenerational transfers and the distribution of earnings. *Econometrica* 49(4): 843–867.

Lucas, R. 1988. On the mechanics of economic development. *Journal of Monetary Economics* 22: 3–42.

OECD. 1997. *Education at a Glance: OECD Indicators.* Paris: OECD.

Persson, T., and G. Tabellini. 1994. Is inequality harmful for growth? *American Economic Review* 84(3): 600–621.

Shaked, M., and J. G. Shanthikumar. 1994. *Stochastic Orders and Their Applications.* Boston: Academic Press.

Tamura, R. 1991. Income convergence in an endogenous growth model. *Journal of Political Economy* 99: 522–540.

van Marrewijk, C. 1999. Capital accumulation, learning and endogenous growth. *Oxford Economic Papers* 51: 453–475.

Viaene, J.-M., and I. Zilcha. 2002a. Capital markets integration, growth and income distribution. *European Economic Review* 46(2): 301–327.

Viaene, J.-M., and I. Zilcha. 2002b. Public education under capital mobility. *Journal of Economic Dynamics and Control* 26: 2005–2036.

III

European Transition and
Inequality

5 Social Transfers and Inequality during the Polish Transition

Michael P. Keane and
Eswar S. Prasad

5.1. Introduction

Beginning in the late 1980s and early 1990s, all the countries of the former Soviet Union and Eastern Europe have, to a greater or lesser extent, undertaken a process of transition away from central planning toward more market-oriented economic systems. However, different countries have chosen very different approaches to the process of transition. The outcomes, in terms of macroeconomic and social indicators, have been quite diverse as well. In general, however, most countries of the former Eastern bloc have experienced poor growth performance and large increases in income inequality during the transition process. The most obvious success story in the process of transition to date has been Poland, which has outstripped other transition economies in terms of growth performance, while at the same time experiencing only modest increases in inequality. Hence, a detailed analysis of the Polish experience, with a view toward asking what the country did right, is of considerable interest.

There has been a lively debate on the efficacy of alternative market-oriented reform strategies, both in terms of the sequencing and magnitude of reforms (see, e.g., Aghion and Blanchard 1994; Dewatripont and Roland 1996). Poland pursued a strategy of rapid and decisive reform that has often been referred to as "shock therapy." This process began in August 1989–January 1990, a period that has become known as the "big bang." Price controls on food were lifted in August 1989 and those on most other products were lifted in January 1990. Numerous other macroeconomic and microeconomic reforms, including restraints on credit for state-owned enterprises, the hardening of their budget constraints, and the opening up of the economy to import competition, were also instituted during this period.

One area in which the Polish reforms lagged behind those of many other transition economies was the privatization of state-owned enterprises (SOEs). Nevertheless, as argued by Pinto, Belka, and Krajewski (1993), even the SOEs that lagged behind in terms of changes in ownership and governance did undertake significant adjustment in response to hard budget constraints and import competition. Thus, the transformation of Poland from a command economy to a market-oriented economy was quite rapid by any measure. Confirming this, Poland has consistently ranked among the top reformers in terms of the various indicators used by the European Bank for Reconstruction and Development (EBRD) in its annual *Transition Report*.[1]

Poland, like other former Eastern bloc countries, experienced substantial declines in output and employment in the early phase of transition.[2] Between 1989 and 1992, the cumulative decline in output was about 20 percent and the official unemployment rate rose from near zero to about 14 percent (table 5.1). Since then, however, the growth performance of Poland has been among the best of the transition economies. Real GDP in 1999 was 22 percent higher than in 1989. In contrast, only a few other transition economies (including Albania, the Czech Republic, Hungary, the Slovak Republic, and Slovenia) managed to keep output to within a few percent, above or below, their pretransition levels. Most other transition economies have still to recover to anywhere close to their pre-transition peaks.

How did Poland succeed in rapidly instituting durable market-oriented reforms despite falling income and rising unemployment? A widely held view is that the process of transition has led to substantial increases in income inequality in almost all the transition economies, thereby complicating the process of reform (see, e.g., Aghion and Commander 1999). How, then, was it possible to maintain broad-based support for market-oriented reforms in Poland?

In this chapter, we use microdata from the Polish Household Budget Surveys (HBS) to show that, in contrast to most other transition economies, the increase in income inequality in Poland during the transition was actually quite modest. In fact, our preferred estimate of the Gini coefficient for the overall individual income distribution actually declined from 0.256 in 1988 to 0.230 in 1992. It then

Table 5.1
Selected macroeconomic indicators for Poland
(annual percentage changes, unless indicated otherwise)

	1986	1987	1988	1989	1990	1991	1992	1993	1994	1995	1996	1997	1998	1999	2000
Real GDP	4.2	2.1	4.0	0.3	−11.4	−7.0	2.6	3.8	5.2	7.0	6.1	6.9	4.8	4.1	5.0
Consumer price index (annual average)	16.5	26.4	60.2	251.1	585.8	70.3	43.0	35.3	32.2	27.8	19.9	14.9	11.8	7.3	9.9
Employment (end-year)	0.3	0.0	−1.0	−0.8	−6.2	−3.9	−3.1	−1.7	1.1	0.3	3.5	1.3	1.4	−1.5	−6.7
Unemployment rate (%) (end-year)	—	—	—	0.1	6.1	11.8	14.3	16.4	16.0	14.9	13.2	8.6	10.5	13.0	15.1

Levels of real GDP in 1999 (1989 = 100) for selected transition economies

	1989			1992
Poland	122	Czech Republic		95
Slovenia	109	Albania		95
Slovak Republic	100	Uzbekistan		94
Hungary	99	Belarus		80

Note: Dashes indicate data are not available.
Sources: IMF (1994) and EBRD Transition Report (various years).

began a gradual increase, reaching levels comparable to the pre-transition period in 1994–1996 and then rising to 0.276 by 1997.

To put this overall increase of 0.02 in context, it is actually rather modest, being only two-thirds the magnitude of the increase observed in the United States in the 1980s (see, e.g., Atkinson, Rainwater, and Smeeding 1995). It is far smaller than the average increase of 0.09 reported by Milanovic (1998) for eighteen Eastern bloc countries. Indeed, our cross-county analysis (see section 5.5 below) suggests that Poland had the smallest increase in inequality of any transition country. Also, note that this still leaves Poland with a Gini value closer to those of the Scandinavian countries (around 0.25) than that of the United States (0.41). (See World Bank 2000.)

We find that social transfers played a critical role in mitigating the increase in income inequality during the Polish transition. In contrast to overall income inequality, inequality in labor earnings increased steadily and substantially during the transition period of 1989–1997. For instance, we estimate that the Gini measure of inequality for individuals in worker-headed households, based only on the labor earnings of those households, increased steadily from 0.252 in 1988, the last full year prior to the transition, to 0.298 in 1997. Thus, the increase in the Gini coefficient for labor earnings (0.046) was more than twice that of the Gini for overall income (0.020).

By attenuating the rise in overall income inequality that might have been generated by the increase in earnings inequality, social transfers may have contributed to maintaining the social and political cohesion that was essential for the reform process. In this regard, it is interesting that social transfers also played a key role in the evolution of between-group income dynamics. A marked increase in the generosity of public sector pensions in 1991 led to a substantial exit of older workers from the labor force onto the pension rolls in 1991–1992 and improved the relative income position of pensioner-headed households. At the same time, other social transfers were increased from 3 percent in 1989 to about 5 percent of GDP by 1992.

As Dewatripont and Roland (1996) point out, such large pensions and social transfers can be rationalized as necessary to achieve initial political support for the big bang reform strategy. Generous pensions, in particular, may be efficacious (in the short run) for reform since they serve a dual purpose: first, paying off the older workers whose earnings capacity seems to have been most adversely affected by the reforms, and second, enabling enterprises to shed less productive workers through early retirement. EBRD statistics indicate that Poland experienced among the most rapid increases in labor productivity of the transition countries.

Analysis of the targeting of transfers in Poland indicates that a substantial proportion was directed not toward households at the bottom of the income distribution but rather toward the middle class and, as noted earlier, toward older workers. Thus, it appears that the transfer system could have been better designed if the goal was purely income support. However, the focus on the middle class and older workers may have been critical for ensuring social stability and setting the stage for rapid reforms.

Recent developments in growth theory (see, e.g., Bénabou 1996) suggest mechanisms whereby greater income inequality may be detrimental for growth. Thus, aside from the political economy considerations noted earlier, maintenance of a high degree of income equality may have also enhanced growth in Poland by broadening the base of individuals with the resources to engage in small-scale entrepreneurial activity. Indeed, according to the EBRD reports, the transition in Poland has been characterized (more than in any other transition country) by an explosion in small-scale entrepreneurial activity. For instance, Poland had almost 2 million private entrepreneurs and 125,000 private commercial enterprises by 1996.

Beginning in 1993, the Polish government reined in the growth of social transfers. At that point, overall inequality began to rise gradually. This suggests that the drop in income inequality from 1989–1992 and the rise from 1993 onward did not follow as a direct consequence of the transition process, but may have been driven largely by fiscal policy choices. Thus, it appears that an increase in inequality is not a necessary consequence of successful transition, but, rather, that inequality dynamics during transition may be strongly influenced by policy choices.

The outline of the chapter is as follows: Section 5.2 describes the data and methods used in our analysis. Section 5.3 presents our results on changes in inequality during the Polish transition, and the role of social transfers in the evolution of inequality. Section 5.4 provides a cross-country perspective on the relationship among transfers, inequality, and growth in the transition countries. Section 5.5 relates the analysis in this paper to the broader literature on the relationship between inequality and growth, and section 5.6 concludes.

5.2   Data and Methods

The empirical analysis in this chapter is based on the Household
Budget Surveys (HBS), a representative sample of Polish households
conducted by the Polish Central Statistical Office (CSO).[3] The CSO
has been collecting detailed microdata on household income and
consumption for more than two decades. Households were surveyed
for a full quarter (until 1992) or for a full month (from 1993 onward)
in order to monitor their income and spending patterns. Supple-
mentary information, including household demographics, is collected
from the same households once every year. The typical sample size
is about 25,000 households per year.

The HBS contains detailed information on sources and amounts of
income for both households and individuals within each household.
Total income is broken down into four main categories: labor income
(including wages, salaries, and nonwage compensation); pensions;
social benefits and other transfers; and other income. Social benefits
include income from unemployment benefits that were introduced in
late 1989. A key point is that the data include measures of the value
of in-kind payments from employers to workers, which have been
an important part of workers' compensation in Poland and other
transition economies. For farm households, farm income and expenditures, as well as consumption of the farm's produce, are also reported. There were no taxes on personal income until 1992. After
that year, we use net incomes in the analysis. The HBS also contains
detailed information on demographic characteristics of all household
members.

We use the aggregate consumer price index (CPI) as the price
deflator. Since there were large price changes in the early years of
transition, we match the price data to the survey period for each
observation by using quarterly CPI data for 1985–1992 and monthly
data for 1993–1997.

The change from quarterly reporting to monthly reporting in 1993
has serious consequences for cross-sectional inequality measurement. Since income and consumption tend to be more volatile at the
monthly compared to the quarterly frequency, this change could
result in an exaggeration of any increase in inequality. In Keane and
Prasad (2002a), we develop a technique for adjusting the 1993–1997
income and consumption data for the increased variability that may
be attributable solely to the shift from quarterly to monthly report-

ing. The basic idea of our approach is to assume that income consists of a permanent or predictable component (determined by education, age, and other observable characteristics of households and their members) plus a mean zero idiosyncratic component. We first regress household income on a large set of controls; these regressions were run separately for each quarter from 1985–1992 and for each month from 1993–1997. We then assume that the variance of the idiosyncratic component would not have jumped abruptly between the fourth quarter of 1992 and the first month of 1993, since, to our knowledge, no dramatic policy changes or exogenous shocks occurred at that point in time. Rather, we assume that the variance of the idiosyncratic component varies smoothly over time (measured in months) according to a polynomial time trend. We estimate this polynomial trend, along with a dummy for the post-1992 period that captures the discrete jump in variance that occurred with the change to monthly income reporting.

The second-stage estimation, where the standard deviations of the income residuals from the first-stage regressions are used as the dependent variable, is done separately for households with different primary income. The results, shown in table 5.2, indicate that the adjustment factor ranges from 0.369 for farmers to 0.044 for

Table 5.2
Regressions using income residuals

	Workers	Farmers	Workers/ farmers	Pensioners
Time	0.001	0.006	0.006	0.000
	(0.002)	(0.006)	(0.006)	(0.001)
Time^2/10^3	0.000	0.188	−0.171	−0.002
	(0.000)	(0.092)	(0.092)	(0.023)
Time^3/10^6	0.001	0.919	0.859	−0.009
	(0.010)	(0.365)	(0.364)	(0.095)
Mean real income	0.207	0.126	0.116	0.367
	(0.014)	(0.013)	(0.021)	(0.027)
Dummy for 93–97	0.165	0.369	0.201	0.044
	(0.028)	(0.102)	(0.098)	(0.026)
Adjusted R^2	0.88	0.65	0.51	0.85
Number of observations	92	92	92	92

Note: The dependent variable is the log standard deviation of the residuals from equation (1). Standard errors are reported in parentheses.

pensioner-headed households.[4] Once we have obtained these adjustment factors, we then scale down the idiosyncratic component (the residuals from the first-stage regressions) of the post-1992 income data for each household to eliminate this jump in variance.

Failure to account for the change in survey frequency may have caused prior studies to greatly overstate the increase in inequality in Poland. For instance, based on statistics computed by the CSO, OECD (1997, 86) reports that the Gini for Poland rose by 0.02 points between 1992 and 1993 alone, which is as large as the increase we find for the entire transition period (see section 5.3.1).[5]

Prior studies of changes in inequality in Poland have often relied on the aggregate data on quantiles of the income distribution published by the CSO in the annual publication *Budzety Gospodarstw Domowych*, which we henceforth refer to as the *Surveys*. Unfortunately, the aggregate income statistics reported by the CSO, as well as those reported by other former communist countries, differ in a number of important ways from economically meaningful measures of income. The official statistics appear to reflect total revenues or "inflows" since they include loans, dissaving, and cash holdings at the beginning of the survey period. For farmers, income includes gross farm revenues, rather than net revenues. This is an important issue as approximately one-fifth of Polish households are either farm households or mixed worker-farmer households. Access to the detailed microdata enables us to make important adjustments in order to obtain a more meaningful measure of income (by excluding non-income revenue items and by calculating net farm income).[6]

Both our procedure for adjusting for the spurious increase in inequality stemming from the switch to the monthly reporting interval, and our corrections for the definitions of income and consumption, rely on access to the HBS microdata.[7] In particular, the variance correction requires access to the data for an extended period of time. Our study is unique in that it is based on the HBS microdata for a long sample period, extending from five years prior to the "big bang" to eight years after. To our knowledge, no prior study of inequality in Poland has adjusted for the change in survey design in 1993, and most have not adjusted for the definitional problems noted earlier.[8]

Table 5.3 reports sample means for some of the variables used extensively in our analysis of inequality.[9] Two interesting features are that the average share of income from transfers and the share of pensioner-headed households increase markedly after the transition. We discuss this in greater detail in what follows. The demographic characteristics of households and household heads remain quite stable during and after the transition. The means of the education dummies indicate a small increase in average levels of educational attainment of household heads in the 1990s (a similar increase occurs in the general population as well).

5.3 Changes in Inequality during the Transition

In this section, we examine various aspects of inequality in Poland over the period 1985–1997. For the years 1993–1997, we use the income and consumption measures that are adjusted (using the procedure described in the previous section) for the increase in idiosyncratic variance that occurred with the shift to a monthly reporting period.

The measures of inequality we examine are based on the distribution of individual income, unless explicitly noted otherwise. A key problem in inequality measurement is how to account for household composition and household economies of scale when measuring household well being, or when assigning individual income or consumption levels to household members. In Keane and Prasad (2001a), we constructed food share (FS)–based equivalence scales for Poland using the Engel (1895) method, which assumes that two households with different demographic composition are equally well off at income levels that enable them to have equal food shares (ratio of expenditure on food to total expenditure on nondurables).[10] In Keane and Prasad (2002a), we document that our results on the evolution of inequality are not sensitive to the choice of equivalence scale.[11] Hence, in what follows, we present results using only the food share–based equivalence scale.[12]

5.3.1 Measures of Overall Inequality

We first examine the evolution of summary measures of overall inequality.[13] Table 5.4 reports Gini coefficients based on total incomes adjusted by the FS equivalence scale. According to the Gini, inequality increased from 0.256 in 1988 to 0.263 in 1989, but then declined in 1990–1992. In fact, by 1992, the Gini had declined to 0.230, which is below the pretransition level.

Table 5.3
Household budget surveys: Sample means for selected years

	1988	1989	1990	1991	1992	1993	1995	1997
Real household income (shares)								
Labor income	0.52	0.53	0.51	0.49	0.49	0.50	0.52	0.56
Transfers	0.23	0.22	0.26	0.32	0.34	0.33	0.33	0.32
Farm income	0.18	0.19	0.16	0.12	0.12	0.11	0.11	0.08
Other income	0.06	0.05	0.06	0.06	0.05	0.07	0.05	0.05
Real household consumption (shares)								
Durables	0.13	0.14	0.11	0.10	0.08	0.08	0.08	0.10
Nondurables	0.87	0.86	0.89	0.90	0.92	0.92	0.92	0.90
Food	0.45	0.46	0.53	0.47	0.44	0.43	0.41	0.38
Household characteristics								
Urban	0.51	0.51	0.51	0.52	0.64	0.66	0.65	0.67
Number of persons in household	3.27	3.27	3.24	3.16	3.14	3.15	3.18	3.12
Primary income source of household								
Workers	0.55	0.55	0.53	0.50	0.49	0.44	0.42	0.42
Farmers	0.10	0.10	0.10	0.09	0.09	0.08	0.08	0.06
Mixed, worker-farmers	0.07	0.07	0.07	0.07	0.06	0.06	0.06	0.06
Pensioners, others	0.28	0.28	0.30	0.34	0.36	0.38	0.39	0.40
Self-employed	—	—	—	—	—	0.05	0.06	0.06

Household head characteristics

Male, 18–30	0.11	0.10	0.10	0.10	0.10	0.10	0.10	0.11
Male, 31–60	0.58	0.59	0.57	0.57	0.57	0.59	0.59	0.58
Male, >60	0.13	0.14	0.14	0.14	0.14	0.13	0.13	0.13
Female, 18–30	0.01	0.01	0.01	0.01	0.01	0.01	0.01	0.01
Female, 31–60	0.09	0.09	0.09	0.09	0.09	0.09	0.09	0.09
Female, >60	0.08	0.08	0.08	0.09	0.09	0.08	0.08	0.08
Age	47.54	47.78	47.90	48.30	48.45	47.96	48.03	48.09
College degree	0.07	0.06	0.06	0.07	0.08	0.09	0.09	0.09
Some college	0.00	0.00	0.00	0.00	0.00	0.01	0.01	0.01
High school	0.20	0.19	0.20	0.21	0.23	0.24	0.24	0.26
Some high school	0.01	0.01	0.02	0.01	0.01	—	—	—
Basic vocational training	0.31	0.33	0.33	0.33	0.33	0.34	0.36	0.35
Primary school	0.34	0.34	0.32	0.32	0.30	0.28	0.26	0.25
Primary school not completed	0.07	0.06	0.05	0.05	0.04	0.04	0.03	0.02

Number of observations (households)

1985	21,560		1992	10,642
1986	25,475		1993	31,966
1987	29,510		1994	31,942
1988	29,287			
1989	29,366		1995	31,874
1990	29,148		1996	31,782
1991	28,632		1997	31,659

Note: The components of income and consumption are shown as (mean) shares of total income and consumption, respectively. Dashes indicate data are not available.

Starting in 1993, however, inequality began to rise and, by 1997, it was at a level significantly higher than the peak attained in 1989. It is important to note, however, that the increase in inequality even by 1997 is hardly dramatic. The increase of 0.020 in the Gini coefficient from 1988 (the year before the transition) to 1997 is smaller than the increase of 0.03 reported for the United States in the 1980s by Atkinson, Rainwater, and Smeeding (1995), or the increase from 0.326 to 0.361 reported for the United Kingdom from 1986 to 1991 in World Bank (1999, 2000).

Next, we examine inequality based on income net of transfers (table 5.4, second row).[14] Interestingly, this reveals a very different picture. The Gini coefficient for income excluding transfers increased by 0.066 from 1988 to 1997, more than three times the increase in the Gini for overall income.

Table 5.4 also reports Gini coefficients for labor income for worker headed households only. These show that inequality in labor earnings increased substantially during the transition (i.e., by 0.046 points between 1988 and 1997), with much of the increase taking place in the early phase. Thus, we see that inequality in labor earnings grew substantially more than inequality in the overall income distribution.

Together, these results suggest that social transfers played a crucial role in inequality dynamics during the Polish transition. Specifically, they appear to have substantially mitigated the increase in income inequality that might otherwise have occurred, given the substantial increase in inequality in labor earnings. We examine the magnitude and targeting of social transfers in more detail later.

Gini coefficients for consumption inequality, based on either total or nondurables consumption, show a pattern similar to those for income inequality. Thus, to conserve space, we focus only on income inequality in much of the analysis that follows.

Next, we examine whether our main results are sensitive to the choice of inequality measure. The Gini coefficient is known to be particularly sensitive to changes around the median of the distribution. The coefficient of variation (and its monotonic transforms, one of which we use here) is more sensitive to changes at the high end of a distribution, while the mean logarithmic deviation is more sensitive to changes near the low end. We report these alternative inequality measures in the bottom rows of table 5.4, in order to determine if they tell a consistent story. In fact, they do. When we

Table 5.4
Poland: Measures of overall inequality

	1985	1986	1987	1988	1989	1990	1991	1992	1993	1994	1995	1996	1997
Gini coefficients													
Total income	0.252	0.254	0.246	0.256	0.263	0.250	0.235	0.230	0.248	0.262	0.255	0.265	0.276
Income excluding transfers	0.373	0.375	0.368	0.385	0.384	0.389	0.404	0.416	0.416	0.437	0.432	0.448	0.451
Nondurables consumption	0.196	0.200	0.205	0.211	0.219	0.209	0.208	0.205	0.222	0.228	0.222	0.227	0.235
Total consumption	0.230	0.234	0.239	0.244	0.258	0.241	0.233	0.227	0.247	0.254	0.247	0.262	0.271
Gini coefficients for worker-headed households													
Labor Income	0.237	0.243	0.240	0.252	0.262	0.268	0.278	0.289	0.285	0.292	0.288	0.295	0.298
Half the square of the coefficient of variation													
Total income	0.085	0.090	0.085	0.091	0.105	0.086	0.079	0.077	0.097	0.103	0.096	0.105	0.112
Income excluding transfers	0.184	0.190	0.186	0.203	0.210	0.207	0.230	0.244	0.265	0.281	0.278	0.294	0.306
Mean log deviation													
Total income	0.075	0.079	0.077	0.078	0.087	0.075	0.071	0.069	0.079	0.086	0.081	0.086	0.093
Income excluding transfers	0.224	0.214	0.213	0.221	0.244	0.247	0.268	0.278	0.404	0.357	0.333	0.317	0.444

Note: The inequality measures shown here are for the individual distributions of income and consumption. Household income and consumption are adjusted using the food share–based equivalence scale and allocated equally to individuals in the household. Income and consumption data for 1993–1997 are adjusted for the change in survey frequency.

use total income, both these measures of inequality also show an upward spike in 1989, followed by a decline in 1990–1992 to below the pretransition level, and a subsequent steady increase during 1993–1997 to a level modestly above that in the pretransition period.[15]

When we look at income net of transfers, both the coefficient of variation (CV) and mean logarithmic deviation show far greater increases in inequality over the transition period than for total income. This pattern is particularly interesting in the case of the CV measure, which is most sensitive to changes at the high end of the distribution. This result stems from the fact that transfers in Poland are focused not only at the low end of the income distribution but extend well into the high end. We give more details on the targeting of transfers below.

To summarize, we find no evidence to support the view, based on aggregate CSO statistics, of a sharp increase in total income inequality following the transition in Poland. For instance, OECD (1997), which uses the CSO aggregates, reports a Gini increase of 0.05 for Poland over the 1989–1996 period, while we find essentially no increase over the same period. Our results also differ markedly in terms of the timing of changes in inequality. The OECD-CSO figures imply that inequality grew tremendously from 1989 to 1993, and that it then stayed rather flat through 1996. Our results indicate that inequality actually fell from 1989–1992. But we find that inequality rose noticeably after 1993 and, especially, in 1996 and 1997. Thus, we find that most of the increase in inequality occurred several years after the big bang, and long after the OECD-CSO figures imply the increase had already ceased.

This difference in timing also has important implications for the interpretation of what occurred during the transition. The OECD-CSO figures for Poland, as well as the comparable figures for other transition economies (e.g., Milanovic 1999), are often interpreted as evidence that substantial increases in inequality are an inevitable concomitant of the process of transition to a market economy. Our results, however, indicate that the change in overall income inequality during the first six years of the transition in Poland was quite modest. Thus, these results suggest that changes in inequality during transition are not inevitable but, rather, may result from particular policy choices.

5.3.2 Winners and Losers in the Transition

We have found no evidence of an increase in overall income inequality in Poland in the immediate aftermath of the big bang, regardless of which of several inequality measures we consider. However, this does not mean that there were not winners and losers in the transition. We now turn to a discussion of how different groups fared in terms of relative income.

In Keane and Prasad (2002a), we report how median total income evolved for four types of households differentiated by main income source of the household head: workers, farmers, mixed worker-farmers, and pensioners. Pensioner-headed households had lower median total income than other groups during the 1985–1989 period, but their relative position improved dramatically after the big bang so as to bring their income up to levels that are comparable the other groups. The main impetus behind the improved relative position of pensioners was a substantial increase in pension availability and generosity that took place in 1991. As a result, we find that pensions contributed importantly to a reduction in inequality.[16]

In addition to the improved relative position of pensioners, other notable features of the transition were an improvement in the relative position of more educated workers[17] and a deterioration in the relative position of more experienced (i.e., older) workers. In Keane and Prasad (2002b), we perform a detailed regression analysis of individual labor earnings data from the HBS. The results indicate that the earnings premium for a college degree relative to a primary school degree increased from 47 percent in 1987 to 102 percent in 1996. But the premium for labor market experience fell sharply in 1990, before recovering to pretransition levels after 1992.

The deterioration in experience premia in the immediate aftermath of the big bang is consistent with the notion of rapid obsolescence of firm- or industry-specific skills during a period of rapid technological change and industrial restructuring (see Svejnar 1996). This, combined with the increased generosity of pensions, explains the surge in the number of pensioner-headed households in 1991–1992 that is obvious in table 5.3. Indeed, self-selection into retirement probably accounts for the recovery in experience premia for older workers that occurred after 1992, since a large number of older workers, particularly in the 55–65 age bracket, retired in 1991–1992.

Specifically, the number of newly granted pensions increased from about 0.6 million per year in 1988–1989 to almost 1.4 million in 1991 (OECD 1998, 65).

Since older workers had the most to lose from the privatization or closure of existing state-owned firms, giving them the option of moving on to the pension rolls may have been a key factor in removing a potential political obstacle to enterprise restructuring and privatization. Furthermore, these early retirements may have contributed to the exceptional rise in labor productivity that occurred in Polish industrial enterprises after 1992 (EBRD 1997).

5.3.3 The Targeting of Transfers

Having discussed the role of transfers in mitigating the rise in overall income inequality during the transition, we now turn to a more detailed analysis of the targeting of transfers.

One simple way to analyze the equalizing role of transfers is to run nonparametric regressions of transfers on income net of transfers. We ran these regressions separately for each year. Figure 5.1 shows the results for 1991. In this figure, households are sorted

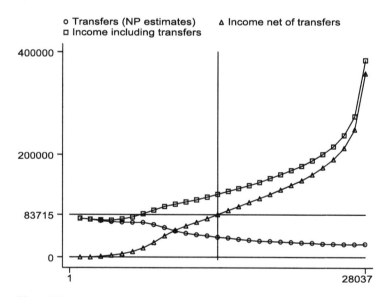

Figure 5.1
Households sorted by income net of transfers

along the X-axis in terms of their level of pretransfer income. The horizontal line shows median real household income net of transfers in 1991; the vertical line shows the observation at the median of the 1991 sample. The key point of this figure is that transfers are not heavily concentrated among households with low pretransfer income. Rather, there are substantial transfers even to households at and even above the median of the pretransfer income distribution.

This pattern is present not just in 1991, but in every year from 1985 to 1997. However, the targeting of transfers changed in important ways during the transition. As a way of summarizing these changes, figure 5.2 shows the fractions of total income accounted for by transfer income, at different percentile points of the pretransfer income distribution, for every year from 1985 to 1997. The key observation from this figure is that ratio of transfer income to total income increased significantly in the early years of transition, at virtually all points of the pretransfer income distribution. At the median, the average share of transfers in total income rose from approximately 20 percent in the pretransition period, to about 35 percent by 1992, before stabilizing at around 28 percent thereafter.

Clearly, these results suggest that transfers could have been better targeted if the goal was purely income support. However, since individuals in the middle class tend to have a significantly higher propensity to vote than individuals at lower income levels, the extension of transfers higher up into the income distribution that occurred in 1990–1992 may have been a mechanism for "buying" the social stability that characterized the transition period.

Also noteworthy is the importance of pensions as a transfer mechanism, and the extent to which transfers were targeted at older workers. We already noted in section 5.3.2 that pension expenditures and the size of the pension rolls increased enormously in the early years of the transition. As shown in table 5.5, total public pension expenditure as a percent of GDP rose from 8 percent in 1989–1990 to almost 15 percent by 1992. The HBS data show a similar pattern, with the share of total income accounted for by pensions rising from 16 percent in 1989 to 25 percent in 1992. The pension replacement rate (average pension as a ratio of average wage) rose from about 52 percent in 1988–1989 to 65 percent in 1991 and remained above 60 percent through 1997 (OECD 1998).

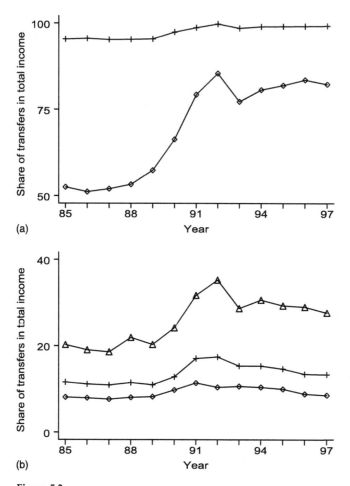

Figure 5.2
(a) Percentiles of pretransfer distribution: 10, 25; (b) Percentiles of pretransfer distribution: 50, 75, 90

The HBS data indicate that, among households headed by a male in the 55–65 age range, the share of pension income in total income rose from 26 percent in 1989 to 50 percent in 1992, remaining at around that level through 1997. For households headed by women in the 52–62 age range, this share rose from 34 percent in 1989 to 49 percent in 1992, before declining slightly to 45 percent by 1997.[18] These figures show the importance of early retirement during the transition.

Table 5.5
Social transfers

	1988	1989	1990	1991	1992	1993	1994	1995	1996	1997
General government expenditures (in percent of GDP)										
Cash transfers to individuals	9.4	11.2	10.6	17.3	19.9	20.4	20.2	19.7	18.7	19.4
Pensions	7.1	8.2	8.1	12.2	14.8	15.0	14.9	14.5	14.3	14.4
Unemployment benefits	0.0	0.0	0.2	1.2	1.7	1.2	1.2	1.2	1.1	1.0
Other benefits	2.3	3.0	2.3	3.9	3.4	4.2	4.1	4.0	3.3	4.0
Mean cash transfers (HBS data)										
Total transfers (avg. ratio to total income)	41154	41792	36254	44948	44694	43486	44171	44860	46786	48197
	(23.4)	(21.8)	(26.3)	(32.2)	(33.6)	(31.6)	(32.8)	(32.7)	(32.4)	(31.3)
Pensions (avg. ratio to total income)	29857	30497	27307	33520	33346	33172	34672	36240	38008	40715
	(17.0)	(15.9)	(19.8)	(24.0)	(25.1)	(24.1)	(25.8)	(26.4)	(26.3)	(26.4)
Other cash benefits (incl. UI) (avg. ratio to total income)	11280	11279	8927	11404	11323	10315	9498	8620	8777	7482
	(6.4)	(5.9)	(6.5)	(8.2)	(8.5)	(7.5)	(7.1)	(6.3)	(6.1)	(4.9)
General government balance (in percent of GDP)	0.0	−7.4	3.1	−6.5	−6.7	−2.9	−3.0	−3.1	−3.4	−3.1
Real GDP (annual % change)	4.0	0.3	−11.6	−7.0	2.6	3.8	5.2	7.0	6.1	6.9

Note: The data on real GDP and government expenditures are taken from various IMF sources. The figures in the middle panel (mean transfers in HBS data) are expressed in terms of 1992Q4 prices.

5.3.4 Summary

Our results suggest that social transfers, especially pensions, played
an important role in the evolution of income inequality during the
Polish transition. The broad patterns are summarized in figure 5.3.
The top panel plots Gini coefficients for both total income and
labor income (for worker-headed households). We see that inequality in labor income grew fairly steadily during the entire 1989–1997
period, but with most of the increase occurring during the early
transition (1989–1992). Despite this, overall income inequality declined substantially in the early transition phase, and only began
to rise in 1993. The bottom panel of figure 5.3 shows social transfers
as a percent of GDP. The dramatic increase in transfers during the
early transition period was sufficient to actually outweigh the effect
of increased earnings inequality, leading to a decline in overall income inequality up through 1992. However, the growth of transfers
was reined in beginning in 1993. And, from 1993 onward, inequality does grow substantially. By 1995, inequality had returned to the
pretransition level, and it rose modestly above that level in 1996–
1997.

   Clearly, the growth in social transfers was crucial in dampening
the rise in overall inequality during the early years of the Polish
transition. Social transfers as a percent of GDP averaged 17.7 percent
during 1990–1997, the highest level in any transition country. The
mean level of transfers across the eighteen transition economies for
which we could find data was substantially lower at 10.8 percent
(see section 5.4). This at least partially explains the fact that Poland
had the smallest increase in inequality during the transition.

   In fact, Gomułka (1998) refers to a "Polish model" of transition,
which is "distinguished by an exceptionally large volume of social
transfers, especially... pensions" that "helped to reduce the social
cost of reform, but is inhibiting Poland's ability to sustain rapid
growth." This theme—that the level of transfers in Poland will hinder future growth—has been sounded by many authors, including
the International Monetary Fund (1994), World Bank (1995), and
OECD (1997). But such dire predictions have yet to be borne out. In
1998–2000, Poland continued to experience strong growth, making it
by far the best-performing transition economy in terms of cumulative growth during the transition. As we describe in sections 5.4

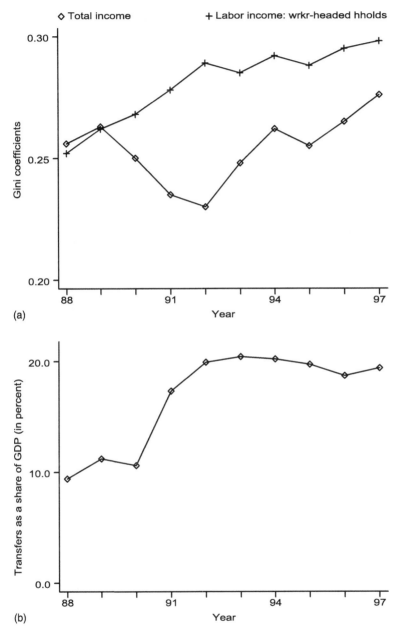

Figure 5.3
Gini coefficients

and 5.5, cross-country evidence, along with recent developments in growth theory, suggest the intriguing possibility that the high level of social transfers in Poland may in fact have been conducive to growth.

5.4   A Cross-Country Perspective on Transfers, Inequality and Growth

In our view, the evidence we provide on transfers and inequality in Poland is also relevant to the broader literature on inequality, redistribution, and growth. Here, we examine the relationship between social transfers, inequality, and growth across the Eastern bloc countries.

The top panel of figure 5.4 plots the relationship between transfers as a percent of GDP and inequality changes during the transition, as measured by changes in the Gini coefficient. The figure contains results for all fourteen countries for which we were able to obtain data on transfers as well as pre- and post-transition Gini coefficients.[19] As expected, countries with higher levels of transfers typically had smaller increases in inequality. The countries with the highest levels of transfers—Poland, Hungary, and Slovenia—also had among the smallest inequality changes during transition.[20]

The bottom panel of figure 5.4 plots the relationship between GDP growth and government transfers as a percent of GDP, for all eighteen countries for which we were able to obtain data on transfers and GDP. The X-axis shows cumulative GDP growth in the first eight years of transition for each country. The relationship is strongly positive, with a simple correlation of 0.67. Note that finding a positive correlation between transfers and growth is particularly surprising given the blatant denominator bias driving the correlation in the opposite direction (i.e., higher output growth increases the denominator of the transfer to GDP ratio).

These findings raise the intriguing possibility that policies that foster income equality may also be conducive to successful transition. In fact, the relationships among transfers, inequality, and growth that we find here for transition economies have also been reported by authors such as Perotti (1996) for a different but much larger sample of industrial and developing countries. This suggests, more generally, that policies that foster income equality may be conducive to growth.

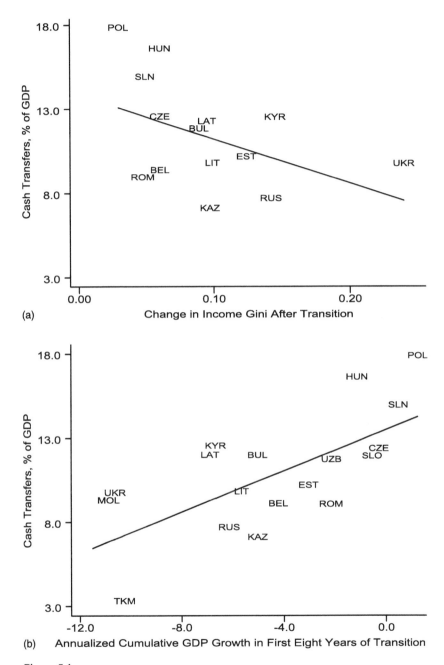

Figure 5.4
Transfers as share of GDP

Of course, the results we have reported only indicate a correlation rather than a causal relationship. It is possible that some omitted factor may actually account for good performance on both the inequality and growth dimensions. However, the patterns we have noted are at least not inconsistent with recent developments in growth theory that imply that redistribution to enhance equality may actually enhance rather than dampen growth.[21] In the next section, we discuss these theories and relate them to the Polish case.

5.5   A Perspective from "New" Growth Theory

A traditional view of the relationship between inequality and growth is that a certain degree of income inequality is conducive to economic growth. The basic idea is that, in a country at a low level of development and with imperfect capital markets, wealth must be concentrated in the hands of a few so they can invest in physical and/or human capital. Kuznets (1955) presented evidence that appears consistent with this view. He found a hump-shaped relationship between inequality and per capita GNP, which he interpreted as evidence that inequality increases in the early stages of development and falls thereafter. It can be further argued that inequality may foster growth even in more advanced economies, provided liquidity constraints remain important, because only wealthy individuals can bear the sunk costs of starting industrial activities. Consistent with this view, Evans and Jovanovic (1989) provide some evidence that capital market constraints affect the decision to become an entrepreneur even in the United States, a country with highly developed capital markets.

But the relationship between growth and inequality has been reexamined by various authors in recent years (see the survey by Aghion, Caroli, and García-Peñalosa 1999). Some of this work has challenged the view that higher inequality is associated with higher rates of growth. Persson and Tabellini (1994), among others, present evidence indicating a negative correlation between inequality and growth.

Recent work in growth theory has rationalized a negative relation between inequality and growth by invoking either borrowing constraints or political economy considerations. For instance, Galor and Zeira (1993) turn on its head the argument that wealth concentration encourages growth when there are liquidity constraints. They present a model with borrowing constraints in which individual productivity is a concave function of human capital and show that redistribution of wealth from the rich to the poor enhances growth because the poor have a higher marginal productivity of investment. Related results have been obtained by Banerjee and Newman (1993), Aghion and Bolton (1997), and Bénabou (1996).

Turning to the political economy models, Alesina and Rodrik (1994) show that income redistribution can enhance growth by reducing political support for taxation of capital. And Perotti (1996) finds empirical support for the view that redistribution can enhance growth by fostering sociopolitical stability. In a similar vein, Roland (1993) and Dewatripont and Roland (1996) argue that transfers can reduce the desire of potential economic losers to block reforms.

How are these models relevant to the Polish case? Clearly, these models do not imply that social transfers are themselves directly beneficial for growth, but rather that transfers affect growth through one of several mechanisms. In the Polish case, the plausible political economy mechanisms seem fairly obvious. Our analysis of winners and losers in the Polish transition suggests that older workers were quite adversely affected, due to declines in experience premia. However, these workers were cushioned by a substantial increase in the availability and generosity of pensions. This led many workers in their 1950s and early 1960s to take early retirement, at generous replacement rates. Furthermore, the mass retirements by older workers in the early phase of the transition had the added benefit that they facilitated enterprise restructuring. This helped Poland achieve better increases in labor productivity than most other transition economies, while at the same time securing the support of pensioners for market-oriented reforms.

The mechanism whereby social transfers mitigate borrowing constraints, thus making it possible for a broader segment of the population to invest in human capital, does not seem relevant to the Polish case. Too little time has passed since the start of the transition for a substantial increase in the stock of human capital (via new investment) to have taken place.

On the other hand, generous transfers may have helped reduce liquidity constraints on small-scale entrepreneurs and the self-employed. Both of these groups have played a key role in Poland's vibrant economic performance since 1990. Indeed, according to OECD (1998, 107), "Poland's recent growth performance rests on a strong entrepreneurial basis, with many dynamic small and medium-sized enterprises (SMEs) and creations of new firms ... SMEs make up the bulk of Poland's 2.2 million registered non-agricultural enterprises ... almost 90 percent [are] micro-enterprises (employing 1 to 5 persons)." Indeed, Poland has seen greater growth in small-scale entrepreneurial activity than has any other transition country.

But evaluating the importance of mechanisms whereby transfers mitigate borrowing constraints on entrepreneurs is made difficult by the potential for intrafamily and intrahousehold transfers. Specifically, the person who receives a transfer may not be the person whose constraint is relaxed and who can therefore start or expand entrepreneurial activity. For example, a pension transfer to a retired older worker may in fact enable his or her children, who might otherwise have had to expend resources caring for the worker, to instead acquire capital. Thus, a simple test of whether transfer recipients were likely to become small-scale entrepreneurs would not shed light on the issue. Further research on mechanisms underlying the exceptional explosion of small-scale entrepreneurial activity in Poland is clearly needed.

5.6 Conclusions

Poland is perhaps the greatest success story of transition. It instituted drastic market-oriented reforms early in the transition process and has received relatively high marks for the extent of its subsequent market-oriented reforms (e.g., in the EBRD's annual *Transition Report*). Like other transition countries, Poland experienced a severe contraction of GDP in the first few years of transition (1990–1992). However, Poland subsequently experienced rapid growth, starting in 1993. Its GDP stood at 22 percent above the pretransition level in 1999, which is a substantially better performance than any other country in the former Eastern bloc.

Another positive aspect of the Polish transition is that it has resulted in very little increase in overall income inequality. This is in sharp contrast to most other transition countries, which have typically seen drastic increases in inequality. Our results indicate that Poland has experienced among the smallest (if not the smallest) increase in inequality of any transition country, and that measures of inequality for Poland remain only modestly above those for the Scandinavian countries.

Our results further indicate that inequality in labor earnings did increase substantially during the Polish transition. However, a striking aspect of government policies during the early years of transition was a sharp increase in social transfers, from about 10 percent of GDP to roughly 20 percent. This is the highest level of transfers (as a share of GDP) of any transition country. We have argued that this increase in transfers substantially mitigated the increase in overall income inequality that might otherwise have resulted from increased earnings inequality.

From these patterns we draw one clear policy conclusion: The Polish experience makes clear that a substantial increase in income inequality is not a necessary concomitant of successful transition. Clearly, it is possible to use high levels of social transfers to maintain income equality, without hindering the transition process or choking off economic growth.

A more speculative hypothesis that is not inconsistent with our findings is that the generous social transfer policy pursued by Poland may have actually promoted the transition process and promoted growth. One mechanism through which social transfers could promote successful transition is by cushioning (or "buying off") groups that would have been most adversely affected by reforms.

For instance, older workers had the most to lose from the privatization or closure of state-owned firms and would have been most adversely affected by enterprise restructuring. But, early in the transition process, Poland substantially increased the availability and generosity of pensions.[22] This induced large numbers of older workers to take early retirement. This may have facilitated transition both by removing potential opposition to reforms by a powerful interest group and by helping to reduce employment at enterprises to more efficient levels and promoting other aspects of enterprise restructuring.[23]

More generally, we found that transfers in Poland have to a great extent been targeted at the middle class rather than just the poor. A number of authors have argued, on political economy grounds, that "the development of a solid, property-owning middle class is essential to the consolidation of capitalism" (Kornai 2000). For further details on these type of arguments, we refer the reader to Havryly-shyn and Odling-Smee (2000), Easterly (2002), and Keane and Prasad (2001b).

Recent developments in growth theory stress another mechanism through which social transfers could promote growth. In environments characterized by liquidity constraints, a more equal income distribution increases the fraction of the population with the resources to engage in small-scale entrepreneurial activity. Thus, social transfers can lead to more equal income distribution, which in turn leads to more small-scale entrepreneurial activity, which in turn promotes growth. In Poland, which had almost 2 million private entrepreneurs by 1996, small-scale entrepreneurial activity has clearly been a key engine of growth—more so than in any other transition country. Further work is needed to determine the extent to which this exceptional explosion in entrepreneurial activity in Poland may be attributable to government transfer policies.

Of course, high social transfer payments do not come without significant costs. These could take the form of distortions induced by disincentives for employment (the result of a generous social safety net), distortions caused by taxation required to finance these transfers, and, more generally, the effects of government budget deficits on overall macroeconomic performance.

In the Polish case, the increase in social transfers during the early phase of the transition was accompanied by a substantial increase in the general government budget deficit (see the bottom panel of table 5.5). De Crombrugghe (1997), for instance, traces the "destabilization" of the Polish budget in 1991–1992 directly to the rise in transfer expenditures. By 1993 the growth in transfer expenditures (as a percent of GDP) had been halted, although pensions and other social benefits remained at a higher level than in the pretransition years.

Our view is that, at least in the early stages of transition, social transfers may have been crucial in setting the stage for rapid reforms, and that this benefit probably outweighed the direct short-term costs of a rising budget deficit. The Polish experience suggests that the prerequisites for this approach to work are a well-functioning set of transfer mechanisms and the commitment to implementing institutional and macroeconomic reforms at a rapid pace. Of course, a danger for the future is that generous social transfers, especially pensions, which in early transition were useful for cushioning older workers and facilitating enterprise restructuring, will remain as entitlements long after their original purpose is no longer operative and become a long-term fiscal burden.

Notes

We thank the staff at the Polish Central Statistical Office, especially Wiesław Łagodziński and Jan Kordos, for assistance with the data. We also thank Krzystof Przybylowski and Barbara Kamińska for excellent translations of the survey instruments and Branko Milanovic for generously sharing his cross-country data with us. We received helpful comments on earlier drafts from Theo Eicher, Omer Moav, Stephan Klasen, an anonymous referee, and the participants of the 2001 and 2002 CESIfo Growth and Inequality conferences. Financial support was provided by the National Council for Eurasian and East European Research. The views expressed in this chapter do not necessarily represent those of the IMF.

1. These indicators measure the progress made by transition countries in many areas of market-oriented reforms including enterprise privatization and reform; price and trade liberalization; and establishment of the rule of law, property rights, and well-functioning financial markets.

2. The reasons for this "transition recession," experienced by all transition economies, are controversial. Some authors stress the contraction of credit to state enterprises (see Calvo and Coricelli 1992), while others stress the aggregate demand contraction, due in part to the opening to import competition and the sharp contraction in exports to other former communist bloc countries (see Berg and Blanchard 1994).

3. Although the survey sample is designed to be representative of the underlying population, nonresponse rates tend to differ across demographic groups. This necessitates the use of sampling weights, although these weights had little effect on any of our main results.

4. Higher-order polynomial terms were insignificant in these regressions, which fit the time path of the idiosyncratic component of variance quite well.

5. One other important change that was made in the 1993 survey was an attempt to obtain a more representative sample of the self-employed. This group's size is believed to have increased markedly since the transition began, resulting in its underrepresentation in the HBS data during the period 1990–1992. However, as shown in Keane and Prasad (2002a), underrepresentation of the self-employed is likely to have led to only a marginal understatement of the extent of inequality in the early years of the transition.

6. It is possible to make some (but not all) of the necessary adjustments to income using information in the aggregate data on categories of income.

7. The aggregate consumption figures published by the Polish CSO, as well as by other former communist countries, often correspond to a measure of total outflows, including saving and repayment of loans. For farm households, consumption includes farm investment and purchases of supplies. An indication of the strange nature of the aggregate consumption data is provided by Milanovic (1998, 41), who reports that in 1993 the Gini for consumption is 0.31, which substantially exceeds the Gini of 0.28 for income. He also reports (33) that in 1993 the ratio of consumption to income is 1.30, an unreasonably high figure. Our access to the detailed micro data enables us to make

necessary adjustments to the categories that are included in consumption. We then find the more plausible results that consumption Ginis are smaller than income Ginis and that the aggregate consumption to income ratio falls in the 0.89 to 0.96 range during the 1985–1997 period.

8. At the time we began our study, the Polish CSO had never before released the HBS microdata. A long negotiation process by the first author during 1992–1993 led to its release. Subsequently, the microdata for the first half of 1993 was released to the World Bank and this data is used in World Bank (1995) and Milanovic (1998). More recently, the data for 1993–1996 have been obtained by researchers at the World Bank. As noted above, a subsample of the HBS is also now available in the through the Luxembourg Income Survey (LIS) for 1987, 1990 and 1992. Thus, no prior researchers have had access to the microdata for the entirety of the extended period that we examine.

9. The sample size falls in 1992 since half of the total sample in that year was used to test the new monthly survey. These monthly data from 1992 were considered unreliable and not made available to us.

10. For details on the estimation of the food share based equivalence scales, and for a comparison with other commonly used equivalence scales, see Keane and Prasad (2001a). We are aware of the potential problems associated with the use of food share–based equivalence scales. However, we were concerned about estimating a complete demand system under conditions when rationing of certain commodities was probably an issue in some years of our sample, but where we do not observe the rationing regimes.

11. Besides our own FS scale, we also used the OECD scale, the McClements scale (which is commonly used in Britain), and the simple per capita scale. Appendix Table B1 in Keane and Prasad (2001a) shows values of different equivalence scales for a representative set of household types.

12. We recomputed many of the results in this chapter using different equivalence scales. Although the levels of inequality were slightly affected by the choice of equivalence scale, patterns of the evolution of inequality over time were robust to this choice.

13. In all cases, we examine the distribution of individual income (or consumption), assigning to each individual the per equivalent income for the household in which the person resides.

14. Since transfers tend to be stable over time, the adjustment factors (used to adjust for the change in survey frequency in 1993–1996) for income net of transfers were nearly identical to those we computed for income including transfers.

15. In Keane and Prasad (2001a, 2002a), we show that similar results hold if one examines alternative inequality measures such as quantile ratios, quantile shares, or kernel density estimates of the income distribution.

16. A similar result is reported by Garner and Terrell (1998), who find that pensions substantially reduced inequality during the early transition years in the Czech and Slovak republics.

17. In Keane and Prasad (2002a), we report that changes in within-group inequality were very different across different groups. Within-group inequality actually fell

among farmer and mixed worker-farmer households during the transition, which, in addition to the roles of pensions and other social transfers, also helps to account for the rather small increase in overall income inequality. The Gini for household income for individuals in worker-headed households rose from 0.189 in 1988 to 0.248 in 1997. This increase of 0.059 is almost three times as great as the 0.020 increase in the Gini for the overall income distribution, and is consistent with the increase in labor income inequality noted earlier.

18. The typical retirement age in Poland is 65 for men and 62 for women. Among households with heads in the 45–55 age range and in lower age ranges, there was a small drop from 1989 to 1992 in the share of income from labor income, but this was mostly offset by an increase in other social benefits rather than pensions. Among households with heads aged 65 and older, pensions constitute 85–90 percent of total income, with labor income accounting for barely 2 percent.

19. The level of transfers is expressed as a percent of GDP and is the average, for each country, from the first year of its transition through 1997. The Gini coefficients are for per capita income and the change is the difference between the value of the coefficient four to five years into the transition and the value of this coefficient before transition. For data and sources, see Keane and Prasad (2002a).

20. Note that higher transfers do not necessarily imply more redistribution. An extreme example is provided by Commander and Lee (1998), who note that transfers in Russia have actually become regressive in the transition.

21. In Keane and Prasad (2002a), we provide a more detailed regression analysis of the relationship between inequality changes and growth in the transition economies. We find a negative relationship even after controlling for initial conditions (including the pretransition level of inequality) and measures of the extent of market-oriented reforms. Grun and Klasen (2001) report similar findings.

22. The Polish situation is considerably different from that in numerous other transition economies, where the real value of pensions and other transfers fell precipitously during transition (both in absolute terms and relative to average wages).

23. Fidrmuc (2000) presents an interesting empirical analysis of voting patterns in transition countries. He notes that various politically powerful groups—including unions and retirees—were more likely to vote for left-wing parties. Notwithstanding their political leanings, these were in fact the regimes that had enough political capital to institute significant reforms. The Polish experience can be seen as one where successive (relatively short-lived) governments during early transition used generous transfers to acquire such political capital and appease groups that had the most to lose, in the short run, from market-oriented reforms.

References

Aghion, Philippe, and Olivier Blanchard. 1994. "On the Speed of Transition in Central Europe." *NBER Macroeconomics Annual* 9: 283–320.

Aghion, Philippe, and Simon Commander. 1999. "On the Dynamics of Inequality in the Transition." *Economics of Transition* 7(2): 275–298.

Aghion, Philippe, and Patrick Bolton. 1997. "A Trickle-Down Theory of Growth and Development with Debt Overhang." *Review of Economic Studies* 64(2): 151–162.

Aghion, Philippe, Eve Caroli, and Cecilia García-Peñalosa. 1999. "Inequality and Economic Growth: The Perspective of the New Growth Theories." *Journal of Economic Perspectives* 37(4): 1615–1660.

Alesina, Alberto, and Dani Rodrik. 1994. "Distributive Politics and Economic Growth." *Quarterly Journal of Economics* 109(2): 465–490.

Atkinson, Anthony B., Lee Rainwater, and Timothy M. Smeeding. 1995. "Income Distribution in OECD Countries: Evidence from the Luxembourg Income Study." OECD Social Policy Studies No. 18. Paris: OECD.

Banerjee, Abhijit, and Andrew F. Newman. 1993. "Occupational Choice and the Process of Development." *Journal of Political Economy* 101(2): 274–298.

Bénabou, Roland. 1996. "Inequality and Growth." *NBER Macroeconomics Annual* 11: 11–74.

Berg, Andrew, and Olivier Blanchard. 1994. "Stabilization and Transition: Poland 1990–1991." In *The Transition in Eastern Europe, Vol. 1: Country Studies*, ed. Olivier Blanchard, Kenneth Froot, and Jeffrey Sachs. Chicago: University of Chicago Press.

Calvo, Guillermo A., and Fabrizio Coricelli. 1992. "Stabilizing a Previously Centrally Planned Economy: Poland 1990." *Economic Policy* 14: 176–226.

Commander, Simon, and Une Lee. 1998. "How Does Public Policy Affect the Income Distribution? Evidence from Russia, 1992–1996." Manuscript, EBRD, London.

de Crombugghe, Alain. 1997. "Wage and Pension Pressure on the Polish Budget." World Bank Policy Research Working Paper No. 1793.

Dewatripont, Mathias, and Gérard Roland. 1996. "Transition as a Process of Large-Scale Institutional Change." *Economics of Transition* 4(1): 1–30.

Engel, E. 1895. "Die Lebenskosten belgischer Arbeiter-Familien früher und jetzt." *Bulletin de l'Institut International de Statistique* 9: 1–129.

Easterly, William. 2002. "The Middle Class Consensus and Economic Development." Working paper, World Bank.

European Bank for Reconstruction and Development (EBRD). Various years. *Transition Report*.

Evans, Davis S., and Boyan Jovanovic. 1989. "An Estimated Model of Entrepreneurial Choice under Liquidity Constraints." *Journal of Political Economy* 97(4): 808–827.

Fidrmuc, Jan. 2000. "Political Support for Reforms: Economics of Voting in Transition Countries." *European Economic Review* 44: 1491–1513.

Galor, Oded, and Joseph Zeira. 1993. "Income Distribution and Macroeconomics." *Review of Economic Studies* 60(1): 35–52.

Garner, Thesia, and Katherine Terrell. 1998. "A Gini Decomposition of Inequality in the Czech and Slovak Republics during the Transition." *Economics of Transition* 6(1): 23–46.

Gomułka, Stanisław. 1998. "The Polish Model of Transformation and Growth." *Economics of Transition* 6(1): 163–171.

Grun, Carola, and Stephan Klasen. 2001. "Growth, Income Distribution and Well-Being in Transition Countries." *Economics of Transition* 9(2): 359–394.

Havrylyshyn, Oleh, and John Odling-Smee. 2000. "Political Economy of Stalled Reforms." *Finance and Development* 37(3): 7–10.

International Monetary Fund (IMF). 1994. "Poland: The Path to a Market Economy." Occasional Paper No. 113.

Keane, Michael P., and Eswar S. Prasad. 2001a. "Consumption and Income Inequality during the Transition to a Market Economy: Poland, 1985–1992." *IMF Staff Papers* 47: 121–154.

Keane, Michael P., and Eswar S. Prasad. 2001b. "Poland: Inequality, Transfers and Growth in Transition." *Finance and Development* 38(1): 50–53.

Keane, Michael P., and Eswar S. Prasad. 2002a. "Inequality, Transfers and Growth: New Evidence from the Economic Transition in Poland." *Review of Economics and Statistics* 84(2): 324–341.

Keane, Michael P., and Eswar S. Prasad. 2002b. "Changes in the Structure of Earnings during the Polish Transition." IMF Working Paper No. 02/135.

Kornai, Janos. 2000. "Making the Transition to Private Ownership." *Finance and Development* 37(3): 12–13.

Kuznets, Simon. 1955. "Economic Growth and Income Inequality." *American Economic Review* 45(1): 1–28.

Milanovic, Branko. 1998. "Income, Inequality and Poverty during the Transition from Planned to Market Economy." World Bank Regional and Sectoral Studies, Washington, DC.

Milanovic, Branko. 1999. "Explaining the Increase in Inequality during Transition." *Economics of Transition* 7(2): 299–341.

OECD. 1997, 1998. "OECD Economic Surveys: Poland." Paris: OECD.

Perotti, Roberto. 1996. "Growth, Income Distribution and Democracy: What the Data Say." *Journal of Economic Growth* 1: 149–187.

Persson, Torsten, and Guido Tabellini. 1994. "Is Inequality Harmful for Growth?" *American Economic Review* 84(3): 600–621.

Pinto, Brian, Marek Belka, and Stefan Krajewski. 1993. "Transforming State Enterprises in Poland: Evidence on Adjustment by Manufacturing Firms." *Brookings Papers on Economic Activity*, 213–270.

Roland, Gerard. 1993. "The Political Economy of Restructuring and Privatization in Eastern Europe." *European Economic Review* 37(2–3): 533–540.

Svejnar, Jan. 1996. "Enterprises and Workers in the Transition: Econometric Evidence." *American Economic Review Papers and Proceedings* 86(2): 123–127.

World Bank. 1995. "Understanding Poverty in Poland." Country Study, World Bank, Washington, DC.

World Bank. 1997–2000. "World Development Indicators." World Bank, Washington, DC.

6   Growth and Inequality: Evidence from Transitional Economies in the 1990s

Oleksiy Ivaschenko

6.1   Introduction

The relationship between income inequality and economic growth has received much attention in the economic literature. The impact of economic development on income inequality, however, remains ambiguous. Even if found to be significant in univariate regressions of income inequality on per capita GDP, the parameter estimate on aggregate income loses its strength and can even reverse sign when other explanatory factors or country-specific dummies are introduced (Deininger and Squire 1998).

However, a common trait of the previous studies linking income inequality and economic growth is that they concentrated primarily on what happens to income distribution during the process of *development*, that is of rising per capita income. In contrast, the countries of Eastern Europe (EE) and the former Soviet Union (FSU) witnessed a sharp contraction in output during the initial stage of the transition.[1] This decline has been accompanied by a marked increase in income inequality, though, not at a uniform rate across the region. In many transitional economies, inequality has reached levels comparable to that observed in highly unequal countries of Asia and Latin America.

These developments in transitional countries pose many intriguing questions. What is the role of economic *decline* (and recovery) in changing income distribution? What specific factors lie behind a noticeable increase in income inequality over the transition? How well do the same factors explain the changes in inequality across different counties?

I attempt to answer these questions in this chapter using a unique panel of inequality estimates constructed for twenty-four transitional countries of EE and the FSU and embracing the period from 1989 to 1998. The fact that the combined population of these countries exceeds 400 million people makes the understanding of the factors driving the changes in income distribution go far beyond a purely research interest. Although it is often argued that policymakers should be more concerned about absolute poverty than income inequality, there are several reasons why one may (or should) care about the latter as well. At a given rate of economic growth, more unequal distribution of income would be associated with a lower rate of poverty reduction, assuming, of course, that the poor partici-pate fully in sharing the gains from growth. Moreover, as suggested in many studies (e.g., Alesina and Rodrik 1994; Birdsall, Ross, and Sabot 1995; Deininger and Squire 1998; Persson and Tabellini 1994; Sylwester 2000; Easterly 2001), an unequal income distribution might itself be detrimental to long-run economic growth for a variety of reasons.[2] The most common arguments for this are that an unequal distribution of income creates pressure for redistributional policies, and hence distorts incentives for working and investing; that it leads to abuse of power by the elite and to sociopolitical instability and, thus, harms the investment environment; and finally that, in the presence of imperfect capital markets, it reduces opportunities for accumulating human capital (such as education and health) and physical assets. From a social welfare point of view, it has also been argued that both utilitarian and nonutilitarian views of welfare sug-gest that income inequality reduces aggregate well-being.[3] These considerations leave no doubt that inequality indeed matters, and in this chapter I investigate which factors underlie the trends in inequality observed in transitional economies.

There is a growing amount of research which attempts to explain the rise in income inequality during the transition. Many existing studies try to figure out the possible factors behind the changes in the distribution of income using either theoretical models of transi-tion (Aghion and Commander 1999; Ferreira 1999; Milanovic 1999) or a Gini decomposition analysis (by income component or recipient) applied to a single country or a set of countries (Garner and Terrell 1998; Milanovic 1999; Yemtsov 2001). Yet a third approach employs cross-country regressions to examine why income inequality is dif-ferent *across* countries at a given point in time (World Bank 2000).

This chapter represents the first attempt to identify factors under-lying the changes in income inequality over time *within* countries rather than to explain differences in inequality levels across countries. Until now a lack of compatible time-series data with sufficient geographical coverage ruled out the possibility of doing this, and I undertake the task using the assembled panel of inequality estimates comparable over time and across countries. I use panel data estimation methods to control for unobservable country-specific effects that result in a missing-variable bias in cross-sectional studies.

The remainder of the chapter is structured as follows. In section 6.2 I present some evidence on the evolution of income inequality and economic growth during the transition. Section 6.3 discusses potential determinants of rising inequality in transitional countries with a reference to existing literature. Section 6.4 describes the data used in the empirical analysis. Section 6.5 is devoted to model specification and description of the estimation technique. Section 6.6 describes regression results. In section 6.7 I examine the robustness of results. Section 6.8 offers a conclusion and presents some policy implications of the findings.

6.2 Growth and Inequality during the Transition

Figure 6.1 shows the relationship between the changes in income inequality and changes in real GDP during 1989–1998. It clearly suggests that better growth performers experienced much smaller increases in income inequality.

There is substantial variation in the regional performance, with the transitional economies of EE performing much better, both in terms of economic growth and distributional outcomes, than the FSU countries. However, there are significant differences within these two groups of countries as well.

Although quite illustrative, inequality and growth dynamics presented in figure 6.1 may be misleading as they do not fully reflect what happened at different stages *within* this period. For instance, given the evidence presented in figure 6.1, one may mistakenly conclude that Poland (POL) and Slovenia (SVN) were growing consistently through the 1990s while other countries were declining, and that inequality was uniformly trending upward during the period. Therefore, in table 6.1 I present the evidence on the evolution of inequality and growth separately for economic decline and economic recovery episodes. This analysis gives us a better idea of the relationship between income distribution and economic growth.

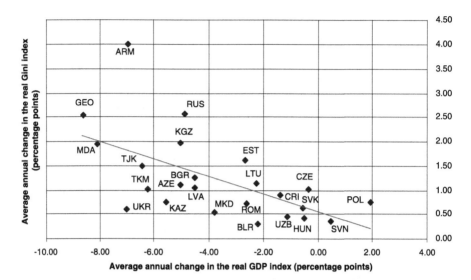

Figure 6.1
The dynamics of income inequality and GDP growth in transitional economies, 1989–1998
Source: Author's calculations using a constructed panel of inequality estimates and the Real GDP index from the Trans/MONEE2000 database, UNICEF, Florence.

Several major observations emerge out of the data in table 6.1. First, no single country escaped economic decline and an increase in income inequality (except Poland) at the start of the transition (see columns 5 and 7, table 6.1).

Second, after the sharp economic decline in the initial period, most of the countries started to recover at some later stage. In general, Eastern Europe and the Baltic states began growing in 1992–1994, while the non-Baltic FSU countries started to grow later or continued to decline as of 1998 (see column 3, table 6.1).

Third, it appears that the economic recovery in the FSU countries was generally associated with declining income inequality. Conversely, recovery in EE countries was accompanied by rising income inequality, although at very modest rates (see columns 6 and 8, table 6.1). This is a very interesting observation since it indicates that the mechanisms behind the inequality trends in EE and the FSU are not necessarily the same.

In what follows, I discuss potential determinants of the changes in income distribution in transitional countries. This discussion serves as a basis for the choice of variables used later in the empirical analysis. Most of the factors that I consider are those commonly found in the literature on the determinants of cross-country inequality, while others are specific to the transitional region circumstances that I expect to be influential in explaining the pattern of income inequality.

6.3   Potential Determinants of Rising Inequality in Transitional Countries

A vast amount of literature exists on the determinants of income inequality that considers both the individual (e.g., increasing returns to skills) and macro-level factors (e.g., inflation, political democracy) affecting income distribution. In this chapter I focus on the latter, although the former might be equally important.

The main factors that I anticipate to affect income inequality in transitional countries are: the level of economic development (measured by per capita GDP), macroeconomic conditions (inflation, unemployment), government involvement in the economy (government consumption, social transfers), structural changes (economic liberalization, privatization, deindustrialization), and forces outside economic domain (political freedom, civil conflicts).

Many attempts to identify a link between income inequality and the level of economic development have been undertaken since the seminal work of Kuznets (1955), who argued for an inverted U–shaped relationship between income inequality and economic development. Although several studies (e.g., Paukert 1973; Ahluwalia 1976) have found a support for such a relationship, most of the recent research does not find economic development to affect income distribution (e.g., Anand and Kanbur 1993; Deininger and Squire 1998; Ravallion 1995).

However, the striking economic decline in EE and the FSU countries in the initial years of the transition, and the subsequent economic recovery, are expected to have had significant implications for income distribution. That is because economic decline and recovery were associated with dramatic and heterogeneous shocks to real incomes, the changes in the real value of social transfers, and other developments in social and economic conditions. Figure 6.1 provides strong support for anticipating a negative relationship between

Table 6.1
The dynamics of income inequality and GDP growth in transitional economies of EE and the FSU

Region/country	Population (mid-1997, millions)	Real GDP index (1989 = 100) at the bottom of decline (year)	in 1998	Avg. annual change in the real GDP index (percentage points) decline period	growth period	Avg. annual change in the Gini index (percentage points) decline period	growth period
1	2	3	4	5	6	7	8
I. FSU							
a. Baltic states							
Estonia	1.5	60.76 (94)	75.70	−7.85	3.74	3.31	−0.65
Latvia	2.5	51.04 (95)	59.30	−8.16	2.75	1.00	1.20
Lithuania	3.7	64.83 (94)	79.53	−7.03	3.67	2.51	−0.26
b. Western CIS							
Belarus	10.2	62.69 (95)	77.75	−6.22	5.02	0.31	0.44
Moldova	4.0	—	32.00	−8.11	—	1.95	—
Russia	147.0	—	55.89	−4.90	—	2.58	—
Ukraine	50.4	—	36.61	−7.04	—	0.69	—
c. Caucasus							
Armenia	3.8	31.63 (93)	41.68	−15.29	2.08	8.42	−0.40
Azerbaijan	7.8	41.86 (95)	49.40	−9.69	2.51	2.05	−0.33
Georgia	5.4	24.60 (94)	31.70	−8.64	—	2.57	—
d. Central Asia							
Kazakhstan	15.3	—	61.20	−5.49	—	0.84	—
Kyrgyz Rep.	4.6	50.39 (95)	60.30	−5.09	—	1.97	—
Tajikistan	6.0	39.19 (96)	41.90	−6.44	—	1.69	—
Turkmenistan	4.6	41.99 (97)	43.75	−6.25	—	1.04	—
Uzbekistan	23.6	83.36 (95)	89.50	−3.18	—	0.48	—

II. Central EE						
Czech Rep.	10.3	84.58 (92)	94.90	-5.14	2.53	0.33	1.46
Hungary	10.2	81.89 (93)	95.20	-4.53	2.66	0.32	0.52
Poland	38.7	82.21 (91)	117.15	-5.22	5.47	-0.34	1.33
Slovak Rep.	5.4	74.97 (93)	99.60	-6.26	4.09	0.41	0.74
III. South EE						
Bulgaria	8.3	63.69 (97)	65.90	-4.54	—	1.27	—
Romania	22.6	74.99 (92)	82.08	-8.34	3.30	0.63	1.37
IV. FY						
Croatia	4.7	59.54 (93)	77.70	-10.11	3.65	0.35	1.36
Macedonia	2.0	67.99 (95)	71.50	-5.34	0.79	0.60	0.41
Slovenia	2.0	82.04 (92)	103.90	-5.99	3.66	0.37	0.40

Note: Dashes indicate data are not available.

Note: Dashes in columns means that by the end of 1998 a country under consideration continued to decline. South EE also includes Albania; the former Yugoslavia (FY) also includes Yugoslavia, FR, and Bosnia-Herzegovina. These countries are not included in the table due to the lack of data.

Sources: Author's calculations using a constructed panel of inequality estimates and the real GDP index and population data from the Trans-MONEE2000 database, UNICEF, Florence.

income inequality and economic development for transitional countries. Nevertheless, as the evidence from table 6.1 indicates, this relationship is hardly universal across countries.

Inflation may have a strong redistributional impact through its effect on individuals whose nominal incomes are not adjusted proportionally to increases in prices; mostly state-sector employees, pensioners, and beneficiaries of various social benefits. That would be an argument for a positive relationship between income inequality and inflation. However, inflation may also have an equalizing impact on income distribution through a progressive tax system by pushing wage earners into higher tax brackets, thus implying less inequality in disposable income. These two effects may well counterbalance each other. In a study of the determinants of inequality for OECD countries (Gustafsson and Johansson 1999), inflation was not found to be significant in explaining inequality. That may not be the case for transitional economies, however, as most of them experienced a sharp rise in inflation at the start of the transition.[4] Moreover, the progressivity of the inflation tax is unlikely to be a mechanism at work in most of the transition countries due to a high occurrence of tax evasion. Hence, I expect inflation to be positively associated with income inequality in the transition region.[5]

Destruction of the old economic system and significant structural changes during the transition caused a substantial rise in unemployment across the region. In many countries the unemployment rate grew from virtually zero to 10–15 percent even when measured by the number of officially registered unemployed.[6] Unemployment is likely to largely affect those in the lower percentile of income distribution. Milanovic (1998) indicates that unemployment in transition countries increased the most among women, young people, and those with lower education. A negative impact of unemployment on income distribution has been confirmed in a number of studies of industrialized countries (Gustafsson and Palmer 1997; Weil 1984), and I anticipate unemployment to have an inequality-increasing effect in transitional economies as well.

In times of economic hardship and increasing unemployment, government-financed projects (e.g., construction) may provide a source of employment and income (with low-skilled labor probably benefiting the most), which serve as a buffer to widening income inequality.[7] The size of the public sector is found to reduce inequality in cross-country studies by Stack (1978) and Boyd (1988). Government involvement in the economy, measured as a share of government consumption in GDP, decreased between 1989 and 1998 in eight out of fifteen states of the FSU (including the Baltic states), increased in five states, and was practically unchanged in the rest. In the EE region, government consumption has declined in only two countries, while in the remainder it has either grown or has been relatively stable. In this chapter I look at the effect of government consumption on income distribution in transitional economies.[8]

Centrally planned economies were dominated to a various extent by state enterprises with administratively set wages. The overwhelming predominance of the state sector in EE and the FSU economies is widely regarded as a main reason for low income inequality in the region before the transition.[9] The process of transition brought about a massive expansion of the private sector and the share of the private-sector employment.[10] This process is likely to increase income inequality due to the wage differential between the state and private sectors. Moreover, the distribution of earnings within the private sector is usually more unequal than in the state sector. That privatization can lead to rising income inequality is argued in theoretical models of transition by Milanovic (1999) and Ferreira (1999). However, due to the poor data on the scope of privatization in transitional countries, the impact of rising private sector on income distribution has not been empirically tested, until this chapter.

Economic liberalization also led to profound changes in the sectoral composition of the economy. There is a clear trend for the industrial sector to shrink, while the evidence for the agricultural sector is mixed—in some countries its relative importance has declined, while in others it has increased.[11] The share of industry in total output in the region declined on average by 25 percent from 1989 to 1998, and in several countries the drop was even more profound. For instance, in the ten years after 1989 the share of the industrial sector declined from 52 percent to 32 percent in Poland, from 58 percent to 33 percent in Slovak Republic, from 59 percent to 25 percent in Bulgaria, and from 50 percent to 35 percent in Russia. It is very likely that the declining industrial-sector employment may have an inequality-increasing impact due to an outflow of labor to sectors with higher wage differentials, for instance, services.[12] A negative relationship between industrial-sector employment and income inequality is confirmed in studies of industrialized countries by Gustafsson and Johansson (1999) and Levy and Murnane (1992), and in this chapter I investigate the effect of de-industrialization on income distribution in the transitional region.

The process of economic transition in EE and the FSU was generally accompanied by the expansion of political democracy. Although a common argument in the literature is that the higher degree of political democracy should be accompanied by a more equal distribution of income (e.g., Gradstein, Milanovic, and Ying 2001; Rodrik 1999), the existing evidence does not show any robust relationship between democracy and inequality in a cross-country regression analysis. Here I investigate whether political democracy affects income inequality in transitional countries.

A number of countries in EE (republics of the former Yugoslavia) and the FSU (Armenia, Azerbaijan, Georgia, Tajikistan, Moldova, and Russia) experienced persistent internal conflicts over the last decade. Since civil conflicts are likely to have strong distributional consequences, I analyze their impact on income inequality in the transitional region. The data used in the empirical analysis and their sources are described in detail in the next section.

6.4   The Data

I construct a panel of inequality estimates using time-series data on income inequality across transitional countries. The majority of observations are drawn from the UNU/WIDER-UNDP World Income Inequality Database (WIID) (Version 1.0, September 2000), which to date represents the latest and most extensive data on inequality for both developed and developing countries.[13] In addition, I augment these data with a few observations from Milanovic (1998) (mainly for 1989) and the latest household surveys conducted by the World Bank (2000) (mainly for 1998–1999).

To minimize problems with data comparability across countries and over time I require inequality data that I select for the panel to be based on the same living standard indicator, have the same sample and enumeration unit, be drawn from nationally representative surveys, and, whenever possible, come from one source.[14] Income inequality is measured by the Gini coefficient with individuals representing the unit of analysis. The coefficients are calculated based on household per capita income. The compiled panel of inequality estimates represents perhaps the most consistent and extensive coverage available for transitional countries to date. It consists of 149 observations covering twenty-five countries in transition from 1989 to 1999.[15] However, due to either missing observations on other variables, or the deletion of observations based on the influence diagnostics tests (as discussed later), only 129 out of 149 originally assembled Gini coefficients are used in the estimation. A detailed description of the data on income inequality used in the empirical analysis and their sources is presented in table 6.A1.

The constructed panel of inequality estimates is far from being perfect, however, as not all of the above comparability requirements could always be met, and the resulting inequality measures are still subject to potential measurement error problems. The use of panel data and panel data estimation methods (to be discussed), however, help diminish some problems with data consistency. The country-specific intercepts in the fixed-effects model setting can absorb, among all other unobservable characteristics, the differences in inequality definition across countries (Deininger and Squire 1998).[16] Nevertheless, the use of panel data cannot remedy all data limitations, and thus the empirical results must be treated with some degree of caution.

I now turn to the definitions and sources of data on explanatory variables. The level of economic development is measured by PPP-adjusted per capita GDP in constant 1992 USD. The data on PPP-adjusted per capita GDP in current USD come from the World Bank World Development Indicators (WDI) 2000 database, and they are then deflated to 1992 prices using the U.S. GDP deflator.

Inflation is measured as the annual percentage change in the consumer price index (CPI) (end-year). As CPI-based inflation is not available for all countries in our sample for 1989 and 1990, the GDP deflator inflation is taken for those years instead. Finally, as neither of the mentioned above indexes could be obtained for Croatia (1989), Macedonia FYR (1989, 1990), and Slovenia (1989) inflation there is measured by the food price index (a subindex of the CPI). All inflation data are drawn from the World Bank WDI 2000 database.

Unemployment represents a share of the labor force that is without work but available for and seeking employment. However, as I have mentioned, unemployment data for transitional countries may substantially understate the actual scope of unemployment. Nonetheless, as no better alternative is available, official estimates are used in most cases. Unemployment data are taken from the

European Bank for Reconstruction and Development (EBRD) *Transition Report 2000*, which provides further reference on the origin of the data for each country.

General government consumption, expressed as a fraction of GDP, refers to all current spending for purchases of goods and services (including wages and salaries). It also includes most expenditures on national defense and security, but excludes government military expenditures that are part of government capital formation. As such, government consumption represents a good measure of the government's involvement in the economy. The data on government consumption come from the World Bank WDI 2000 database.

Industrial employment represents a share of industry in total employment. I was able to obtain only 105 observations covering twenty-four countries (EBRD 2000). As other explanatory variables contain more observations, the use of these employment data in the model estimation would substantially reduce a number of observations on other variables. Since the sample is relatively small, I consider that inappropriate. Therefore, I use a share of industry value added in GDP as a proxy for industrial-sector employment.[17] This provides us with a substantially larger number of observations. The data come from the World Bank WDI 2000 database.

Private-sector employment equals the number of people employed in the private sector as a percentage of total employment. Data availability, however, represents a severe constraint here, as practically no data prior to 1993–1994 exist. I have managed to collect fifty-one observations using IMF country reports, a number not sufficient for our purposes. Thus, in the regression analysis I use a share of the private sector in GDP as a proxy for the private-sector employment. Since I have found high correlation between the size of the private sector and the private-sector employment in our sample (for those observations that are available), and in view of the lack of an alternative, such a proxy is considered to be justifiable. These data and their more extensive descriptions are available in EBRD (2000).

Economic liberalization (which is largely reflected in structural changes) is measured with the Cumulative Liberalization Index (De Melo, Denizer, and Gelb 1996), which reflects the progress with economic reforms on several fronts: internal (price) liberalization, external (foreign trade) liberalization, and the extent of privatization and banking-sector reform.[18]

The progress in the introduction of political rights and civil liberties during the transition is measured using the Index of Political Freedom (IPF) (Freedom House 2001), which represents an arithmetic average of the political rights and civil liberties indexes. The political rights index reflects the extent to which people in a country can participate in the political process. The civil liberties index measures the freedoms to develop views, institutions, and personal autonomy apart from the state.

The effect of civil conflicts on income inequality is measured using a dummy variable set equal to one for each year since an internal conflict has taken place in a given country.[19] In our sample the countries affected by civil conflicts are Croatia, Macedonia FYR, Armenia, Azerbaijan, Georgia, Moldova, Tajikistan, and Russia.[20] The historical information on civil conflicts in the region is obtained from the Reuters Foundation.[21]

Table 6.A2 provides the descriptive statistics of the data used in the regression analysis. Table 6.A3 shows the matrix of the Pearson correlation coefficients.

6.5   Model Specification and Estimation

The primary interest of this study is to explain the changes in income inequality in transitional economies, and I thus estimate income inequality as a function of various potential explanatory variables presented here. The base model specification is

$$\text{GINI}_{(it)} = \alpha_i + \beta_0^*\text{GDPPC}_{(it)} + \beta_1^*\text{GDPPC\_S}_{(it)} + \beta_2^*\text{INFL}_{(it)}$$

$$+ \beta_3^*\text{UNEMP}_{(it)} + \beta_4^*\text{CONSG}_{(it)} + \beta_6^*\text{INDVA}_{(it)}$$

$$+ \beta_7^*\text{PRIVS}_{(it)} + \varepsilon_{(it)}; \qquad i = 1, \dots, \text{N}; t = 1, \dots, \text{T}, \qquad (1)$$

where i represents country index, t denotes time period, GINI is the Gini coefficient of income inequality, α_i is a country-specific intercept, GDPPC is PPP-adjusted GDP per capita (1992 constant USD), GDPPC_S is its squared value, INFL is annual inflation as measured by the year-to-year change in the consumer price index, UNEMP is a share of unemployed in total labor force, CONSG is general government consumption as a percentage of GDP, INDVA is industry value added as a percentage of GDP, PRIVS is the private-sector share in GDP, and $\varepsilon_{(it)}$ is an error term. The assumption on $\varepsilon_{(it)}$ is that $\varepsilon_{(it)} \sim IID(0, \sigma_\varepsilon^2)$. All variables (including the Gini coefficient) enter the regressions in the natural log form. The natural log of $(1 + INFL/100)$ is used for INFL variable in the estimations to deal with negative and very high values of INFL. The natural log of $(1 + UNEMP)$ is used for UNEMP variable in the estimations since the unemployment rate equals zero for many countries at the start of the transition. A squared value of GDPPC (with GDPPC expressed in the natural log form) is included into the regression to account for the potential quadratic relationship between income inequality and per capita GDP.

In view of the large body of literature exploring the effect of income distribution on economic growth, one may be quick to point out the possible problem with the given model specification arising from the potential existence of a reverse causality between inequality and growth. I argue that the transition economies of EE and the FSU represent a unique case when the possibility of causality from income distribution to economic growth can be ruled out, at least for the period under investigation, since the reasons for the economic collapse and subsequent recovery in the region had clearly nothing to do with the distribution of income. This is confirmed by the Granger causality tests (Granger 1969). I have tested whether income inequality Granger-causes economic growth using from one to five lags, which provides 87 to 22 observations, respectively. In *none* of the cases did the test statistic indicate that I could reject the null hypothesis that the Gini coefficient *does not* Granger-cause per capita GDP.[22]

I estimate equation (1) using the assembled panel for twenty-four transitional countries covering a period from 1989 to 1998. The use of panel data produces several well-known advantages. The most important is that it allows one to control for unobservable time-invariant country-specific effects that result in a missing-variable bias, an often encountered problem when cross-section data are used. This problem is recognized in Bourguignon and Morrison (1998), Bruno, Ravallion, and Squire (1995), Deininger and Squire (1998), Forbes (2000), Ravallion (1995), and other studies.

To control for unobservable country-specific characteristics I introduce country-specific intercepts in the fixed-effects model setting. The addition of fixed effects to the model also helps alleviate potential heteroscedasticity problems stemming from possible differences across countries (Greene 1997).

There might be another reason for preferring the fixed-effects model to the random-effects model. A crucial assumption for the random-effects model is that country-specific terms (α_i) are uncorrelated with the other explanatory variables. Its violation makes random-effects estimates biased and inconsistent (Greene 1997). The use of the fixed-effects model avoids this problem as individual effects are allowed to be correlated with other regressors. To test whether the country-specific effects are correlated with the exogenous variables, I conduct a Hausman test.[23] While the test statistic suggests that I cannot reject the null hypothesis for the base model, the results of a Hausman test are found to be sensitive to the model specification and sample selection. Therefore, I prefer to use the fixed-effects model.

More important, the fixed-effects model is chosen since the main goal of this study is to investigate what factors have caused substantial changes in income inequality over time within countries rather than to explain variation in inequality across countries.[24] Thus, the use of the fixed-effects estimator, which is also called the "within" estimator, is very appropriate since it allows one to focus on how changes in within-country characteristics are related to changes in within-country inequality. The fixed-effects model is also more suitable when the focus is on a specific set of countries and the inference is restricted to these countries (Baltagi 1995, 10). Moreover, the country-specific effects have been found to be statistically significant.[25] This implies that if the model is estimated without taking them into account (i.e., if a single overall intercept is included instead of country dummies) the estimated coefficients will be biased.

The fixed-effects estimation technique, however, is not perfect. First, random-effects estimates are more efficient than fixed-effects ones given that all necessary assumptions are satisfied. Second, the fixed-effects model is very costly in terms of the lost degrees of freedom, which may represent a particular problem for the relatively small sample. To overcome this problem, I estimate the model in deviations from the country means.[26] This within-countries estimator is identical to the least squares dummy variable (LSDV) estimator obtained if a dummy variable is included for each country (as in the original formulation of equation (1)), but the resulting R^2 is lower (Greene 1997, 619).

Third, it has been argued (Barro 1997, 37; Temple 1999) that the fixed-effects technique eliminates the cross-sectional information and, hence, lowers precision of the estimates. This problem is, of course, especially acute if most of the variation in the data is due to cross-country differences. While in nontransition countries most (approximately 90%) of the variation in inequality is due to variation across countries (Deininger and Squire 1996; Li, Squire, and Zou 1998; Quah 2001), in transition countries a substantial source of the variation in inequality over the last decade is attributable to the profound changes in inequality over time (see table 6.A2). Hence, the use of the fixed-effects estimation for transitional countries seems to be appropriate. In addition, if one bears in mind that inequality comparisons across countries are likely to be much less reliable than inequality comparisons for a single country over time, despite all efforts to assemble the inequality estimates that are as consistent as possible both across space and time, the reliance on mostly variation over time in inequality is even desirable.

Given all considerations outlined here, I prefer to use the fixed-effects model since its advantages seem to outweigh its weaknesses given the data and research purposes. Nevertheless, to check the robustness of the results to the estimation technique the random-effects model is also estimated. The empirical results are described later in the chapter. The panel that I estimate is unbalanced as a number of time-series observations differ across countries. However, assuming that observations are missing randomly, consistency of the fixed-effects estimator is not affected. The fixed-effects model is estimated with OLS, which, given the assumed properties of residuals, is the best linear unbiased estimator (Hsiao 1986).

6.6 The Regression Results

I first estimate a "full" version of equation (1) with both the log of per capita GDP (GDPPC) and its squared value (GDPPC_S) included among the explanatory variables. This allows capturing a potential threshold effect in the relationship between income inequality and per capita GDP.

It is worth noting that up to now most of the attempts to test for a U-shaped relationship between income inequality and economic development have used cross-sectional regressions. This approach may be conceptually incorrect when studying the intertemporal relationship between income inequality and per capita income. If one wants to see whether inequality changes with economic development, longitudinal data are needed (Deininger and Squire 1998). Here the use of the panel data provides an obvious advantage over purely time-series or cross-sectional data.

However, to test for any kind of a quadratic relationship between income inequality and per capita GDP is not the main purpose of this study. Here I undertake an attempt to identify specific factors behind the changes in inequality in the transitional region. While economic growth represents a good aggregate measure of the economy's health since it reflects the outcome of multiple complex processes taking place at all levels of the economy, it alone does not seem to be a satisfactory explanation of the inequality pattern. That is why in equation (1) I also introduce other potential explanatory forces into play. In addition, I estimate an alternative specification of equation (1) where I include only GDPPC (but not GDPPC_S) among the regressors to test for the linear relationship between income inequality and per capita GDP. Finally, since some of the explanatory variables in the model appear to be significantly correlated, I try several alternative specifications to investigate the robustness of the parameter estimates.[27] The regression results from estimating different modifications of equation (1) are reported in table 6.2.[28]

The regression results indicate a statistically strong relationship between income inequality and per capita GDP. There is stronger support for a quadratic rather than a linear relationship.[29] The parameter estimates on GDPPC and GDPPC_S indicate that the relationship between income inequality and economic growth depends on where a country stands in terms of its per capita GDP. More specifically, they suggest that for a country below (above) some threshold level of development the process of economic growth would be associated with falling (rising) income inequality. It is worth noting that many transition countries (mostly those in the FSU) had either already been below the estimated threshold level of per capita GDP (see table 6.2) at the start of the transition, or slipped below this level as a result of an economic decline, and thus are expected to have negative relationship between growth and inequality. The linear specification indicates that a 10 percent decline in per capita income would increase the Gini coefficient at the mean by 0.48 percentage points (see column 3, table 6.2). That income inequality might increase during recessions was confirmed in a number of studies of the

Table 6.2
Fixed-effects estimates from the regression of the Gini coefficient on selected explanatory variables: All countries

Explanatory variable	Full model (quadratic relationship)	Full model (linear relationship)	Reduced model 1 (quadratic relationship)	Reduced model 2 (quadratic relationship)
1	2	3	4	5
Intercept				
GDPPC	−4.190***	−0.157**	−3.650***	−4.912***
	(1.084)	(0.063)	(1.131)	(1.208)
GDPPC_S	0.239***		0.203***	0.272***
	(0.064)		(0.067)	(0.072)
INFL	0.033***	0.034***	0.024*	
	(0.013)	(0.013)	(0.013)	
UNEMP	−0.001	−0.023	0.035*	0.086***
	(0.021)	(0.021)	(0.020)	(0.019)
CONSG	−0.014	−0.023	−0.061	−0.090*
	(0.047)	(0.050)	(0.048)	(0.052)
INDVA	−0.288***	−0.350***	−0.375***	
	(0.072)	(0.074)	(0.073)	
PRIVS	0.105***	0.091***		
	(0.027)	(0.028)		
Number of countries	24	24	24	24
Number of observations	129	129	129	129
R^2 adj.	0.65	0.61	0.61	0.52
F-value	32.66	31.97	33.33	12.14
Estimated threshold level (PPP-adjusted GDP per capita, 1992 USD)	6405		8015	8337

Note: All variables are in the natural log form. Standard errors are presented in parentheses. The model is estimated in deviations from the group means. The Yule-Walker (iterated) method was used to correct for serial correlation and heteroskedasticity.
*indicates significance at 10 percent level; **indicates significance at 5 percent level; ***indicates significance at 1 percent level (two-tailed tests).

United States (Meier 1973; Metcalf 1969; Thurow 1970). So, given that economic decline in many transition countries reached an un-precedented scale, the adverse changes in the distribution of income are not surprising.

Inflation is found to increase income inequality, although the esti-mated coefficient in one of the specifications turns out to be only marginally significant.[30] The magnitude of the effect, however, does not appear to be large. A 10 percent increase in inflation would raise inequality at the mean by at most 0.08 Gini points (see table 6.2). I have also tested (using the LSDV specification) for a threshold effect of inflation as one would expect that it is only the inflation above a particular level that affects income distribution. Indeed, when I include among the explanatory variables in equation (1) dummies for inflation levels instead of INFL, a clear threshold effect is appar-ent. I find (see column 2, table 6.3) that hyperinflation (annual CPI exceeds 500 percent) is associated with a 9.5 percent higher income inequality compared to the situation of the relative macroeconomic stability (annual inflation below 20 percent).

Unemployment rate does not seem to have an impact on inequal-ity in the base model (see column 2, table 6.2). It is very likely, how-ever, that the parameter estimate on unemployment is contaminated due to a high correlation of the unemployment rate with other indi-cators of structural changes, namely de-industrialization and priva-tization (see table 6.A3). Indeed, when I eliminate PRIVS from the estimation, the coefficient on UNEMP becomes positive and margin-ally significant (see column 4, table 6.2). Finally, when INDVA and INFL are also omitted from the regression, the parameter estimate on UNEMP becomes statistically significant at a 1 percent level (see column 5, table 6.2). The magnitude of the coefficient suggests that a 1 percentage point increase in the unemployment rate at the mean would raise the Gini coefficient at the mean by 0.33 points.

The lack of robustness of the effect of unemployment on income inequality may also be due to the following factors. First, a likely inequality-increasing effect of growing unemployment can be coun-terbalanced by an increasing flow of unemployment benefits. Sec-ond, it is also possible that the increase in between-groups inequality stemming from larger unemployment could be offset by a more equal distribution of income among transfer recipients (Milanovic 1999). Third, it has been argued that in developing countries the unemployment statistics can in fact reflect the extent of the informal

Table 6.3
Estimates from the regression of the Gini coefficient on selected explanatory variables: All Countries

Explanatory variable 1	Model with inflation dummy (LSDV) 2	Model with CLI (LSDV) 3	Model with IPF (LSDV) 4	Model with war dummy (pooled regression) 5
Intercept				4.370***
				(0.365)
GDPPC	−3.834***	−2.993**	−4.005***	
	(1.225)	(1.217)	(1.230)	
GDPPC_S	0.216***	0.162**	0.225***	
	(0.073)	(0.073)	(0.073)	
Inflation > 500	0.091**	0.106***	0.089**	0.163***
dummy[a]	(0.038)	(0.037)	(0.038)	(0.036)
UNEMP	0.007	−0.014	0.003	−0.002
	(0.025)	(0.025)	(0.025)	(0.022)
CONSG	−0.035	−0.044	−0.045	−0.049
	(0.054)	(0.051)	(0.054)	(0.046)
INDVA	−0.242***	−0.199**	−0.205**	−0.360***
	(0.081)	(0.079)	(0.086)	(0.074)
PRIVS	0.098***	0.020	0.097***	0.117***
	(0.032)	(0.039)	(0.032)	(0.028)
CLI		0.034***		
		(0.011)		
IPF			−0.016	
			(0.013)	
War dummy				0.125**
				(0.050)
Number of countries	24	24	24	24
Number of observations	129	129	129	129
R^2 adj.	0.999	0.999	0.999	0.61
F-value	4290.35	4573.36	4194.15	15.73
Estimated threshold level (PPP-adjusted GDP per capita, 1992 USD)	7255	10432	7293	

Note: All variables are in the natural log form. Standard errors are presented in parentheses. Yule-Walker (iterated) method was used to correct for serial correlation and heteroskedasticity.

[a] excluded category is inflation < 20 percent annual. The coefficients on other categories (21–50, 51–100, 101–500) are not reported since they are not significant.

*indicates significance at 10 percent level; **indicates significance at 5 percent level; ***indicates significance at 1 percent level (two-tailed tests).

sector employment and self-employment, which are generally associated with higher income inequality (Ferreira and Litchfield 1998). Finally, the quality of the unemployment data can also be a simple and quite probable explanation of why the effect of unemployment is not very robust. These data, as was mentioned before, are mostly based on official unemployment records, which may severely underestimate not only the actual scope of unemployment, but also the changes in the rate of unemployment over time.[31] Thus, their use in the estimation may induce a substantial downward bias in the parameter estimate on unemployment.

With regard to government consumption, I do not find it to influence income distribution. Although the sign of the parameter estimate is as anticipated, the coefficient on CONSG is only marginally significant in one of the specifications (see table 6.2). The *size* of government consumption (as a share of GDP) may have poor predictive power since the total effect of this factor on income distribution clearly depends on the composition of government expenditures and progressivity of taxes used to finance them. Also, the variation in the share of GDP devoted to public consumption is substantially higher across countries than over time (see table 6.A2). The estimation method that relies on the intertemporal variation does not capture the potential effect of government consumption on the levels of income inequality *across* countries.

The parameter estimate on INDVA supports our hypothesis that deindustrialization increases inequality.[32] The coefficient from the full model (see column 2, table 6.2) suggests that a 10 percent decline in the share of the industrial sector would lead to a 0.88 percentage point increase in the Gini coefficient at the mean. The parameter estimate implies that in Ukraine, for example, where the share of industrial sector in total output dropped from 48 percent in 1989 to 34 percent in 1998, the Gini coefficient increased by 2.17 percentage points over the period due to this factor alone, thus explaining a third of the total increase in income inequality.

There is a statistically strong positive relationship between income inequality and the size of the private sector. The estimated coefficient suggests that a 10 percentage point increase in the share of the private sector in the economy would result in a 0.83 point increase in the Gini coefficient. The magnitude of the effect does not seem to be very large. However, if one bears in mind that transitional countries have witnessed a substantial growth of the private sector, it is clear that the rising private-sector employment plays a crucial role in explaining the increase in income inequality.

I next look at the effect of economic liberalization on income inequality using the Cumulative Liberalization Index (CLI) as an explanatory variable in the regressions. The regression results (see column 3, table 6.3) indicate that the process of liberalization is associated with rising income inequality.[33] The CLI is by construction highly correlated with the structural indicators used in my analysis (see table 6.A3). Nevertheless, the parameter estimate on CLI is significant at a 1 percent level even when all other variables are included. The coefficient on PRIVS, however, becomes insignificant in this case. The parameter estimate on CLI indicates that a 10 percent increase in the CLI at the mean would be associated with a 0.27 point increase in the Gini coefficient at the mean. The effect of economic liberalization on income distribution is highly robust to the model specification.

I next investigate the impact on the distribution of income of the factors outside economic domain. Transitional countries have made different progresses in the introduction of political rights and civil liberties during the transition, which makes it interesting to see whether the progress on the political freedom front has any implications for the distribution of income. To do this, I use the IPF described earlier. It is worth noting that the IPF is highly correlated with some other variables (see table 6.A3). For instance, it is positively associated with the progress in economic reforms and negatively with the occurrence of civil conflicts.[34] It is noteworthy that the regression results do not indicate that the extent of political rights and civil liberties has an independent impact on income inequality (see column 4, table 6.3). That does not preclude, though, the possibility that the degree of political democracy may affect income inequality indirectly (Gradstein, Milanovic, and Ying 2001).

A number of countries in the transitional region experienced the periods of civil conflicts and wars over the last decade. Therefore, I also look at the impact of civil wars on income inequality by estimating the pooled regression with a dummy for civil conflicts constructed as discussed earlier.[35] Since this dummy is highly correlated with the level of per capita GDP (see table 6.A3), I omit GDPPC and GDPPC_S from the estimation. The regression results (see column 5, table 6.3) indicate that civil conflicts are associated with a 13.3 percent rise in income inequality.[36]

6.7 Sensitivity Analysis

In this section, I investigate the robustness of my findings. I first check whether the results are sensitive to the definition of the dependent variable. Although most of the Gini coefficients in the data set are based on disposable income, there are several data points based on other welfare concepts (see table 6.A1). As a first check of the robustness of the results described in section 6.6, I perform the estimation using disposable income Gini coefficients only. Since several Gini indexes in our sample come from other sources than the main data series used (the WIDER database) (see table 6.A1), I also examine the sensitivity of the findings to the omission of these observations. Finally, I estimate the model by including only those Gini coefficients that are based on the same welfare definition *within* countries.[37] The resulting parameter estimates are reported in table 6.4.[38]

Similarly to the results reported in table 6.2 (quadratic specification), all estimations shown in table 6.4 strongly support a U-shaped relationship between income inequality and per capita GDP. The estimated coefficients on GDPPC and GDPPC_S are larger than their counterparts in table 6.2.[39] Although the parameter estimates on INDVA and PRIVS differ somewhat from sample to sample (see columns 2–4, table 6.4), which is quite natural given the variation in the representation of countries and time periods across the samples, they are generally in line with those reported in table 6.2. I note that the coefficient on inflation is significant in one case only (see column 2, table 6.4). In the light of our finding that there is a clear threshold effect in the relationship between inflation and inequality this result is not surprising, since the samples differ in the number of high-inflation observations.

I am aware of the literature that advises to make a regression-based additive adjustment of the Gini coefficients based on different concepts for the purpose of cross-country comparisons. This approach, however, hinges on a very strong assumption, namely that the differences in Gini coefficients based on different concepts are the same across countries and over time. For transition countries, this assumption clearly does not hold. For instance, the comparison of the consumption-based Gini coefficient with the disposable income-based one obtained from the *same* survey data indicate that the former is 2 percentage points *higher* than the latter in Poland, is

Table 6.4
Fixed-effects estimates from the regression of the Gini coefficient on selected explanatory variables: Robustness to the definition of the dependent variable and the choice of the data series

Explanatory variable 1	Full model (disposable income Gini coefficients only) 2	Full model (the WIDER database Gini coefficients only) 3	Full model (Gini coefficients based on the same definition within countries) 4
Intercept			
GDPPC	−6.623***	−6.910***	−5.727***
	(1.395)	(1.243)	(1.293)
GDPPC_S	0.388***	0.399***	0.334***
	(0.083)	(0.073)	(0.077)
INFL	0.032**	0.007	0.013
	(0.016)	(0.013)	(0.015)
UNEMP	0.023	0.025	0.019
	(0.025)	(0.021)	(0.024)
CONSG	−0.043	−0.079	−0.062
	(0.067)	(0.051)	(0.060)
INDVA	−0.179*	−0.287***	−0.205**
	(0.107)	(0.069)	(0.101)
PRIVS	0.133***	0.082***	0.113***
	(0.032)	(0.029)	(0.029)
Number of countries	18	21	23
Number of observations	100	110	113
R^2 adj.	0.58	0.66	0.55
F-value	18.44	29.48	18.35
Estimated threshold level (PPP-adjusted GDP per capita, 1992 USD)	5084	5758	5284

Note: All variables are in the natural log form. Standard errors are presented in parentheses. The model is estimated in deviations from the group means. The Yule-Walker (iterated) method was used to correct for serial correlation and heteroskedasticity.
*indicates significance at 10 percent level; **indicates significance at 5 percent level; ***indicates significance at 1 percent level (two-tailed tests).

of the same magnitude in Russia, and is 5 percentage points lower in Georgia (World Bank 2000). Thus, for these countries such an adjustment can hardly be an improvement. In this situation the only solution is to use observations on inequality that are "as fully consistent as possible" (Atkinson and Brandolini 2001).

That is what I attempt to do in this chapter. It is important to note also that since I use the fixed effects estimation any adjustments to the Gini coefficients based on the *same* concept *within* countries would be canceled out anyway. Moreover, when I estimate the pooled regression by including dummies for Gini coefficients based on different concepts, I do not find those dummies to be significant.[40]

I also investigate the robustness of the results to the use of the random effects rather than fixed effects estimation technique. The regression results (see table 6.5) indicate that the fixed effects and random effects estimates are generally very similar.

I next verify to what extent the results could be driven by observations for a particular time period. The parameter estimates are found to be fairly robust to the removal of any single period from the estimation.[41] I note, however, that the coefficient on inflation shows to be insignificant when the model is estimated without data for 1993. That is not surprising since for most countries in the transitional region 1993 was the year of hyperinflation. Thus, the elimination of this year from the estimation is likely to substantially underestimate the impact of inflation on the distribution of income.

As the countries in the sample differ widely in their levels of development and growth experiences during the transition (despite being collectively referred to as transitional economies), it is necessary to investigate the robustness of the results to the regional coverage. I first test the robustness of the results with respect to countries by removing one country at a time. Although the values of the coefficients (not reported here) fluctuate slightly, their magnitudes and significance levels are largely in line with those reported.

In view of the countries' differences in institutional characteristics and macroeconomic performance during the transition, I then estimate the model separately for the FSU and EE regions. I do not argue that such a division of countries into subsamples is perfect as countries within EE and the FSU regions are not homogenous, but it seems to be a natural choice in many respects. First, economic decline in EE was on average less profound and persistent than in the FSU. Second, income inequality in EE has increased much less

Table 6.5
Random-effects estimates from the regression of the Gini coefficient on selected explanatory variables: All countries

Explanatory variable 1	Full model (quadratic relationship) 2	Full model (linear relationship) 3	Reduced model 1 (quadratic relationship) 4	Reduced model 2 (quadratic relationship) 5
Intercept	19.749*** (4.288)	6.638*** (0.464)	17.926*** (4.218)	20.524*** (4.682)
GDPPC	−3.427*** (1.030)	−0.234*** (0.046)	−2.811*** (1.011)	−3.673*** (1.115)
GDPPC_S	0.190*** (0.061)		0.151*** (0.060)	0.197*** (0.066)
INFL	0.027** (0.013)	0.025* (0.014)	0.021 (0.014)	
UNEMP	−0.003 (0.020)	−0.017 (0.020)	0.027* (0.016)	0.073*** (0.016)
CONSG	−0.036 (0.047)	−0.057 (0.048)	−0.080* (0.046)	−0.094* (0.052)
INDVA	−0.312*** (0.073)	−0.352*** (0.075)	−0.389*** (0.071)	
PRIVS	0.080*** (0.027)	0.068** (0.028)		
Number of countries	24	24	24	24
Number of observations	129	129	129	129
R^2 adj.	0.64	0.62	0.63	0.53
Estimated threshold level (PPP-adjusted GDP per capita, 1992 USD)	8374		13422	11260

Note: All variables are in the natural log form. Standard errors are presented in parentheses.
*indicates significance at 10 percent level; **indicates significance at 5 percent level; ***indicates significance at 1 percent level (two-tailed tests).

than in the FSU. Third, in contrast to the FSU, most EE countries already had at least some rudimentary elements of the market economy (e.g., a private sector) before the transition, and were much more effective with reform implementation during the transition. Finally, social safety nets in EE during the transition are widely recognized to have been much stronger than in the FSU.

The results of separate estimations for the FSU and EE are presented in table 6.6. A number of interesting observations can be made based on them. First, when the estimation is performed separately for the FSU and EE countries, a U–shaped relationship between income inequality and the level of economic development becomes less evident for the FSU and collapses completely for EE. The estimation of the respecified model (excluding GDPPC_S to test for the linear relationship) indicates that the inequality-development relationship is in fact linear within these regions. Moreover, the parameter estimate on GDPPC is negative for the FSU region, but positive for EE countries (see columns 4–5, table 6.6). These results are consistent with the found for the whole sample threshold effect in the relationship between income inequality and economic development. In fact, while the FSU countries mostly fell below the estimated threshold level of per capita GDP, EE countries were positioned mostly above the threshold. The estimated coefficients on GDPPC suggest that a $1,000 increase in per capita GDP (constant 1992 prices) at the region-specific means would be associated with a 2.12 Gini point decrease in income inequality at the mean in the FSU and a 0.89 Gini point increase in income inequality at the mean in EE.

A question of great interest is what makes economic growth push income inequality in different directions in the FSU and EE? It could be that explanation lies in the institutional environment in which the growth takes place. For instance, the levels of rent seeking and corruption in the FSU have been much higher than in EE. That may be one explanation of why income inequality in the former region has risen despite a dramatic economic decline.[42] It is also important to note that while the FSU countries were experiencing economic decline over most of the transition decade, the EE countries were growing.[43] The impact of economic recessions and recoveries on income distribution is not necessarily symmetric.

Inflation is found to have a significant impact on income inequality in the FSU countries, but not in EE. This result clearly comes from much higher inflation in the former region. In contrast to the FSU

Table 6.6
Fixed-effects estimates from the regression of the Gini coefficient on selected explanatory variables: EE versus the FSU

Explanatory variable 1	Full model FSU (quadratic relationship) 2	Full model EE (quadratic relationship) 3	Full model FSU (linear relationship) 4	Full model EE (linear relationship) 5
Intercept				
GDPPC	−2.766**	−3.424	−0.314***	0.252***
	(1.373)	(2.679)	(0.095)	(0.089)
GDPPC_S	0.146*	0.212		
	(0.082)	(0.154)		
INFL	0.039**	−0.031	0.039**	−0.026
	(0.019)	(0.020)	(0.019)	(0.020)
UNEMP	−0.014	0.047*	−0.028	0.031
	(0.042)	(0.024)	(0.042)	(0.021)
CONSG	−0.006	−0.076	−0.021	−0.046
	(0.072)	(0.061)	(0.073)	(0.055)
INDVA	−0.301**	−0.233**	−0.339**	−0.203**
	(0.127)	(0.094)	(0.129)	(0.091)
PRIVS	0.060	0.100***	0.044	0.118***
	(0.051)	(0.038)	(0.041)	(0.036)
Number of countries	15	9	15	9
Number of observations	65	64	65	64
R^2 adj.	0.72	0.67	0.70	0.65
F-value	20.83	20.11	22.88	21.99
Estimated threshold level (PPP-adjusted GDP per capita, 1992 USD)				

Note: All variables are in the natural log form. Standard errors are presented in parentheses. The model is estimated in deviations from the group means. The Yule-Walker (iterated) method was used to correct for serial correlation and heteroskedasticity.
*indicates significance at 10 percent level; **indicates significance at 5 percent level; ***indicates significance at 1 percent level (two-tailed tests).

countries, many of which experienced hyperinflation (with annual inflation measured in hundreds percent), most EE countries witnessed inflation rates relatively modest by transitional standards.

Deindustrialization appears to be associated with rising income inequality in both EE and the FSU regions. This finding is robust to the alternative model specifications. The estimated coefficients from the linear specifications (see columns 4–5, table 6.6) suggest that a 10 percent decline in the share of industrial sector in the economy would be associated with a 1.17 and 0.54 percentage point increase in the Gini index at the region-specific means in the FSU and EE, respectively.

The parameter estimates on PRIVS suggest that the growing private sector had an inequality-increasing effect exclusively in EE countries. This result is robust to the model specification. For instance, when INDVA is omitted from the regression, the coefficient on PRIVS becomes even more significant for EE, but remains insignificant for the FSU. The differential impact of privatization in two regions is striking given that the private sector expanded markedly in all economies. It is clearly a look at what makes privatization processes in EE and the FSU different that may provide the explanation. For instance, one consequence of the growing private sector in EE was a significant increase in returns to education and a rise in wage disparities (World Bank 2000). Conversely, privatization in the FSU countries did not substantially raise educational premiums, probably because of the excess supply of highly skilled labor.

Unemployment is not found to affect income distribution. The parameter estimate is only marginally significant for EE in one specification (see column 3, table 6.6). I have also tried several other specifications of the model and the results (not shown here) generally suggest that the exclusion of at least one variable reflecting the structural change in the economy, such as PRIVS or INDVA, from the linear model makes the coefficient on UNEMP significant (at a 10% level) for EE, but not for the FSU. The share of government consumption in GDP does not appear to explain the distributional outcomes neither in EE nor in the FSU.

With regard to the impact of CLI and IPF on income distribution in EE and the FSU, the regression results suggest that economic liberalization was associated with rising income inequality in both regions (see columns 2–3, table 6.7). The extent of political freedom, however, does not affect income inequality in either region.[44]

Table 6.7
Estimates from the regression of the Gini coefficient on selected explanatory variables:
EE versus the FSU

Explanatory variable	Model with CLI (LSDV) FSU	Model with CLI (LSDV) EE	Model with war dummy (pooled regression) FSU	Model with war dummy (pooled regression) EE
1	2	3	4	5
Intercept			4.440***	4.510***
			(0.488)	(0.626)
GDPPC	−0.386***	0.243***		
	(0.105)	(0.096)		
Inflation > 500	0.122**	0.006	0.208***	−0.026
dummy[a]	(0.059)	(0.051)	(0.047)	(0.059)
UNEMP	−0.050	0.001	−0.005	0.047
	(0.041)	(0.025)	(0.036)	(0.031)
CONSG	−0.082	−0.046	−0.024	−0.209***
	(0.084)	(0.055)	(0.078)	(0.058)
INDVA	−0.222*	−0.201*	−0.376***	−0.286**
	(0.133)	(0.103)	(0.102)	(0.136)
PRIVS			0.132***	0.068*
			(0.050)	(0.040)
CLI	0.039***	0.041***		
	(0.019)	(0.008)		
IPF				
War dummy			0.112*	0.193***
			(0.067)	(0.061)
Number of countries	15	9	15	9
Number of observations	65	64	65	64
R^2 adj.	0.999	0.999	0.69	0.64
F-value	2705.14	8450.25	15.71	10.57
Estimated threshold level (PPP-adjusted GDP per capita, 1992 USD)				

Note: All variables are in the natural log form. Standard errors are presented in parentheses. Yule-Walker (iterated) method was used to correct for serial correlation and heteroskedasticity.

[a] excluded category is inflation < 20 percent annual. The coefficients on other categories (21–50, 51–100, 101–500) are not reported since they are not significant.

*indicates significance at 10 percent level; **indicates significance at 5 percent level; ***indicates significance at 1 percent level (two-tailed tests).

I also look at the impact of civil conflicts on income distribution separately for EE and the FSU regions using the pooled regressions. The regression results (see columns 4–5, table 6.7) indicate that the periods of civil wars were associated with rising income inequality in both regions.

Finally, it is worth noting that the results obtained from the separate estimations for EE and the FSU must be treated with caution due to the relatively small regional samples.

6.8   Conclusions

The main goal of this chapter is to identify the factors that caused dramatic changes in income inequality in the transitional countries of EE and the FSU throughout the 1990s. The empirical analysis is performed using a unique panel of inequality estimates that cover twenty-four transitional countries over the period 1989–1998. The econometric approach employs panel data estimation methods.

I find support for a normal U-shaped relationship between income inequality and per capita GDP for the transitional region as a whole. It suggests that for a country below (above) some threshold level of development economic growth is associated with falling (rising) income inequality. Specifically, the relationship between income inequality and economic growth is shown to be negative for countries of EE, but positive for those of the FSU. The results suggest that economic recovery-promoting policies may certainly have an equalizing effect on income distribution in some transition countries. However, at least in the short run, there can be a trade-off between economic growth and income inequality in other countries.

Although undoubtedly important, the relationship between income inequality and economic growth does not represent the main focus of this study. I have searched for specific economic factors and noneconomic forces that determine the changes in income distribution during the transition.

The empirical results indicate that economic liberalization and structural adjustments are associated with rising income inequality. More specifically, I find that a 10 percent increase in the CLI at the mean is associated with a 0.27 and 0.34 percentage point increase in the Gini coefficient at the region-specific means in the FSU and EE countries, respectively. De-industrialization has a strong impact on income distribution in both regions. A 10 percent decline in the share of industrial sector in the economy is related to a 1.17 and 0.54 percentage point increase in the Gini coefficient at the mean in the FSU and EE countries, respectively. Although the economies of both EE and the FSU regions have been substantially privatized during the transition, the evidence suggests that a rapidly growing private sector has contributed to rising income inequality in EE countries only. A 10 percent growth in the share of private sector in the economy is associated with a 0.31 percentage point increase in the Gini coefficient at the mean in these countries.

It is important to note that some increase in income inequality due to structural reforms associated with the transition from centrally planned to market economy is largely inevitable and should not be considered in the negative light. These reforms may have sizable longer-term rewards by strengthening incentives, creating new jobs, and fostering economic growth. Ultimately, it is better to be unequally rich than equally poor. Nevertheless, the policies aimed at facilitating the transition of workers from the public to the private sector, and from the manufacturing sector to services, may be of paramount importance for the distributional outcomes of the reforms. Although there is some evidence to suggest that unemployment may be positively associated with income inequality, the effect is not robust to model specification.

The degree of government involvement in the economy through government consumption generally does not seem to have an impact on income distribution. I find that hyperinflation makes the distribution of income more unequal. This finding may certainly contribute to the explanation of why income inequality in the FSU countries (most of which experienced hyperinflation at the start of the transition) increased much more than in EE countries, where inflation levels have been relatively moderate. The important policy implication of this finding is that macroeconomic stabilization not only fosters economic recovery, but is also beneficial in terms of distributional outcomes.

Finally, I have also investigated the role of some forces outside economic domain in determining income inequality in transition economies. The empirical evidence indicates that civil conflicts are associated with rising income inequality. On average, they lead to a 13.3 percent higher income inequality. The extent of political rights and civil liberties, measured by the IPF, is not found to affect income distribution. Nevertheless, this index is strongly correlated with the indicators of structural changes in the economy, suggesting that political rights and civil liberties are likely to affect income distribution indirectly.

To conclude, the avenue of research undertaken in this chapter appears promising, for it reveals forces influencing income distribution in transitional countries. However, I certainly have not exhausted all factors explaining the dynamics of income inequality in the transitional region, and thus further research here may be beneficial.

6.9 Appendix

Table 6.A1
Description of the Inequality Data Used in the Empirical Analysis

Region/country 1	Start 2	End 3	No. of obs. 4	Gini index (start) 5	Gini index (end) 6	Max. value (year) 7	Welfare measure 8	Area/population coverage 9	Sample/reference unit 10	Source (year) 12
I. FSU										
a. Baltic states										
Estonia	1989	1998	9	23.00	36.97	36.97 (98)	DI, GI (90)	All/All	HH/HH pc	WIID, BM (89)
Latvia	1989	1998	5	22.50	32.10	32.60 (97)	DI, GI (89)	All/All	HH/HH pc	WIID, BM (89)
Lithuania	1989	1999	6	22.50	34.00	35.04 (94)	DI, GI (89)	All/All	HH/HH pc	WIID, BM (89), WB (99)
b. Western CIS										
Belarus	1989	1999	5	22.80	26.00	26.00 (99)	DI, GI (89)	All/All	HH/HH pc	WIID, BM (89), WB (99)
Moldova	1993	1997	2	36.50	42.00	42.00 (97)	DI, GI (93)	All/All	HH/HH pc	BM (93), WB (97)
Russia	1989	1996	5	23.80	37.83	37.83 (96)	GI	All/All	HH/HH pc	WIID, BM (89)
Ukraine	1989	1999	6	25.80	32.00	32.00 (99)	DI, GI (97)	All/All	HH/HH pc	WIID, WB (99)
c. Caucasus										
Armenia	1990	1998	6	26.90	59.00	62.14 (95)	DI, GI (90)	All/All	HH/HH pc	WIID, WB (98)
Azerbaijan	1995	1999	2	44.00	43.00	44.00 (95)	CS	All/All	HH/HH pc	WB
Georgia	1989	1997	4	31.30	51.86	58.71 (96)	DI, GI (88, 90)	All/All	HH/HH pc	WIID

d. Central Asia										
Kazakhstan	1990	1996	4	29.70	35.00	35.00 (96)	DI, GI (90, 93)	All/All	HH/HH pc	WIID, WB (96)
Kyrgyz Republic	1990	1997	3	30.80	47.00	55.30 (93)	DI, GI (90)	All/All	HH/HH pc	WIID, BM (93), WB (97)
Tajikistan	1989	1990	2	31.80	33.40	33.40 (90)	GI	All/All	HH/HH pc	WIID
Turkmenistan	1989	1993	3	31.60	35.80	35.80 (93)	DI, GI (89, 90)	All/All	HH/HH pc	WIID
Uzbekistan	1990	1994	3	31.50	33.00	33.30 (93)	DI, GI (90, 94)	All/All	HH/HH pc	WIID
II. Central EE										
Czech Republic	1989	1997	9	19.36	27.64	28.14 (96)	DI	All/All	HH/HH pc	WIID
Hungary	1989	1997	7	21.41	24.58	24.58 (97)	DI	All/All	HH/HH pc	WIID
Poland	1989	1998	9	25.05	32.00	34.20 (97)	DI	All/All	HH/HH pc	WIID, WB (98)
Slovak Rep.	1989	1997	9	18.06	23.36	24.83 (96)	DI	All/All	HH/HH pc	WIID
III. South EE										
Bulgaria	1989	1997	8	24.47	34.59	34.78 (96)	DI, GI (89, 91)	All/All	HH/HH pc, HH (89, 98)	WIID
Romania	1989	1997	9	23.24	30.27	31.18 (95)	DI	All/All	HH/HH pc	WIID
IV. FY										
Croatia	1989	1998	4	25.10	33.30	33.30 (98)	DI	All/All	HH/HH pc	WIID
Macedonia	1990	1997	5	34.90	36.65	36.94 (96)	DI	All/All	HH/HH pc	WIID
Slovenia	1991	1998	4	22.71	25.00	25.05 (93)	DI	All/All	HH/HH pc	WIID, WB (98)

Sources: UNU/WIDER-UNDP World Income Inequality Database, Version 1.0, September 12, 2000, provides further reference on the source and estimation methodology for each data point drawn from this database. The data by Branko Milanovic are from appendix 4, "The Original Income Distribution Statistics," in his book *Income, Inequality and Poverty during the Transition from Planned to Market Economy* (1998). The data by the World Bank are taken from appendix D, "Poverty and Inequality Tables," in the book *Making Transition Work for Everyone: Poverty and Inequality in Europe and Central Asia* (World Bank 2000).

Note: Disposable income (DI) is equal to *gross income* (GI) minus payroll and direct personal income taxes (PIT). Gross income consists of earnings from labor, cash social transfers, self-employment income, other income (gifts, income from property) and in-kind consumption (e.g., agricultural products grown on a household's plot of land). It is argued (Milanovic 1998) that the difference between gross and disposable incomes is negligible for transition countries (especially for the pretransition period) as gross income already excludes payroll taxes withdrawn at the source, and PIT is minimal (less than one percent of gross income). That allows one to use the Gini coefficients based on gross incomes as the benchmarks for the levels of income inequality observed before the transition (mostly for the FSU countries, for which the pretransition disposable income Gini indexes are not available). It is very important to have these pretransition observations in the sample since the evidence suggests that most of the variation in income inequality over time has taken place over the initial period of transition and economic collapse. As the first transition period surveys were often conducted a few years into the transition process, by taking the estimates of inequality derived solely from these surveys one would significantly underestimate the changes in inequality over time (which is what I want to explain).

The Gini coefficients for Romania and Macedonia are based on disposable monetary income, which does not include in-kind consumption. These Gini coefficients are likely to overestimate the *levels* of inequality, but not the *changes* in inequality. Note that two data points (Azerbaijan, 1995, 1999) are Gini coefficients based on *consumption* (CS). These observations are used due to the lack of alternatives. They are not found to influence the overall results. The Gini index for 1988 is used in the absence of 1989 data.

The data coming from the Family Budget Surveys (FBS) (mostly 1989 data in our sample) are not completely representative and may underestimate inequality as FBS excluded pensioner-headed households and households headed by the unemployed. However, the estimates of inequality obtained from transition-year surveys can also be downward-biased due to decreased response rates among the rich, inadequate coverage of informal sector incomes, etc. (for a detailed discussion of these and other data issues see Milanovic 1998). It is not clear, though, how all these biases would, on the net, affect the *changes* in inequality. In any case, there is not much that one can do about these sorts of problems except trying to use observations that are "as fully consistent as possible" (Atkinson and Brandolini 2001). That was a guiding principle in the compilation of the data.

Table 6.A2
Descriptive Statistics and Variance Decomposition

Variable	Mean	Min	Max	Std. Dev. Overall	Between	Within
GINI	30.5	17.8	62.1	9.21	7.87	5.14
GDPPC	6322.4	1649.9	13764.9	2789.40	2680.60	1191.45
INFL	247.7	−7.6	9750.0	945.22	669.02	793.09
UNEMP	7.9	0.0	38.8	7.39	6.84	3.89
CONSG	18.0	6.0	27.4	4.96	4.27	2.90
INDVA	38.2	15.3	67.4	8.71	5.30	7.02
PRIVS	38.4	5.0	75.0	21.44	13.64	17.55
CLI	2.6	0.0	7.7	2.11	1.21	1.81
IPF	3.4	1.5	7.0	1.60	1.44	0.89

Source: Author's calculations.

Note: The number of observations for all variables is 129. The overall and within (over time) standard deviations are calculated over all 129 observations. The between (across countries) standard deviation is calculated over the means for twenty-four countries.

GDPPC = GDP per capita, PPP-adjusted USD in 1992 prices;

INFL = Inflation rate, measured by the year-on-year change in CPI (percent);

UNEMP = Share of unemployed in total labor force (percent);

CONSG = Government consumption as share of GDP (percent);

INDVA = Share of industry value added in GDP (percent);

PRIVS = Private sector share in GDP (percent);

CLI = Cumulative Liberalization Index (score);

IPF = Index of Political Freedom (score).

Table 6.A3
The matrix of the Pearson correlation coefficients

	GINI	GDPPC	INFL	UNEMP	CONSG	INDVA	PRIVS	WAR_D	CLI	IPF
GINI	1.00	—	—	—	—	—	—	—	—	—
GDPPC	-0.75 (0.00)	1.00	—	—	—	—	—	—	—	—
INFL	0.15 (0.10)	-0.25 (0.01)	1.00	—	—	—	—	—	—	—
UNEMP	0.26 (0.00)	-0.12 (0.18)	-0.05 (0.55)	1.00	—	—	—	—	—	—
CONSG	-0.24 (0.01)	0.14 (0.11)	-0.04 (0.68)	-0.01 (0.99)	1.00	—	—	—	—	—
INDVA	-0.62 (0.00)	0.41 (0.00)	0.14 (0.10)	-0.42 (0.00)	0.05 (0.58)	1.00	—	—	—	—
PRIVS	0.30 (0.00)	-0.11 (0.22)	-0.22 (0.01)	0.52 (0.00)	-0.12 (0.17)	-0.51 (0.00)	1.00	—	—	—
WAR_D	0.56 (0.00)	-0.43 (0.00)	0.35 (0.00)	0.09 (0.30)	-0.27 (0.00)	-0.29 (0.00)	-0.02 (0.86)	1.00	—	—
CLI	0.25 (0.00)	0.04 (0.68)	-0.27 (0.00)	0.68 (0.00)	0.04 (0.63)	-0.51 (0.00)	0.81 (0.00)	-0.05 (0.56)	1.00	—
IPF	0.11 (0.20)	-0.37 (0.00)	0.27 (0.00)	-0.49 (0.00)	-0.11 (0.22)	0.21 (0.02)	-0.57 (0.00)	0.31 (0.00)	-0.59 (0.00)	1.00

Note: All variables except WAR_D, CLI and IPF are in the natural log form. $\ln(1 + \text{INFL}/100)$ and $\ln(1 + \text{UNEMP})$ are used for respectively INFL and UNEMP. WAR_D is a dummy variable equal to 1 for each year since an internal conflict has taken place in a given country. The values in parentheses indicate Prob. $> |r|$ under H_0: Rho $= 0$; (0.00) means that the p-value is less than 0.005. Dashes indicate data are not available.

Notes

I am grateful to Arne Bigsten, Francois Bourguignon, Bjorn Gustafsson, Stephan Klasen, Michael Lokshin, Per Lundborg, Jukka Pirtillä, Ali Tasiran, an anonymous referee and seminar participants at the 2001 Panel Data Workshop at Gothenburg University, 2001 Jamboree Conference at Mannheim University, 2001 CESifo Conference in Munich, 2001 WIDER Conference in Helsinki, and 2002 CESifo Conference in Elmau for useful comments on an earlier draft of this chapter. I am entirely responsible for all remaining errors.

1. In many countries of the FSU the outputs declined to 30–40 percent of their pre-transition levels.

2. A number of recent studies (e.g., Forbes 2000) suggest, however, that in the short run the relationship between inequality and growth could be positive.

3. Grun and Klasen (2001) applied a set of inequality-adjusted indicators of well-being to measure aggregate welfare in transition countries. They found that an adjustment for inequality significantly influences the ranking of transition countries in terms of their absolute levels of well-being and the achievements in well-being over time.

4. In our sample, the mean annual inflation is 248 percent, and the maximum is 9,750 percent (Turkmenistan 1993).

5. The regressivity of the inflation tax and imperfect indexation have been found, using micro-level data, to increase income inequality in Brazil during the years of high inflation (Ferreira and Litchfield 1998).

6. The official unemployment statistics are likely to significantly understate the real level of unemployment. Indeed, unofficial estimates indicate significantly higher levels of unemployment. Moreover, many people are registered as employed even when they are not receiving payment for their labor.

7. Government consumption, however, can affect the distribution of income not only on the expenditure side, but also through the tax collection.

8. Another mechanism for government to influence income distribution is through social security transfers. These transfers are found to reduce inequality in a cross-country study of both advanced and developing countries by Milanovic (1994), but appear insignificant in a study of OECD countries by Gustafsson and Johansson (1999). I do not analyze the impact of social transfers in this chapter due to the lack of data.

9. The level of income inequality in EE and the FSU before the transition was widely considered to be lower than in the rest of the world (Atkinson and Micklewright 1992).

10. In many transitional countries the share of private sector in total economy has increased from barely existing to from 50 to 60 percent.

11. Diminishing relative importance of the industrial and/or agricultural sector was offset by the growing relative importance of services sector, which in many countries has increased 1.5–2 times.

12. Note that if the labor force moves from the remaining state-owned industrial sector to the private sector, the potential effect of this on income distribution would be captured by the privatization variable.

13. About half of the WIID database is formed by K. Deininger and L. Squire's 1996 database. However, for the transitional region most of the data in the database come from the UNICEF/IRC TransMonee2000 Database, Florence.

14. In the original WIID database most of the countries are represented with multiple time series of inequality estimates that often are not compatible.

15. As there are only five observations for 1999, in the estimation they are used as 1998 values.

16. This is true, however, only if these differences are *systematic*. I am thankful to a referee for pointing this out to me.

17. As a check of how good this proxy is, I estimate the model with the industrial employment variable as well. The results (discussed in what follows) indicate that industry value added is a very good proxy indeed.

18. The data are updated up to 1998.

19. The assumption is that the effect of civil conflict (if any) on income inequality is likely to persist for a certain period.

20. In the case of Russia, I refer to the military conflict in Chechnya.

21. See ⟨http://www.alertnet.org⟩.

22. The results of these tests are not shown but are readily available upon request from the author.

23. H_0 is that there is no correlation. The test statistic is distributed as X_k^2, where k denotes the dimension of the slope vector β (Baltagi 1995, 68).

24. The random effects estimator combines the within and between estimators, thus giving some weight to the cross-country variation.

25. F-test of the null hypothesis that country-specific effects are not significant yields an F-value of 6.14, which is higher than a critical value of 2.07. This means that I can reject the hypothesis that there are no country-specific effects of omitted variables. The same test was conducted for time effects. In this case the $F_{9,88}$ statistic was 2.10, indicating that it is not possible to reject the hypothesis of no time-specific effects. Hence, the use of the one-way model is appropriate.

26. Specifying the original formulation of equation (1) as $y_{it} = \alpha_i + \beta'X_{it} + \varepsilon_{it}$, the formulation in terms of deviations from the country means becomes:

$$(y_{it} - \bar{y}_i) = \beta'(X_{it} - \bar{X}_i) + (\varepsilon_{it} - \bar{\varepsilon}_i), \quad \text{where } \bar{y}_i = \Sigma y_{it}/t; \bar{X}_i = \Sigma X_{it}/t; \bar{\varepsilon}_i = \Sigma \varepsilon_{it}/t.$$

27. I note here that the test of multicollinearity for the linear model indicates that the highest condition index equals 4.17, which is below a cutoff point of 10 suggested in the literature. Hence, I do not have a problem of severe collinearity in the estimation of the model.

28. To detect outliers and influential cases, I have conducted influence diagnostics such as the studentized residuals, the "hat" matrix, the COVRATIO statistic, DFFITS, and DFBETAS (Belsley, Kuh, and Welsch 1980; Bollen and Jackman 1985). I then deleted those observations that were detected influential by at least three tests. These observations turned out to be Moldova (1990), Russia (1998), Tajikistan (1998), and Uzbekistan (1989). However, when the model is estimated with these outliers included the results are very similar to those reported in table 6.2.

29. I have also estimated the model with GDPPC and GDPPC_S being the only explanatory variables. The parameter estimates (not shown here) on both terms are statistically significant at 1 percent and 5 percent levels respectively (negative for GDPPC and positive for GDPPC_S). The F-test statistics for their joint significance is 45.71 (significant at a 1% level). Adjusted R^2 for the model is equal to 0.46.

30. The recent study by the World Bank (2000) has found that inflation *volatility* is also associated with distributional costs in the transitional region.

31. Unemployment data can also be a poor indicator of labor market conditions since in many transition countries adjustments in the labor market manifested themselves in underemployment and nonpayment of wages rather than in the shedding of labor.

32. I note that when the model is estimated using the available observations on the industrial sector employment as a share of total employment (100 observations, 23 countries), instead of those on INDVA, the parameter estimate is nearly identical to the one on INDVA reported in table 6.2. These estimation results are not reported here for brevity.

33. This finding is in contrast to that reported in the World Bank (2000), where they use the same reform index as I do, but a smaller sample of countries (20) and a different estimation technique (a pooled regression rather than fixed effects).

34. Note that the higher value of the IPF means fewer political rights and civil liberties.

35. The fixed effects model cannot be estimated in this setting. Thus I perform a pooled regression. A pooled regression refers to an OLS regression with a single overall intercept.

36. The civil war dummy remains significant at a 5 percent level even when GDPPC and GDPPC_S enter the regression. The estimated effect, however, is slightly lower in this case than the one reported.

37. Note that the estimation of the model in deviations from the country means requires that the Gini coefficients are as comparable as possible *within* countries over time but not necessarily across countries. For this reason, the use of consumption-based Gini coefficients for Azerbaijan (see table 6.A1) does not cause a problem since like is compared with like. The same applies to the disposable monetary income Gini coefficients for Romania and Macedonia.

38. Unfortunately, I cannot test the robustness of our findings to the use of alternative measures of inequality, as only the Gini coefficients are available.

39. One may not conclude here on the quality of different data series, though, as the changes in the parameter estimates could be driven by exclusion of the observations for particular countries and/or time periods.

40. The comparison category is Gini coefficient based on the household per capita disposable income.

41. These results are not shown here but are available from the author upon request.

42. I do not have sufficient longitudinal data on the levels of corruption in transitional countries to run the fixed effects regression. However, a simple regression of the average Gini coefficient during the transition period on the corruption perception index for sixteen transition countries of EE and the FSU indicates that higher corruption is associated with larger income inequality (the parameter estimate is significant

at a 7% level). The regression results are not shown here but are available from the author upon request.

43. This is reflected in the composition of our sample, where the majority of observations for the FSU and EE countries cover the periods of economic decline and economic recovery, respectively.

44. The results are not reported here but are available from the author upon request. I have also estimated several alternative specifications with IPF, but the parameter estimate on IPF is found to be insignificant.

References

Aghion, P., and S. Commander. 1999. "On the Dynamics of Inequality in the Transition." *Economics of Transition* 7(2): 275–298.

Ahluwalia, M. S. 1976. "Income Distribution and Development: Some Stylized Facts." *American Economic Review* 66: 125–135.

Alesina, A., and D. Rodrik. 1994. "Distributive Politics and Economic Growth." *Quarterly Journal of Economics* 109(2): 465–490.

Anand, S., and S. M. R. Kanbur. 1993. "Inequality and Development: A Critique." *Journal of Development Economics* 41: 19–43.

Atkinson, A., and A. Brandolini. 2001. "Promise and Pitfalls in the Use of 'Secondary' Data Sets: Income Inequality in OECD Countries as a Case Study." *Journal of Economic Literature* 39(2): 771–799.

Atkinson, A., and J. Micklewright. 1992. *Economic Transformation in Eastern Europe and the Distribution of Income.* Cambridge: Cambridge University Press.

Baltagi, B. H. 1995. *Econometric Analysis of Panel Data.* West Sussex, UK: John Wiley and Sons Ltd.

Barro, R. J. 1997. *Determinants of Economic Growth: A Cross-Country Empirical Study.* Cambridge: The MIT Press.

Belsley, D., E. Kuh, and R. E. Welsch. 1980. *Regression Diagnostics: Identifying Influential Data and Sources of Collinearity.* New York: Wiley.

Birdsall, N., D. Ross, and R. Sabot. 1995. "Inequality and Growth Reconsidered: Lessons from East Asia." *The World Bank Economics Review* 9(3): 477–508.

Bollen, K. A., and R. W. Jackman. 1985. "Regression Diagnostics: An Expository Treatment of Outliers and Influential Cases." *Sociological Methods and Research* 13: 510–542.

Bourguignon, F., and C. Morrison. 1998. "Inequality and Development: The Role of Dualism." *Journal of Development Economics* 57: 233–257.

Boyd, R. L. 1988. "Government Involvement in the Economy and the Distribution of Income: A Cross-National Study." *Population Research and Policy Review* 7: 223–238.

Bruno, M., M. Ravallion, and L. Squire. 1995. "Equity and Growth in Developing Countries: Old and New Perspectives on the Policy Issues." Paper prepared for the IMF Conference on Income Distribution and Sustainable Growth, Washington, DC.

Deininger, K., and L. Squire. 1996. "A New Data Set Measuring Income Inequality." *World Bank Economic Review* 10(3): 565–591.

Deininger, K., and L. Squire. 1998. "New Ways of Looking at Old Issues: Inequality and Growth." *Journal of Development Economics* 57: 259–287.

De Melo, M., C. Denizer, and A. Gelb. 1996. "From Plan to Market: Patterns of Transition." The World Bank Policy Research Paper No. 1564. Washington, DC.

Easterly, W. 2001. "The Middle Class Consensus and Economic Development." The World Bank Development Research Group Working Paper No. 2346. Washington, DC.

European Bank for Reconstruction and Development (EBRD). Various years. *Transition Report.*

Ferreira, F. H. G. 1999. "Economic Transition and the Distributions of Income and Wealth." *Economics of Transition* 7(2): 377–410.

Ferreira, F. H. G., and J. Litchfield. 1998. "The Roles of Structural Factors and Macroeconomic Instability in Explaining Brazilian Inequality in the 1980s." LSE Discussion Paper No. DARP 41.

Forbes, K. J. 2000. "A Reassessment of the Relationship between Inequality and Growth." *American Economic Review* 90(4): 869–887.

Freedom House. Index of Political Freedom. Available online at ⟨www.freedomhouse. org⟩.

Garner, T. I., and K. Terrell. 1998. "A Gini Decomposition Analysis of Inequality in the Czech and Slovak Republics during the Transition." *Economics of Transition* 6(1): 23–46.

Gradstein, M., B. Milanovic, and Y. Ying. 2001. "Democracy and Income Inequality: An Empirical Analysis." The World Bank Development Research Group Working Paper No. 2561. Washington, DC.

Granger, C. W. J. 1969. "Investigating Causal Relations by Econometric Models and Cross-Spectral Methods." *Econometrica* 37(3): 425–438.

Greene, W. H. 1997. *Econometric Analysis*, 3d ed. New York: Prentice-Hall International Inc.

Grun, C., and S. Klasen. 2001. "Growth, Income and Well-Being in Transition Countries." *Economics of Transition* 9(2): 359–394.

Gustafsson, B., and M. Johansson. 1999. "In Search of Smoking Guns: What Makes Income Inequality Vary Over Time in Different Countries?" *American Sociological Review* 64: 585–605.

Gustafsson, B., and E. Palmer. 1997. "Changes in Swedish Inequality: A Study of Equivalent Income 1975–1991." In *The Changing Distribution of Economic Well-Being— International Perspectives*, ed. P. Gottschalk, B. Gustafsson, and E. Palmer, 293–325. Cambridge, UK: Cambridge University Press.

Hsiao, C. 1986. *Analysis of Panel Data*. Cambridge, UK: Cambridge University Press.

Kuznets, S. 1955. "Economic Growth and Income Inequality." *American Economic Review*: 1–28.

Levy, F., and R. J. Murnane. 1992. "U.S. Earnings Levels and Earnings Inequality: A Review of Recent Trends and Proposed Explanations." *Journal of Economic Literature* 30: 1333–1381.

Li, H., L. Squire, and H. Zou. 1998. "Explaining International and Intertemporal Variations in Income Inequality." *Economic Journal* 108: 1–18.

Meier, T. 1973. "The Distributional Impact of the 1970 Recession." *Review of Economics and Statistics* 55: 214–224.

Metcalf, C. 1969. "The Size Distribution of Personal Income during the Business Cycle." *American Economic Review* 59: 657–668.

Milanovic, B. 1994. "Determinants of Cross-Country Income Inequality: An 'Augmented' Kuznets' Hypothesis." The World Bank Development Research Group Working Paper No. 1246. Washington, DC.

Milanovic, B. 1998. *Income, Inequality and Poverty during the Transition from Planned to Market Economy*. Washington, DC: The World Bank.

Milanovic, B. 1999. "Explaining the Increase in Inequality during Transition." *Economics of Transition* 7(2): 299–343.

Paukert, F. 1973. "Income Distribution at Different Levels of Development: A Survey of Evidence." *International Labour Review* 108: 97–125.

Persson, T., and G. Tabellini. 1994. "Is Inequality Harmful for Growth?" *American Economic Review* 84(3): 600–621.

Quah, D. 2001. "Some Simple Arithmetic on How Income Inequality and Economic Growth Matter." CESifo Working Paper.

Ravallion, M. 1995. "Growth and Poverty: Evidence for Developing Countries in the 1980s." *Economic Letters* 48: 411–417.

Rodrik, D. 1999. "Democracies Pay Higher Wages." *Quarterly Journal of Economics* 114: 707–738.

Stack, S. 1978. "The Effect of Direct Government Involvement in the Economy on the Degree of Inequality: A Cross-National Study." *American Sociological Review* 43: 880–888.

Sylwester, K. 2000. "Income Inequality, Education Expenditures, and Growth." *Journal of Development Economics* 63: 379–398.

Temple, J. 1999. "The New Growth Evidence." *Journal of Economic Literature* 37: 112–156.

Thurow, L. 1970. "Analyzing the American Income Distribution." *American Economic Review* 60: 261–269.

Weil, G. 1984. "Cyclical and Secular Influences on the Size Distribution of Personal Incomes in the UK: Some Econometric Tests." *Applied Economics* 16: 749–755.

World Bank. 2000. *Making Transition Work for Everyone: Poverty and Inequality in Europe and Central Asia*. Washington, DC.

Yemtsov, R. 2001. "Inequality and Income Distribution in Georgia." Discussion Paper No. 252. World Bank, Washington DC, and IZA, Bonn.

IV

The Political Economy of
Inequality

7

(Re-)Distribution of
Personal Incomes,
Education, and Economic
Performance across
Countries

Günther Rehme

7.1 Introduction

According to the Kuznets (1955), hypothesis *redistribution* that makes the income distribution more unequal should be beneficial in the earlier stages of development. The opposite would hold at later stages of development.

Following Perotti (1996), at least four theoretical approaches can be identified that link inequality, redistribution, and growth. All of them predict that growth increases as equality increases. Indeed a number of studies such as Alesina and Rodrik (1994), Persson and Tabellini (1994), or Perotti himself find that growth is *negatively* associated with income inequality across countries. This has established what may be called the *Conventional Consensus View* (CCV).

However, based on inequality data compiled by Deininger and Squire (1996) that consensus has been challenged by, for example, Li and Zou (1998), Forbes (2000), Barro (2000), and others who find a *nonrobust* or even *positive* association, especially for rich countries. These results may thus be called the *New Challenge View* (NCV).[1]

Whatever the association between growth and inequality might be, it would entail important consequences for the effect of redistribution on growth. One should bear in mind that income inequality and (income) redistribution are two distinct things. But they are related as follows: The economic system produces an income distribution and then the state intervenes to redistribute income by levying taxes and granting subsidies to satisfy some welfare target. After the state intervention, another income distribution emerges that may look quite different from the one before the intervention. The net effect of the intervention is usually called *redistribution*. Thus, a comparison between the distribution of personal incomes before and after taxes provides one with a picture of the level of redistribution.

The evidence about the link between *redistribution* and growth across countries is mixed.[2] For instance, Perotti (1993), Alesina and Rodrik (1994), and Persson and Tabellini (1994) show that redistribution causes lower growth. However, empirical studies such as Easterly and Rebelo (1993), or Sala-i-Martin (1996) find that there is a positive relation across countries. These results can be reconciled with theory by models along the lines of, for example, Galor and Zeira (1993), Saint-Paul and Verdier (1996), Chiu (1998), or Aghion, Caroli, and García-Peñalosa (1999).

This chapter focuses on schooling and argues that public education, its finance and the way it is undertaken (schooling technology) are important determinants of income inequality *and* growth.

In the model, human capital simultaneously determines growth and income inequality. In this framework the chapter identifies two redistribution mechanisms. On the one hand, redistribution occurs by means of direct fiscal redistribution from the well-off to the not-so-well-off. On the other hand, there is redistribution through taxes used for expenditure on public education, which redistributes income by changing the relative wages. It is shown that growth and pre-tax and post-tax income inequality—measured by the Gini coefficient—are first increasing and then decreasing in human capital. For a given level of human capital a less efficient education technology implies lower growth, but also lower after-tax income inequality and higher measured income redistribution. The intuition for this is straightforward: To maintain a given level of public education a less efficient education sector requires higher, redistributive taxes. In contrast, a more skill-intensive technology does not affect the education sector directly, but it implies higher growth and more inequality and lower measured redistribution for a given level of human capital.

Most of the recent NCV proponents have based their results on *unadjusted* inequality measures using the secondary data set of Deininger and Squire (1996). As shown by Atkinson and Brandolini (2001), there are pitfalls when using these data. In particular, they argue that "there is no real alternative to seeking data sets where the observations are as fully consistent as possible; at the same time, the choice of definition on which to standardize may affect the conclusions drawn" (796).

Therefore, this chapter uses reliable and consistently defined income data from the Luxembourg Income Study (LIS) for a sample of relatively rich countries. With these data the model's implications are then set against the empirical evidence. The data suggest the following:

The association between the education as well as the distributional variables and growth is not very strong. More secondary as well as tertiary education or more spending on overall education appear to be associated with higher growth. Pre-tax *and* post-tax income inequality are *negatively* related to growth, even when controlling for fertility.[3] Thus, the situation after redistribution is not conducive to growth, suggesting that more redistribution might raise long-run growth.

These findings are interpreted in light of research based on *unadjusted* measures of inequality, which mixes Gini coefficients for income before and after taxes. It is argued that the coefficients on *unadjusted* Gini coefficients are most likely to be biased upwards.

Controlling for standard variables such as initial income or fertility, the data reveal that the government expenditure on (all levels of) education is negatively associated with pre-tax and post-tax income inequality and positively related to redistribution.

Thus, the data suggest that the typical (rich) country would have higher growth and less inequality if it spent more on education given its education technology. If the latter becomes worse, higher inequality and lower growth might ensue, once policy reactions have responded to that change.

The chapter is organized as follows: Section 7.2 presents the theoretical model and derives testable predictions. Section 7.3 confronts the model with empirical evidence. Section 7.4 provides concluding remarks.

7.2 The Model

Consider an economy that is populated by N (large) members of two representative dynasties of infinitely lived individuals. The two dynasties are made up of *high-skilled* people, L_h, and *low-skilled* people, L_l, where L_h, L_l denote the total numbers of the respective agents in each dynasty. The difference between the agents is "lumpy," that is, *either* an individual has received education certified in the form of a degree and is then considered high-skilled *or* it has no degree and remains in the low-skilled labor pool.

By assumption the population is stationary with $L_h \equiv xN$ and
$L_l \equiv (1 - x)N$, where x denotes the percentage of high-skilled people
in the population. Each individual supplies one unit of either high-
or low-skilled labor inelastically over time. Furthermore, the high-
skilled agents own an equal share of the total capital stock, which is
held in the form of shares of many identical firms operating in a
world of perfect competition. Thus, high-skilled agents receive wage
and capital income and make investment decisions, whereas low-
skilled agents do not, as they do not own capital by assumption.

Aggregating over firms overall output is produced according to

$$Y_t = B_t K_t^{1-\alpha} H^\alpha, H^\alpha = [(L_h + L_l)^\alpha + \beta L_h^\alpha], \qquad 0 < \alpha < 1, \qquad (7.1)$$

where K_t denotes the aggregate capital stock including disembodied
technological knowledge, H measures effective labor in production,
and B_t is a productivity index. The production function is a *reduced
form* of the following relationship: By assumption *effective labor* depends on tasks requiring *basic skills* and tasks requiring *high skills*.
These tasks are *imperfect substitutes* in production. On the other hand,
low- and high-skilled people are taken to be *perfect substitutes* in performing *basic* tasks. Thus, high-skilled people always perform the
tasks of low-skilled people in the model, but low-skilled people can
never execute tasks that require a degree. See Rehme (1999) for more
details.

The parameter β measures skill-biased productivity differences,
that is, it captures how *productively* tasks, which require high skills,
contribute to the generation of output in relation to tasks requiring
low skills.[4] Notice that each type of labor alone is *not* taken to be an
essential input in production.

The government runs a balanced budget and uses its tax revenues
to finance public education and to grant direct transfers to the low-
skilled workers.[5] Thus, the chapter contemplates two redistributive
mechanisms. On the one hand resources are redistributed directly
from the currently working, relatively rich high-skilled people to the
currently working, relatively poor low-skilled individuals. On the
other hand there is intertemporal redistribution from the currently
working high-skilled to the future high-skilled individuals whose
parents in turn may be low- or high-skilled.

For this the government taxes the accumulated factor of production, that is, it taxes the high-skilled agents' capital income at a constant rate $\vartheta \equiv \tau + \phi$. The capital stock (wealth) of the representative

high-skilled agent is $k_{ht} = K_t/L_h$ so that $G_t = \vartheta r_t k_{ht} L_h = \vartheta r_t K_t$, where r_t denotes the return on capital. This implies that $G_t/(r_t K_t) = \vartheta$ for all t. Thus, real resources $\vartheta r_t K_t = (\tau + \phi) r_t K_t$ are taken from the private sector where the amount $\tau r_t K_t$ is used to finance public education, which generates high-skilled agents.[6] In turn the amount $\phi r_t K_t$ is granted as transfers to the low-skilled and captures that the government corrects for post-education income differentials.[7]

In general, public education depends on government resources and other factors such as high-skilled labor itself. That is captured by the following *reduced form* of the education technology[8]

$$x = \left(\frac{\tau}{c}\right)^\epsilon \quad \text{where } 0 < \epsilon < 1, \ c \geq 1 \ x_\tau > 0, \text{ and } x_{\tau\tau} < 0. \tag{7.2}$$

Thus, if the government channels more resources into education, it will generate more high-skilled people. However, doing this becomes more difficult at the margin, as more resources provided to the education sector lead to a decreasing marginal product of those resources due to congestion effects.

The parameter c measures the *efficiency* by which resources are used in education. One may think about $1/c$ is as a survival rate in a particular education program. If the latter is higher it would make funds more efficient when generating graduates and the study times were of equal length.

In turn, ϵ measures the *productivity* of the whole education sector. A lower ϵ implies that the education sector is more productive and that a marginal increase in taxes would increase education output relatively more. This productivity may depend on the duration of studies, the quality of education, student-teacher ratios, or how capital (computers) and students are combined for given resources in efficiency units (τ/c).

7.2.1 The Private Sector

There are as many identical, price-taking firms as individuals and the firms face perfect competition and maximize profits. By assumption they are subject to knowledge spillovers, which take the form $B_t = A(K_t/N)^\eta = A k_t^\eta$ with $\eta \geq \alpha$. Thus, the *average* stock of capital, $k_t = K_t/N$, which includes disembodied technological knowledge, is the source of a positive externality.[9] Then simplify by setting $\eta = \alpha$, which allows one to concentrate on steady state behavior. For a justification see Romer (1986). As the firms cannot influence the externality, it does not enter their decision directly so that

$$r = (1 - \alpha)Ak_t^\alpha K_t^{-\alpha}H^\alpha,$$

$$w_h = \alpha Ak_t^\alpha K_t^{1-\alpha}[(L_h + L_l)^{\alpha-1} + \beta L_h^{\alpha-1}], \tag{7.3}$$

$$w_l = \alpha Ak_t^\alpha K_t^{1-\alpha}(L_h + L_l)^{\alpha-1}.$$

All agents act price-takingly and have logarithmic utility. (In the rest of the chapter, time subscripts are dropped for convenience.) The low-skilled do not invest and consume their entire wage and transfer income. Thus, their intertemporal utility is given by

$$\int_0^\infty \frac{c_l^{1-\nu} - 1}{1 - \nu} e^{-\rho t}\, dt \quad \text{where } c_l = w_l + \phi r \frac{K}{L_l}. \tag{7.4}$$

In contrast, the high-skilled own all the assets that are collateralized one-to-one by capital. A representative high-skilled agent takes the paths of r, w_h, w_l, ϑ as given and solves

$$\max_{c_h} \int_0^\infty \frac{c_h^{1-\nu} - 1}{1 - \nu} e^{-\rho t}\, dt \tag{7.5a}$$

$$s.t. \quad \dot{k}_h = w_h + (1 - \vartheta)rk_h - c_h \tag{7.5b}$$

$$k_h(0) = \text{given}, \quad k_h(\infty) = \text{free}. \tag{7.5c}$$

This problem is standard and involves the following growth rate of consumption:

$$\gamma \equiv \frac{\dot{c}_h}{c_h} = \frac{(1 - \vartheta)r - \rho}{\nu}, \tag{7.6}$$

which depends on the after-tax return on capital. As the high-skilled agents own the initial capital stock equally and as they have identical utility functions, their investment decisions are the same. But then the wealth distribution will not change over time, and only high-skilled agents continue to own equal shares of the total capital stock over time.

7.2.2   Market Equilibrium

For the rest of the chapter normalize the population by setting $N = 1$ so that the factor rewards in (7.3) are given by

$$r = (1 - \alpha)A(1 + \beta x^\alpha), \quad w_h = \alpha A k_t(1 + \beta x^{\alpha-1}), \quad \text{and} \quad w_l = \alpha A k_t.$$

The return on capital is constant over time and wages grow with the capital stock. Note that $w_l(t)$ does not directly depend on x. It only does so indirectly through k_t and so $\gamma(x)$ when $t \neq 0$. See, for example, Johnson (1984).

As $w_h = w_l(1 + \beta x^{\alpha-1})$, high-skilled labor receives a premium over what their low-skilled counterpart gets, regardless of whether high-skilled labor is taken as scarce or not. This reflects that the high-skilled may always (perfectly) substitute for low-skilled labor so that both types of labor receive the same wage w_l for routine tasks and that performing high-skilled tasks is remunerated by the additional amount $w_l \beta x^{\alpha-1}$.

The wage premium depends on the percentage of high-skilled labor in the population, grows over time at the rate γ, and is decreasing in x for a *given* capital stock.[10] On the other hand the (relative) wage premium w_h/w_l increases when production is getting more (high-)skill biased (higher β).[11]

From the production function $\gamma_y = \gamma_k$ so that for given x per capita output and the capital-labor ratio grow at the same rate. With constant N and x total output also grows at the same rate as the aggregate capital stock. From (7.6) the consumption of the representative high-skilled agent grows at γ.

Each high-skilled worker owns $k_{h0} = K_0/L_h$ units of the initial capital stock. Equation (7.5b) implies $\dot{k}_h = w_h + (1 - \vartheta)r k_h - c_h$ so that $\gamma_{k_h} = (w_h - c_h)/k_h - (1 - \vartheta)r$ where $(1 - \vartheta)r$ is constant. In steady state, $\gamma_{k_h} = \gamma_k$ is constant by definition. But w_i/k, $i = h, l$ is constant as well, because

$$\frac{w_h}{k_t} = \frac{\alpha A k_t(1 + \beta x^{\alpha-1})}{k_t} = \alpha A(1 + \beta x^{\alpha-1}) \quad \text{and} \quad \frac{w_l}{k_t} = \alpha A,$$

which implies $\gamma_k = \gamma$. But then consumption of the low-skilled also grows at the rate γ. Thus, the economy is characterized by *balanced growth* in *steady state* with $\gamma_Y = \gamma_K = \gamma_y = \gamma_k = \gamma_{c_h} = \gamma_{c_l}$. From (7.6), (7.7), and $\tau = cx^{1/\epsilon}$, one obtains

$$\gamma = \frac{(1 - cx^{1/\epsilon} - \phi)(1 - \alpha)A(1 + \beta x^\alpha) - \rho}{\nu}, \tag{7.7}$$

which is first increasing and then decreasing, that is, concave in x.[12]

Thus, in the model it is possible that an economy has high-skilled workers, but does not necessarily do better than another economy with less high-skilled people.

For given $x \in (0,1)$ the effect of a change in the productivity of the education sector is given by $dy/d\epsilon = (\ln(x)cx^{1/\epsilon}r)/(\epsilon^2 v) < 0$. One also verifies $dy/d\phi < 0$, $dy/dc < 0$ and $dy/d\beta > 0$ for given x.

Proposition 7.1 The long-run growth rate γ is first increasing and then decreasing in x. For given x, a less productive education technology (higher ϵ) or a less efficient use of public resources in education (higher c) imply lower growth, whereas a more skill-biased technology (higher β) implies higher growth. An increase in direct, purely redistributive transfers to the low-skilled (higher ϕ) lowers long-run growth.

7.2.3 Income Inequality

The chapter concentrates on simple inequality measures for current income such as the Lorenz curve and the Gini coefficient, because the latter has been used extensively in the recent growth literature. Note that average current income before (g) and after (n) taxes depends on time and is given by $\mu^g \equiv w_l(1-x) + w_h x + rk_t$ and $\mu^n \equiv w_l(1-x) + \phi r k_t + w_h x + (1 - \phi - \tau)rk_t$. However, the *gross* and *net* income shares of the *low-skilled* are constant and given by

$$\sigma_l^g \equiv \frac{w_{lt}(1-x)}{\mu_t^g} = \frac{\alpha(1-x)}{1 + \beta x^a}, \tag{7.8a}$$

$$\sigma_l^n \equiv \frac{w_{lt}(1-x) + \phi r k_t}{\mu_t^n} = \frac{\alpha(1-x) + \phi(1-\alpha)(1 + \beta x^a)}{(1 + \beta x^a)(1 - (1-\alpha)cx^{1/\epsilon})}, \tag{7.8b}$$

where use has been made of $\tau = cx^{1/\epsilon}$. The corresponding Lorenz curve (LC), which relates cumulative population shares to cumulative income shares, is presented in figure 7.1. The LC has a kink at the point A at which $(1-x)$ percent of the population receive σ_l percent of total income. The Gini coefficient is then calculated as

$$G = 1 - 2\left[\frac{(1-x)\sigma_l}{2} + x\sigma_l + \frac{(1-\sigma_l)x}{2}\right] = 1 - (\sigma_l + x),$$

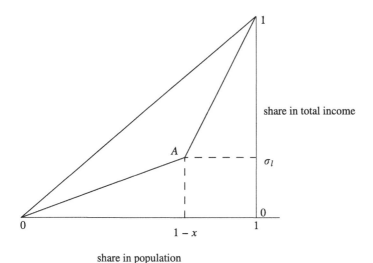

Figure 7.1
Ordinary Lorenz curve

where the expression in square brackets represents the area under the LC.

It is easy to see that $\sigma_l^n > \sigma_l^g$ so that the low-skilled get a larger share of income after taxes than before taxes. If point A corresponds to the situation before taxation then the income distribution after taxes would have a kink at a point strictly above A and would imply a less unequal income distribution. See Atkinson (1970). Furthermore, the Gini coefficients for *gross* (G^g) and for *net* (G^n) incomes, namely,

$$G^g = 1 - (\sigma_l^g + x) \quad \text{and} \quad G^n = 1 - (\sigma_l^n + x), \tag{7.9}$$

would report that as well, because $\sigma_l^n > \sigma_l^g$ implies $G^g > G^n$. Thus, taxation for education as well as direct transfers have a long-run redistributive impact reflected in the difference between the respective Gini coefficients. For that reason the chapter uses (see, e.g., Lambert 1993, chap. 2)

Definition 7.1 (Redistribution): Income redistribution is measured by $\Pi \equiv G^g - G^n$ and captures the long-run redistributive impact of taxation used for education and of the direct transfers granted to the low-skilled workers.

Table 7.1
Numerical simulation

x	G^g	G^n	Π	γ	τ
0.10	0.386	0.342	0.044	0.0195	0.027
0.15	0.392	0.345	0.047	0.0201	0.054
0.20	0.390	0.339	0.051	0.0202	0.089
0.25	0.382	0.327	0.056	0.0200	0.131
0.30	0.370	0.310	0.059	0.0194	0.179

Note: Parameter values: $\alpha = 0.7$, $\beta = 1.13$, $c = 1.43$, $\epsilon = 0.58$, $\phi = 0.13$, $v = 3.55$, $\rho = 0.01$.

The difference in Gini coefficients is given by

$$\Pi = \sigma_l^n - \sigma_l^g = \frac{(1 - \alpha)(\phi(1 + \beta x^\alpha) + \alpha(1 - x)cx^{1/\epsilon})}{(1 + \beta x^\alpha)(1 - (1 - \alpha)cx^{1/\epsilon})}. \tag{7.10}$$

Growth, inequality and redistribution are complicated functions of x. In order to get an impression of its qualitative features, I have calibrated the model using the chapter's data for thirteen OECD countries. Focusing on the percentage of the population with tertiary education, which ranges from 10 to 26 percent with a sample mean of 15 percent, table 7.1 presents simulations based on "reasonable" parameter values.

Thus, income inequality—as measured by the Gini coefficient—as well as growth first increases, and then decreases with a rising number of people with tertiary education.[13] These simulated effects are small. In particular, they are smaller for the growth rate than for the distributional variables.

Clearly, measured redistribution is higher if the government directly transfers more resources to the low-skilled (higher ϕ). However, in the relevant range measured redistribution is also increasing in x and hence in τ. But there is no clear (functional) relation between inequality and redistribution. For instance, when plotting $\Pi(x)$ against $G^g(x)$, it would be possible that two values of Π are associated with the same G^g. Furthermore, higher x implies higher redistribution Π but also first higher and then lower growth.

Proposition 7.2 For a given production and education technology and many parameter constellations (β, c, ϵ), the Gini coefficients (G^g, G^n) for pre-tax or post-tax income inequality are inverted U–shaped in x.

Thus, for sufficiently high x an increase in it would lower pre-tax and post-tax income inequality. Furthermore, such an increase would often also widen the gap between them and so redistribution as defined here.

The results have to be interpreted with caution as they are sensitive to changes in the institutional and production features. For changes in the latter it is not difficult to verify

Proposition 7.3   For a given level of human capital (x),

1. a more skill-biased production (higher β) entails higher pre-tax and (even) higher post-tax inequality and so lower redistribution;

2. a less efficient use of public resources in education (higher c) or a less productive education sector (higher ϵ) imply no change in pre-tax, but a reduction in post-tax inequality and hence more redistribution.

The first result follows because a higher β has a direct and positive bearing on the wages of the high-skilled and pre-tax capital income, but has no direct effect on tax revenues. As a consequence, there is lower redistribution. The intuition for the second result is the following: If it is relatively more difficult to generate more high-skilled people, higher taxes are called for. Thus, if two economies have the same x the one with a *less* productive education sector must use more resources to have that x, thereby redistributing relatively more income.[14]

7.3   Empirical Evidence

7.3.1   *Data and Methodology*

Human capital is measured by the percentage of the *population* from 25 to 64 years of age that has attained *at least* upper secondary education (SECP) or *at least* university-level (tertiary) education (TERP). Data for these variables are provided by the OECD for 1996 and thirty-four countries.[15] They collapse the time series dimension into a single number by attaching weights to the human capital composition of different generations at a particular point in time and are taken to represent a long-run process which is approximated by their time-averages over the sample period.[16]

The nature of the human capital data also serves as a justification for the methodology employed. Although authors such as Caselli, Esquivel, and Lefort (1996) argue that growth should be investigated by means of *dynamic* panel data methods, these methods may have their own problems as, for example, argued by Barro (1997, 37) or Temple (1999, 132). Therefore, the chapter uses time-averaged data and concentrates on simple statistics, the properties of which may also be relevant for more sophisticated methods.

A valuable source for data on income distributions for many countries is the Luxembourg Income Study (LIS), which satisfies many minimum quality requirements and provides a consistent data source. Thus, income inequality is measured by Gini coefficients based on LIS data.[17] Then averages of the Gini coefficients for each country are taken for the period 1970–1990 and are meant to reflect long-run within-country inequality. For a similar procedure, see Deininger and Squire (1998, 268).

The income and recipient concept employed here is *gross* or *net* income per household where the latter has been adjusted by the square root of household members. These concepts are *strictly* adhered to. On the importance of income and recipient concepts in the measurement of inequality, see, for instance, Cowell (1995) or Atkinson (1983).

Finally, long-run growth rates were calculated using the Penn World Table (Mark 5.6) from Summers and Heston (1991). All the other data are taken from Barro and Lee (1994). Combining these data sources with LIS data yields a sample of thirteen relatively rich countries for the period 1970–1990 for which reliable (good) inequality data are available.

7.3.2 Findings

The Gini coefficient for individual households' *gross* incomes is denoted by LIS.G and that for individual households' *net* incomes by LIS.N. Furthermore, RE ≡ LIS.G − LIS.N denotes redistribution. In the sample the Gini coefficients are characterized as follows.

Over the sample period income inequality has risen in some countries, but not in all. Redistribution has increased in almost all of them. For instance, in the United States the Gini coefficient went up from 35.05 in 1974 to 41.81 in 1997. Thus, there was a marked increase in pre-tax income inequality. For the same period the Gini coefficient for net income goes up from 31.46 in 1974 to 37.24 in 1997. On the other hand, redistribution (RE) goes up from 3.59 in 1974 to 4.57 in 1997. Thus, policy in the United States has corrected slightly increasingly for some of the increase in pre-tax inequality. A similar picture holds for the United Kingdom so that higher inequality in pre-tax incomes often seems to be associated with more redistribution within countries over time.

Sweden has low pre-tax inequality that fell over the period (1967: 32.05; 1995: 26.2). It reduced redistribution from 6 in 1967 to 4.2 in 1995. Thus, Sweden and the United States have very different pre-tax income inequality, but redistribute approximately the same. On period averages the United States redistributes more (RE: 4.4) than, for example, Germany (RE: 3.7), France (RE: 2.49) or Canada (RE: 3.4). All the latter countries have lower pre-tax inequality than the United States.

Clearly, growth of GDP per capita should be controlled for by many factors. This is done here by means of simple growth regressions and by focusing on parsimonious models. Following a common procedure, a benchmark model with often used robust regressors is used to add education and distributional variables to see what the latter contribute to the "explanation" of long-run growth across countries.

The benchmark model used here for i countries is $\gamma_i = \alpha + \beta_1 LY70_i + \beta_2 LAFERT_i + \beta_3 CVLIB_i + \epsilon_i$, where LY70 denotes the (natural) logarithm of GDP per capita in 1970, LAFERT represents the logarithm of the average fertility rate for the period 1960–1984, CVLIB is Gastil's index of civil liberties (from 1 to 7; 1 = most freedom) for the period 1972–1989, and ϵ_i is a disturbance term. According to the estimated coefficients, CVLIB does not really add to the "explanation" of growth and is dropped in the subsequent analysis, because it is not the main variable of interest.[18]

In table 7.2 model (1) is the reduced benchmark model. In all models the estimated coefficient on LY70 is always negative and that on fertility (LAFERT) is negative in ten out of the sixteen models. The estimates then suggest the following.

The association between the human capital as well as the distributional variables and growth is not very strong. Most of the coefficients on these variables are statistically insignificant. However, even small effects may have important and economically significant consequences in the long run.[19]

Table 7.2
Growth regressions

	(1)	(2)	(3)	(4)	(5)	(6)	(7)
Const.	23.225	23.375	16.656	16.374	23.008	24.755	22.129
	(6.344)	(5.209)	(5.959)	(6.198)	(5.708)	(6.867)	(8.886)
	[0.004]	[0.001]	[0.023]	[0.030]	[0.004]	[0.006]	[0.038]
LY70	−2.262	−2.587	−1.825	−1.844	−2.563	−2.449	−2.121
	(0.638)	(0.541)	(0.641)	(0.649)	(0.580)	(0.707)	(0.985)
	[0.005]	[0.001]	[0.021]	[0.022]	[0.002]	[0.007]	[0.064]
LAFERT	−0.534	0.407	2.413	2.253	0.434	−0.656	0.025
	(0.905)	(0.840)	(1.340)	(1.306)	(0.894)	(0.945)	(1.681)
	[0.568]	[0.639]	[0.109]	[0.123]	[0.640]	[0.506]	[0.988]
SECP		0.029	0.036	0.036	0.030		
		(0.012)	(0.011)	(0.012)	(0.013)		
		[0.039]	[0.014]	[0.015]	[0.049]		
TERP						0.019	0.018
						(0.027)	(0.028)
						[0.501]	[0.535]
GEDU							
LIS.G			−0.077				−0.030
			(0.043)				(0.059)
			[0.108]				[0.630]
LIS.N				−0.067			
				(0.039)			
				[0.121]			
RE					0.025		
					(0.102)		
					[0.814]		
R^2	0.642	0.783	0.846	0.842	0.784	0.661	0.671
Obs.	13	13	13	13	13	13	13

Note: The dependent variable is the average growth rate of real GDP per capita over the period 1970–1990. The estimation method is OLS. Standard errors are shown in parentheses and t-probabilities are reported in square brackets.

1. The coefficients on education are positive in all models. However, secondary education (SECP) appears to contribute more to linear "explanations" of long-run growth than tertiary education (TERP) or education expenditure (GEDU). As an indication notice the relatively high R^2s in models (2)–(5). For instance, the latter models suggest that an increase of one standard deviation (11 percentage points) in the percentage of people aged 25–65 who have at least upper secondary education (SECP) raises long-run growth by 0.3 to 0.4 percentage points. Models (6)–(9) suggest that growth

Table 7.2
(continued)

(8)	(9)	(10)	(11)	(12)	(13)	(14)	(15)	(16)
22.954	25.886	22.403	21.092	22.102	22.972	20.497	20.911	23.334
(9.439)	(7.857)	(6.585)	(8.665)	(9.062)	(7.091)	(8.241)	(8.469)	(6.931)
[0.041]	[0.011]	[0.008]	[0.041]	[0.041]	[0.012]	[0.034]	[0.036]	[0.008]
−2.236	−2.554	−2.235	−2.059	−2.196	−2.287	0.183	−1.990	−2.270
(1.032)	(0.797)	(0.653)	(0.978)	(1.015)	(0.702)	(1.609)	(0.910)	(0.687)
[0.062]	[0.013]	[0.008]	[0.069]	[0.063]	[0.012]	[0.912]	[0.057]	[0.009]
−0.266	−0.712	−0.424	−0.061	−0.352	−0.425	0.183	−0.009	−0.538
(1.644)	(1.006)	(0.938)	(1.740)	(1.703)	(0.987)	(1.609)	(1.528)	(0.956)
[0.875]	[0.499]	[0.662]	[0.973]	[0.842]	[0.678]	[0.912]	[0.996]	[0.587]
0.017	0.024							
(0.029)	(0.031)							
[0.569]	[0.470]							
		0.086	0.071	0.082	0.106			
		(0.116)	(0.135)	(0.146)	(0.133)			
		[0.477]	[0.611]	[0.590]	[0.449]			
			−0.017			−0.031		
			(0.065)			(0.057)		
			[0.810]			[0.596]		
−0.016				−0.003			−0.022	
(0.053)				(0.063)			(0.051)	
[0.773]				[0.960]			[0.672]	
	−0.050				−0.051			−0.007
	(0.139)				(0.137)			(0.123)
	[0.724]				[0.719]			[0.954]
0.664	0.666	0.663	0.665	0.663	0.668	0.654	0.650	0.642
13	13	13	13	13	13	13	13	13

would be raised by 0.08 to 0.1 percentage points when increasing by one standard deviation (4.8 percentage points) the percentage of people aged 25–65 who have at least tertiary education (TERP). In turn, a one-standard-deviation change (1.04 percentage points) of more education expenditure would increase the growth rate by around 0.08 to 0.1 percentage points.

2. The coefficients on redistribution (RE) are ambiguous and statistically insignificant. When controlling for SECP they are positive, but they are negative in all other cases. All coefficients on RE suggest that it does not add much to "explaining" the cross-country variation in growth rates.

3. When controlling for initial income *and* fertility, the coefficients on pre-tax *and* on post-tax income inequality are statistically insignificant but they are always *negative*, no matter whether one also controls for education (SECP, TERP, or GEDU). For instance, when controlling for secondary education SECP in models (2)–(5) a one-standard-deviation change in pre-tax inequality (LIS.G) of 3.67 lowers the long-run growth rate by 0.28 percentage points. The same change for post-tax inequality (LIS.N) amounts to 3.88 and lowers the growth rate by 0.26. But when controlling for tertiary education (TERP) or overall spending on education (GEDU), these effects become smaller.

4. Pre-tax income inequality (LIS.G) appears to be more strongly, negatively related to growth than post-tax income inequality (LIS.N), as the coefficients for the latter are consistently closer to zero than those found for LIS.G.

The findings suggest that more inequality in gross incomes seems to imply lower growth for the typical country in the sample. Then the state intervenes by redistribution. That intervention does not appear to affect growth very much in the typical country. However, the resulting inequality in personal incomes *after* taxes is still *negative*. But that means that the state may *not* have intervened *enough* to generate a situation where after-tax income inequality would not negatively affect growth anymore.

The negative association between pre-tax *or* post-tax income inequality and growth also allows for an interpretation of results based on some forms of *unadjusted* inequality measures.[20]

Lemma 1 If the "true" association between growth and pre-tax income inequality, measured by the Gini coefficient, is negative, then the estimated coefficients on unadjusted inequality measures based on mixes of Gini coefficients for net and for gross incomes are most likely to be biased upwards.

But then the estimated non-negative signs found on the coefficients for *unadjusted* inequality measures allow for another interpretation: The "true" association between pre-tax inequality and growth is negative. Post-tax inequality depends on pre-tax inequality and redistribution. If one uses the mix-generated *unadjusted* inequality measure, one really runs a regression on a variable containing information about pre-tax inequality and redistribution, which are two different things. Thus, a positive coefficient in a growth regression may also indicate that pre-tax inequality *negatively* "affects" growth and redistribution strongly *positively* "affects" growth.

Table 7.3 presents the "effects" of some widely used determinant factors on income inequality and redistribution.

These regressions indicate that initial income and fertility are negatively related to equality and redistribution. In turn, government spending on overall education (GEDU) is consistently *negatively* associated with pre-tax and post-tax inequality, but it is *positively* related to redistribution.

7.3.3   The Role of the Schooling Technology

A common measure of the (internal) inefficiency in schooling is the dropout rate. Recently, the OECD has provided data on dropout rates for students enrolled at the university-level tertiary education, covering many OECD countries for the 1990s.[21] Differences in these rates are taken to reflect structural differences that have not changed much *across* countries and over a long time horizon. Thus, the results below are only suggestive.

With this variable, called DROP, regressions have been run which control for policy responses by means of interaction terms. The regression results that are available on request indicate that most of the relationships are statistically insignificant. The point estimates in turn suggest that when controlling for the dropout rate, DROP, and for policy reactions (e.g., GEDU*DROP), more education and more spending on it may raise growth and reduce income inequality but also redistribution. However, when looking at the total effect of education expenditure GEDU (tertiary education, TERP) around the sample mean, it turns out that more education expenditure GEDU (tertiary education, TERP) seems to lower income inequality but raises redistribution and growth.

The coefficients on the dropout rate DROP appear to confirm that countries where it is more difficult to generate education have lower inequality. But they also seem to be those that redistribute less. But the latter is only true if one controls for the interaction terms. The total effect is that around the sample mean an increase in DROP raises pre-tax and post-tax inequality but lowers redistribution and growth.

Table 7.3
Determinants of inequality

Dependent variable	(1) LIS.G	(2) LIS.G	(3) LIS.G	(4) LIS.N	(5) LIS.N	(6) LIS.N	(7) RE	(8) RE	(9) RE
Const.	−87.562	−79.199	−43.246	−104.390	−92.394	−59.485	14.814	11.109	13.734
	(36.683)	(35.545)	(42.709)	(41.330)	(37.240)	(45.991)	(17.153)	(16.805)	(22.422)
	[0.038]	[0.053]	[0.341]	[0.030]	[0.035]	[0.232]	[0.408]	[0.525]	[0.557]
LY70	10.903	10.627	7.789	12.268	11.872	9.275	−1.158	−1.035	−1.243
	(3.687)	(3.527)	(3.939)	(4.154)	(3.695)	(4.241)	(1.724)	(1.668)	(2.068)
	[0.014]	[0.015]	[0.083]	[0.014]	[0.011]	[0.060]	[0.517]	[0.550]	[0.565]
LAFERT	23.036	21.910	18.214	23.728	22.114	18.730	−0.525	−0.026	−0.296
	(5.236)	(5.066)	(5.519)	(5.899)	(5.307)	(5.943)	(2.448)	(2.395)	(2.897)
	[0.001]	[0.002]	[0.011]	[0.002]	[0.002]	[0.014]	[0.835]	[0.992]	[0.921]
CVLIB			−3.163			−2.896			−0.231
			(2.289)			(2.465)			(1.202)
			[0.204]			[0.274]			[0.852]
GEDU		−0.876	−1.438		−1.256	−1.771		0.388	0.347
		(0.626)	(0.722)		(0.655)	(0.777)		(0.296)	(0.379)
		[0.195]	[0.081]		[0.088]	[0.052]		[0.222]	[0.387]
R²	0.660	0.720	0.774	0.620	0.730	0.770	0.051	0.204	0.207
Obs.	13	13	13	13	13	13	13	13	13

Note: Estimation by OLS. Standard errors in parentheses and t-probabilities in square brackets.

In terms of the model this suggests that c and ϵ may not be independent of one another. Furthermore, one may argue that they are also related to β. For instance, Wälde (2000) shows that the structure of education systems (elitist vs. egalitarian) may influence the skill intensity in production. In that sense the estimates here would support such an argument.

7.4 Concluding Remarks

This chapter argues that education directly affects growth and income inequality. In the model pre-tax and post-tax income inequality—measured by the Gini coefficient—as well as growth are first increasing and then decreasing in education. It is shown that a less efficient schooling system would require more redistributive education expenditure for a given level of education.

The data, which are based on *consistent* concepts for the measurement of inequality, provide some evidence that, when controlling for various factors such as initial income or fertility, long-run growth is higher for countries that (1) spend more on education, and (2) have lower pre-tax and lower post-tax income inequality. The data also suggest that countries with a more productive, public education technology exhibit lower income inequality and higher growth. The chapter does not find an indication that higher pre-tax or post-tax income inequality is good for growth in rich countries.

The consistent negative relation between pre-tax and post-tax inequality and growth in the data suggests that mixing Gini coefficients based on gross or on net incomes is most likely to produce an upward bias when measuring the effect of *unadjusted* measures of inequality on growth. It also indicates that a rich country could raise growth and lower pre-tax and post-tax inequality, given its education technology, if it spent more on public education. However, a more precise disentanglement of the interaction between education policy and education technology, and their effects on growth and inequality appears to be called for and should be an interesting topic for further research.

Notes

I am grateful for helpful comments made by Theo Eicher, Danny Quah, Cecilia García-Peñalosa, and the participants at the conference Growth and Inequality: Issues and Policy Implications at CESifo, Munich, and Schloss Elmau, Bavaria, in 2001/2, and the

Development Conference on Growth and Poverty at UNU/WIDER in Helsinki, May 2001. I have also benefited from useful conversations with Ingo Barens, Volker Caspari, and Rafael Gerke. Furthermore, I owe a special thanks to Rafael Doménech and an anonymous referee for their insightful comments and suggestions. Of course, all errors are my own.

1. Banerjee and Duflo (2000) have recently attempted to reconcile the two conclusions, but they ended up with a negative result. Based on Deininger and Squire's data and the use of *unadjusted* inequality measures, they show that the data cannot really tell us very much about the relationship between inequality and growth, especially once one accounts for possible nonlinearities.

2. This literature is surveyed by, for example, Bénabou (1996), Bertola (2000), Aghion, Caroli, and García-Peñalosa (1999), or Zweimüller (2000).

3. For instance, Barro (2000) finds for his data and for unadjusted inequality measures that inequality is *positively* associated with growth when looking at a subsample of rich countries and when including fertility as an additional control variable.

4. A constant β implies that the diversity in it across countries is structurally fixed for a long time. Thus, the paper abstracts from skill-biased technical change and should, therefore, be viewed as complementary to research along the lines of, for example, Galor and Tsiddon (1997), Acemoglu (1998), or Caselli (1999).

5. There is evidence (available on request) that across countries capital income taxes are indeed significantly positively related to expenditure on education. Constancy of the tax rate is imposed in order to focus on long-run, time-consistent equilibria with steady-state, balanced growth. For a discussion of private vs. public education, see, for instance, Glomm and Ravikumar (1992) or Fernandez and Rogerson (1998).

6. In the model, agents are endowed by the same *basic* ability and receive basic training that is produced and provided costlessly. Education always means higher education. Ex ante everybody is a candidate for receiving (higher) education and once chosen to be *in* the education process will complete the degree. Thus, the education sector is characterized by continuous excess demand due to rationing, which seems realistic for most education systems. Furthermore, the education process is taken to be sufficiently productive in converting no skills into high skills. The model ignores problems arising from the time spent receiving education by assuming that education is provided as a public good and that all people spend the same time in school, but attend different courses leading to different degrees. Opportunity costs of education might easily be introduced into the model by subtracting a fixed amount of happiness from a high-skilled person for having spent time in school. The chapter's results would not change in that case.

7. Of course, redistribution may take other forms in reality. For instance, suppose that in contrast to this model's assumptions education is privately costly. Public expenditures on higher education might then be regressive if higher-income families have better access to educational opportunities. Redistribution in the form of social transfers might in fact have a growth impact by loosening liquidity constraints that prevent individuals in poor families from taking advantage of educational opportunities. In that sense redistribution corrects for ex ante (wealth or income) inequality in the chapter, because education is provided costlessly and ex ante the family background of a student does not matter in the model. Second, there is redistribution ex post that corrects for inequality in income after education has taken place.

8. Underlying this equation is the description of an education sector with spillovers from, for instance, high-skilled to new high-skilled people or where the capital equipment such as computers makes the education technology very productive. A more formal, OLG-based justification of the setup is available on request.

9. Here the assumption is that regardless of the source of new ideas or blueprints production is undertaken so that all agents are affected relatively equally from knowledge spillovers. The results would not change if the externality depended on the *entire* capital stock instead.

10. On this see, for instance, Bound and Johnson (1992), Katz and Murphy (1992), or Autor, Krueger, and Katz (1998).

11. The idea that skill-biased technological change within firms with its corresponding demand for high-skilled labor and the (education system's) supply of high-skilled people are in a "run" determining wage inequality over time can, e.g., be found in Tinbergen (1975).

12. This follows because $d\gamma/dx = (1/v)[-\Delta_1 + \Delta_2]$, where $\Delta_1 = (c/\epsilon)x^{1/\epsilon-1}(1-\alpha) \cdot A(1+\beta x^{\alpha})$ and $\Delta_2 = (1 - cx^{1/\epsilon} - \phi)(1-\alpha)A\alpha\beta x^{\alpha-1}$. For $x \to 0$ we have $d\gamma/dx = +\infty$. When $x \to 1$ we have $d\gamma/dx = -(1/\epsilon)c(1-a)A(1+\beta) + (1-c\phi)(1-\alpha)A\alpha\beta < 0$. Furthermore, $d\Delta_1/dx > 0$ and $d\Delta_2/dx < 0$ imply $d^2\gamma/dx^2 < 0$. These properties capture that expanding education may lead to lower growth under some especially congestive circumstances. See, for example, Temple (1999, 140).

13. In an economy with income growth such as the one modelled here this property of the Gini coefficients often follows by construction. See Fields (1987) or Amiel and Cowell (1999).

14. Recall that the result is conditional on (observable) x. Given that policy may react to a change in fundamentals there is nothing to preclude the possibility that a change in them produces different effects in total. Notice also that the result applies only when income inequality is measured by the Gini coefficient. For instance, a higher ϵ may increase income inequality (given τ) when measuring it by the concept of Generalized Lorenz Curve Dominance. See Shorrocks (1983). Thus, the results depend on which measurement concept one uses.

15. See OECD (1998), Table A1.2A.

16. For a critical assessment of other frequently employed data sources measuring human capital see de la Fuente and Doménech (2000).

17. As a sensitivity check, I have also used data from the World Income Inequality Database (WIID) in Helsinki and found that the paper's results are robust for samples with more countries when using slightly less rigorous consistency requirements. These results are available on request.

18. The estimate for β_3 was 0.082 with a standard error of 0.378 and a t-probability of 0.832.

19. Bearing in mind that due to the consistency requirement the sample size is small and although given statistical insignificance the focus of this chapter is on the point estimates and their economic significance, but not on inferential statistics. On the distinction between statistical and economic significance see, for example, McCloskey (1985) or McCloskey and Ziliak (1996).

20. Suppose one mixes Gini coefficients for *net* and *gross* incomes to get an *unadjusted* inequality index I, which is then used in growth regressions.

The model really run: $\gamma_i^u = a + bG_i^g + cG_i^n + \epsilon_i$,

The model run: $\gamma_i^u = a' + b_i' I(G_i^g, G_i^n) + \epsilon_i'$,

where γ_i^u is the residual of the regression of γ_i on a vector of control variables. For simplicity assume that the control variables are not correlated or even orthogonal to the distributional variables. Commonly γ_i^u is called the *unexplained* part of the growth rate. The latter is attempted to be explained by $I(\ )$ in the models above. In general, $G_i^g = G_i^n + R_i^A$ for country i. This is true by the definition of R_i^A as a measure of redistribution. Not every observation in G_i^g may necessarily have a corresponding matching value of G_i^n in the data set. However, values of G_i^n are included by many NCV proponents in order to boost the number of observations. Now what is basically done is to create $I_i = G_i^g + G_i^n$. But this means $I_i = G_i^g + \tilde{G}_i^g - \tilde{R}_i^A$ where $\tilde{G}_i^g$ and $\tilde{R}_i^A$ may be unknown *if* there is no matching value for G_i^g available in the data set. This implies that their estimate for b', call it $\hat{b}'$, would contain information of the distribution of *gross* incomes, but also information on *redistribution*. Thus, the model they run is $\gamma_i^u = a + bG_i^g + c\tilde{G}_i^g - c\tilde{R}_i^A + \epsilon_i$ which puts a restriction on the effect that $\tilde{R}_i^A$ exerts. Relaxing it and noting that $\tilde{G}_i^g$ and $\tilde{R}_i^A$ are unknown, when there are no matching values in G_i^g, the regression is really run on values of *known* Gini coefficients for gross incomes, some *unknown* Gini values for gross income, and some *unknown* values for redistribution. But consequently their "true" model is

$$\gamma_i^u = a + bG_i^g + c\tilde{G}_i^g + d\tilde{R}_i^A + \epsilon_i,$$

where $d = -c$. But this suggests the following argument: The estimates for b and c have often been found to be *negative* in earlier contributions. Furthermore, there is an empirical literature that shows that the estimate for d is likely to be positive. Thus, one has an upward bias for the estimate of b'. This bias may be so strong that one may even get a positive estimate for $b' = b + c + d$, that is, $\hat{b}' \geq 0$ is compatible with $\hat{b} < 0$, $\hat{c} < 0$ and $\hat{d} > 0$.

21. See OECD (2000), Table C4.1.

References

Acemoglu, D. 1998. Why do new technologies complement skills? Directed technical change and wage inequality. *Quarterly Journal of Economics* 113: 1055–1089.

Aghion, P., E. Caroli, and C. García-Peñalosa. 1999. Inequality and economic growth: The perspective of the new growth theories. *Journal of Economic Literature* 37: 1615–1660.

Alesina, A., and D. Rodrik. 1994. Distributive politics and economic growth. *Quarterly Journal of Economics* 109: 465–490.

Amiel, Y., and F. A. Cowell. 1999. *Thinking about Inequality*. Cambridge, UK: Cambridge University Press.

Atkinson, A. B. 1970. On the measurement of inequality. *Journal of Economic Theory* 2: 244–263.

Atkinson, A. B. 1983. *The Economics of Inequality*, 2d ed. Oxford: Clarendon Press.

Atkinson, A. B., and A. Brandolini. 2001. Promise and pitfalls in the use of "secondary" data-sets: Income inequality in OECD countries as a case study. *Journal of Economic Literature* 39: 771–799.

Autor, D., A. Krueger, and L. Katz. 1998. Computing inequality: Have computers changed the labour market. *Quarterly Journal of Economics* 63: 1169–1213.

Banerjee, A. V., and E. Duflo. 2000. Inequality and growth: What can the data say? Working Paper 7793, NBER.

Barro, R. J. 1997. *Determinants of Economic Growth: A Cross-Country Empirical Study.* Cambridge: The MIT Press.

Barro, R. J. 2000. Inequality and growth in a panel of countries. *Journal of Economic Growth* 5: 5–32.

Barro, R. J., and J.-W. Lee. 1994. Sources of economic growth. *Carnegie Rochester Conference Series on Public Policy* 40: 1–46.

Bénabou, R. 1996. Inequality and growth. In *NBER Macroeconomics Annual 1996*, ed. B. S. Bernanke and J. J. Rotemberg, 11–73. Cambridge: The MIT Press.

Bertola, G. 2000. Macroeconomics of distribution and growth. In *Handbook of Income Distribution*, vol. 1, ed. A. B. Atkinson and F. Bourguignon, 477–540. Amsterdam: Elsevier.

Bound, J., and G. Johnson. 1992. Changes in the structure of wages in the 1980s: An evaluation of alternative explanations. *American Economic Review* 82: 371–392.

Caselli, F. 1999. Technological revolutions. *American Economic Review* 89: 78–102.

Caselli, F., G. Esquivel, and F. Lefort. 1996. Reopening the convergence debate: A new look at cross-country growth empirics. *Journal of Economic Growth* 1: 363–389.

Chiu, W. H. 1998. Income inequality, human capital accumulation and economic performance. *Economic Journal* 108: 44–59.

Cowell, F. A. 1995. *Measuring Inequality*, 2d ed. Hemel Hempstead, UK: Prentice Hall/Harvester Wheatsheaf.

de la Fuente, A., and R. Doménech. 2000. Human capital in growth regressions: How much difference does data quality make? Working Paper 262, OECD.

Deininger, K., and L. Squire. 1996. A new data set measuring income inequality. *World Bank Economic Review* 10: 565–591.

Deininger, K., and L. Squire. 1998. New ways of looking at old issues: Inequality and growth. *Journal of Development Economics* 57: 259–287.

Easterly, W., and S. Rebelo. 1993. Fiscal policy and economic growth. An empirical investigation. *Journal of Monetary Economics* 32: 417–458.

Fernandez, R., and R. Rogerson. 1998. Public education and income distribution: A dynamic quantative evaluation of education-finance reform. *American Economic Review* 88: 813–833.

Fields, G. S. 1987. Measuring inequality change in an economy with income growth. *Journal of Development Economics* 91: 611–625.

Forbes, K. J. 2000. A reassessment of the relationship between inequality and growth. *American Economic Review* 90: 869–887.

Galor, O., and D. Tsiddon. 1997. Technological progress, mobility, and economic growth. *American Economic Review* 87: 363–382.

Galor, O., and J. Zeira. 1993. Income distribution and macroeconomics. *Review of Economic Studies* 60: 35–52.

Glomm, G., and B. Ravikumar. 1992. Public versus private investment in human capital: Endogenous growth and income inequality. *Journal of Political Economy* 100: 818–834.

Johnson, G. E. 1984. Subsidies for higher education. *Journal of Labor Economics* 2: 303–318.

Katz, L. F., and K. M. Murphy. 1992. Changes in relative wages, 1963–1987: Supply and demand factors. *Quarterly Journal of Economics* 107: 35–78.

Kuznets, S. 1955. Economic growth and income inequality. *American Economic Review* 45: 1–28.

Lambert, P. J. 1993. *The Distribution and Redistribution of Income: A Mathematical Analysis*, 2d ed. Manchester, UK: Manchester University Press.

Li, H., and H.-F. Zou. 1998. Income inequality is not harmful for growth: Theory and evidence. *Review of Development Economics* 2: 318–334.

McCloskey, D. N. 1985. The loss function has been mislaid: The rhetoric of significance tests. *American Economic Review* 75: 201–205.

McCloskey, D. N., and S. T. Ziliak. 1996. The standard error of regressions. *Journal of Economic Literature* 34: 97–114.

OECD. 1998. *Education at a Glance 1998*. Paris: OECD.

OECD. 2000. *Education at a Glance 2000*. Paris: OECD.

Perotti, R. 1993. Political equilibrium, income distribution, and growth. *Review of Economic Studies* 60: 755–776.

Perotti, R. 1996. Growth, income distribution, and democracy: What the data say. *Journal of Economic Growth* 1: 149–187.

Persson, T., and G. Tabellini. 1994. Is inequality harmful for growth? *American Economic Review* 84: 600–621.

Rehme, G. 1999. Education, economic growth and personal income inequality across countries. Working Paper ECO 99/42, European University Institute, Florence, Italy.

Romer, P. M. 1986. Increasing returns and long-run growth. *Journal of Political Economy* 94: 1002–1037.

Saint-Paul, G., and T. Verdier. 1996. Inequality, redistribution and growth: A challenge to the conventional political economy approach. *European Economic Review* 40: 719–728.

Sala-i-Martin, X. 1996. A positive theory of social security. *Journal of Economic Growth* 1: 277–304.

Shorrocks, A. F. 1983. Ranking income distributions. *Economica* 50: 1–17.

Summers, R., and A. Heston. 1991. The Penn World Table (Mark 5): An expanded set of international comparisons, 1950–1988. *Quarterly Journal of Economics* 106: 327–368.

Temple, J. 1999. The new growth evidence. *Journal of Economic Literature* 37: 112–156.

Tinbergen, J. 1975. *Income Distribution: Analysis and Policies.* Amsterdam: North-Holland.

Wälde, K. 2000. Egalitarian and elitist education systems as the basis for international differences in wage inequality. *European Journal of Political Economy* 16: 445–468.

Zweimüller, J. 2000. Redistribution, inequality and growth. *Empirica* 27: 1–20.

8

The Impact of Tax Policy on Inequality and Growth: An Empirical and Theoretical Investigation

Theo S. Eicher,
Stephen J. Turnovsky, and
Maria Carme Riera Prunera

8.1 Introduction

Vast literatures exist analyzing the relationship between economic growth and income inequality, on the one hand, and between taxation and economic growth, on the other. This chapter combines these strands of the growth literature and examines the effects of tax policy on both income inequality and growth. This analysis requires an explicitly specified sector of skill accumulation, since the growth and inequality effects stemming from fiscal policy actions do not impinge on all sectors of the economy equally. The key feature of our model is that we introduce both raw (unskilled) labor, together with human capital (skills) and physical capital, into a two-sector framework that incorporates the accumulation of both skills and physical accumulation. In addition, government expenditure is introduced as a productive factor in the production of new output, together with a distortionary income tax. The production characteristics of the two sectors are sufficiently general to permit our simulations to allow for the diverse cross-country experiences with regards to taxation, inequality, and growth.[1] These features are integrated into a nonscale growth model, the implications of which have been shown to adhere closely to the economic performance of industrialized countries, and which replicates the distinctly nonlinear nature of inequality in the United States with relative ease (Jones 1995).

The results derived in the chapter draw attention to the fact that the nonscale growth model not only fits the U.S. data well for the long run (as first shown by Jones 1995), but also that our parameterization of the model is able to track important aspects of the short-run evolution of the economy. Specifically, we show that the initial phase of the transitional adjustment of the skill premium in response to changes in the tax code is inherently nonlinear, a feature that closely follows the U.S. skill premium experienced in the 1980s.

Our simulations also relate well to the literature on the macro-economic effects of tax reforms. Studies examining tax reforms show that higher taxes tend to discourage investment rates (Auerbach and Hassett 1991; Cummins, Hassett, and Hubbard 1994, 1996) and that income taxes seem to increase wealth inequality, compared to the distributional neutrality of a consumption tax, as some authors have pointed out (Perroni 1995; Felder 1997). The empirical studies show that the impact of tax changes depends on the mechanism underlying the production of knowledge, as well as on the complementarity between knowledge and physical capital, a feature also shared by our model.

We choose as our benchmark the dramatic changes in the U.S. tax code in the early 1980s and the ensuing, significant changes in the skill premium. Any growth model that seeks to speak to the discussion on policy, taxation, and inequality must be able to replicate key events in the data to render its implications relevant. A key feature of the data in the 1980s was the nonmonotonic nature of the response of the skill premium to changes in the tax code. This is a transition that is difficult for a conventional one-sector growth model or a two-sector endogenous growth model to explain. This is because in either case the transitional adjustment path is a one-dimensional locus and therefore can generate only monotonic adjustments. In contrast, Eicher and Turnovsky (1999) have shown that the transitional path in a two-sector nonscale model can easily be non-monotonic (depending upon the nature of the underlying shock), and is thus capable of explaining the nonlinear characteristics of the data. The original Eicher-Turnovsky model included knowledge, in the form of a public good, and here we modify their original formulation to include endogenous private skill formation.

In our simulations, using actual tax rates for the 1980s, we find that the model replicates both key steady-state variables of the economy as well as tracking the short-run, nonlinear transition path of the skill premium fairly closely. Most importantly we are able to highlight that the speed of adjustment during the transition, and the magnitude of the change in inequality is a function of the externalities in production and education sector.

The previous literature on the topic is separated into two strands: the growth and inequality literature, and the growth and taxation models. Existing explanations for the observed patterns of inequality have focused on sectoral mobility (from agriculture to industry),[2] capital market imperfections,[3] sociopolitical (in)stability and redistribution,[4] or skill-biased technical change.[5] In contrast, the tax reform literature centered on macroeconomic variables, such as employment and accumulation. These studies show how higher taxes discourage investment rates (e.g., Auerbach and Hassett 1991) or labor supply (e.g., Eissa 1996). Models that actually correlate changes in the tax structure with changes in growth (e.g., Auerbach 1996) focus on the distorting effects of current tax structure, and not on the productive services that the government might finance—to the benefit of economic growth.

The structure of the chapter is as follows. Section 8.2 presents the nonscale model with endogenous skill formation. Section 8.3 describes the general equilibrium and stationary states, and section 8.4 outlines how tax reforms in the 1980s correlate both with the predictions of the model and the evolution of real inequality. Section 8.5 concludes.

8.2   A Two-Sector Nonscale Economy

We begin by outlining the structure of a two-sector nonscale model that features exogenous population growth and endogenously growing physical and human capital. We focus on a decentralized economy in which population, N, is assumed to grow at the steady rate $\dot{N}/N = n$. The government plays a simple role. It taxes final income and uses the proceeds to finance the purchases of a productive input that increases productivity in the final output sector.

8.2.1   Individual Agents

Individual i produces final output, Y_i, and gross additions to human capital, J_i, in separate sectors, each subject to externalities according to the Cobb-Douglas production functions:

$$Y_i = \alpha_F \theta^{b_N} [\psi H_i]^{b_H} [\phi K_i]^{b_K} K^{c_K} H^{c_H} G_S^{c_G}, \tag{1a}$$

$$J_i = a_J (1 - \theta)^{e_N} [(1 - \psi) H_i]^{e_H} [(1 - \phi) K_i]^{e_K} K^{f_K} H^{f_H}. \tag{1b}$$

Each individual is endowed with a unit of labor, θ of which is allocated to the production of new output and $(1 - \theta)$ to the production of new human capital. In addition, he allocates a fraction ψ of his current human capital, H_i, to the production of final output, and the balance $(1 - \psi)$ to the accumulation of further human capital. Likewise, he allocates a fraction ϕ of his physical capital, K_i, to the production of final output and the rest $(1 - \phi)$ to the human capital sector. The production of new output is subject to positive externalities arising from the aggregate stock of physical capital, K, human capital, H, as well as the services, G_S, provided by government spending, G, on a productive input. The public good is assumed to be rival, but excludable, so that $G_S = G/N$. The constants α_F, a_J represent exogenous technological shift factors to the production functions. To allow for positive externalities from all factors in both sectors, b_i and c_i represent the private productive elasticities and e_i and f_i represent the externalities.

All agents are identical so that aggregate and individual quantities are related by

$$Y = NY_i, \qquad K = NK_i, \qquad H = NH_i. \tag{2}$$

Government expenditure is proportional to aggregate output, while government services derived by the individual agent are proportional to individual output, in accordance with

$$G = gY = gNY_i; \qquad G_S = gY_i, \tag{3}$$

and substituting (3) into (1a) we can rewrite the production function as

$$Y_i = a_F \theta^{b_N/(1-c_G)} [\psi H_i]^{b_H/(1-c_G)} [\phi K_i]^{b_K/(1-c_G)} K^{c_K/(1-c_G)} H^{c_H/(1-c_G)}, \tag{1a'}$$

where $a_F \equiv (\alpha_F g^{c_G})^{1/(1-c_G)}$.

Allowing for depreciation of both human and physical capital (δ_K, δ_H), the rate at which the individual accumulates the two types of capital is described by

$$\dot{K}_i = (1 - \tau_y)Y_i - C_i - T_i - (\delta_K + n)K_i, \tag{4a}$$

$$\dot{H}_i = J_i - (\delta_H + n)H_i. \tag{4b}$$

According to (4a), income is taxed at the rate τ_y, and in addition we allow for lump-sum taxation, T_i.

Agents maximize their intertemporal utility function

$$\frac{1}{1-\gamma} \int_0^\infty (C_i)^{1-\gamma} e^{-\rho t} \, dt \qquad \rho > 0; \gamma > 0, \tag{5}$$

subject to the production functions (1a) and (1b), the accumulation constraints (4a) and (4b), and the usual initial conditions. His decision variables are (1) the rate of consumption, C_i; (2) the sectoral allocation of labor, θ; human capital, ψ, physical capital, ϕ and (3) the rates of accumulation of physical and human capital. The optimality and transversality conditions to this problem can be summarized as follows:

$$C_i^{-\gamma} = v_i, \tag{6a}$$

$$v_i b_N (1 - \tau_y) \frac{Y_i}{\theta} = \mu_i e_N \frac{J_i}{1 - \theta}, \tag{6b}$$

$$v_i b_H (1 - \tau_y) \frac{Y_i}{\psi} = \mu_i e_H \frac{J_i}{1 - \psi}, \tag{6c}$$

$$v_i b_K (1 - \tau_y) \frac{Y_i}{\phi} = \mu_i e_K \frac{J_i}{1 - \phi}, \tag{6d}$$

$$b_K (1 - \tau_y) \frac{Y_i}{K_i} - \delta_K - n + \frac{\mu_i}{v_i} e_K \frac{J_i}{K_i} = \rho - \frac{\dot{v}}{v}, \tag{6e}$$

$$b_H (1 - \tau_y) \frac{v_i}{\mu_i} \frac{Y_i}{K_i} - \delta_H - n + e_H \frac{J_i}{H_i} = \rho - \frac{\dot{\mu}}{\mu}, \tag{6f}$$

together with the transversality conditions

$$\lim_{t \to \infty} v_i K_i e^{-\rho t} = \lim_{t \to \infty} \mu_i H_i e^{-\rho t} = 0, \tag{6g}$$

where v_i, μ_i are the respective shadow values of physical capital and human capital.

Equation (6a) equates the marginal utility of consumption to the shadow value of capital. Equations (6b), (6c), and (6d) determine the sectoral allocations of labor, human capital, and physical capital such that their respective after-tax marginal products are equated across sectors. Equation (6e) equates the marginal return to investing in an additional unit of physical capital to the return on consumption, both measured in terms of units of final output. Analogously, (6f) equates the marginal return to human capital to the return on consumption, both expressed in units of human capital. In both cases the return to the asset reflects the fact that the additional unit will be allocated across the two sectors.

8.2.2   The Aggregate Economy

To derive the behavior of the aggregate economy we first sum (1a′) and (1b) over the N individuals in the economy. We may express the resulting quantities in terms of the aggregates

$$Y = a_F \theta^{s_N} \phi^{s_K} \psi^{s_H} K^{\sigma_K} H^{\sigma_H} N^{\sigma_N},$$ (7a)

$$J = a_J (1 - \theta)^{e_N} (1 - \phi)^{e_K} (1 - \psi)^{e_H} K^{\eta_K} H^{\eta_H} N^{\eta_N},$$ (7b)

where[6]

$$s_N \equiv \frac{b_N}{1 - c_G}; \qquad s_K \equiv \frac{b_K}{1 - c_G}; \qquad s_H \equiv \frac{b_H}{1 - c_G},$$

$$\sigma_K \equiv \frac{b_K + c_K}{1 - c_G}; \qquad \sigma_H \equiv \frac{b_H + c_H}{1 - c_G}; \qquad \sigma_N \equiv 1 - \frac{b_H + b_K}{1 - c_G},$$

$$\eta_H \equiv e_H + f_H; \qquad \eta_K \equiv e_K + f_K; \qquad \eta_N \equiv 1 - e_H - e_K.$$

Next, we introduce the government and consider the aggregate accumulation equations. We assume that the government finances its expenditure in accordance with a balanced budget, which, aggregated over N individuals, can be expressed as

$$\tau_y N Y_i + N T_i = g N Y_i,$$

or, in terms of the aggregate quantities

$$\tau_y Y + T = g Y.$$ (8)

Summing (4a) and (4b) over the individuals in the economy, and applying the government budget constraint (8), the aggregate rates of capital accumulation can be expressed as

$$\dot{K} = (1 - g) Y - C - \delta_K K,$$ (9a)

$$\dot{H} = J - \delta_H H,$$ (9b)

where Y, J are defined in (7a) and (7b).

8.2.3   Balanced Growth Equilibrium

Before describing the dynamics, we characterize the balanced growth equilibrium. This is defined to be a growth path along which all variables grow at constant, but possibly different, rates. In accordance with U.S. data, we assume that the output/capital ratio, Y/K, is constant. A key feature of the nonscale model is that the equilibrium percentage growth rates of human and physical capital, $\hat{H}$ and $\hat{K}$, respectively are determined entirely by production conditions. Taking the differentials of the production functions (7a) and (7b), and solving, we obtain

$$\hat{H} = \left[\frac{\eta_N(1 - \sigma_K) + \sigma_N \eta_K}{(1 - \eta_H)(1 - \sigma_K) - \sigma_H \eta_K} \right] n \equiv \beta_H n, \tag{10a}$$

$$\hat{K} = \hat{Y} = \hat{C} = \left[\frac{\sigma_N(1 - \eta_H) + \sigma_H \eta_N}{(1 - \eta_H)(1 - \sigma_K) - \sigma_H \eta_K} \right] n \equiv \beta_K n, \tag{10b}$$

and thus the per capita growth rate of output (capital) is

$$\hat{Y} - n = \frac{[(1 - \eta_H)(\sigma_H + \sigma_N + \sigma_K - 1) + \sigma_H(\eta_H + \eta_N + \eta_K - 1)]n}{(1 - \eta_H)(1 - \sigma_K) - \sigma_H \eta_K}. \tag{10c}$$

It is evident from (10a) and (10b) that the magnitudes of the relative sectoral growth rates depend upon the assumed production elasticities in conjunction with the population growth rate. Equation (10c) implies that countries converge to identical output per capita growth rates if either their production technologies are identical, or their production functions exhibit constant returns to scale. If production technologies differ across countries, growth rates exhibit conditional convergence. The fact that (10c) implies that the per capita growth rate of output in general depends upon the population growth rate, n, is a double-edged sword. The evidence on the correlation between population growth and output growth is ambiguous (see, e.g., Barro and Sala-i-Martin 1995). On the other hand, the growth rate has the great advantage that it is no longer a function of the *absolute size* of the population, N, as in previous R&D-based models, an implication that is soundly rejected by the data.

Finally, the possibly differential equilibrium growth rates of physical capital and knowledge are reflected in the growth rates of their respective shadow values, v, μ. Using the optimality conditions (6), these can be shown to grow in accordance with

$$\hat{v} - \hat{\mu} = (\beta_H - \beta_K)n, \tag{10d}$$

where since agents are identical we drop the subscript i.

8.3   Dynamics of a Two-Sector Model

To derive the equilibrium dynamics about the balanced growth path, we define the following stationary variables:

$$y \equiv Y/N^{\beta_K}; \qquad k \equiv K/N^{\beta_K}; \qquad c \equiv C/N^{\beta_K}; \qquad h \equiv H/N^{\beta_H};$$

$$j \equiv J/N^{\beta_H}; \qquad q \equiv v/\mu N^{(\beta_H - \beta_K)}.$$

For convenience, we refer to y, k, c, and h as *scale-adjusted* quantities.[7] This allows us to rewrite scale-adjusted output and human capital as

$$y = a_F \theta^{s_N} \phi^{s_K} \psi^{s_H} k^{\sigma_K} h^{\sigma_H}, \tag{11a}$$

$$j = a_J (1 - \theta)^{e_N} (1 - \phi)^{e_K} (1 - \psi)^{e_H} k^{\eta_K} h^{\eta_H}. \tag{11b}$$

The optimality conditions then enable the dynamics to be expressed in terms of these scale-adjusted variables, as follows. First, substituting (11a) and (11b) into the labor allocation condition, (6b), the human capital allocation condition, (6c), and the physical capital allocation condition, (6d) yields the three relationships:

$$(1 - \tau_y) a_F q b_N \theta^{s_N - 1} \phi^{s_K} \psi^{s_H} k^{\sigma_K} h^{\sigma_H}$$
$$= a_J e_N (1 - \theta)^{e_N - 1} (1 - \phi)^{e_K} (1 - \psi)^{e_H} k^{\eta_K} h^{\eta_H}, \tag{12a}$$

$$(1 - \tau_y) a_F q b_H \theta^{s_N} \phi^{s_K} \psi^{s_H - 1} k^{\sigma_K} h^{\sigma_H}$$
$$= a_J e_H (1 - \theta)^{e_N} (1 - \phi)^{e_K} (1 - \psi)^{e_H - 1} k^{\eta_K} h^{\eta_H}, \tag{12b}$$

$$(1 - \tau_y) a_F q b_K \theta^{s_N} \phi^{s_K - 1} \psi^{s_H} k^{\sigma_K} h^{\sigma_H}$$
$$= a_J e_K (1 - \theta)^{e_N} (1 - \phi)^{e_K - 1} (1 - \psi)^{e_H} k^{\eta_K} h^{\eta_H}. \tag{12c}$$

In principle, we can solve these three relationships for the allocation of labor, human capital, and physical capital across the production and education sectors:

$$\theta = \theta(q(1 - \tau_y), h, k); \qquad \partial\theta/\partial q > 0, \mathrm{sgn}(\partial\theta/\partial h) = \mathrm{sgn}(\sigma_H - \eta_H),$$

$$\mathrm{sgn}(\partial\theta/\partial k) = \mathrm{sgn}(\sigma_K - \eta_K), \tag{13a}$$

$$\psi = \psi(q(1 - \tau_y), h, k); \qquad \partial\psi/\partial q > 0, \mathrm{sgn}(\partial\psi/\partial h) = \mathrm{sgn}(\sigma_H - \eta_H),$$

$$\mathrm{sgn}(\partial\psi/\partial k) = \mathrm{sgn}(\sigma_K - \eta_K), \tag{13b}$$

$$\phi = \phi(q(1 - \tau_y), h, k); \qquad \partial\phi/\partial q > 0, \mathrm{sgn}(\partial\phi/\partial h) = \mathrm{sgn}(\sigma_H - \eta_H),$$

$$\mathrm{sgn}(\partial\phi/\partial k) = \mathrm{sgn}(\sigma_K - \eta_K). \tag{13c}$$

Intuitively, an increase in the relative value of physical capital, q, attracts resources to the output (capital-producing) sector; labor, human capital, and physical capital therefore move from human capital production to final output production. An increase in the stock of either form of capital raises the productivity of both sectors in proportion to an amount that depends upon the respective productive elasticity. Resources will therefore move toward the sector in which the input has the greater production elasticity (is more productive).

Using the optimality conditions, the dynamics of the system can be expressed in terms of the redefined stationary variables by

$$\dot{k} = k\left[(1-g)a_F\theta^{s_N}\phi^{s_K}\psi^{s_H}k^{\sigma_K-1}h^{\sigma_H} - \delta_K - \frac{c}{k} - \beta_K n\right], \tag{14a}$$

$$\dot{h} = h[a_J(1-\theta)^{e_N}(1-\phi)^{e_K}(1-\psi)^{e_H}k^{\sigma_K}h^{\eta_H-1} - \delta_H - \beta_H n], \tag{14b}$$

$$\dot{q} = q\Bigg\{\left(\frac{e_H}{1-\psi}\right)(a_J(1-\theta)^{e_N}(1-\phi)^{e_K}(1-\psi)^{e_H}k^{\eta_K}h^{\eta_H-1})$$

$$- \left(\frac{b_K}{\phi}\right)(1-\tau_y)(a_F\theta^{s_N}\phi^{s_K}\psi^{s_H}k^{\sigma_K-1}h^{\sigma_H})$$

$$- (\delta_H - \delta_K) - (\beta_H - \beta_K)n\Bigg\}, \tag{14c}$$

$$\dot{c} = \frac{c}{\gamma}\Bigg\{\left(\frac{b_K}{\phi}\right)(1-\tau_y)(a_F\theta^{s_N}\phi^{s_K}\psi^{s_H}k^{\sigma_K-1}h^{\sigma_H})$$

$$- (\rho + \delta_K) + [\gamma(1-\beta_K)-1]n\Bigg\}, \tag{14d}$$

where $\theta(.)$, $\psi(.)$, $\phi(.)$ are determined by (13). To the extent that we are interested in the per capita growth rates of physical and human capital, they are given by $\dot{k}/k + (\beta_K - 1)n$ and $\dot{h}/h + (\beta_H - 1)n$, respectively.

The steady state to this system, denoted by "$\sim$" superscripts, can be summarized by

$$\frac{(1-g)\tilde{y}}{\tilde{k}} - \frac{\tilde{c}}{\tilde{k}} = \beta_K n + \delta_K, \tag{15a}$$

$$\frac{\tilde{j}}{\tilde{h}} = \beta_H n + \delta_H, \tag{15b}$$

$$\frac{\tilde{j}}{\tilde{h}} \left(\frac{e_H}{1 - \tilde{\psi}} \right) - \delta_H - \beta_H n = (1 - \tau_y) \frac{\tilde{y}}{\tilde{k}} \frac{b_K}{\tilde{\phi}} - \delta_K - \beta_K n, \tag{15c}$$

$$(1 - \tau_y) \frac{\tilde{y}}{\tilde{k}} \frac{b_K}{\tilde{\phi}} - \delta_K - \beta_K n = \rho + (1 - \gamma)(1 - \beta_K)n, \tag{15d}$$

together with the two production functions (11a, 11b), and the sectoral allocation conditions (13).

These nine equations determine the steady-state equilibrium in the following sequential manner. First, equation (15b) yields the *gross* equilibrium growth rate of knowledge, $\tilde{j}/\tilde{h} = \tilde{J}/\tilde{H}$, in terms of the returns to scale, β_H, and the rates of population growth and depreciation. Next, given $\tilde{j}/\tilde{h}$, equations (15c) and (15d) determine the sectoral allocation of human capital, $\tilde{\psi}$, such that the rate of return on investing in human capital, given by the left hand side of (15c), equals the rate of return on consumption, given by the right-hand side of (15d). Having determined the allocation of human capital, $\tilde{\psi}$, dividing (12a) and (12b), respectively, by (12c) yields the corresponding sectoral allocation of labor, $\tilde{\theta}$, and physical capital, $\tilde{\phi}$. Having determined $\tilde{\phi}$, (15c) and (15d) determine the output-capital ratio such that the rate of return on physical capital equals the (common) rate of return on consumption and human capital. Then having obtained the output-capital ratio, (15a) determines the consumption-capital ratio consistent with the growth rate of capital necessary to equip the growing labor force and replace depreciation. Given $\tilde{\theta}$, $\tilde{\psi}$, $\tilde{\phi}$, $\tilde{y}/\tilde{k}$, and $\tilde{j}/\tilde{h}$, the scale-adjusted production functions determines the stocks of physical capital, $\tilde{k}$, and human capital, $\tilde{h}$, and thus $\tilde{y}$. Finally, having derived $\tilde{\theta}$, $\tilde{\psi}$, $\tilde{\phi}$, $\tilde{h}$, $\tilde{k}$, any of the three sectoral allocation conditions determine the long-run equilibrium relative shadow value of the two assets, $\tilde{q}$.

A more formal characterization of the transitional dynamics is provided in the appendix. The dynamics underlying our analysis are based on the linearization of the fourth-order system (14). In order for the dynamics to describe a unique stable adjustment path, we require that the number of unstable roots equal the number of jump variables (2). Unfortunately, the system is too complex to yield intuitive formal stability conditions that ensure well-behaved saddlepoint behavior. Nevertheless, we assume that this condition is met, as indeed it is in all of our numerical simulations. For the purposes of this chapter, the analysis of changes in tax regimes on inequality, using simulation analysis, the formal stability conditions are of only secondary importance.

8.3.1 The Impact of Public Policy on Inequality

Our concern is to analyze the dynamic response of the economy to changes in income tax rates. We seek to go beyond qualitative results and simulate variations in tax rates that reflect the significant policy events that occurred in the United States during the 1980s. To understand and interpret the adjustments in the economy in response to tax changes, it is useful to first derive the qualitative nature of the long-run equilibrium.

An immediate manifestation of the nonscale characteristic of the model as seen from equations (10a) and (10b) is that the steady-state equilibrium growth rates, of both capital goods are independent of the tax rate τ_y (see Jones 1995; Eicher and Turnovsky 1999). This is a major advantage of the model, since the evidence shows no lasting impact of tax policy on long-run growth (Stokey and Rebelo 1995; Easterly and Rebelo 1993; Jones 1995). The fact that long-run growth is not affected by public policy does not rule out substantial effects of tax policy on economic variables in the short and intermediate term. The magnitude of such effects is depends on the speed of adjustment in the economy. We address this point further in our simulations.

Since taxes do not influence the long-run growth, the equilibrium sectoral asset allocations, $\tilde{\theta}$, $\tilde{\psi}$, and $\tilde{\phi}$, are also independent of the tax rate. From (15d), we know that a lower tax rate reduces only the output-capital ratio in the long run, which, in turn, leads to a lower consumption-capital ratio in order for the equilibrium growth rate of final output to remain unchanged. Again, the sectoral allocations may vary significantly during the transition and impact the skill premium, as we show in our simulations.

The impact on the steady-state scale adjusted stocks of physical and human capital are, respectively,

$$\frac{\partial \tilde{k}/\partial \tau_y}{\tilde{k}} = \frac{(\eta_H - 1)}{(1 - \tau_y)[(1 - \sigma_K)(1 - \eta_H) - \sigma_H \eta_K]} < 0, \tag{16a}$$

$$\frac{\partial \tilde{h}/\partial \tau_y}{\tilde{h}} = -\frac{\eta_K}{(1 - \tau_y)[(1 - \sigma_K)(1 - \eta_H) - \sigma_H \eta_K]} < 0. \tag{16b}$$

Thus a decline in the tax rate will increase the long-run scale-adjusted stocks of both physical and human capital. Assuming that $\eta_K < 1 - \eta_H$, so that human capital is relatively more important than physical capital in the production of new human capital, then the tax cut will have a relatively larger positive impact on physical capital. This assumption, which is conventional throughout the two-sector endogenous growth models, is equivalent here to $\eta_N > f_K + f_H$, thus imposing an upper bound on the externalities in the human capital sector.

Much of the focus of our simulations shall be on income inequality, which we measure by the skill premium

$$w_R \equiv 1 + \frac{r_H}{w} = 1 + \frac{\partial Y / (\psi H)}{\partial Y / (\theta N)} = 1 + \frac{b_H}{b_N} \frac{\theta}{\psi} \frac{N}{H} > 1, \tag{17}$$

where w is the marginal product of unskilled workers and, r_H, the marginal product of human capital, represents the return to skills. Essentially, the relative skill premium is the base wage received for raw labor plus the marginal product of skills in the final goods sector, scaled by the return to raw labor.

Recalling the definition of h, we see that since a reduction in the tax rate on final output increases h (and therefore H) in the long run, it reduces the skill premium as defined by (17). The short-run response may be quite different, however, and requires a detailed simulation of the adjustment. This is because h is fixed in the short run, so that the short-run adjustments in the skill premium operate entirely through the short-run allocations of raw labor θ and human capital ψ. Indeed, in the short run a decrease in τ_y (equivalent to an increase in q) attracts resources to the output (physical-capital) producing sector. If raw labor is more sectorally mobile than human capital (i.e., θ responds more intensely than ψ), then the tax cut will be associated with a short-run rise in the skill premium, before ultimately declining over time.

The differential adjustment in the long and short run of the skill premium is novel to the literature. It requires a nonlinear transition path that is particular to this strand of growth models. In previous models, the transition speed was constant throughout the entire adjustment. In our model, not only the speed of adjustment of all variables changes over time, but their transition is also nonmonotonic.

8.4   Response of Skill Premia to Tax Reforms

One key question of the growth literature is whether the theoretical policy guidance derived from models is empirically relevant. Hence, the purpose of the simulations in this section is twofold. First, we would like to confirm that reasonable parameter values generate plausible steady-state values to key economic variables. This would confirm whether this class of models is capable of generating growth rates of output and skills, as well as allocations of resources to the two sectors that are reasonable, given observed real-world quantities. This endeavor is of key concern since the Solow model generates excessively large rates of convergence (see Barro and Sala-i-Martin 1992), while the first-generation growth models (e.g., Romer 1990) generate key variables and convergence rates that depend implausibly on the size of the population.

Our second purpose is to gain insights into the qualitative nature of the transition path followed by the economy in response to a tax shock. If our benchmark economy replicates transition paths that are similar to those observed in the data, our simulations can be taken as policy guidance. We ask how well these transition paths implied by the model correlate with the actual observed changes in inequality following specific changes in the U.S. tax code. As mentioned earlier, our benchmark is the dramatic change in the tax code in the United States in the 1980s.

Table 8.1 reports the values we employ for our fundamental parameters. Insofar as possible, these are consistent with those suggested by previous calibration exercises.[8] Our benchmark economy assumes that the individual production function and the individual education function exhibit constant returns to scale in the private

Table 8.1
Benchmark parameters

Production function	$\alpha_F = 1$, $b_N = 0.41$, $b_K = 0.31$, $b_H = 0.28$
	$c_G = 0.1$, $c_K = 0$, $c_H = 0$
Education sector	$a_J = 1$, $e_N = 0.30$, $e_K = 0.20$, $e_H = 0.50$
	$f_K = 0$, $f_H = 0$
Preferences	$\rho = 0.04$, $\gamma = 2.5$
Depreciation/Population	$\delta_K = 0.05$, $\delta_H = 0.05$, $n = 0.015$
Fiscal policy	$g = 0.1$, $\tau_y = 0.15152$

factors of production. The private shares of raw labor, physical capital, and human capital—0.41, 0.31, and 0.28, respectively—in the production function for output correspond to the estimates obtained for non-oil-producing countries by Mankiw, Romer, and Weil (1992). In the base calibration, we assume $g = 0.10 = c_G$, which corresponds to government expenditure flow being set at its socially optimal level. Government services are external to the private individual, which introduces increasing returns to scale in the aggregate production function. The benchmark calibration abstracts from externalities in aggregate physical and human capital.

Information on the education function is sparse. We feel that the most important input in augmenting the stock of human capital is human capital, followed by raw labor, with physical capital being the least important. Thus we set $e_H = 0.50$, $e_N = 0.30$, $e_K = 0.20$ as a plausible benchmark, with the relative magnitudes of e_H, e_K being consistent with the endogenous growth models of human capital. Analogously, the benchmark calibrations assume the absence of externalities in the two capital goods.

The key policy variable we consider is the income tax rate, and the experiment we analyze and try to replicate are the short-run effects of the accumulated tax cut that occurred in the United States under the Reagan regime in 1980–1985. Following Mendoza, Razin, and Tesar (1994) and Carey and Tchilinguirian (2000), we obtain a measure for an effective tax rate on total household income illustrated in figure 8.1.[9]

We choose to focus on the U.S. economy because the United States underwent significant changes in its tax code during the Reagan years, especially during the first term 1980–1984. Figure 8.1 clearly shows the legacy of the Reagan administration, with substantial, successive tax cuts in 1980–1981 from 15.152 percent to 11.031 percent in 1985. We choose the 1980–1981 tax rate as our benchmark and analyze a reduction to 11.031 percent, its value in 1985. These years capture the most significant changes in the U.S. tax code in the past fifty years. The U.S. skill premium time series figure 8.2 reveals an additional reason why this time period is especially attractive.

The relative wage hardly moved during the mid- to late-1970s, until the Reagan tax reforms were instituted. After the first, large tax cut was instituted the relative wage dropped briefly only to rise precipitously until 1984. Clearly, the effect of taxes on relative wages is a function of time lags and an array of interrelated economic fac-

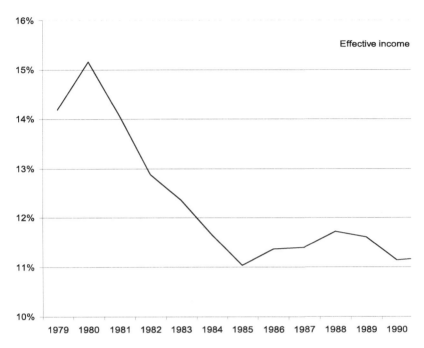

Figure 8.1
Effective U.S. income taxes
Source: OECD (1984, 1997).

tors. However, the model developed earlier incorporates key economic variables, such as investment in education and physical capital. Hence, we would like to explore how successful the model would be in explaining the markedly nonlinear trend in the skill premium, since it coincides with U.S. tax changes during the same period of time.

A key aspect to note in figure 8.2 is that the relative wage movement is *nonmonotonic*. Although taxes fell between 1980 and 1985, the relative wage first dips and then recovers. One interpretation is to assume that factors external to the model account for such nonmonotonicities. An alternative explanation we explore here is to see whether the growth model can replicate such nonmonotonic adjustments as part of its intrinsic dynamics. Indeed, we know from Eicher and Turnovsky (1999) that the transition path in nonscale economies may be characterized by significant nonmonotonicities in the state variables. In particular, we have shown that both the initial state of the economy and the size of the tax cut may influence the

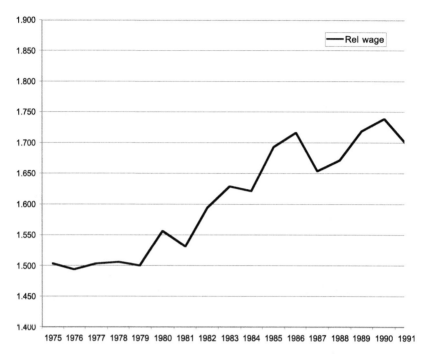

Figure 8.2
U.S. skill premium (college/high school)
Source: U.S. Census Bureau (2000). Mean earnings of workers 18+ by educational attainment.

actual transition to the new steady state. This result, established in simulations for a model without human capital in Eicher and Turnovsky (1999), is extended here for the case incorporating human capital. This characteristic of the nonscale growth model stands in sharp contrast with both the Solow model, as well as with the first-generation endogenous growth models (e.g., Romer 1990), in which transitions are represented either by monotonic adjustments in all key variables, or by instantaneous jumps to the balanced growth path.

The benchmark parameters in table 8.1 yield a set of benchmark values of key economic variables reported in table 8.2a. With the only externality being in government expenditure, which is excludable, the long-run growth rates of the per capita stocks of capital are zero. The share of labor allocated to the production of final output is about 85 percent, the share of capital allocated to production is 86

Table 8.2a
Initial benchmark equilibrium values

$\widehat{Y/N}$	$\widehat{H/N}$	$\tilde{\theta}$	$\tilde{\varphi}$	$\tilde{\psi}$	$\widetilde{Y/K}$	$\widetilde{C/Y}$
0	0	0.845	0.861	0.691	0.344	0.711

Table 8.2b
New steady-state equilibrium

$\widehat{Y/N}$	$\widehat{H/N}$	$\tilde{\theta}$	$\tilde{\varphi}$	$\tilde{\psi}$	$\widetilde{Y/K}$	$\widetilde{C/Y}$
0	0	0.845	0.861	0.691	0.332	0.702

percent and about 31 percent of the skills are used in the human capital sector. The implied equilibrium output-capital ratio is 0.34, and the consumption-output ratio is 0.71. All of these simulated equilibrium values coincide with those found in standard OECD data. Although less information exists on the sectoral allocation of assets, we feel the implied fractions are reasonable.

We can now analyze the dynamics predicted by the model following an accumulated reduction in the tax rate to 11.031 percent by considering the new steady-state equilibrium as reported in table 8.2b. As discussed, the only long-run responses to the tax cut are reductions in the ratios of output to capital and consumption to output. The sectoral allocations of raw labor, physical capital, and human capital remain unchanged. As mentioned earlier, this invariance of the growth rate to tax policy is indeed a feature of the U.S. long-run growth rate.

More interesting, however, is the determination of the extent to which variations in the skill premium, as generated by the model, correlate with U.S. data in the short run as described in figure 8.2. During 1980–1985 the skill premium initially fell, then rose, and subsequently fell for one period, before continuing to rise during the next two periods. Figure 8.3A shows that the this nonscale model not only replicates the steady-state variables well, but also that the simulations also mimic the short-run transition of the skill premium in response to the Reagan tax cuts simulations quite successfully as well. As panel (i) of figure 8.3A shows, on impact the skill premium declines, it then increases for uniformly for approximately four years, after which it begins to decline. The explanation for that can be seen by considering panels (ii) and (iii).

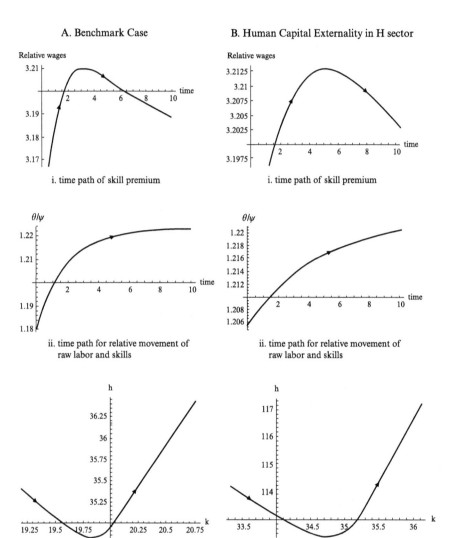

A. Benchmark Case

i. time path of skill premium

ii. time path for relative movement of
raw labor and skills

iii. phase diagram human and
physical capital

B. Human Capital Externality in H sector

i. time path of skill premium

ii. time path for relative movement of
raw labor and skills

iii. phase diagram human and
physical capital

Figure 8.3
Dynamic adjustments

The immediate impact of the reduction in the income tax rate is to attract resources away from the human capital sector to the output sector; θ, ψ, ϕ all increase on impact (see 13a–c). In particular, human capital is reallocated more rapidly than unskilled labor, hence the ratio θ/ψ falls. With the initial stock of human capital fixed, this implies a corresponding immediate reduction in the skill premium. The higher fraction of labor and skills attracted to the final output sector reduces their respective shadow values in that sector relative to the human capital sector, so that both θ, ψ begin to fall. Furthermore, with the greater initial mobility of human capital, its shadow value declines relative to that of raw labor so that as a reaction to the initial fall in θ/ψ is that θ/ψ now begins to rise, and indeed it continues to do so monotonically. This causes the skill premium to begin rising.

At the same time, the reduction in the tax rate raises the return on physical capital relative to that of human capital, and thus physical capital begins to accumulate, while the rate of growth of human capital declines below the population growth rate, so that the "scale-adjusted" human capital actually declines. With human capital increasing in relative scarcity, this increases the skill premium further, thus accentuating the effect of the rising relative shares θ/ψ.

Over time, the effects of the reallocation of factors become less important, revert, and cause the skill premium to decline. First, as raw labor and skills are gradually restored toward their respective (unchanged) steady-state sectoral allocations, θ/ψ increases at a reduced rate, slowing down the rising skill premium. In addition, as physical capital is accumulated, this raises the productivity of human capital, slowing down its initial decline, and inducing its accumulation as well. This is illustrated by the V-shape of the phase diagram relating human and physical capital in panel (iii). As human capital increases, this puts downward pressure on the skill premium, and eventually this effect dominates, in which case the skill premium begins to decline. This decline occurs after approximately four years.[10]

Figure 8.3B illustrates the same time paths in the case where the human capital production function is subject to an externality from aggregate human capital, of the amount $f_H = 0.10$. The steady state with this externality is essentially unchanged from table 8.2b; however, the speeds of adjustment differ. While the qualitative characteristics of the adjustments are essentially unchanged, this externality decreases the magnitudes of both negative eigenvalues that determine the speed of convergence. Hence both the initial adjustment and the adjustment to the long-run steady state are slowed. As a consequence, the peak in the relative wage occurs after five, rather than three to four years.

We also conducted sensitivity analyses to gauge the effects of variations in other externalities. In all cases the shapes are generally as indicated in figure 8.3A–B, but again, the speeds of adjustment are affected. Introducing a human capital externality in the final output sector speeds up the adjustment during the early phases and reduces it during the latter phases. As a consequence, the peak in the skill premium occurs after only two periods. A physical capital externality in either sector slows down the adjustment throughout the entire transition, although its impact is more moderate than is that of a comparable externality due to human capital. Finally, increasing the externality due government expenditure has a similar effect to that of human capital; it raises the speed of adjustment in the short term, but reduces it during the latter stages of the transition. By contrast, the speed of convergence is essentially invariant with respect to the share of output claimed by the government. The sensitivity analysis thus reveals that how effective tax reductions are in fostering increases in factor accumulation, or reductions in inequality will depend on the nature of the economy. Those economies that have fewer human capital externalities will see less of a rise in the relative wage in the short run and a prolonged deviation from the steady state. However, the larger the share of government purchases in output, and the greater the externality associated with such services, the more muted the relative wage response.

8.5   Conclusion

The purpose of the chapter has been to examine the relevance of the most recent strand of growth models in predicting steady states and transitions in response to policy experiments. We derive qualitative results and simulate the model to examine specifically how the model predicts the transition of the skill premium to changes in the income tax. The policy experiment that we have in mind is the historic Reagan tax cuts of the early 1980s.

We show that the model simulates the steady states, convergence speeds, and the actual nonlinear adjustment pattern of the skill premium exceedingly well. In addition, we highlight that how fast and in which fashion the skill premium adjusts is a function of the externalities in production, either human, physical or of public services. The implication for the policy effects is clear. Lower taxes change the incentives for factor accumulation, and hence the return to all factors. While long-term adjustments may not be significant, they may not preclude dramatic changes in short run variations of the skill premium.

8.6 Appendix: Characterization of Transitional Dynamics

Henceforth we assume that the stability properties are ensured so that we can denote the two stable roots by μ_1, μ_2, with $\mu_2 < \mu_1 < 0$. The key variables of interest are physical capital, and technology. The generic form of the stable solution for these variables is given by

$$k(t) - \tilde{k} = B_1 e^{\mu_1 t} + B_2 e^{\mu_2 t}, \tag{A.1a}$$

$$h(t) - \tilde{h} = B_1 v_{21} e^{\mu_1 t} + B_2 v_{22} e^{\mu_2 t}, \tag{A.1b}$$

where B_1, B_2 are constants and the vector

$$\begin{pmatrix} 1 & v_{2i} & v_{3i} & v_{4i} \end{pmatrix}' \qquad i = 1, 2$$

(where the prime denotes vector transpose) is the normalized eigenvector associated with the stable eigenvalue, μ_i. The constants, B_1, B_2, appearing in the solution (10) are obtained from initial conditions and depend upon the specific shocks. Thus suppose that the economy starts out with given initial stocks of capital and knowledge, k_0, a_0 and through some policy shock converges to $\tilde{k}, \tilde{a}$. Setting $t = 0$ in (A.1a) and (A.1b) and letting $d\tilde{k} \equiv \tilde{k} - k_0$, $d\tilde{h} \equiv \tilde{h} - h_0$, B_1, B_2 are given by

$$B_1 = \frac{d\tilde{h} - v_{22} d\tilde{k}}{v_{22} - v_{21}}; \qquad B_2 = \frac{v_{21} d\tilde{k} - d\tilde{h}}{v_{22} - v_{21}}. \tag{A.2}$$

In studying the dynamics, we are interested in characterizing the slope along the transitional path in $h - k$ space. In general, this is given by

$$\frac{dh}{dk} = \frac{B_1 v_{21} \mu_1 e^{\mu_1 t} + B_2 v_{22} \mu_2 e^{\mu_2 t}}{B_1 \mu_1 e^{\mu_1 t} + B_2 \mu_2 e^{\mu_2 t}} \tag{A.3}$$

and is time varying. Note that since $0 > \mu_1 > \mu_2$, as $t \to \infty$ this converges to the new steady state along the direction $(dh/dk)_{t \to \infty} = v_{21}$, for all shocks. The initial direction of motion is obtained by setting $t = 0$ in (12) and depends upon the source of the shock.

It is convenient to express the dynamics of the state variables in phase-space form:

$$
\begin{pmatrix} \dot{k} \\ \dot{h} \end{pmatrix} = \begin{pmatrix} \dfrac{(\mu_1 v_{22} - \mu_2 v_{21})}{v_{22} - v_{21}} & \dfrac{(\mu_2 - \mu_1)}{v_{22} - v_{21}} \\ \dfrac{(\mu_2 - \mu_1)v_{21}v_{22}}{v_{22} - v_{21}} & \dfrac{(\mu_2 v_{22} - \mu_1 v_{21})}{v_{22} - v_{21}} \end{pmatrix} \begin{pmatrix} k - \tilde{k} \\ h - \tilde{h} \end{pmatrix}. \tag{A.4}
$$

By construction, the trace of the matrix in (A.4) $= \mu_1 + \mu_2 < 0$ and the determinant $= \mu_1\mu_2 > 0$, so that (A.4) describes a stable node. The dynamics expressed in (A.1) and (A.4) are in terms of the scale adjusted quantities, from which the growth rates of per capita capital and knowledge can be derived.[11]

Equations (A.1a) and (A.1b) highlight the fact that with the transition path in k and h being governed by two stable eigenvalues, the speeds of adjustment for physical capital and human capital are neither constant nor equal over time. In addition, with output being determined by the two types of capital, the transition of output is also not constant over time, but a simple composite of the transition characteristics of h and k as determined in (A.4).

Notes

We thank Uwe Walz, Danny Quah, Walter Fisher, and participants at the Munich Inequality and Growth Conferences in May 2001 and January 2002 for helpful comments on earlier drafts.

1. Cross-country evidence on the effect of growth on inequality and on that of inequality on growth is inconclusive (see Anand and Kanbur 1993; Deininger and Squire 1998; and Forbes 2000), while historical and recent time series shows a diversity of experiences (Williamson 1991, 1999; Gottschalk and Smeeding 1997). For a review see, Aghion, Caroli, and García-Peñalosa (1999).

2. See Kuznets (1955).

3. See Galor and Zeira (1993).

4. See Bertola (1993), Alesina and Rodrik (1994), Persson and Tabellini (1994), and Alesina and Perotti (1995).

5. See Eicher (1996), García-Peñalosa (1994), and Galor and Tsiddon (1996).

6. The elasticity σ_N reflects the assumption that the government good is rival but excludable. If it were a pure public good $\sigma_N = (1 - \sigma_K - \sigma_H)/(1 - c_G)$.

7. Under constant returns to scale, these scale-adjusted quantities are just regular per capita quantities.

8. See Lucas (1988), Jones (1995), Ortigueira and Santos (1997), and Ogaki and Reinhart (1998).

9. τ_y = taxes on income, profit, and capital gains divided by the sum of (1) unincorporated surplus of private unincorporated enterprises, (2) households' property and entrepreneurial income, and (3) wages and salaries of dependent employment. Our tax data are OECD Revenue Statistics and OECD National Accounts.

10. In the more distant future (around 50 years) the decline in the skill premium is reversed and it converges—albeit slowly—to its long-run steady state, which lies below its original starting point. However, this is not relevant for the impact of the policy shock we are considering.

11. Note that the representation of the transitional dynamics in $k - h$ space takes full account of the feedbacks arising from the jump variables, q and c; these are incorporated in the two eigenvalues.

References

Aghion, P., E. Caroli, and C. García-Peñalosa. 1999. "Inequality and Economic Growth: the Perspective of the New Growth Theories." *Journal of Economic Literature* 37(4): 1615–1660.

Alesina, A., and D. Rodrik. 1994. "Distributive Politics and Economic Growth." *Quarterly Journal of Economics* 109(2): 465–490.

Alesina, A., and R. Perotti. 1995. "Taxation and Redistribution in an Open Economy." *European Economic Review* 39(5): 961–979.

Anand, S., and S. M. R. Kanbur. 1993. "Inequality and Development: A Critique." *Journal of Development Economics* 41(1): 19–43.

Auerbach, A. 1996. "Tax Reform, Capital Allocation, Efficiency and Growth." In *Economic Effects of Fundamental Tax Reform*, ed. H. Aaron and W. Gale. Washington DC: The Brookings Institution.

Auerbach, A., and K. Hassett. 1991. "Recent U.S. Investment Behavior and the Tax Reform Act of 1986: A Disaggregate View." *Carnegie-Rochester Conference Series on Public Policy* 35: 185–215.

Barro, R. J., and X. Sala-i-Martin. 1992. "Convergence." *Journal of Political Economy* 100: 223–251.

Barro, R. J., and X. Sala-i-Martin. 1995. *Economic Growth*. New York: McGraw-Hill.

Bertola, G. 1993. "Factor Shares and Savings in Endogenous Growth." *American Economic Review* 83(5): 1184–1198.

Carey, D., and H. Tchilinguirian. 2000. "Average Effective Tax Rates on Capital, Labour and Consumption." OECD Working Paper no. 31.

Cummins, J., K. Hassett, and R. G. Hubbard. 1994. "A Reconsideration of Investment Behavior Using Tax Reforms as Natural Experiments." *Brookings Papers on Economic Activity* 2: 1–59.

Cummins, J., K. Hassett, and R. G. Hubbard. 1996. "Tax Reforms and Investment: A Cross-Country Comparison." *Journal of Public Economics* 62(1–2): 237–273.

Deininger, K., and Lyn Squire. 1998. "New Ways of Looking at Old Issues: Inequality and Growth." *Journal of Development Economics* 57: 259–287.

Easterly, W., and S. Rebelo. 1993. "Fiscal Policy and Growth: An Empirical Investigation." *Journal of Monetary Economics* 32: 417–458.

Eicher, T. 1996. "Interaction between Endogenous Human Capital with Technological Change." *Review of Economic Studies* 63: 127–144.

Eicher, T., and S. Turnovsky. 1999. "Convergence in a Two-Sector Nonscale Growth Model." *Journal of Economic Growth* 4: 413–428.

Eissa, N. 1996. "Tax Reforms and Labor Supply." In *Tax Policy and the Economy*, vol. 10, ed. J. Poterba, 119–151. Cambridge: The MIT Press for the National Bureau of Economic Research.

Felder, S. 1997. "Tax Reform in a Two-Class Growth Model." *Empirical Economics* 22(2): 273–291.

Forbes, K. 2000. "A Reassessment of the Relationship between Inequality and Growth." *American Economic Review* 90(4): 869–887.

Galor, O., and D. Tsiddon. 1996. "Income Distribution and Growth: The Kuznets Hypothesis Revisited." *Economica* 63(250): S103–S117.

Galor, O., and J. Zeira. 1993. "Income Distribution and Macroeconomics." *Review of Economic Studies* 60(1): 35–52.

García-Peñalosa, C. 1994. "Inequality and Growth: A Note on Recent Theories." *Investigaciones Económicas* 18(1): 97–116.

Gottschalk, P., and T. M. Smeeding. 1997. "Cross-National Comparisons of Earnings and Income Inequality." *Journal of Economic Literature* 35(2): 633–687.

Jones, C. I. 1995. "Time-Series Tests of Endogenous Growth Models." *Quarterly Journal of Economics* 110: 495–525.

Kuznets, S. 1955. "Economic Growth and Income Inequality." *American Economic Review* 45(1): 1–28.

Lucas, R. E. 1988. "On the Mechanics of Economic Development." *Journal of Monetary Economics* 22: 3–42.

Mankiw, N. Gregory, David Romer, and David N. Weil. 1992. "A Contribution to the Empirics of Economic Growth." *Quarterly Journal of Economics* 107(5): 407–437.

Mendoza, E. G., A. Razin, and L. L. Tesar. 1994. "Effective Tax Rates in Macro-economics Cross-Country Estimates of Tax Rates on Factor Incomes and Consumption." *Journal of Monetary Economics* 34: 297–323.

OECD. Various years. "Main Aggregates." *Statistical Bulletins*.

Ogaki, M., and C. Reinhart. 1998. "Measuring Intertemporal Substitution: The Role of Durable Goods." *Journal of Political Economy* 106: 1078–1098.

Ortigueira, S., and M. S. Santos. 1997. "On the Speed of Convergence in Endogenous Growth Models." *American Economic Review* 87: 383–399.

Perroni, C. 1995. "Assessing the Dynamic Efficiency Gains of Tax Reform when Human Capital is Endogenous." *International Economic Review* 36(4): 907–925.

Persson, T., and G. Tabellini. 1994. "Is Inequality Harmful for Growth? Theory and Evidence." *American Economic Review* 84: 600–624.

Romer, P. 1990. "Endogenous Technical Change." *Journal of Political Economy* 98: S71–S103.

Stokey, N. L., and S. Rebelo. 1995. "Growth Effects of Flat-Rate Taxes." *Journal of Political Economy* 103(3): 519–550.

U.S. Census Bureau. 2000. Available online at ⟨http://www.census.gov/population/socdemo/education/tableA-3.txt⟩. 1/25/2001.

Williamson, J. G. 1991. *Inequality, Poverty and History*. Oxford: Blackwell.

Williamson, J. G. 1999. "Globalization and the Labor Market: Using History to Inform Policy." In *Growth, Inequality and Globalization*, P. Aghion and J. G. Williamson. Cambridge: Cambridge University Press.

V

Technology and Natural Resources and Inequality

9 Inequality and Economic Growth: Do Natural Resources Matter?

Thorvaldur Gylfason and
Gylfi Zoega

9.1 Introduction

For a long time, many economists were of the view that economic
efficiency and social equality were essentially incompatible, almost
like oil and water. The perceived but poorly documented trade-off
between efficiency and equality was commonly regarded as one of
the main tenets of modern welfare economics. One of the key
ideas behind this perception was that increased inequality could
increase private as well as social returns to investing in education
and exerting effort in the hope of attaining a higher standard of
life. Redistributive policies were supposed to thwart these tendencies and blunt incentives by penalizing the well-off through taxation
and by rewarding the poor. Economic efficiency—both static and
dynamic—was bound to suffer in the process, or so the argument
went.

More often than not in recent empirical work, measures of income
inequality have turned out to have a negative effect on economic
growth across countries. Thus Alesina and Rodrik (1994), Persson
and Tabellini (1994), and Perotti (1996) report that inequality hurts
growth. Barro (2000) assesses the relationship between economic
growth and inequality in a panel of countries over the period from
1965 to 1995 and finds—by studying the interaction of the Gini index
and the initial level of income in a growth regression—that increased
inequality tends to retard growth in poor countries and boost
growth in richer countries.[1] However, Barro finds no support for a
relationship between inequality and growth in his sample as a
whole. Forbes (2000) finds that the relationship between inequality
and growth becomes positive in a pooled regression when country
effects are included. She claims that country-specific, time-invariant,

omitted variables generate a significant negative bias in the estimated coefficients reflecting the effects of inequality on growth in
pure cross sections and mentions corruption and the level of public
education as two candidates in this regard. Banerjee and Duflo
(2000b) claim that this result is misleading, and arises from imposing
a linear structure on highly nonlinear data.

The previously mentioned empirical results—showing, by and
large, that rapid economic growth tends to go along with less, not
more, inequality—call for an explanation. Thus far, the explanations on offer involve showing how inequality affects growth either
directly or indirectly through its effects on public policy, including taxes and transfers and education expenditures. We now briefly
describe some of these theories before returning to our proposed
thesis, which involves natural resources as a joint determinant of
both inequality and growth.

First, large inequalities of income and wealth may trigger political
demands for transfers and redistributive taxation. To the extent
that transfers and taxation distort incentives to work, save and
invest, inequality may impede growth. It is not clear, however, that
this type of political-cum-fiscal explanation necessarily implies an
inverse relationship between inequality and growth, for it is possible
that during the redistribution phase increased equality and a drop in
growth go hand in hand, especially in panel data that reflect developments over time country by country as well as cross-sectional
patterns. Perotti (1996) finds little empirical support for this type of
explanation. Moreover, in democratic countries with an unequal
distribution of income and with many poor people, the electorate
may vote for more and better education as well as higher taxes and
transfers (Saint-Paul and Verdier 1993, 1996), thus obscuring the
relationship between inequality and growth. Absent democracy,
dictators may still find it in their own interest to redistribute incomes
and reform education in order to promote social peace and
strengthen their own hold on political power (Alesina and Rodrik
1994). Easterly and Rebelo (1993) report empirical results that suggest that increased inequality is associated with both higher taxes
and more public expenditure on education in a large sample of
countries in the period 1970–1988.

In second place, the initial extent of inequality probably makes
a difference. An equalization of incomes and wealth in countries
with gross inequities, such as Brazil where the Gini index is sixty,

would seem likely to foster social cohesion and peace and thus to strengthen incentives rather than weaken them, whereas in places like Denmark and Sweden, where the Gini index is 25 and incomes and wealth are thus already quite equitably distributed by world standards, further equalization might well have the opposite effect. Excessive inequality may be socially divisive and hence inefficient: It may motivate the poor to engage in illegal activities and riots, or at least to divert resources from productive uses, both the resources of the poor and those of the state. Social conflict over the distribution of income, land, or other assets can take place through labor unrest, for instance, or rent seeking that can hinder investment and growth (Benhabib and Rustichini 1996).[2] Alesina and Perotti (1996) report empirical evidence of an inverse relationship between inequality and growth through sociopolitical instability.[3]

Third, national saving may be affected by inequality if the rich have a higher propensity to save than the poor (Kaldor 1956). In this case inequality may be good for growth in that the greater the level of inequality, the higher is the saving rate and hence also investment and economic growth. Against this Todaro (1997) suggests that the rich may invest in an unproductive manner—count their yachts and expensive cars. Barro (2000) finds no empirical evidence of a link between inequality and investment.

Fourth, increased inequality may hurt education rather than helping it as suggested by the political-economy literature referred to at the beginning of this brief discussion. If so, increased inequality may hinder economic growth through education. Galor and Zeira (1993) and Aghion (1998) argue that this outcome is likely in the presence of imperfect capital markets. If each member of society has a fixed number of investment opportunities, imperfect access to credit, and a different endowment of inherited wealth, the rich would end up using many of their investment opportunities while the poor could only use a few. Therefore, the marginal return from the last investment opportunity of the rich would be much lower than the marginal return of the last investment opportunity of the poor. Redistribution of wealth from the rich to the poor would increase output because the poor would then invest in more productive projects at the margin. This argument can also be applied to investment in human capital if we assume diminishing returns to education. In this case, taking away the last few quarters of the university education of the elite and adding time to the more elementary education of the poor would raise output and perhaps also long-run growth, other things being the same. Income redistribution would reverse the decline in investment in human capital resulting from the credit-market failure.[4]

The distribution of income and wealth may also affect the amount of public and private investment in education. When a large part of the population is poor, it may be more likely that the majority of voters will support expenditures on public education aimed at the poor, as argued by Saint-Paul and Verdier (1993, 1996) and corrobo-rated empirically by Easterly and Rebelo (1993), but the effect could also, in principle, go the other way. If so, the more deprived and detached from the mainstream population is the poorer segment, the less likely the poor are to participate in or affect the outcome of elections. As a result the general level of education may suffer— the more so, the more capital-constrained is the poorer segment of the population. A virtuous circle may arise when redistribution of income leads to an increase or improvement in human capital, which then induces voters to prefer higher expenditures on education, which again pulls more workers out of poverty, and so on. At an empirical level, we would expect increased equality to enhance eco-nomic growth through its effect on education, and vice versa. That is, more and better general education may be expected to reduce public tolerance against extreme inequality and thus to reduce inequality through the political process, thereby stimulating economic growth. These processes can be mutually reinforcing; that is, if increased social equality encourages education and economic growth, this does not mean that more and better education cannot similarly, and simultaneously, enhance equality and growth.

The previous models all have the same basic structure: Inequality affects some unknown intermediate variable X which, in turn, makes a difference for economic growth. In this chapter we take a different approach: we view both economic growth and inequality of incomes as well as of educational attainment and of land as endogenous var-iables and argue that the inverse relationship between inequality and growth does not imply causality one way or the other. We propose an explanation which, in contrast to the ones surveyed in the litera-ture reviewed briefly earlier, involves a variable that is exogenous to most economic models. This variable is the abundance of, or rather dependence on, natural resources, which we measure by the amount of natural capital per person and the share of natural capital in national wealth, respectively. We will argue, on theoretical grounds as well as empirically, that a direct relationship between natural resource intensity and inequality, on the one hand, and between natural resource intensity and growth, on the other hand, can help account for the inverse cross-sectional relationship between inequality and growth that is observed in the data, assuming that natural resources are given. The first relationship—between natural resource intensity and inequality—was documented by Bourguignon and Morrison (1990) in a sample of thirty-five developing countries in 1970, while the second relationship—between natural resource intensity and growth—has been scrutinized by a number of authors in recent years, beginning with Sachs and Warner (1995). Moreover, we assume that the ownership of natural resources tends to be less equally distributed than other assets within as well as across countries. To the extent that this is not the case at the outset, we assume that rent seeking and other forces, frequently compounded by a lack of democracy, will see to it that the natural resources end up in the hands of a relatively small minority—a military regime, say, or a royal family.

The chapter proceeds as follows. In section 9.2, we set out our view of the way in which natural resources can affect inequality and growth. In section 9.3, we describe the data that we use to measure income inequality and also gender inequality in education; we also discuss inequality in the distribution of land. In section 9.4, we present simple cross-country correlations between three different measures of education, three different measures of inequality and economic growth, and thus allow the data to speak for themselves. In section 9.5, we attempt to dig a little deeper and report the results of cross-sectional multiple regression analysis where growth is traced to natural resource intensity, education and inequality as well as to other factors commonly used in growth regression analysis (investment and initial income), and where some of the determinants of growth, including education and inequality, are explicitly modeled as endogenous variables. Section 9.6 concludes the discussion.

9.2 Resources, Distribution, and Growth

An important potential weakness of the many stories purporting to explain the relationship between inequality and growth is that both of these variables are endogenous. This leaves open the possibility that a third, exogenous variable is affecting both, thus giving rise to the inverse correlation between the two. Specifically, a country's abundance of, or dependence on, natural resources can under many circumstances be viewed as exogenous to models of economic growth and also to models attempting to explain the extent of income inequality. But even if we treat natural resources as exogenous, we are aware that both natural resource extraction and reserves can respond to economic forces; for example, oil prices can influence oil production as well as oil exploration. We do not address this problem in this paper, but we acknowledge its potential importance; at some point, this problem will need to be addressed. Here we want to let it suffice to explore the possibility that natural resource ownership impinges on both inequality and growth and thus illuminates the inverse relationship between inequality and growth that has been observed in cross-sectional data.

We will now show how natural resource dependence is inversely related to both equality and growth in a standard growth model. Thereafter, we will test this prediction empirically in a sample of eighty-seven industrial and developing countries in the period 1965–1998. Our theoretical model can be summarized as follows: Workers can earn a living either by working in the primary sector extracting natural resources from the soil or the sea or through paid employment in the manufacturing sector, including services. Because human capital is equally spread across the population, wage income in manufacturing is the same for all workers. However, due to the whims of nature, or the competition for the rent generated by the natural resource, earnings in the primary sector are unequal at each point in time. It follows that the more time workers devote to natural resource extraction, the more unequal the distribution of income. And growth is also affected. If we assume, quite plausibly, that the manufacturing industry provides greater opportunities for learning and innovation, it follows that the more time workers spend in the primary sector, the lower will be the rate of growth. Hence, abundant natural resources cause both inequality and slow growth by tempting workers away from industries where technology and output are more likely to progress and grow and where earnings are more equally shared. Elsewhere (Gylfason and Zoega 2001b) we show how saving and investment—and hence also growth—can depend inversely on natural resources. The intuition is again straightforward: When physical capital is less important in the production technology, the optimal rate of saving is lower. Therefore, the optimal level of steady-state capital is lower. If we now postulate learning-by-investing (as in Romer 1986), the rate of technological progress and the rate of growth of output per capita will consequently both be lower.

Our hypothesis has the advantage that here we have an exogenous variable that affects the two endogenous variables in a predictable way, and this makes any empirical testing of the theory more robust. We will show how the relationship between inequality and growth can arise in the presence of natural resources. If natural resources affect both inequality and growth, then this could shed new light on the statistical relationship between inequality and growth. But to do this we need to identify, on theoretical grounds as well as empirically, the relationship between natural resources and inequality, on the one hand, and between natural resources and growth, on the other hand. It is to this task that we now turn.

9.2.1   Allocation of Time

Imagine a world in which natural resources generate a constant flow of riches. All one has to do is go out and pick the fruits of nature, be they diamonds, fish, or oil. This could involve passively standing beneath an apple tree or a coconut palm and picking up the fruits that fall to the ground or one could have to exert oneself looking for fruits, diamonds or fish, to take a few examples. The value of each bundle of the natural resource is equal to R and the likelihood of finding a bundle increases with the time spent searching. Now imagine that amid the bounties of nature there is a manufacturing industry that uses labor and capital to produce output without using or depending in any way on the natural resource. Assume, crucially for our argument, that workers face a more challenging and stimulating work environment in the manufacturing industry, because manufacturing is more likely to foster learning and innovation. In particular, assume that there is learning-by-investing in manufacturing.

Workers have a choice when it comes to their work effort: They can spend part of or all of their time trying their luck picking fruits or they can take a paid job in industry. Each individual has to decide how much time to spend picking fruits and how much time to spend in paid employment. We denote the fraction of time spent in productive employment by β and the fraction spent picking fruits by $1 - \beta$.

Now assume that the discovery of a bundle of natural resources valued R is a random event and follows a Poisson distribution. Denote the number of such discoveries by the random variable N. The random event is then defined as "a worker finds a bundle of the natural resource during a unit of time" and has the following density:

$$f(N) = \frac{e^{-\gamma(1-\beta)} [\gamma(1 - \beta)]^N}{N!} \qquad \text{for } N = 0, 1, 2, \ldots, \tag{1}$$

where the mean arrival rate—that is, the expected number of discoveries by a given worker or, equivalently, the probability that a discovery will be made by the worker within a unit of time—is $E(N) = \gamma(1 - \beta)$. The expected number of discoveries for the representative individual is thus a linear function of the fraction of time spent searching. The larger the share of time spent in nature, the more bundles will be discovered. The parameter γ measures search effectiveness.

There are L individuals (identical by assumption) spending part of their time searching. The aggregate income from the natural resource is then

$$Y^n = NLR. \tag{2}$$

The expected value and the variance of N given by the Poisson distribution are both equal to $\gamma(1 - \beta)$. Since all individuals are identical, it follows that the variance across the population in the number of discoveries of the natural resource bundles per unit of time is also equal to $\gamma(1 - \beta)$. We now have the following result: The variance of the distribution of income emanating from the natural resource is an increasing function of the time devoted by each worker to the natural resource–based sector—primary sector, for short. Define income per capita by lower-case letters. We then have

$$E(y^n) = \gamma(1 - \beta)R, \qquad \text{var}(y^n) = \gamma(1 - \beta)R \tag{3}$$

The expected per capita income or rent from the natural resource as well as the variance of this per capita income across the population of workers is an increasing function of the abundance of the resource R and also an increasing function of the time spent procuring it $1 - \beta$.

We now turn to the manufacturing industry, which offers workers an alternative to wandering around nature. This industry uses capital and labor to produce output and offers opportunities for learning and innovation. The production function is

$$Y_i = (qK_i)^\alpha (K\beta L_i)^{1-\alpha} \tag{4}$$

Here q denotes the quality of capital and takes a value between zero and one,[5] K_i and L_i denote the capital and labor used by firm i and K is the aggregate capital stock in the manufacturing sector. As in Romer (1986) the aggregate capital stock is a proxy for the accumulated knowledge that has been generated in the past through investment at all firms. This is what sets manufacturing apart from the primary sector; it uses capital and the installation of new units of capital generates a flow of ideas that raises productivity in a labor-augmenting fashion. In contrast, the primary sector does not offer similar opportunities for learning and innovation.

We assume a perfectly competitive market for labor and capital. Assuming symmetric equilibrium, so that $K = kL$, gives the following first-order conditions for maximum profit, and also for equilibrium in the two factor markets:

$$\frac{dY_i}{dL_i} = (1 - \alpha)kq^\alpha(\beta L)^{1-\alpha} = \beta w \tag{5}$$

$$\frac{dY_i}{dK_i} = \alpha q^\alpha(\beta L)^{1-\alpha} = r + \delta, \tag{6}$$

where w is the real wage, r is the real interest rate and δ is the rate at which installed capital loses its usefulness over time, as a result of economic obsolescence as well as physical wear and tear (Scott 1989).[6]

The representative worker/consumer has to make two decisions each moment of his infinite life. He has to decide how much to consume and save and how much time to spend working in the manufacturing sector rather than trying his luck in the primary sector. We assume that he cannot do both at the same time. Hence a decision to spend more time in the primary sector causes him to spend less time in paid employment making manufactures. Moreover, we assume that time spent in the primary sector is costly: A direct cost η is incurred for each moment spent. Finally, there is a tax on wages t_w and also a tax on income from the natural resources t_n.

The worker maximizes the discounted sum of future utility from consumption:

$$\max_{\beta,c} \int_0^\infty \log(c_t)e^{-\rho t}\,dt, \tag{7}$$

where ρ is the discount rate, subject to

$$\dot{a}_t = ra_t + \beta w(1 - t_w) + \gamma(1 - \beta)R(1 - t_n) - \gamma(1 - \beta)\eta - c_t.$$

By assumption, the worker does not gain any utility (or suffer disutility) in the primary sector, nor from being employed. The worker has assets a, which he accumulates if his earnings exceed expenditures (henceforth, we omit time subscripts). His earnings come from three sources: There is interest income on assets ra, which is tax-free, there is wage income from employment βw, taxed at t_w, and there is the value of the primary goods he picks or produces $(1 - \beta)R$, taxed at t_n. The worker then incurs the direct cost η and consumes c per unit of time. A necessary condition for optimal consumption is

$$c = \frac{1}{\lambda}, \tag{8}$$

where λ denotes the shadow price of wealth. Consumption is at an optimum when the marginal utility of consumption is equal to the shadow price of wealth at each instant. More interesting is equation (9), which helps determine the optimal allocation of time:

$$w(1 - t_w) = \gamma R(1 - t_n) - \eta. \tag{9}$$

The left-hand side of equation (9) shows the marginal benefit from working longer in manufacturing net of taxes, while the right-hand side shows the marginal benefit from fruit picking, also net of taxes. While each worker takes wages w as given, wages do nevertheless respond to market forces. Combining equations (5) and (9) gives the following equation:

$$(1 - \alpha)kq^\alpha L^{1-\alpha}\beta^{-\alpha}(1 - t_w) = \gamma R(1 - t_n) - \eta. \tag{10}$$

Solving for β gives

$$\beta = \left[\frac{(1 - \alpha)kq^\alpha L^{1-\alpha}(1 - t_w)}{\gamma R(1 - t_n) - \eta}\right]^{1/\alpha}. \tag{11}$$

The time spent in industrial employment β is decreasing in the value of the natural resource R and search effectiveness γ as well as in taxes on wage income t_w, and increasing in the accumulated knowledge in the manufacturing industry kL ($=K$), the productivity of capital q, taxes on natural resources t_n and the cost of utilizing the natural resource η.

9.2.2 Work and Growth

We can now describe the various ways in which natural resources affect the allocation of labor in our model.

• The discovery of natural resources R raises the reward to producing primary output and reduces the optimal time spent in manufacturing.

• A decrease in the cost of producing primary output η and an increase in search effectiveness γ have an effect identical to that of a resource discovery: labor leaves manufacturing for the primary sector.

• The structure of the tax system affects the allocation of time. The higher are taxes on wages t_w and the lower are taxes on income or rent from natural resource extraction t_n, the more time is devoted to producing primary goods.

• History matters because past learning-by-investing in the industrial sector determines current knowledge as reflected by k and hence also real wages. The more advanced the manufacturing sector, the higher the wages it can afford to pay and the more time workers spend in manufacturing.

The last point explains why natural resource abundance and dependence do not have to go together. Abundance of natural resources is a significant impediment to growth only if productivity and wages in the manufacturing sector are low, that is, if there is little accumulated knowledge and expertise in the sector. But the presence of abundant natural resources can prevent manufacturing from "taking off," thereby preventing innovation and learning from taking place:

• When R is sufficiently high, or when productivity in the manufacturing sector is sufficiently low, it can be optimal not to spend any time in manufacturing. In this case, growth never takes off.

Education provides a possible solution to this dilemma by increasing labor productivity in manufacturing:

· Education can increase knowledge, and thereby also labor productivity which, like past learning-by-doing, lifts wages and draws workers to the manufacturing industry from the primary sector.

We now turn to the remaining necessary condition for maximum utility, the Euler equation giving optimal growth of consumption:

$$\frac{\dot{c}}{c} = r - \rho. \tag{12}$$

Equations (6) and (12) give the optimal rate of growth of consumption and output:

$$g = \alpha q^{\alpha}(\beta L)^{1-\alpha} - \delta - \rho. \tag{13}$$

Growth is an increasing function of β, the share of time spent producing manufactures rather than primary goods.

There are two market failures in the model. The first is the standard one that firms, when investing, neglect the gains from learning and knowledge spillovers to other firms. In contrast, a social planner uses the average product of capital—not the private marginal product—to measure the cost of capital. Second, workers compare the current benefit from spending time in the two sectors but ignore the growth effect of industrial employment: by spending more time in the manufacturing industry they, collectively, would raise the marginal product of capital, the interest rate and economic growth. This makes their wages grow more rapidly. By withdrawing labor from the primary sector, workers would invest in a higher future wage. However, each worker has only a very small effect on growth imparting an external benefit to others.

We can now summarize the relationship between natural resources and growth.

· A rise in the natural resource rent R attracts more people to the primary sector in the hope of securing a piece of the action. These people leave the manufacturing sector, thereby lowering the private marginal product of capital, the rate of interest and the rate of growth of consumption and output. This is the Dutch disease working through the labor market (Paldam 1997).

• When abundant natural resources reduce the incentive to provide good education (Gylfason 2001), this reduces labor productivity and wages, hence reinforcing the incentive to stay in the natural resource sector. An abundant natural resource—a high value of R—attracts workers and this effect is reinforced by bad education which drives people away from industrial employment.

• If natural resources reduce the quality of society's institutions, this could manifest itself in a reduction in the private cost of rent seeking η. Moreover, less developed capital markets are likely to generate a lower quality capital stock q, which depreciates at a higher rate δ (Gylfason and Zoega 2001a, 2001b).

We can now combine these insights with the earlier result showing that the variance of income or rent emanating from the natural resource sector is

$$\text{var}(y^n) = \gamma(1 - \beta)R. \tag{14}$$

Equations (13) and (14) show that while economic growth is increasing in β, inequality—measured by the variance of income—is decreasing in β. According to our thesis, any variable that increases the value of β is likely to stimulate growth and reduce inequality. Equation (11) shows that an abundance of natural resources—relative to the level of technological know-how—will lower the value of β. In contrast, any variable that raises labor productivity and wages in the manufacturing sector will raise β, increase growth and reduce inequality. The knowledge that has been generated through past investment and production is one such factor. Another factor is the level of education. Education that raises productivity and wages in industry will discourage workers from spending time in the natural resource sector and hence raise growth and reduce inequality. At last, the tax system can affect growth and equality: A high tax on natural resource rents and a low tax on wages increases the value of β, hence raising growth and reducing inequality.

9.3   Measuring Inequality

In what follows, we make use of three different measures of inequality. Take income inequality first. The Gini index measures the

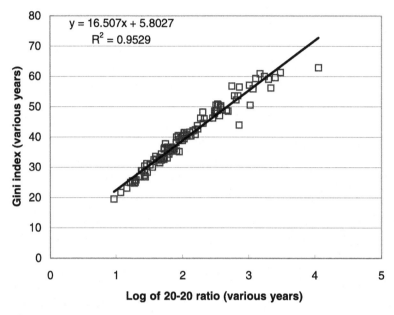

Figure 9.1
The Gini index and the 20-20 ratio

extent to which income (or, in some cases, consumption) among individuals or households within an economy deviates from a perfectly equal distribution. A Gini index of 0 represents perfect equality, while a Gini index of 100 means perfect inequality. As figure 9.1 shows, the Gini index is closely correlated with the log of the ratio of the income or consumption of the 20 percent of households with the highest incomes to the income or consumption of the 20 percent of households with the lowest incomes (the "20/20 ratio"). In our sample, the 20/20 ratio is lowest (2.6, Gini = 19.5) in the Slovak Republic and highest in Sierra Leone (57.6, Gini = 62.9). The regression line through the scatter in figure 9.1 shows that each ten-point increase in the Gini index goes along with roughly a doubling of the 20/20 ratio. Thus, for example, the Nordic countries have a Gini index of 25 and a 20/20 ratio of 3 whereas the United Kingdom has a Gini index of 35 and a 20/20 ratio of 6. The corresponding figures are 30 and 4 for Germany and 40 and 8 for the United States as well as for China and Russia. The data come from nationally representative household surveys and refer to different years between 1983–1985 and 1998–1999 (World Bank 2000, Table 2.8). The data refer to either (a) per-

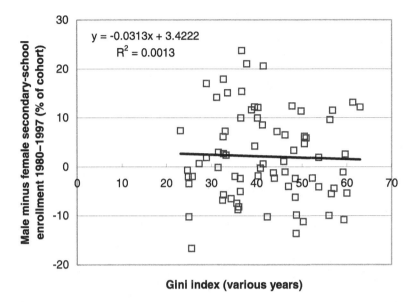

Figure 9.2
Income inequality and gender inequality

sonal or household incomes before taxes and transfers or (b) consumption expenditures and, hence, implicitly incomes after taxes and transfers. Whenever possible, consumption was used rather than income (World Bank 2000). The Gini index of income inequality is available for seventy-five of the eighty-seven countries in our sample.

Our second inequality measure is intended to reflect one aspect of social inequality, that is, the unequal access of males and females to education. We take the difference between the average secondary-school enrollment rates of males and females in 1980–1997 to represent gender inequality in education. In a majority of cases where the rates are different, more males than females go to secondary school. In some cases, however, more females than males attend secondary schools. Even so, we use the arithmetic rather than absolute difference between male and female enrolment rates as our inequality measure. This means that we view a change from a situation where, say, the secondary-school enrollment rate for males is 17 percentage points higher than that for females (as in Egypt) to a situation where the secondary-school enrollment rate for females is 17 percentage points higher than that for males (as in Finland) as a decrease in gender inequality. Surprisingly, figure 9.2 shows that there is in

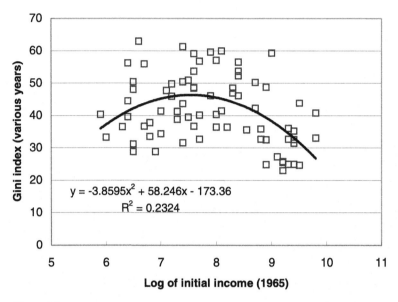

Figure 9.3
Income inequality and initial income: The Kuznets curve

our sample no discernible correlation between income inequality as measured by the Gini index and gender inequality of education as measured by the excess of male over female secondary-school enrollment. Thus economic and social inequality, as measured here, do not necessarily go hand in hand.

Our cross-country data support the notion of a Kuznets curve: Income inequality tends to increase with income at low levels of income and to decrease with income at higher levels of income, as shown in figure 9.3. Galor and Moav (1999) suggest the following interpretation of the Kuznets curve: in early stages of development, when investment in physical capital is the main engine of economic growth, inequality spurs growth by directing resources toward those who save and invest the most, whereas in more mature economies human capital accumulation takes the place of physical capital accumulation as the main source of growth, and inequality impedes growth by hurting education because poor people cannot fully finance their education in imperfect credit markets. On the other hand, the gender inequality of education varies inversely and linearly with initial income, without any visible tendency for gender inequality to increase with income at low levels of income (figure 9.4).

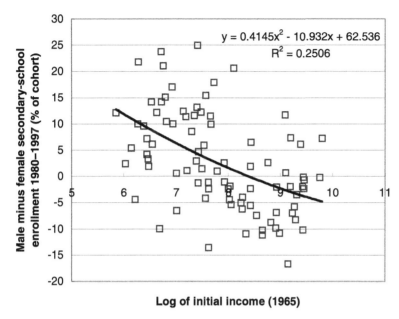

Figure 9.4
Gender inequality and initial income

The third measure of inequality that we will use is the Gini index for the distribution of land. This measure is taken from Deininger and Olinto (2000), and covers fifty of the eighty-seven countries in our sample. Figure 9.5 shows that, almost without exception, land is less equally distributed than income in our sample. Spearman's rank correlation between the two measures is 0.57.

9.4 Cross-Country Patterns in the Data

In this section, we allow the data to speak for themselves in the form of a series of bivariate cross-sectional correlations. We first take a look at the correlations between our three measures of inequality and economic growth, all of which are unambiguously negative in our data: Greater inequality in the distribution of income and land as well as in access to education tends to go together with lower rates of growth. We then move on to show that two of the three measures of inequality increase from country to country in tandem with the share of natural capital in national wealth. This opens up the possibility that it is the variation in natural capital in the sample that

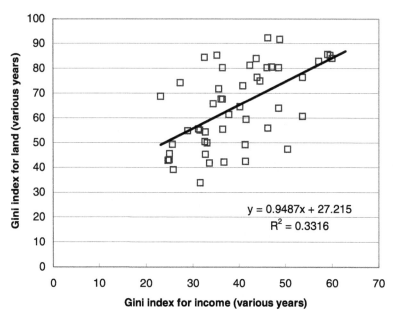

Figure 9.5
Distribution of income and land

generates the apparent relationship between inequality and growth: When natural resources become more important, inequality rises and growth recedes. This was the prediction of our model in section 9.2. At last, we also show that income inequality and three different measures of education are inversely related, while education and growth are positively correlated. This finding accords with earlier research indicating that education, by reducing inequality and fostering growth, can help clarify the inverse relationship between inequality and growth that is observed in the data. Unlike natural resource abundance, however, education is probably best viewed as an endogenous variable, a possibility that we address explicitly in the regression analysis presented in section 9.5.

9.4.1 Inequality and Growth

Let us now begin by looking at the cross-country pattern of income inequality and economic growth. Figure 9.6 shows a scatterplot of the annual rate of growth of gross national product (GNP) per capita from 1965 to 1998 (World Bank 2000, Table 1.4) and the inequality

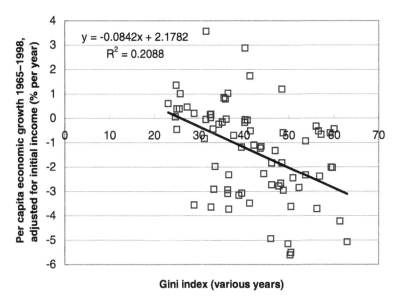

Figure 9.6
Income inequality and economic growth

of income or consumption as measured by the Gini index (World Bank 2000, Table 2.8). The growth rate has been adjusted for initial income: the variable on the vertical axis is that part of economic growth that is not explained by the country's initial stage of development, obtained as a residual from a regression of growth during 1965–1998 on initial GNP per head (i.e., in 1965) as well as the share of natural capital in national wealth, taken from World Bank (1997). The seventy-five countries shown in the figure are represented by one observation each.[7] The regression line through the scatterplot suggests that an increase of about twelve points on the Gini scale from one country to another is associated with a decrease in per capita growth by 1 percentage point per year on average. Twelve points on the Gini scale correspond roughly to the difference between income inequality in the United Kingdom (Gini = 36) and in Sweden and Japan (Gini = 25). The relationship in figure 9.6 is statistically significant (Spearman's rank correlation is −0.50). If rich countries and poor are viewed separately, a similar pattern is observed in both groups (not shown). Shaving one percentage point off any country's annual growth rate is a serious matter because the (weighted) average rate of per capita growth in the world economy

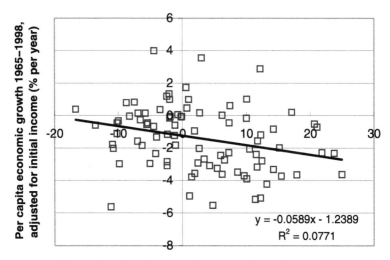

**Male minus female secondary-school enrollment 1980–1997
(% of cohort)**

Figure 9.7
Gender inequality and economic growth

since 1965 has been about 1.25 percent per year. We see no signs of the positive cross-sectional relationship between inequality and growth in rich countries reported by Barro (2000), nor do we see any evidence of the nonlinearity in the panel relationship documented by Banerjee and Duflo (2000a,b).

Figures 9.7 and 9.8 tell a similar story. Here we see the cross-country pattern of per capita growth as measured in Figure 9.6 and gender inequality of education (figure 9.7) and land inequality (figure 9.8). The pattern is not as clear as in figure 9.6, but it is still statistically significant (Spearman's rank correlation is −0.32 and −0.37, respectively). The number of countries is seventy-five and fifty in the two figures. All countries for which the requisite data are available are included in all the figures in the paper, without exception.

9.4.2 Natural Resources, Inequality, and Growth

In figure 9.9, we measure natural resource dependence by the share of natural capital in national wealth in 1994—namely, the share of natural capital in total capital, which comprises physical, human,

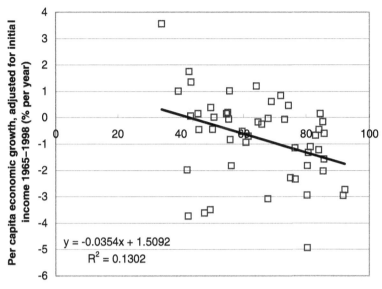

Figure 9.8
Land inequality and economic growth

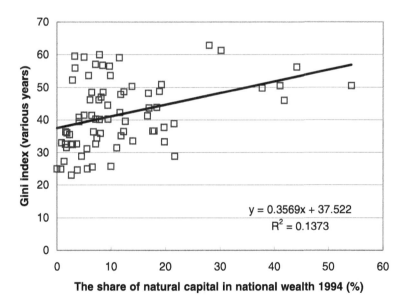

Figure 9.9
Income inequality and natural capital

and natural capital (though not social capital; see World Bank 1997). The natural capital variable is intended to come closer to a direct measurement of the intensity of natural resources across countries than the various proxies that have been used in earlier studies, mainly the share of primary (i.e., nonmanufacturing) exports in total exports or in gross domestic product (GDP) and the share of the primary sector in employment or the labor force. The latter proxies may be prone to bias due to product and labor market distortions.

Figure 9.9 shows that the share of natural capital in national wealth is positively correlated with income inequality as measured by the Gini index. Spearman's rank correlation is 0.41. Notice the cluster of five countries (Niger, Guinea-Bissau, Madagascar, Mali, and Zambia, in descending order) in the northeast corner of the figure with a natural capital share above 35 and Gini above 45. Even if this cluster is removed from the sample, the pattern remains statistically significant. Notice, further, the two countries (Sierra Leone and the Central African Republic) with a natural capital share of around 30 and Gini above 60. If this pair of observations is omitted, the pattern remains significant. If, however, both clusters (i.e., all seven countries) are removed from the sample, the remaining pattern becomes insignificant in a statistical sense. In this sense, this group of seven African countries in the northeast corner of the figure explains the inverse correlation. Even so, we are inclined to keep these African countries in our sample. We find it instructive that no country with a natural capital share above 25 has a Gini coefficient below 45.

Figure 9.10 shows that the natural capital share is also positively correlated with gender inequality as measured by the male minus female secondary-school enrollment rate. Spearman's rank correlation is 0.32. The pattern observed is statistically significant with or without the seven African countries mentioned above. Moreover, there is a positive albeit insignificant correlation between land inequality and natural capital in our sample (not shown); Spearman's rank correlation is 0.19.

From figures 9.9 and 9.10 combined with figure 9.11, which shows that the natural capital share varies inversely with per capita economic growth from 1965 to 1998 across the same group of countries, we conclude that these findings may help explain the inverse cross-sectional relationship between inequality and growth shown in figures 9.6 and 9.7. In figure 9.11, the rank correlation between nat-

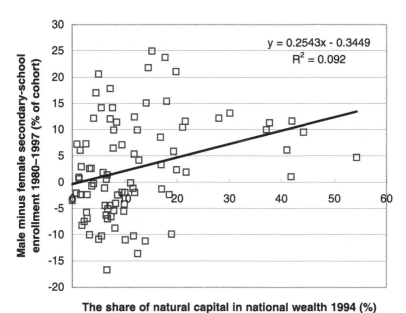

Figure 9.10
Gender inequality and natural capital

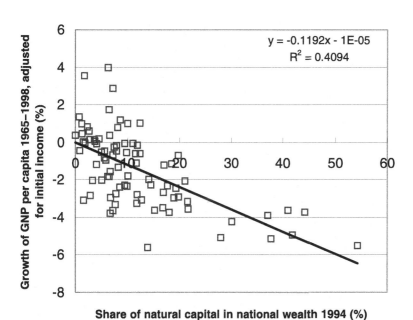

Figure 9.11
Natural capital and economic growth

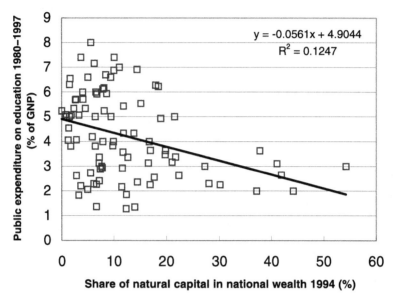

Figure 9.12
Natural capital and expenditure on education

ural capital and growth ($r = -0.64$) is statistically significant, and remains so even if the two clusters in the southwest corner and the northeast corner of the figure are excluded from the sample (see Gylfason and Zoega 2001b).

At last, figure 9.12 shows that, in our sample, natural capital is also inversely and significantly correlated with public expenditure on education ($r = -0.32$). Natural capital is also inversely and significantly related to years of schooling for girls and secondary-school enrollment for both genders (not shown).

9.4.3   Inequality and Education

Let us now consider the three measures of education inputs, outcomes, and participation and how they vary with inequality and economic growth. Figure 9.13 shows a scatterplot of public expenditure on education from 1980 to 1997 as reported by UNESCO (see World Bank 2000, Table 2.9) and income inequality. Public expenditure on education varies a great deal from country to country. In the 1990s, some countries spent as little as 1 percent of their GNP

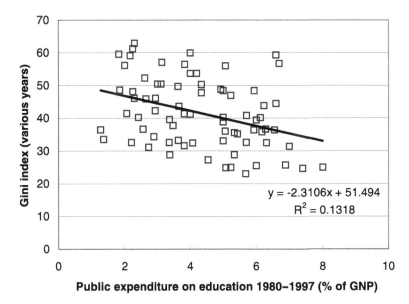

Figure 9.13
Expenditure on education and income inequality

on education (Haiti, Indonesia, Myanmar, Nigeria, and Sudan). Others have spent between 8 percent and 10 percent of their GNP on education, including St. Lucia, Namibia, Botswana, and Jordan, in descending order. Public expenditure is admittedly an imperfect measure of a nation's commitment to education, not least because some nations spend more on private education than others. Moreover, public expenditure on education may be supply-led and of mediocre quality, and may thus fail to foster efficiency, equality, and growth, in contrast to private expenditure on education, which is generally demand-led and thus, perhaps, likely to be of a higher quality. Even so, this yardstick should reflect at least to some extent the government's commitment to education. The regression line through the seventy-four observations in figure 9.13 suggests that an increase in public expenditure on education by one percent of GNP from one country to the next is associated with a decrease of 2.3 points in the Gini index. The relationship is statistically significant ($r = -0.36$).

Figure 9.14 shows scatterplots of the expected number of years of schooling for females from 1980 to 1997 and income inequality. This

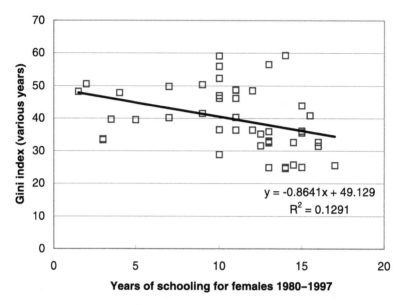

Figure 9.14
Years of schooling and income inequality

indicator of schooling is intended to reflect the total education resources, measured in school years, that a girl will acquire over her lifetime in school or as an indicator of an education system's overall state of development. In figure 9.14, the regression line through the forty-six observations, one per country, suggests that an increase by one year of the schooling that an average girl at the age of school entry can expect to receive is associated with a decrease in the Gini index, namely, increased equality, by almost one point. The relationship is statistically significant ($r = -0.49$). Unlike the relationship in figure 9.13, the one in figure 9.14 is significantly nonlinear (not shown), suggesting that the marginal effect of increased education on equality is rising in the level of education—that is, there may be increasing returns to schooling in terms of equality. Sen (1999), among others, emphasizes the importance of educating girls in developing countries. The corresponding relationship for males (not shown) is virtually the same as for females.

In figure 9.15, we present a scatterplot of secondary-school enrollment and income inequality. The pattern is clear: an increase in secondary-school enrollment by 5 percent of each cohort goes hand in hand with a decrease in the Gini index by one point. The data

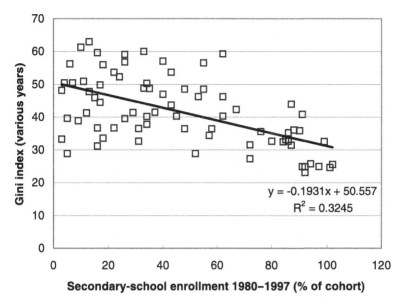

Figure 9.15
School enrollment and income inequality

exhibit a similar, albeit not quite as strong, relationship between secondary-school enrollment and gender inequality (not shown). The same applies to figures 9.13 and 9.14: Public expenditure on education and years of schooling for girls are also inversely related to gender inequality (not shown). All three measure of education are positively correlated with economic growth (not shown).

These patterns seem to suggest that more and better education goes along with less inequality as well as more rapid growth and that human capital, like natural capital, thus can perhaps help explain the inverse relationship between inequality and growth that we observe in the data. To find out, we need to dig a little deeper.

9.5   Regression Analysis

Table 9.1 reports seemingly unrelated regression (SUR) estimates of a system of five equations for the eighty-seven countries in our sample for the years 1965–1998. The equations reveal how natural capital intensity can affect growth through various channels: through investment, education and inequality, as well as directly.

9.5.1   The Model and Estimation

The first equation shows how economic growth depends on (a) the logarithm of initial per capita income (i.e., in 1965), defined as income in 1998 divided by an appropriate growth factor, (b) the share of natural capital in national wealth (which comprises physical, human and natural capital), (c) the share of gross domestic investment in GDP in 1965–1998, (d) the log of the secondary-school enrollment rate (the log in order to capture diminishing returns to education), (e) the Gini index, and (f) gender inequality of education as measured by the difference between male and female secondary-school enrollment rates in 1980–1997. This equation can be interpreted either as a description of endogenous long-run growth or of medium-term growth in the neoclassical model where economic growth is exogenous in the long run. Initial income is intended to capture conditional convergence. Natural capital is another exogenous determinant of growth. Investment and education are intended to capture the contribution of physical and human capital accumulation to growth. The inequality measures reflect the hypothesized effects of income and gender inequality on growth.

The second equation shows the relationship between the investment rate and the natural capital share (as spelled out in Gylfason and Zoega 2001b; the underlying explanation is that increased dependence on natural resources reduces the share of physical capital in GDP and thereby weakens the incentive to save and invest by our extension of the Golden Rule).

The third equation shows how the enrolment rate depends on initial income (because wealthy countries can afford to spend more on education) as well as on natural capital (as in Gylfason 2001; Gylfason and Zoega 2001b; the idea behind this formulation is that the natural-resource-intensive sector may find it profitable to use workers with fewer skills than the manufacturing sector).

The fourth equation shows the relationship among the Gini index, initial income (i.e., the Kuznets curve), and the natural capital share that we documented in section 9.4. The fifth and last equation shows the relationship between gender inequality and the natural capital share. To recapitulate, our hypothesis from section 9.2 is that because natural resource ownership tends to be less equally distributed than other assets, countries that depend heavily on their natural resources tend to have a less equal distribution of income, education, and land than countries that are less dependent on their natural wealth.

The recursive nature of the system and the conceivable correlation of the error terms in the four equations make SUR an appropriate estimation procedure (Lahiri and Schmidt 1978). However, the fact that ordinary least squares (OLS) estimates of the system (not shown) are almost identical to the SUR estimates shown in table 9.1 indicates that the correlation of error terms across equations is of minor consequence. In our data, each country is represented by a single observation. This is because our data on natural resources are limited to a single year, 1994. In view of this, our analysis is confined to a cross section of countries, even if panel data on income distribution have recently become available (Deininger and Squire 1996). An extension of our analysis to panels must await richer data on natural capital. This may be important because some writers (e.g., Forbes 2000) have reported panel regression results on inequality and growth that seem to go against some of the results that have been obtained from cross-sectional studies (but see Banerjee and Duflo 2000b, who disagree with Forbes 2000 and also Bénabou 1996).

9.5.2 Empirical Results

All the coefficient estimates shown in table 9.1 are economically and statistically significant, with one exception. The coefficient on initial income in the growth equation indicates a conditional convergence speed of 1.3 percent per year. The direct effect of the natural capital share on growth is -0.05 and the indirect effects through investment and education are $-0.20 * 0.11 = -0.022$ and $-(0.03) * 1.08 = -0.032$. The additional indirect effect of the natural capital share on growth via the Gini index is $0.30 * (-0.04) = -0.012$. The total effect of natural capital on growth is, therefore, about -0.12 (for given initial income). Hence, the income distribution channel accounts for about one-tenth of the total effect of natural capital intensity on growth.

Of additional interest here are the effects of education and inequality on growth. The first equation in the table shows the direct effect of education on growth to be $1.08 / E = 0.025$, evaluated at the mean value of the secondary-school enrollment rate, $E = 0.43$; this means that an increase in the enrollment rate by ten percentage

Table 9.1
Regression results

Dependent variable	Initial income	Initial income squared	Natural capital share	Investment rate	Enrollment rate (log)	Gini index	Gender inequality	R²	Countries
Economic growth	−1.26 (6.05)		−0.05 (5.19)	0.11 (3.82)	1.08 (3.88)	−0.04 (2.84)	−0.01 (0.76)	0.68	74
Investment rate			−0.20 (3.98)					0.15	87
Enrollment rate	0.54 (11.31)		−0.03 (6.29)					0.70	87
Gini index	48.88 (3.54)	−3.20 (3.69)	0.30 (2.84)					0.31	74
Gender inequality			0.25 (2.98)					0.09	87

Note: Estimation method: SUR. t-ratios are shown within parentheses. Constant terms are not reported to conserve space.

points from one country to another increases growth by 0.25 of a percentage point. The direct effect of increased income inequality on growth is also rather strong: an increase in the Gini index by fifteen points, which corresponds to the difference between Norway (Gini = 26) and the United States (Gini = 41), from one place to another is associated with a decrease in growth by 0.6 percentage points which, in turn, is about a half of the average per capita growth in our sample over the period under review. On the other hand, we do not find significant evidence of a negative effect of increased gender inequality of education and economic growth; the coefficient reported in the top line of table 9.1 is negative, true, but small and insignificant. Even so, an increase in the natural capital share increases both types of inequality significantly and substantially. Thus, an increase in the natural capital share by 10 percentage points from one country to another increases the Gini index by three points and the difference between male and female secondary-school enrollment rates by 2.5 percentage points; the latter type of increased inequality, however, does not significantly hamper growth.

It is interesting to note that the inclusion of the natural capital share and the secondary-school enrollment rate in the growth equation does not reverse the sign of the estimated coefficient of the Gini index. In particular, the relationship between growth and inequality remains negative, in contrast to the results of Forbes (2000). However, the size of the income distribution effect is reduced by about a half by the inclusion of the natural capital and school enrollment variables. This seems to suggest that in growth equations without natural capital and education, the income distribution variable picks up a good part of the influence of the omitted variables. Our cross-sectional results bear out a long-term relationship between inequality and growth while the pooled estimation of Forbes (2000) reflects short- to medium-term relationships by her own reckoning. It is also possible that the inclusion of omitted, country-specific variables other than natural capital and education could reverse the sign of the coefficient of the Gini index.

Notice, at last, that the data support the notion of a Kuznets curve relating income inequality and initial income. There is, however, no comparable nonlinear relationship between gender inequality and initial income. In our data, initial income has no significant effect on investment across countries.

9.5.3   Other Possibilities

We have experimented with several variations of the model specification in table 9.1.

First, we added natural capital per person as a proxy for natural resource abundance in order to distinguish between natural resource abundance and natural resource intensity (as in Gylfason and Zoega 2001b). By intensity, or dependence, we mean the importance of natural resources to the national economy, while abundance refers to the supply (per capita) of the natural resources. Some countries— Australia, Canada, and the United States, to name a few—have abundant natural resources but are not particularly dependent upon them, not any more. Our argument has been that it is natural resource dependence that matters for inequality and growth. We do not expect Australia, Canada, or the United States to suffer from their abundance of natural resources, far from it. When we add natural capital per person as an independent explanatory variable to each equation in table 9.1, it turns out that natural resource abundance encourages economic growth, investment and education and reduces gender inequality, but has no effect on income inequality. In other respects, the results remain virtually the same as in table 9.1. This means that increased dependence on natural resources hurts growth, as we hypothesized, while increased abundance helps (for more, see Gylfason and Zoega 2001b).

Next, we entered the natural capital share and the Gini index of income inequality multiplicatively rather than additively in our growth equation in order to study the interaction between the two variables. Now the coefficient of the multiple is -0.0011 (with $t = 3.72$). This means that the negative effect of natural resource dependence on growth varies directly with income inequality: The more unequal the distribution of income, the greater is the adverse effect of natural resource dependence on growth. Evaluated at the mean value of the Gini index in our sample (42), the effect of the natural capital share on growth is -0.05 as in table 9.1. This new specification also means that the negative effect of income inequality on growth varies directly with natural resource dependence: The greater the natural capital share, the greater is the adverse effect of income inequality on growth. Evaluated at the mean value of the natural capital share in our sample (12), the effect of income inequality on economic growth is -0.013, which is smaller than the coefficient of the Gini index in the first equation in table 9.1. When we replace the Gini index of income inequality in the above experiment with our measure of gender inequality or of land inequality, we obtain the same results: The greater the natural capital share, the greater is the adverse effect of increased inequality on growth.

Third, we replaced our gender inequality measure (the arithmetic difference between male and female secondary-school enrollment rates) by the absolute difference between male and female enrolment rates. The new measure means that a change from a situation where more boys than girls go to school to one where more girls than boys go to school leaves gender inequality unchanged if the numbers are the same. When we reestimate our system using this new measure, increased gender inequality reduces economic growth directly: The coefficient on gender inequality in the first equation in table 9.1 is now -0.05 with $t = 2.09$. In this case, however, the effect of the natural capital share on gender inequality becomes small and statistically insignificant (the coefficient is 0.08 with $t = 1.47$). In other respects, the regression results (not shown) are very similar to those reported in table 9.1.

Our fourth and last experiment involves Africa and Latin America. When we add a dummy variable for Africa to each equation in our model, in case Africa might be different from other regions, as some studies have shown, the dummy coefficient has the expected sign everywhere, but it is statistically significant only in the equations for education and the Gini index. The annual rate of per capita growth in Africa is thus 0.75 of a percentage point smaller than elsewhere according to our results (not shown), but the difference is not significant ($t = 1.73$). The investment rate is almost 2 percentage points lower in Africa than elsewhere, but again the difference is insignificant ($t = 1.38$). The secondary-school enrollment rate is 15 percentage points lower in Africa than elsewhere (evaluated at the sample mean), and this difference is significant ($t = 3.23$). Gender inequality in education is also significantly greater in Africa than elsewhere, by almost five percentage points ($t = 2.15$). There is, on the other hand, no significant difference between the Gini index in Africa and the rest of our sample. All the estimates shown in table 9.1 remain essentially intact in the presence of the African dummy. When we add a dummy variable for Latin America (with or without Central America) rather than for Africa, the dummy has no effect on growth, investment, or education, but it does matter for distribution;

specifically, the Latin dummy reduces gender inequality by 7.5 percentage points ($t = 2.48$) and increases the Gini index of income inequality by ten points ($t = 3.20$). Again, our estimates in table 9.1 remain unchanged. We conclude that the specification of our model in table 9.1 is sufficiently broad to render the inclusion of regional dummy variables superfluous.

9.6 Conclusion

The inverse empirical relationship between inequality and economic growth across countries that has emerged from several recent studies has spurred several authors to suggest various potential theoretical explanations for the relationship. These explanations have generally been of the following kind: Inequality is bad for some variable X—for example, education—and X is good for growth, so increased inequality hurts growth by hurting X. We approach this issue from a different angle: We argue that a country's dependence on its natural resources influences both inequality and growth. We show—both theoretically and empirically—how variations in the share of natural resources in national wealth can help explain the inverse relationship between inequality and economic growth across countries.

The essence of our story is this: If the distribution of ownership of natural resources is more unequal than the distribution of other forms of wealth, the inequality of the distribution of income, education, or land is directly related to the share of natural resources in national income. Specifically, we show—in the context of an endogenous growth model of the simplest kind—how natural resources can reduce growth and increase inequality by attracting workers away from higher technology industries. Our data appear to confirm this prediction: they suggest that the Gini index of income inequality as well as gender inequality varies directly with the share of natural capital in national wealth. The data also bear out an inverse relationship between economic growth and the share of natural capital in national wealth.

Differences in human capital across countries appear also to help explain the inverse cross-country correlation between economic growth and inequality. More and better education—measured by secondary-school enrollment, years of schooling, or public expenditure on education—is associated with less inequality and more rapid growth in our data. This suggests a clear role for public policy in combating the potentially adverse effects of excessive dependence on natural resources on income inequality and growth. In addition, tax policy can be used to combat the adverse effect of natural resources on inequality and growth. When income or rent from natural resource extraction is taxed at a higher rate than wage income, this discourages workers from spending time in the natural resource sector, raises the marginal product of capital in manufacturing, increases the real rate of interest and thereby also the rate of growth of output and consumption per capita.

Our regression results suggest that natural capital intensity reduces growth directly as well as indirectly by reducing equality, secondary-school enrollment rates and investment rates. This leaves an important role for public policy, which can be used to encourage growth by enhancing equality, among other things. We conclude that the trade-off between equality and (dynamic) efficiency is affected by both natural and human capital, as well as by tax policy.

Notes

Thorvaldur Gylfason gratefully acknowledges financial support from *Jan Wallanders och Tom Hedelius Stiftelse* in Sweden. Gylfi Zoega acknowledges with thanks helpful comments from Theo Eicher, Stephen Turnovsky, and other participants of the CESifo conferences on Growth and Inequality: Issues and Policy Implications.

1. This empirical finding does not support the claim of García-Peñalosa (1995) that in rich countries increased inequality discourages education and growth by increasing the number of poor people who cannot afford education whereas in poor countries increased inequality encourages education and growth by increasing the number of rich people who can afford education.

2. Further, Aghion (1998) suggests that excessive inequality may be associated with macroeconomic volatility through credit cycles because of unequal access to credit and thus to investment opportunities, and that this may hurt investment and growth.

3. See also Aghion, Caroli, and García-Peñalosa (1999).

4. For a further discussion of recent empirical literature on inequality and growth, see Bénabou (1996).

5. Like Scott (1989), we distinguish between quantity and quality. If some investment projects miss the mark and fail to add commensurately to the capital stock, we have $q < 1$. There are three ways to interpret q: (a) as an indicator of distortions in the allocation of installed capital due to a poorly developed financial system, trade restrictions, or government subsidies that attract capital to unproductive uses in protected industries or in state-owned enterprises where capital may be less productive than in the private sector (Gylfason, Herbertsson, and Zoega 2001); (b) as the ratio of the economic cost (i.e., minimum achievable cost) of creating new capital to the actual cost of investment (Pritchett 2000)—that is, K is then measured on the basis of actual costs,

which may overstate its productivity; or (c) as a consequence of aging: the larger the share of old capital in the capital stock currently in operation, namely, the higher the average age of capital in use, the lower is its overall quality (Gylfason and Zoega 2001a). For our purposes, the three interpretations are analytically equivalent. However, we assume that the quality of capital has remained constant in the past, which means that all units of capital are of the same quality. In other words, we are not interested here in the implications of having different vintages of capital.

6. The parameters q and δ can both be modeled as endogenous choice parameters (as in Gylfason and Zoega 2001a), but here we treat them as exogenous magnitudes for simplicity, even if we acknowledge that depreciation may depend on quality, through obsolescence.

7. All countries for which the requisite data are available are included in all the figures in the chapter, without exception.

References

Aghion, Philippe, with Eve Caroli and Cecilia García-Peñalosa. 1998. "Inequality and Economic Growth." Part I in *Growth, Inequality and Globalization: Theory, History and Policy*, Philippe Aghion and Jeffrey G. Williamson. Cambridge: Cambridge University Press.

Aghion, Philippe, Eve Caroli, and Cecilia García-Peñalosa. 1999. "Inequality and Economic Growth: The Perspective of the New Growth Theories." *Journal of Economic Literature* 37: 1615–1660, December.

Alesina, Alberto, and Roberto Perotti. 1996. "Income Distribution, Political Instability, and Investment." *European Economic Review* 40: 1203–1228, June.

Alesina, Alberto, and Dani Rodrik. 1994. "Distributive Politics and Economic Growth." *Quarterly Journal of Economics* 109: 165–190, May.

Banerjee, Abhijit V., and Esther Duflo. 2000a. "Inequality and Growth: What Can the Data Say?" Working Paper No. 00–09, Department of Economics, MIT.

Banerjee, Abhijit V., and Esther Duflo. 2000b. "A Reassessment of the Relationship Between Inequality and Growth." Unpublished manuscript, Department of Economics, MIT.

Barro, Robert J. 2000. "Inequality and Growth in a Panel of Countries." *Journal of Economic Growth* 5: 5–32, March.

Bénabou, Roland. 1996. "Inequality and Growth." NBER *Macroeconomics Annual*.

Benhabib, Jess, and Aldo Rustichini. 1996. "Social Conflict and Growth." *Journal of Economic Growth* 1: 124–142, March.

Bourguignon, François, and C. Morrison. 1990. "Income Distribution, Development and Foreign Trade." *European Economic Review* 34: 1113–1132, September.

Bruno, Michael. 1984. "Raw Materials, Profits, and the Productivity Slowdown." *Quarterly Journal of Economics* 99: 1–28, February.

Deininger, Klaus, and Pedro Olinto. 2000. "Asset Distribution, Inequality, and Growth." Working Paper No. 2375, World Bank, Development Research Group.

Deininger, Klaus, and Lyn Squire. 1996. "A New Data Set Measuring Income Inequality." *World Bank Economic Review* 10: 565–591, September.

Easterly, William, and Sergio Rebelo. 1993. "Fiscal Policy and Growth: An Empirical Investigation." *Journal of Monetary Economics* 32: 417–458, December.

Forbes, Kristin J. 2000. "A Reassessment of the Relationship Between Inequality and Growth." *American Economic Review* 90: 869–887, September.

Galor, Oded, and Omer Moav. 1999. "From Physical to Human Capital: Inequality in the Process of Development." CEPR Discussion Paper No. 2307, December.

Galor, Oded, and Joseph Zeira. 1993. "Income Distribution and Macroeconomics." *Review of Economic Studies* 60: 35–52, January.

García-Peñalosa, Cecilia. 1995. "The Paradox of Education or the Good Side of Inequality." *Oxford Economic Papers* 47(2): 265–285.

Gylfason, Thorvaldur. 2001. "Natural Resources, Education, and Economic Development." *European Economic Review* 45: 847–859, May.

Gylfason, Thorvaldur, and Gylfi Zoega. 2001a. "Obsolescence." CEPR Discussion Paper No. 2833, June.

Gylfason, Thorvaldur, and Gylfi Zoega. 2001b. "Natural Resources and Economic Growth: The Role of Investment." CEPR Discussion Paper No. 2743, March.

Gylfason, Thorvaldur, Tryggvi Thor Herbertsson, and Gylfi Zoega. 2001. "Ownership and Growth." *World Bank Economic Review* 15: 431–449, October.

Kaldor, Nicholas. 1956. "Alternative Theories of Distribution." *Review of Economic Studies* 23: 83–100.

Lahiri, Kajal, and Peter Schmidt. 1978. "On the Estimation of Triangular Structural Systems." *Econometrica* 46: 1217–1221.

Paldam, Martin. 1997. "Dutch Disease and Rent Seeking: The Greenland Model." *European Journal of Political Economy* 13: 591–614, August.

Perotti, Robert. 1996. "Growth, Income Distribution, and Democracy: What the Data Say." *Journal of Economic Growth* 5: 149–187, June.

Persson, Torsten, and Guido Tabellini. 1994. "Is Inequality Harmful for Growth?" *American Economic Review* 84: 600–621, June.

Pritchett, Lant. 2000. "The Tyranny of Concepts: CUDIE (Cumulated, Depreciated, Investment Effort) Is *Not* Capital." *Journal of Economic Growth* 5: 361–384, December.

Romer, Paul M. 1986. "Increasing Returns and Long-Run Growth." *Journal of Political Economy* 94: 1002–1037, October.

Sachs, Jeffrey D., and Andrew M. Warner. 1995. "Natural Resource Abundance and Economic Growth." NBER Working Paper 5398, Cambridge. Revised 1997, 1999.

Saint-Paul, Gilles, and Thierry Verdier. 1993. "Education, Democracy and Growth." *Journal of Development Economics* 42: 399–407.

Saint-Paul, Gilles, and Thierry Verdier. 1996. "Inequality, Redistribution and Growth: A Challenge to the Conventional Political Economy Approach." *European Economic Review* 40: 719–728.

Scott, Maurice Fitzgerald. 1989. *A New View of Economic Growth*. Oxford, UK: Clarendon Press.

Sen, Amartya. 1999. *Development as Freedom*. Oxford: University Press.

Todaro, Michael P. 1997. *Economic Development*. London: Longman.

World Bank. 1997. "Expanding the Measure of Wealth: Indicators of Environmentally Sustainable Development." Environmentally Sustainable Development Studies and Monographs Series No. 17, World Bank, Washington, DC.

World Bank. 2000. *World Development Indicators 2000*. Washington, DC: World Bank.

10 Wage Inequality and the Effort Incentive Effects of Technical Change

Campbell Leith,
Chol-Won Li, and
Cecilia García-Peñalosa

10.1 Introduction

The recent increase in earnings inequality in a number of industrialized countries is by now a well-documented event. Countries have differed in their experiences, with the most pronounced increases taking place in the United Kingdom and the United States. An important component of this increase in inequality has been the rise in the educational wage differential. Between 1980 and 1988, the wage ratio of university graduates to workers with no qualification increased by almost 8 percent in the United Kingdom, and the wage ratio of college to high school graduates rose by some 25 percent in the United States over the period 1979–1995.[1]

The main explanation for the upsurge in wage inequality has been the hypothesis of an acceleration in *skill-biased technological change*. In particular, it has been argued that the development of new information technologies has resulted in a shift in the relative demand for labor in favor of those with greater skills (see Berman, Bound, and Griliches 1994).[2] The aim of this chapter is twofold. First, it contributes to the theoretical literature on the relationship between technological progress and relative wages by examining how, in the presence of imperfect information in the labor market, technical change can affect not only demand but also the *effective supply* of skills. Second, imperfect information will generate equilibrium unemployment, and will allow us to account for a fact that has largely been ignored by previous explanations of the rise in the skill premium—namely, that the increase in the relative wage has been accompanied by an increase in unemployment rates for *both* skilled and unskilled workers (see the discussion in section 10.2).

Our argument is based on the efficiency wage model of Shapiro and Stiglitz (1984), whereby imperfect information on the part of firms about whether or not employees are shirking forces the former to pay wages above the market clearing level, which in turn leads to unemployment. The combination of high wages and the risk of remaining unemployed if found shirking and fired, induces optimal effort on the part of workers. We introduce technological progress into this framework. We stress that an important feature of new technologies is that they not only create new jobs, they also destroy old ones. When an innovation arrives, some workers retain their jobs but others are reallocated between jobs or made redundant.[3] This process affects the effort incentives of workers, and hence the effective labor supply. That is, changes in the rate of technical change alter the trade-off between pay and unemployment that firms face, and will affect equilibrium wages and employment.

In our model, the net impact of technical change on wages is ambiguous. Faster technical change increases the discounted wage flow but, since it also raises turnover, it reduces the probability of remaining with the current employer. Hence it may increase or decrease the present value of being employed, depending on parameter values. We consider two types of workers, skilled and unskilled, and assume that it is easier to monitor the effort levels of the unskilled, and that it is easier for a skilled worker that has lost her job to immediately find a new one, as her transferable skills make her more adaptable to the new technology than an unskilled worker. These differences imply that the incentives of the two types of workers will not be affected in the same way by a change in the rate of technical progress, and that consequently the relative (effective) supply of workers will shift.

A number of results emerge. First, if technical change is biased, in the sense that it increases the demand for skilled workers relative to that for the unskilled, then the incentive mechanism may strengthen or partially offset the impact of demand on relative wages. A more surprising finding is that if technical change is *skill-neutral*, in the sense that it leaves the relative demand for labor unchanged, an increase or fall in the rate of technical change will still change the relative wage. Third, we show that a *reduction* in the rate of technical change can generate an increase in the skill premium, which is consistent with the productivity slowdown experienced during the 1970s and 1980s.

The model also generates patterns of unemployment that fit the data. As we see in detail in section 10.2, previous work cannot explain the increase in both the skilled and unskilled unemployment rates alongside the increase in relative wages. The efficiency wage model implies that there is equilibrium unemployment in all labor markets. Moreover, changes in the rate of technical change will affect both wages and employment. In this context it is possible for a decline in the rate of technological progress to increase the wages of the skilled relative to the unskilled and reduce the level of employment for both types of workers.

This chapter contributes to two recent strands in the growth literature, both of which have not received as much attention as they merit. The first one is concerned with the relationship between unemployment and technological progress, pioneered by Aghion and Howitt (1994); the second is the literature on growth and imperfect information in the labor market, where the cost of training a worker is assumed to depend on her ability, which is not known to the firm (see Eicher and Kalaitzidakis 1997; Eicher 1999). Our modeling strategy differs from the former in that we consider how technical change affects the supply rather than the demand for labor, and from the latter in the type of information asymmetry considered.

The chapter proceeds as follows. Section 10.2 discusses the existing literature on technical change and the skill premium and argues that there are a number of empirical regularities that they have difficulty explaining. Section 10.3 outlines the model and considers the incentive effects of technological progress. In section 10.4 we use the model to analyze the impact of technical progress on the skill-premium and show that both skill-biased and skill-neutral technological progress affect the relative wage. We then show in section 10.5 how our framework can generate a simultaneous increase in the relative wage and in the unemployment rates of both types of workers and argue that differences in unemployment benefits and employment protection legislation can explain the different experiences of continental Europe relative to the United States and the United Kingdom. We summarize our results and discuss further policy implications in section 10.6.

10.2   Problems with Existing Explanations of the Increase in Relative Wages

The early empirical literature on the increase in relative wages in the 1980s found little support for the role of supply or international trade as potential explanations.[4] Theoretical work has consequently concentrated on modeling the way in which new technologies shift the relative demand for labor. Recent empirical work has, however, documented the importance of both international trade and changes in the supply of skills. Feenstra and Hanson (1999) find that when we measure trade by the degree of "outsourcing," increased competition from newly industrializing countries can account for a large fraction of the change in the relative wage in the United States. Supply effects have been documented by Card and Lemieux (2001), who show that, once the labor force is decomposed into cohorts, there has been a slowdown in the rate of growth of educational attainment of those cohorts that have experienced the greatest increase in the education premium. Still, they find that there has been an increase in the returns to education for all cohorts which may well be due to technological change.

The existing theoretical literature has, however, encountered two problems when trying to fit the evidence. The first one is the productivity slowdown. The 1970s and 1980s witnessed a sharp reduction in rates of total factor productivity (TFP) growth, with TFP growth in the United States falling from 3 percent in the mid-1960s to around 1 percent by the late 1980s, and by even more in the United Kingdom, France, and Germany.[5] Yet most work explaining wage inequality through technical change relies on an *increase* in the rate of technological progress.[6] The reason is that this approach is based on the hypothesis, first put forward by Nelson and Phelps (1966), that the main difference between educated and non-educated workers is the greater capacity of the former to absorb and implement new technologies. The relative demand for skilled labor will then only increase if there is faster technical change that forces firms to employ skilled workers to implement the new technologies.

A second question that explanations of the increase in the skill premium must answer is: Why is it that changes that should have affected all industrial economies in roughly the same way—such as competition from newly industrializing countries or biased technical change—have not had similar effects on relative wages? The standard explanation is that in the United States and the United Kingdom, flexible labor markets permitted an adjustment of wages in response to the increase in the relative demand for skills; in Europe, wage rigidities left the skill premium constant, leading, instead, to an increase in unskilled unemployment.

As was first pointed out by Nickell and Bell (1995, 1996), unemployment rates were much higher in the 1980s than in the 1970s for both skilled and unskilled workers. This increase in unemployment took place in both the North American and the European economies. Neither the demand-based explanations nor the hypothesis of an increase in the supply of unskilled labor are capable of accounting for the simultaneous shift in relative wages and the increase in unemployment for both types of workers. An exception is the search model developed by Acemoglu (1999). Yet, in his setup, the mechanism that triggers the changes is an acceleration of the rate of skill-biased technical change. By using a supply-side approach based on an efficiency-wage model we are capable of providing a framework in which productivity, relative wages, and unemployment can move in a way consistent with the evidence.

10.3   The Model

10.3.1   Features of the Economy

10.3.1.1   Workers

Time is continuous and denoted by t. There are H skilled and L unskilled workers, and $E_i(t)$ and $U_i(t)$, $i = H, L$ denote the number of workers employed and unemployed, respectively. This means $H = E_H(t) + U_H(t)$ and $L = E_L(t) + U_L(t)$. All workers have identical preferences, are risk-neutral, and their intertemporal utility function is time-additive.[7] This implies that the real rate of interest is given by the rate of time preference, ρ, which is common to all consumers. We assume that agents consume all their labor income, $w_i(t)$, as they receive it. They also decide whether or not to exert effort when employed. The instantaneous utility function when employed is $w_i(t) - \varepsilon T_i(t)$, where $\varepsilon T_i(t)$ is the disutility of effort and ε can take values of either 0 or 1. $T_i(t)$ is an index of the level of technology which is specific to each type of labor since, as we will see later, skilled and unskilled workers operate different technologies.

We assume that technological progress is the only way in which workers are separated from firms in equilibrium. There is a probability η_i that, following a technological innovation which destroys her job, a worker immediately finds a job elsewhere. This assumption captures the observation of Davis and Haltiwanger (1992) that job-to-job reallocation represents a substantial fraction of worker turnover. In what follows we assume $\eta_H > \eta_L$, that is, that the rate of job-to-job reallocation is larger for skilled than for unskilled workers, reflecting the fact that the former have more transferable skills making adoption of new technologies easier.

The return to a worker from being employed and not shirking, denoted by $V_i^N(t)$, is defined by the following "asset" equation, where $V_i^U(t)$ is the value of being unemployed. The interest rate, ρ, times asset value $V_i^N(t)$ must equal the flow benefits

$$\rho V_i^N(t) = w_i(t) - \varepsilon T_i(t) + b_i(t)[V_i^U(t) - V_i^N(t)] + \dot{V}_i^N(t) \tag{1}$$

of being an employed nonshirker, which consists of the real wage $w_i(t)$, the disutility of effort, $\varepsilon T_i(t)$, and capital gains/losses. The rate of worker dislocation, $b_i(t)$, is endogenous and as we will see below results from the fact that technological progress destroys jobs. With probability $b_i(t)$ the worker suffers the capital loss associated with moving from employment to unemployment, $V_i^U(t) - V_i^N(t)$. The term $\dot{V}_i^N(t)$ captures the capital gains/losses arising from changes in wages due to productivity growth and the dynamics of employment adjustment.

The value of being an employed shirker, denoted by $V_i^S(t)$, follows a similar recursive equation,

$$\rho V_i^S(t) = w_i(t) + [b_i(t) + s_i][V_i^U(t) - V_i^S(t)] + \dot{V}_i^S(t), \tag{2}$$

where the probability of entering unemployment is increased by s_i, the probability of being found shirking. This probability is specific to each category of worker and, in line with the literature on worker monitoring, we assume $s_L > s_H$.

Last, the value of being unemployed is

$$\rho V_i^U(t) = z T_i(t) + a_i(t)[V_i^N(t) - V_i^U(t)] + \dot{V}_i^U(t). \tag{3}$$

$z T_i(t)$ is unemployment benefit and $a_i(t)$ the probability of exiting unemployment. Since in equilibrium no worker shirks, the only way the worker can reenter employment is if an innovation creates new jobs.

10.3.1.2   Production

We assume that we are in a small open economy, where the prices of the N varieties of good are exogenously determined in world markets. A particular variety is produced by one type of labor only. Let

n_H be the number of varieties produced by skilled workers and n_L the number produced by unskilled workers, with $N = n_L + n_H$. Supposing that all unskilled-produced goods have the same price, P_L, and that all skill-produced varieties have price $P_H = 1$, we can write aggregate output as

$$Y = \int_0^{n_L} P_L Q_L(j)\, dj + \int_0^{n_H} Q_H(n_L + j)\, dj. \tag{4}$$

The production of final goods takes place according to a Cobb-Douglas technology in which only labor is used,

$$Q_L(j) = A x_L^\alpha(j) = A x_L^\alpha, \tag{5a}$$

$$Q_H(j) = A x_H^\alpha(j) = A x_H^\alpha, \tag{5b}$$

where $0 < \alpha < 1$, A is a scale parameter, and $x(j)$ is employment in the production of good j. Firms maximize profits by equating the marginal product of labor to the real wage, which implies the inverse labor demand functions $w_i = \alpha A P_i / x_i^{1-\alpha}$. We define the index of technical progress as $T_i = n_i^{1-\alpha}$, and let $\omega_i \equiv w_i / T_i$ denote the productivity-adjusted wage. We can then express the demand functions as

$$\omega_i = \frac{\alpha A P_i}{(n_i x_i)^{1-\alpha}}, \tag{6a}$$

$$= \frac{\alpha A P_i}{E_i^{1-\alpha}}, \tag{6b}$$

where $E_i = n_i x_i$ is total employment of type i workers.

10.3.1.3 Technical Change
Technical change is exogenous and takes the form of expanding variety. The rate of growth of unskilled-produced and skilled-produced varieties are, respectively,

$$g_L = \frac{\dot{n}_L}{n_L} \quad \text{and} \quad g_H = \frac{\dot{n}_H}{n_H}. \tag{7}$$

We say that (1) technical change is neutral whenever $g_H = g_L = g$, and (2) technical change is skill-biased (deskilling) whenever $g_H > g_L$ ($g_H < g_L$). To understand these definitions, recall the relative demand for labor. From equation (6b) we have

$$\frac{E_{Ht}}{E_{Lt}} = \left(\frac{w_{Lt}/P_{Lt}}{w_{Ht}}\right)^{1/(1-\alpha)} \frac{n_{H_0}}{n_{L_0}} e^{(g_H - g_L)t}, \tag{8}$$

where n_{i0} is the initial number of type i varieties. When the rates of growth of the two types of varieties are the same, the two labor demand functions shift proportionally, leaving the relative demand for skills unchanged. This is what we term *skill-neutral* technical change. A faster (slower) rate of growth of skill-produced varieties implies that the relative demand for skills increases (decreases) over time, namely, results in *skill-biased* (deskilling) technical change.

10.3.2 The Incentive Effects of Technological Progress

10.3.2.1 Labor Reallocation

A key feature of technological progress is that new jobs are created as old jobs are destroyed. To understand how these effects work in our model, consider the labor demand functions (6a). The number of workers used to produce a given variety depends on the number of varieties of intermediate goods and on the equilibrium wage. Log-differentiating equation (6a) and using (7), we obtain

$$-\dot{x}_i = x_i \left(g_i + \frac{1}{1-\alpha} \frac{\dot{\omega}_i}{\omega_i}\right). \tag{9}$$

The number of jobs lost in a given variety in a unit time interval, $-\dot{x}_i$, is proportional to the number of jobs that existed with a coefficient determined by the rate of increase in real wages and by the rate of technological progress. If all workers who are separated from firms could not find jobs elsewhere, $-\dot{x}_i$ would be equivalent to the number of individuals becoming unemployed in a given variety. However, recall that we have assumed that a fraction η_i of workers who are separated from firms are immediately recruited by a new firm. Therefore, the number of workers joining the unemployment pool from a given variety is $-(1 - \eta_i)\dot{x}_i$, and the probability of a given worker becoming unemployed is $b_i = -(1 - \eta_i)\dot{x}_i/x_i$. We then have

$$b_i = (1 - \eta_i)\left(g_i + \frac{1}{1-\alpha}\frac{\dot{\omega}_i}{\omega_i}\right)$$

$$= (1 - \eta_i)\left(g_i - \frac{\dot{E}_i}{E_i}\right). \tag{10}$$

The total number of workers of type i becoming unemployed during a unit time interval is $n_i b_i x_i$. The number of unemployed workers who find jobs is $a_i U_i$. Therefore, changes in employment are $\dot{E}_i = a_i U_i - n_i x_i b_i$, which upon rearrangement gives

$$a_i = \frac{\eta_i \dot{E}_i + (1 - \eta_i) g_i E_i}{U_i}. \tag{11}$$

10.3.2.2 Incentive Effects

We can now examine the impact of technological progress on workers' effort incentives and its effect on the wage-employment trade-off. Firms ensure that workers do not shirk by setting $V_i^N = V_i^S$, which using equations (1) and (2) can be solved for productivity-adjusted wages ω_i. Let $v_i^U \equiv V_i^U / T_i$ and $v_i^N \equiv V_i^N / T_i$ be the productivity-adjusted values of being unemployed and employed respectively. The individual no-shirking condition (NSC) can then be expressed as

$$\omega_i = [\rho - (1 - \alpha) g_i] \left(v_i^U + \frac{\varepsilon}{s_i} \right) + \varepsilon + (1 - \eta_i) \frac{g_i - \dot{E}_i / E_i}{s_i} \varepsilon - \dot{v}_i^N, \tag{12}$$

where v_i^U is to be determined.

Using (1) and (2), the condition $V_i^N = V_i^S$ can also be expressed as $v_i^N - v_i^U = \varepsilon / s_i$. Differentiating, we have $\dot{v}_i^N = \dot{v}_i^U$, which together with equations (3) to (11) implies

$$v_i^U = \frac{z + \dfrac{\varepsilon}{s_i} \cdot \dfrac{\eta_i \dot{E}_i + (1 - \eta_i) g_i E_i}{U_i} + \dot{v}_i^N}{\rho - (1 - \alpha) g_i}. \tag{13}$$

These two equations together determine the combinations of wages and unemployment that ensure that workers do not shirk. Before obtaining the equilibrium NSC it is worth examining in detail the incentive effects of technical change. Equation (12) gives the combinations of ω_i and E_i that prevent shirking for a given v_i^U, and shows how they are affected by technical change. On the one hand, technological progress results in increased returns to employment, implying that workers lose more if they are found to be shirking. It therefore tends to strengthen the disciplinary effect of unemployment, allowing firms to reduce the wage for a given level of employment. We call this the *employment capitalization* effect of productivity growth.[8]

On the other, there is what we call a *job destruction effect*. Recall that $b_i = (1 - \eta_i)(g_i - \dot{E}_i/E_i)$ is the probability of a worker becoming unemployed, and its inverse, $1/b_i$, is the average duration of employment. As g_i increases, employment duration falls, weakening the disciplinary effect of unemployment. Firms are required to raise ω_i in order to extract effort from workers. The strength of the job destruction effect depends on the extent of job-to-job reallocation. If the latter is high, the expected duration of employment is long, and the impact of job destruction weakens.

Technical change also affects the employment-wage trade-off through v_i^U, as the greater the value of being unemployed, the higher the wage needed to prevent shirking. From equation (13), a higher g_i reduces the effective discount rate at which the unemployed capitalize future benefits and makes unemployment a more attractive option, tending to raise ω_i. We call this the *unemployment capitalization effect*. The last effect operates through the job acquisition rate a_i. Its inverse $1/a_i$ is the average duration of unemployment. As g_i rises, duration falls and the disciplinary effect of unemployment weakens. This is termed the *job creation effect*. Note that as *more* jobs are created, real wages rise.

Equations (12) and (13) together yield the equilibrium NSC

$$\dot{E}_i = E_i \frac{(\omega_i - z)\dfrac{s_i}{\varepsilon} + \left[(1 - \alpha) - \dfrac{(1 - \eta_i)i}{i - E_i}\right]g_i - \rho - s_i}{1 + \dfrac{\eta_i i}{i - E_i}}. \tag{14}$$

In steady state, where $\dot{E}_i = 0$, this condition reduces to

$$\omega_i = z + \varepsilon + \frac{\varepsilon}{s_i}\left[\rho - (1 - \alpha)g_i + \frac{(1 - \eta_i)}{1 - E_i/i}g_i\right]. \tag{15}$$

Firms need to use a combination of higher wages and unemployment to prevent shirking. The steady state NSC thus implies an upward-sloping relationship between the wage and the level of employment. The four incentive effects we discussed earlier combine into two competing tendencies. First, the term $(\rho - (1 - \alpha)g_i)$ is the effective discount rate and captures the employment and unemployment capitalization effects. Since the flow benefits from unemployment are necessarily less than the flow benefits from employment, the employment capitalization effect dominates, and

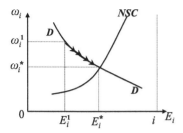

Figure 10.1
Equilibrium in the labour market

a higher g_i reduces the effective discount rate and hence the no-shirking wage. Second, the job destruction and job creation effects are also combined in a single term capturing the probabilities of entering and exiting unemployment, as $a_i + b_i = (1 - \eta_i)g_i/(1 - E_i/i)$. Through these probabilities faster technical change increases job turnover, implying that workers have less incentive to avoid shirking and firms need to increase the wage. Either of these two net effects may dominate.

10.3.3 Equilibrium and Comparative Statics

The equilibrium wage and employment level are given by the intersection of the demand function with the steady state NSC, which are, respectively,

$$\omega_i = \frac{\alpha A P_i}{E_i^{1-\alpha}},$$ (DD)

$$\omega_i = z + \varepsilon + \frac{\varepsilon}{s_i}\rho + \frac{\varepsilon}{s_i}\left[\frac{1 - \eta_i}{1 - E_i/i} - (1 - \alpha)\right]g_i.$$ (NSC)

As depicted in figure 10.1, the demand function is monotonically decreasing and the NSC monotonically increasing, yielding a unique equilibrium, (E_i^*, ω_i^*). Note from equation (14) that whenever the wage is greater than ω_i^*, then $\dot{E}_i > 0$, while for $\omega_i < \omega_i^*$, $\dot{E}_i < 0$. This implies that the equilibrium is stable, with firms moving along the demand function until the equilibrium is reached.

We can now examine the effect of technological change on the equilibrium. Differentiating the steady state NSC with respect to g_i, we have

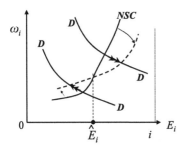

Figure 10.2
The impact of a productivity slowdown

$$\frac{d\omega_i}{dg_i} \begin{cases} > 0 & \text{for } E_i > \hat{E}_i \\ = 0 & \text{for } E_i = \hat{E}_i, \\ < 0 & \text{for } E_i < \hat{E}_i \end{cases} \quad \text{where } \hat{E}_i = \frac{\eta_i - \alpha}{1 - \alpha} i < i. \tag{16}$$

Whether a change in g increases or decreases the productivity-adjusted wage depends on the equilibrium level of employment relative to a critical value, $\hat{E}_i$. Figure 10.2 illustrates the case of a reduction in the rate of technological change. A lower g_i pivots the NSC curve around $\hat{E}_i$, from the solid to the dotted curve. If employment is initially above $\hat{E}_i$, then the wage falls and employment rises, while if employment is initially below $\hat{E}_i$, ω_i increases and E_i decreases. The intuition for this result is simple. For high levels of employment, the duration of any unemployment is likely to be small. A productivity slowdown then reduces job turnover, weakens the incentives to shirk, and allows firms to cut the real wage. When employment is low, the net capitalization effect dominates, and wages rise following a decrease in g_i.

Note that the job-to-job reallocation rate plays a crucial role in shaping the relationship between technological progress and wages, as it determines the threshold level of employment $\hat{E}_i$. For a given level of employment, the larger η_i is, the weaker the job creation destruction effect is, and hence the more likely it is that an increase in the rate of technical change reduces the equilibrium wage.

The rest of the comparative statics are straightforward. A higher unemployment benefit shifts the NSC upward, increasing the wage and reducing employment; while an increase in either the probability of being caught shirking, the rate of job-to-job reallocation, or the supply of labor tend to reduce the wage and raise employment. A lower P_i shifts the demand function leftward, resulting in a lower equilibrium wage and level of employment.

10.4   Relative Wages

We are now in a position to examine the effect of technical change on the skill premium. Let $\Omega_t \equiv w_{Ht}/w_{Lt}$ be the relative wage at time t. Using the demand functions (6), the skill premium can be expressed as

$$\Omega_t = \left(\frac{n_{H0}}{n_{L0}}\right)^{1-\alpha} \left(\frac{E_{Lt}}{E_{Ht}}\right)^{1-\alpha} \frac{1}{P_{Lt}} e^{(1-\alpha)(g_H - g_L)t}. \tag{17}$$

In the absence of incentive effects or rigidities, the levels of employment are simply equal to the supplies of the two types of labor. Equation (17) then encompasses the three hypotheses that have been put forward to explain the recent increase in the skill premium: the relative supply of skills; the effect of international trade, captured by a change in the relative price of unskilled-produced goods P_{Lt}; and skill-biased technical change, as reflected in any difference in the rate of innovation of the two types of goods, $g_H - g_L$.

Introducing incentive considerations implies that wages will depart from their market-clearing levels, and adds a further mechanism through which technological progress can affect relative wages. There are two important ways in which the supply-side effect differs from the demand-side impact of technical change. First, in contrast to the existing literature, an increase in the skill premium can be consistent with a *reduction* in the rate of technological change. Second, as we will see in what follows, technical change may increase the skill premium even if it is *skill-neutral*.

10.4.1   Biased Technical Change and the Productivity Slowdown

That skill-biased technical change increases the relative wage in our model will come as no surprise. Still, it is worth examining how the supply-side effects interact with the standard demand-side impact. Because of the importance of the productivity slowdown during the 1980s, let us consider the effect of a fall in the rate of technological change. Suppose, more precisely, that we start from a situation of neutral technical change, with $g_L = g_H$, and technical progress becomes skill-biased through a reduction in g_L to g_L', while g_H remains constant. As a result of this slowdown in technical progress, the economy experiences a productivity slowdown.

Now consider what happens to wages. The skilled labor market remains unchanged, employment remains constant and the real wages of skilled workers keep growing at rate $(1 - \alpha)g_H$. In the unskilled labor market, the NSC curve pivots. As we saw before, two situations are possible. If the initial level of employment is above (below) the threshold $\hat{E}_L$, then the productivity adjusted wage ω_L falls (rises) and, as a result, the skill premium, ω_H/ω_L, rises (falls).

This creates the possibility that a similar productivity slowdown has resulted in a larger increase in the skill-premium in the United States and the United Kingdom relative to continental Europe because $\hat{E}_L$ is higher in Europe than in the United States/ United Kingdom, ceteris paribus. A recent study by Boeri (1999), finds evidence that there is more job-to-job reallocation in Europe than in the United States (which suggests that η_L, and therefore $\hat{E}_L$, is indeed higher in Europe than the United States/United Kingdom). His argument is that, as a result of tighter labor protection regulation in Europe, there is an "intermediate" labor market status between employment and unemployment. In other words, workers that are about to be fired can remain in their jobs for a period of time, which will give them the chance of finding a new position, thus moving from one job to another without a spell of unemployment in between. In the United States, weak employment protection implies that workers enter unemployment as soon as they are given notice of termination.

Note that for $E_L > \hat{E}_L$, the real unskilled wage, $w_{Lt} = \omega_L(n_{L0})^{1-\alpha}e^{(1-\alpha)g_Lt}$, may actually fall when g_L falls.[9] If the fall in g_L is large enough, then the reduction in the productivity adjusted wage could, for a period of time, offset the effect of improving productivity and we would simultaneously observe an increase in the skill premium, a productivity slowdown, and a reduction in the real wages of the unskilled.

10.4.2 Skill-Neutral Technical Change

Now suppose that the number of the two types of varieties increase at the same rate, $g_H = g_L = g$, and that there is a reduction in the rate of technical change. What would be the impact on the relative wage?

The first thing to note is that there is no demand effect as the demand for both types of workers shifts proportionally. The only impact stems from the impact of a lower g on the effective supply, and hence on productivity-adjusted wages.

Consider the ratio of the productivity-adjusted wages, ω_H/ω_L. Differentiating, we have

$$\frac{d(\omega_H/\omega_L)}{dg} = \frac{1}{\omega_L}\left[\frac{d\omega_H}{dg} - \frac{\omega_H}{\omega_L}\frac{d\omega_L}{dg}\right], \tag{18}$$

where

$$\frac{d\omega_i}{dg} = \frac{(1-\alpha)(E_i - \hat{E}_i)}{\dfrac{s_i(i - E_i)}{\varepsilon} + \dfrac{1 - \eta_i}{1 - \alpha}\dfrac{g}{\omega_i}\dfrac{iE_i}{i - E_i}}.$$

Equation (18) implies that skill-neutral technical change can affect inequality by having a different impact on the effort incentives of the two types of workers. As we saw in section 10.4.1, slower technological progress may increase or decrease productivity-adjusted wages depending on whether the net capitalization or the job creation-destruction effect dominates. Which effect dominates depends crucially on the value of $\hat{E}_i$ which, in turn, depends upon, η_i.

In order to look at possible patterns of wage inequality, we calibrate the model and obtain numerical examples. We choose the following parameter values:

Preferences:	$\rho = 0.04$, $\varepsilon = 1$	Labor market:	$L = 1, H = 1$	
Technology:	$\alpha = 0.6$, $A = 4.1$		$s_H = 0.02$, $s_L = 0.2$	
Prices:	$P_H = 1$, $P_L = 0.66$		$z = 0$, $\eta_L = 0.75$,	
			$\eta_H = 0.99$	

The values of ρ and α are standard, corresponding to a rate of time preference of 4 percent and labor income share of 60 percent. The cost of effort and the scale parameter A have been arbitrarily chosen. The price of the skill-produced good is used as a numeraire, and it is assumed to be about 50 percent higher than that of the unskilled good in world markets. There are no unemployment benefits. The probability of a shirker being caught is assumed to be ten times as large for unskilled than for skilled workers.

The choice of job-to-job reallocation parameters is not obvious, as evidence is sparse. Evidence on transfers following job destruction suggests that in Germany 32 percent of all separations result in reemployment within one week, and in Canada 53 percent of workers were in a new job within three weeks.[10] Because we are using annual values in the calibrations, the corresponding rates of job-to-job reallocation should be much higher. We can obtain an indirect estimate from the evidence presented by Davis and Haltiwanger (1992). They find that, in the United States, total worker reallocation in a year—namely, the proportion of workers that change employers or transit from employment to joblessness during a year—was 36.8 percent over the period 1972–1986. We can then use unemployment rates to estimate the proportion of those separated from an employer who have another job within a year. Our estimates give a value of η_H between 0.944 and 0.994, and of η_L between 0.77 and 0.977. In our benchmark calibration we use the values $\eta_H = 0.99$ and $\eta_L = 0.75$, representing the greatest difference between the two categories of workers implied by these estimates.[11]

Values for the benchmark economy are depicted in the first three columns of table 10.1. We consider the effect of a reduction in the rate of productivity growth from 5 percent to 1 percent. For the benchmark economy, a reduction in g increases ω_H and reduces ω_L. A high value of η_H implies that the job creation destruction effect almost disappears in the skilled labor market. The net capitalization effect then leads to a higher equilibrium skilled wage. In the unskilled labor market, low rates of job-to-job reallocation imply that the job creation-destruction effect dominates, resulting in a lower unskilled wage. That is, ω_H increases and ω_L falls, leading to a higher-skill premium accompanied by a reduction in the real unskilled wage.

In the next two columns, we raise the rate of unskilled job-to-job reallocation, η_L, from 0.75 to 0.8. This significantly reduces the level of inequality at all levels of technical progress. This confirms the idea that labor market policies in Europe which raise the rate of job-to-job reallocation for unskilled workers may help explain the smaller increases in inequality observed in Europe.

Finally, we reduce the rate of shirker detection for unskilled workers, s_L, from 0.2 to 0.1. As can be seen in the final two columns of table 10.1, this also serves to reduce the skilled wage premium at all rates of technical progress. The intuition is straightforward.

Table 10.1
Inequality and the productivity slowdown

	$\eta_L = 0.75$ and $s_L = 0.2$			$\eta_L = 0.8$ and $s_L = 0.2$		$\eta_L = 0.75$ and $s_L = 0.1$	
	ω_H	ω_L	ω_H/ω_L	ω_L	ω_H/ω_L	ω_L	ω_H/ω_L
$g = 0.05$	2.67	1.70	**1.57**	1.68	**1.49**	1.79	**1.40**
$g = 0.03$	2.73	1.67	**1.63**	1.66	**1.54**	1.74	**1.47**
$g = 0.01$	2.88	1.64	**1.75**	1.64	**1.72**	1.68	**1.68**

A high s_L implies a weaker trade-off between wages and unemployment (i.e., a flatter NSC curve), and consequently the fall in g results in a small wage change. Again, to the extent that employers operating in European labor markets are constrained by employment protection legislation from firing "shirking" workers, this may account from the different trends in the skill premium in Europe relative to the United States and the United Kingdom.

10.5   The Wage-Employment Puzzle

As we have already argued, one of the problems of existing explanations of the increase in relative wages is that they have difficulty accounting for the increases in unemployment rates for both skilled and unskilled workers during the 1980s. In contrast, our framework can generate a simultaneous increase in the wage premium and in unemployment for both types of workers. There are in fact several circumstances under which this may happen. One possibility is that the changes in employment and wages are only due to a technological slowdown. Suppose that we are in a situation in which $E_H < \hat{E}_H$ and $E_L < \hat{E}_L$. A reduction in the rate of technical change will pivot the NSC in the two labor markets, leading to an increase in the productivity-adjusted wages and a reduction of employment levels in both markets. If the skilled wage increases more sharply than the unskilled wage, then the skill premium and unemployment rates will increase together.

However, we saw in section 10.2 that there is strong evidence supporting the role of increased competition in the market for low-skill manufactures from newly industrializing countries in explaining the increase in the skill premium. In this section we argue that a reduction in the rate of skill-neutral technological progress, together with this effect can simultaneously generate the observed changes in employment and relative wages.

10.5.1 Replicating the U.S. Data

Consider the following scenario. Suppose that η_H is large and η_L is small, so that we are initially in an equilibrium where $E_H < \hat{E}_H$ and $E_L > \hat{E}_L$. A reduction in the rate of technical change will pivot the NSC in the two labor markets. For skilled workers, the extent of job creation destruction is relatively small, and the fall in g will have the effect of increasing productivity-adjusted wages and reducing employment levels. In the unskilled market, the opposite will happen, ω_L falls and E_L rises. As we saw in section 10.4.1, this reduction in the productivity-adjusted wage may well result in a lower real unskilled wage. Suppose that at the same time there is a fall in P_L, which will reduce the demand for unskilled workers. As we can see in figure 10.3, if the demand shift is sufficiently large this will result in a fall in unskilled employment. That is, the combination of the productivity slowdown and the reduction in the world price of low-skill manufactures, results in an increase in the skill premium and an increase in both skilled and unskilled unemployment. The reasons for the increase in unemployment are, however, different in the two labor markets. Skilled employment falls because the strength of the net capitalization effect requires the disciplining of workers through unemployment, while unskilled unemployment is the direct effect of a lower price for their output.

To illustrate these effects, we calibrate the model to match U.S. data. Productivity growth in the United States fell from 3 percent to

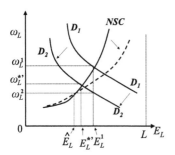

Figure 10.3
The unskilled labor market

1 percent between 1970 and 1990. We choose parameters so that such a reduction in g together with a fall in the price of the unskilled good replicate that the data on unemployment and the skill premium. We fix the following parameters: α, ρ, z, ε, P_H, and s_L, and let the data determine the rest. This yields

Preferences:	$\rho = 0.04$, $\varepsilon = 1$	Labor market:	$L = 1$, $H = 1$,
Technology:	$\alpha = 0.6$, $A = 3.0387$		$s_H = 0.045$
Prices:	$P_H = 1$, $P_L = 0.660$		$s_L = 0.7$, $z = 0$,
			$\eta_H = 0.995$
			$\eta_L = 0.74$

Table 10.2 reports the results. The first row replicates the situation in 1970, with a skill premium of 1.49 and low rates of unemployment of 1.7 and 5.27 for skilled and unskilled workers, respectively.[12] The second row considers the effect on wages and employment of a fall in the price of the unskilled-produced good from $P_L = 0.660$ to $P_L' = 0.568$. (i.e., by 16%). The next row adds to that a fall in g. For the unskilled, a low reallocation rate implies that the productivity slowdown partly offsets the increase in unskilled unemployment, while it reinforces the increase in the skill premium. For the skilled, a lower g results in a higher wage and unemployment rate. A demand shift due to increased import penetration together with a fall in the rate of (skill-neutral) technical progress can thus account for the simultaneous increase in the skill premium and the unemployment rates for both educated and noneducated workers.

10.5.2 Unemployment Benefits and Job-to-Job Reallocation

In this section we argue that labor market policies can indeed help explain differences in inequality between Europe and the United

Table 10.2
Simulating unemployment and wages in the United States

	ω_H	$1\text{-}E_H$	ω_L	$1\text{-}E_L$	ω_H/ω_L
$g = 0.03$, $P_L = 0.660$	**1.836**	**1.7**	**1.232**	**5.27**	**1.49**
$g = 0.03$, $P_L = 0.568$	1.836	1.7	1.109	15.85	1.65
$g = 0.01$, $P_L = 0.568$	1.844	2.8	1.085	11.00	1.70

Table 10.3
Changes in unemployment benefits and job-to-job reallocation

Labor market parameters	Technical change and prices	ω_H	$1\text{-}E_H$	ω_L	$1\text{-}E_L$	ω_H/ω_L
$z = 0.05$	$g = 0.03$, $P_L = 0.660$	1.839	2.2	1.240	7.3	1.49
$\eta_L = 0.7435$	$g = 0.01$, $P_L = 0.568$	1.870	6.2	1.121	18.1	1.67
$z = 0.12$	$g = 0.03$, $P_L = 0.660$	1.849	3.42	1.260	10.9	1.47
$\eta_L = 0.7435$	$g = 0.01$, $P_L = 0.568$	1.930	13.3	1.180	28.5	1.63
$z = 0.12$	$g = 0.03$, $P_L = 0.660$	1.849	3.42	1.233	5.9	1.50
$\eta_L = 0.90$	$g = 0.01$, $P_L = 0.568$	1.930	13.3	1.175	27.1	1.63

States, although we need the more complex depiction of the labor market used in this chapter. A common argument is that a major difference between the U.S. and European labor markets is the level of unemployment benefits. In the late 1980s, benefit-replacement ratios were 12 percent in the United States, 19 percent in the United Kingdom, and 28 percent in both Germany and Sweden (OECD 1994). In our model, benefit-replacement ratios, captured by the parameter z, play an important role in determining the position of the NSC curve relative to the demand curve, and hence the magnitude of the impact of changes in other parameters. Table 10.3 considers an economy identical to that in table 10.2, except that unemployment benefit is now greater. In the first two rows, we consider a situation where $z = 0.05$ (rather than 0, as in our simulated U.S. economy), and we examine what happens to wages and employment as the rate of productivity growth falls from 3 percent to 1 percent, and the price of unskilled-produced goods drops from 0.660 to 0.568. The initial relative wage is still 1.49. However, following the shocks, there is a smaller increase in inequality (to 1.67 rather than 1.70), and a greater increase in unemployment for both types of workers. Rows 3 and 4 consider an economy with an even higher replacement ratio, $z = 0.12$, and show that following the shocks there is an even smaller increase in the skill premium (11% compared to 14% in the simulated U.S. economy) and a greater increase in unemployment rates.

To explore the possibility that a package of European labor market policies may account for the smaller increase the wage premium in Europe, the last two rows of table 10.3 consider an economy with a higher benefit replacement ratio, $z = 0.12$, and a higher job-to-job reallocation rate for unskilled workers, $\eta_L = 0.90$,[13] than our calibrated U.S. economy. This change implies that in response to the technology and price shock there is an even weaker increase in the relative wage and an even greater increase in unemployment than in the previous case. If we compare this economy with the one in table 10.2, the differences are large: the skill premium increases by 9 percent rather than 14 percent, while skilled and unskilled unemployment rates rise by 9.9 percent and 21 percent, respectively, rather than by 1.1 percent and 5.73 percent.

The intuition for the effect of changes in either z or η is the same. The higher the unemployment benefit or the greater the probability of being immediately reallocated to a new job, the weaker the disciplinary effects of unemployment. Consequently, large changes in employment are required in order to maintain workers on the NSC curve after a change in the rate of productivity growth.

10.6 Summary and Further Policy Implications

In contrast to most of the literature linking inequality and technical progress, this chapter shifts the emphasis to the supply side, arguing that incorporating job flows arising from technical progress into a model of efficiency wages allows us to model the impact of technical change on workers' effort incentives. The impact of technical change on wages is ambiguous and depends crucially on two competing factors—technical progress not only increases expected labor income through what we call the employment capitalization effect (and thereby reduces incentives to shirk), it also introduces the possibility that workers will become unemployed as a result of technical even if they do not shirk (thus increasing incentives to shirk through the job destruction-creation effect). To the extent that technical change is more likely to result in unemployment for unskilled workers (as $\eta_H > \eta_L$), the productivity slowdown reduces their incentives to shirk, allowing firms to cut unskilled wages without compromising workers' effort levels. This is the case even when technical progress is skill-neutral.

Our analysis suggests that labor market policies which affect the costs of unemployment and the ease of job-to-job transfer can account for a different response in Europe and the United States/ United Kingdom to a similar productivity slowdown. The role of η_i, the rate of job-to-job reallocation, has been shown to be crucial. Consistent with the study by Boeri (1999), we have argued that

European employment protection legislation, by implicitly allowing workers time to search for a new job when their existing job is lost due to technical change, implies that unskilled workers in Europe are less likely to enter unemployment than their American counterparts, even if unskilled unemployment rates are higher in Europe. Additionally, higher replacement ratios in Europe further reduce the expected costs of unemployment for the unskilled. As a result unskilled wages in Europe have to be maintained to prevent shirking behavior. In the United States, workers are more sensitive to changes in labor turnover due to technical change, hence firms can use the productivity slowdown as an opportunity to reduce unskilled wages.

It is also possible to interpret the rate of job-to-job transfer, η, as a parameter capturing the relative effectiveness of job search of the employed relative to the unemployed since, in steady state, it measures the proportion of new jobs filled directly by workers leaving a job rather than exiting unemployment. Seen in this light, policies which raise the job search skills of the unemployed, may actually raise inequality by reducing η.

Any attempt to reduce unemployment by improving the job search skills of the unemployed, will make existing workers more vulnerable to competition from the unemployed and allow firms to reduce wages, ceteris paribus. Since the unemployment rates are higher for unskilled workers, this will have a disproportionate affect on the unskilled. However, policies that seek to reduce inequality by slowing the rate of labor turnover will not only increase unemployment, but by reducing new job opportunities to the unemployed are also likely to increase the duration of unemployment.

This highlights the fact that policies that tend to reduce inequality have a cost in terms of unemployment: High job-to-job reallocation rates (due to job protection legislation and high replacement ratios) result in less inequality at the expense of greater changes in employment. The argument that there is a trade-off between inequality and unemployment, and that differences in labor market regulations imply high inequality and low unemployment in the United States and low inequality and high unemployment in Europe, is not new. An essential feature of our approach is that lower inequality is often obtained at the expense of higher rates of unemployment for both skilled and unskilled workers, rather than reducing only unskilled employment (see table 10.3). This has important implications for the policymaker and may affect the chances of generating support for particular policy measures.

Notes

We would like to thank participants at the CESifo conferences on Growth and Inequality: Issues and Policy Implications for helpful comments on an earlier draft of this paper, which was originally published in discussion paper form as Leith and Li (2001). We would also like to thank Theo Eicher, Raji Jataraman, Nobuhiro Kiyotaki, and seminar participants at the Universities of Stirling, Otaru and Hokkaido, the Kansai Macroeconomics Workshop, and the Bank of Japan for their comments.

1. See Acemoglu (2000).

2. This hypothesis has been theoretically explored by Eicher (1996), Galor and Tsiddon (1997), Greenwood and Yorukoglu (1997), Acemoglu (1998), and Caselli (1999), among others.

3. The importance of this process has been documented by Davis and Haltiwanger (1992). They find that in the United States, between one-third and one-half of total worker reallocation (between employers or from employment to joblessness) is due to shifts in employment opportunities across firms.

4. See Murphy and Welch (1992) and Berman, Bound, and Griliches (1994).

5. See OECD (2001).

6. A number of papers have attempted to reconcile an acceleration technical progress with the observed productivity slowdown, arguing that it takes time to implement new technologies (see Greenwood and Yorukogklu 1997; Aghion and Howitt 1998, chap. 8; and Galor and Tsiddon 1997, respectively). Yet, productivity has fallen over a twenty-year period, which seems too long as an experimentation period.

7. The assumption of risk neutrality is made for reasons of tractability. We conjecture that introducing risk aversion would raise the costs of unemployment such that the job flows induced by technological change would have an even greater impact on inequality through the channels we describe here.

8. It is analogous to what Aghion and Howitt (1994) call the capitalization effect of growth on labor demand, which increases the return of creating a new job and makes it profitable for firms to hire more workers.

9. A fall in the real wage of the lowest decile of the earnings distribution was observed in the United States during the 1980s (OECD 1993).

10. See OECD (1996).

11. During this period the unemployment rates for high-education and low-education workers were 2 percent and 7.8 percent, respectively (Nickell and Bell 1995). The flow into unemployment of type i workers can be expressed as $f_i = 0.368 * E_i(1 - \eta_i)$, assuming the same reallocation rate for skilled and unskilled workers. The stock of unemployment is then $U_i = f_i/a_i$, where a_i is the probability of exiting unemployment in a year. Assuming a_i lies between 1 and 0.1 (i.e., between 10% and 100% of workers find a job within a year), we get the preceding values.

12. We use observations for the average unemployment rates over the period 1971–1974 from Nickell and Bell (1995).

13. A higher rate of job-to-job reallocation in Europe than in the United States is consistent with the evidence in Boeri (1999).

References

Acemoglu, D. 1998. "Why Do New Technologies Complement Skills? Directed Technical Change and Wage Inequality." *Quarterly Journal of Economics* 113: 1055–1090.

Acemoglu, D. 1999. "Changes in Unemployment and Wage Inequality: An Alternative Theory and Some Evidence." *American Economic Review* 89: 1259–1278.

Acemoglu, D. 2000. "Technical Change, Inequality, and the Labour Market." NBER Working Paper No. 7800.

Aghion, P., and P. Howitt. 1994. "Growth and Unemployment." *Review of Economic Studies* 61: 477–494.

Aghion, P., and P. Howitt. 1998. *Endogenous Growth Theory*. Cambridge: The MIT Press.

Berman, E., J. Bound, and Z. Griliches. 1994. "Changes in the Demand for Skilled Labor within U.S. Manufacturing Industries: Evidence from the Annual Survey of Manufactures." *Quarterly Journal of Economics* 109: 367–365.

Boeri, T. 1999. "Enforcement of Employment Security Regulations, On-the-Job Search and Unemployment Duration." *European Economic Review* 43: 65–89.

Card, D., and T. Lemieux. 2001. "Can Falling Supply Explain the Rising Return to College for Younger Men? A Cohort-Based Analysis." *Quarterly Journal of Economics* 116: 705–746.

Caselli, Francesco. 1999. "Technological Revolutions." *American Economic Review* 89: 78–102.

Davis, S. J., and J. Haltiwanger. 1992. "Gross Job Creation, Gross Job Destruction and Employment Reallocation." *Quarterly Journal of Economics* 107: 819–863.

Eicher, T. S. 1996. "Interactions between endogenous human capital and technological change." *Review of Economic Studies* 63: 127–144.

Eicher, T. S. 1999. "Training, Adeverse Selection and Appropriate Technology." *Journal of Economic Dynamics and Control* 23: 272–246.

Eicher, T. S., and P. G. Kalaitzidakis. 1997. "The Human Capital Dymension to Foreign Direct Investment: Training, Adverse Selection, and Firm Location." In *Trade, Dynamics, and Growth*, ed. B. Jensen and K. Y. Wong, 337–364. Ann Arbor: Michigan University Press.

Feenstra, R. C., and G. H. Hanson. 1999. "The Impact of Outsourcing and High-technology Capital on Wages: Estimates for the United States, 1979–1990." *Quarterly Journal of Economics* 114(3): 907–940.

Galor, Oded, and Daniel Tsiddon. 1997. "Technological Progress, Mobility, and Economic Growth." *American Economic Review* 87: 363–382.

Greenwood, Jeremy, and Mehmet Yorukoglu. 1997. "1974." *Carnegie-Rochester Conference Series on Public Policy* 46: 49–95.

Leith, C., and C.-W. Li. 2001. "Wage Inequality and the Effort Incentive Effects of Technological Progress." CESifo Working Paper No. 513.

Murphy, K. M., and K. Welch. 1992. "The Structure of Wages." *Quarterly Journal of Economics* 107: 285–326.

Nelson, R., and E. Phelps. 1966. "Investments in Humanns, Technological Diffusion, and Econmic Growth." *American Economic Review* 56: 69–75.

Nickell, Stephen, and Brian Bell. 1995. "The Collapse in the Demand for the Unskilled and Unemployment across OECD Countries." *Oxford Review of Economic Policy* 11: 40–62.

Nickell, Stephen, and Brian Bell. 1996. "Changes in the Distribution of Wages and Unemployment in OECD Countries." *The American Economic Review* 86(2): 302–309.

OECD. 1993. *Employment Outlook.* Paris, July.

OECD. 1994. *Employment Outlook.* Paris, July.

OECD. 1996. *Employment Outlook.* Paris, July.

OECD. 2001. *Employment Outlook.* Paris, July.

Shapiro, C., and J. E. Stiglitz. 1984. "Equilibrium Unemployment as a Worker Discipline Device." *American Economic Review* 74: 433–444.

Index